READINGS IN
MASS COMMUNICATION

READINGS IN
MASS COMMUNICATION

Concepts and Issues
in the Mass Media

Michael C. Emery
San Fernando Valley State College
Ted Curtis Smythe
California State College at Fullerton

WM. C. BROWN COMPANY PUBLISHERS
Dubuque, Iowa

Consulting Editor
  Curtis D. MacDougall
  Northwestern University

Third Printing, 1973

Printed in the United States of America

Contents

Part Two

REVOLUTION IN THE MASS MEDIA

Part Three

MULTIPLYING MEDIA DEBATES

Part Four

APPENDIX

Preface

The rush for knowledge about the real world of the mass media has accelerated during the last ten years so that today one of the most popular college classes is the one which introduces students to dramatic innovations in media style, format and production—often for the first time in their lives.

Even newspapers, those old unchangeables, have taken strides so as to cause veteran editors and critics to wonder where the old days have gone. As for television, the "old days" were the early 1960's! It is this wild change—both in society and in the media—that we have attempted to grab hold of long enough to study. Change in the concepts by which we view the functions and roles of the mass media, change in the media themselves and change in the criticism we voice about media performance.

The throttle is wide open for more drastic changes in the seventies. Our hope is that this collection of articles, excerpts from speeches and reports about the media, will help the reader carefully examine the true extent of these changes. Future trends of a useful nature might then receive the support of thoughtful people, whether they be professionals or media consumers.

The first of the three major sections, "Changing Concepts of the Function and Role of the Mass Media," focuses on suggestions of mass media specialists on how to fundamentally change the media. What can the people do about television, for example, if poor programming continues to be the order of the day? A considerable amount of book space has been devoted to two of these suggestions regarding: (1) means of increasing access of the people to the mass media, and (2) means of increasing nongovernmental control of the mass media.

The cry "revolution" became a cliché in the sixties. Yet there is a genuine "Revolution in the Mass Media," the title of Part II. An examination of the multitude of changes includes three groups: the traditional media, such as daily newspapers, radio and television; the "alternative media," as they call themselves, underground newspapers and minority journalism; and the "persuasive" forms of the media, the powerful and much misunderstood forces of advertising and public relations.

Evidence that much of media life is not understood and appreciated is seen in the increasing number of arguments—sometimes they are debates—about the content of the media. Part III, obviously titled "Multiplying Media Debates," examines this content and the criticism and furor evoked by it. Two of the five subsections deal with television, one with the press, one with the treatment of minorities in the mass media and the last one specifically with examples of content change.

The book's three parts are interrelated. Trends in society and in the mass media have brought about the conditions which have fostered new functions and roles. As the media have plowed new ground in order to meet changing conditions, they have harvested criticism. The Appendix to this book contains three national reports on press performance which show how the press has been criticized. Also included are questions for further study taken from the task force report of the National Commission on the Causes and Prevention of Violence.

Not all of these articles conveniently fit into our categories. Not all of the articles we wanted would even fit into the book. This deserves a word of explanation.

Several excellent articles were simply too long. Some of these resisted editing—they could not be "boiled," to use an old editor's expression for cutting copy drastically. A few others would have been ruined by any editing. So, we sought shorter articles in those few cases. An example is Jerome A. Barron's seminal article on "Access to the Press: A New First Amendment Right," which appeared first in *Harvard Law Review* in 1967. To publish this article in full would have taken most of the first part of this book. Since Professor Barron has expressed his fundamental concept in other articles, we have used one of these. When required, articles were edited for timeliness and clarity.

Our selection of articles should not be construed as agreement with the opinions expressed therein. We disagree, either singly or together, with many of the opinions, particularly in Parts I and III.

We do agree, however, that what these writers and critics say deserves wide exposure and thoughtful consideration. We hope that through discussion with colleagues or in classrooms, the inadequacies of some positions will become apparent.

We did not try to give both sides to all questions. Our reasoning is twofold: we want to present as many new suggestions as possible, and we feel that the present situation or the "conventional wisdom" is already well-stated and well-known in most cases.

The selections we have made are based on the premise that these are the major concepts, trends or issues that American mass media will face in the seventies. We will appreciate criticism and suggestions for improving our selection, both of content and of articles. Changes in American mass media ought to be reflected by changes in the book itself.

The editors express their appreciation for the guidance and encouragement of Richard C. Crews, our editor at WCB. We also extend our thanks to colleagues who offered suggestions for articles. And a special note of thanks to those authors and publishers who gave us permission to reprint their work. While they are responsible for the content of their articles, we take full responsibility for the selection.

Michael C. Emery

Ted Curtis Smythe

With the hope that the information and persuasive media will—through alert, aggressive and unselfish actions—help to further elevate the rising level of consciousness in this land.

Part One

Changing Concepts:
The Function and Role
of the Mass Media

Our opinions of CBS News Correspondent Walter Cronkite, the investigative reporters of the *New York Times* or the owner of the local cable television company depends on our basic concepts about the role of television news, newspapers or media corporations. Causing alterations in these viewpoints are the same tremendous technological and societal pressures which have forced reevaluations throughout all levels of the population. Part I tackles these basic media concepts.

People always have worried about how the media affects, or could be made to affect, society. English kings feared the power of the poor printer; in 1972 advertisers wonder how best to use new television developments to their advantage. But as economic and social conditions play upon purposes served by the media, and affect support for media organizations, the concepts themselves undergo serious change. For example, during the sixties nearly every journalism convention sponsored a panel discussion on "Free Press-Fair Trial." While this simplistic slogan is still with us and deserves continued scrutiny (for one reason the issue of television cameras in courtrooms has not been resolved), there are other more vibrant concepts now before the public. The exhaustive discussion of these ideas lies ahead and our selections try to place them in a useful framework for hard judgment.

Our first article, by Edwin Diamond, former senior editor at *Newsweek*, is an overview of these newer thoughts and practices which confront Americans and their mass media in the seventies. His basic concern is shared by numerous authors—how can we increase the "voices" in the mass media so as to offer more diverse viewpoints and information? A worry of others, how can we do this without destroying what general credibility can be claimed by the media? Diamond argues "there is virtue in diversity—in sharpened news coverage and in widened access to print and to the cameras."

One of the most significant suggestions for increasing diversity in print media is elaborated in Jerome A. Barron's concept of "Access to the Press." Barron, associate professor of law at George Washington University, asserts that newspapers, as with radio and television, should be *required* to provide "the public with a balanced presentation of controversial public issues" by permitting representatives of less popular viewpoints to gain access to the press. His concept grows out of the FCC's "fairness doctrine" for radio and television.

Clifton Daniel, associate editor of the *New York Times*, responds to Barron's concept. Daniel agrees that there is a problem of access, but that "its dimensions are not great and the solutions proposed are not practical." He sharply questions the application of "access laws," arguing that judges are not editors, and disputes Barron's broadcasting analogy claiming that the First Amendment does not permit such an interpretation.

While the "access" debate concerns newspapers and magazines, changes have also occurred in our views of broadcasting's role and function. During the fifties the questions of extending stations and of advertiser influence were paramount; in the sixties the need for increasing channel capacity and for developing an independent non-commercial network was espoused. This resulted in a law requiring that new television sets have both VHF and UHF capability and led to the Corporation for Public Broadcasting, which is supported by appropriations from Congress.

Because of the technological nature of the electronic media, which permits government controls through the Federal Communication Commission (FCC), we have selected only those articles which suggest ways in which the FCC or the public can increase access to the media. Finally, we include a serious rebuttal to some of the FCC's recent actions and proposals.

In our first article, Nicholas Johnson, commissioner on the FCC, backgrounds the contemporary arrangements between the FCC and the broadcast industry. His article is based on testimony delivered at hearings on S. 2004, the "Pastore Bill," which would greatly increase protection for present broadcast station owners. Johnson attacks that principle by declaring that the FCC must *increase competition* for available broadcast frequencies and *increase representative ownership* of broadcast facilities.

In the second article, also by Johnson, he goes beyond this emphasis on what the FCC must do and focuses instead on what the citizen and citizen groups may do. Basically, this article suggests ways to influence the development of and programming practices of television. Johnson's contention is that groups should challenge current broadcast license holders and either seek to win their frequencies or to cause them to change their practices. He includes the dates on which broadcast licenses will expire within given states, for use in challenging broadcast license holders. He cites the Texarkana KTAL-TV case, where local groups did some fact-finding and then, "armed with the threat of a license renewal hearing. . .went directly to the station's management and hammered out *an agreement* in which the station promised it would make a number of reforms, or forfeit its license."

This threat of community pressure is what worries Richard W. Jencks, Vice President, CBS Washington. He argues, for instance, that private groups exploit the power of the FCC, forcing a weak station "to enter into a contract under which it will be required to do many things which the Commission itself either *cannot do, does not wish to do* or *has not yet decided to do."*

Finally, that veteran of network news wars Fred W. Friendly tackles the promise of cable TV (CATV) for the seventies. He reviews briefly the development of broadcasting in America. The lesson he wants to impart is that the same patterns *should not* occur in cable television. "The current monopoly," he claims, "could give way to a new Tower of Babel, in which a half-hundred voices scream in a cacophonous attempt to attract the largest audience." His solution for protecting the promise of CATV is for public interests to vie with private interests for ownership of cable systems. The revenues from subscribers would support quality programming. Now is the time to keep all options open, Friendly claims, else "this new rocket will fly off in its own mercantile orbit beyond everyone's control."

The problem of access to the mass media is only one of the new concepts shattering our perspectives on the role and function of the mass media. Suggestions for a press council have been revived in recent years, indicating perhaps that the time has finally come for an idea that has been kicking around for more than two decades. The concept was first put forth in reports issued by the "Hutchins Commission" in 1947. Since then, many countries have formed their own national press councils. But not in the United States. Critics have increasingly sought some means of improving press performance, however, and have turned to some form of a national press council as a partial means of improvement.

Our excerpt to lead off this section is from a task force report of the National Commission on the Causes and Prevention of Violence. The report proposes the establishment of a national center for media study. Central to its concise argument for a national center is the assumption that the media do not have the "capacity for self-evaluation and self-criticism" but that they "are capable of improving their performance under the stimulus of responsible criticism." An independent national center for media study would provide such stimulus, the report asserts.

Other critics have long pointed out that America's press is essentially a local press, not national, so they have sought to develop the concept of community media councils. In fact, some of these councils have already been tried and, generally, have been found successful, as Donald E. Brignolo reports. Brignolo surveys the historical development of the idea before discussing the procedures undertaken in four experimental councils. He concludes that the experiments have "demonstrated that a community press council can function effectively in this country without infringing upon the publisher's freedom." He even sees the "acceptance of the idea that an advisory body, set up to evaluate newspaper performance, can be beneficial to both the public and the press."

Press councils are an "external" means of controlling the performance of the press. Many professionals are advocating instead an "internal" control as a means of improving press performance. One of these controls is the ombudsman.

The newspaper ombudsman's function is outlined by Norman E. Isaacs, formerly executive editor of the *Louisville Courier-Journal* and *Times*. Isaacs cites the example at the *Courier-Journal* where for several years an ombudsman has been hearing charges from the public and acting to bring about change when he finds valid complaints. Isaacs claims that the ombudsman has not only reduced the type of error which required corrections, but the idea apparently has earned the respect of the public. He suggests that other publishers should take some constructive steps "to convince the citizenry of our essential fairness, of our dedication to accuracy and of our willingness to listen."

Another means of internal control of mass media is growing in the United States. This is the concept of "reporter power." As with the ombudsman, the concept of reporter power is an import from Europe. Edwin Diamond explores recent developments in the efforts of reporters to gain greater control over policy on the newspapers and magazines for which they work. Their success varies from publication to publication, as do the methods they use. So far, Diamond reports, reporters do not want to run management. They do, however, want a greater voice in shaping management's decisions, particularly those decisions regarding editorial-news policies and practices.

During the sixties the Federal Freedom of Information Act was signed into law. It has given the press the right of access to the files of many governmental agencies, as have "right to know laws" in several states. This victory of the sixties was one more step in working out the adversary relationship between government and press.

The social tensions of the sixties and early seventies have, however, created another issue—one that federal courts have not yet considered. This is the "confidential" relationship between news source and reporter. Abraham S. Goldstein, dean of the Yale University Law School, suggests the need for "a more sensitive law of confidential communications" in the federal government, to protect sources of news from overly zealous investigators. Some of the more powerful mass media organizations have too often negotiated individual cases, Goldstein suggests. He hopes they will, in the future, fight out in the courts the principles of confidential relationship between source and newsman.

The agreement of the U.S. Supreme Court in May, 1971 to decide whether a newsman had the constitutional right to refuse a grand jury the source of information obtained in confidence was considered vital for clarification. But the arguments between Justice Department and news media were expected to continue past the one decision. Also at stake was the issue of whether unused television film could be subpoenaed or whether it could be considered "privileged" as a reporter's notes are in many instances.

Dr. Frank Stanton, president of CBS, refused to comply with a subpoena requesting he provide a house subcommittee with materials used in preparation of the controversial documentary, "The Selling of the Pentagon." The subpoena mentioned unused film clips. Dr. Stanton's testimony to the Staggers subcommittee, published here, was in the face of threats of contempt action against him and CBS and again raised the question of who actually controls broadcasting.

Our final section is devoted to the issue of "relevancy"—one of the mod words of our times. We have juxtaposed two articles to illuminate two approaches to "advocacy in news reporting."

Carey McWilliams, long-time editor of *The Nation*, leads off with a survey of the development of reform journalism or muckraking. He writes largely about what his magazine has been publishing in the past decade, but also outlines contributions by others. The thrust of his article, however, is that reform journalism can and should be conducted by the mass media because "good investigative journalism takes time, money and commitment on the part of a publisher." McWilliams also pointedly comments on the adverse effect of the FCC's "personal attack" doctrine in the making of documentaries and on the effect of libel laws as they are used against small publications.

Dr. J.K. Hvistendahl also reaches into the past to substantiate what he calls a fourth revolution in American journalism—the advent of activist or "truth-as-I-see-it" reporting. Dr. Hvistendahl supports the idea that the journalistic activist "has a right (indeed an obligation) to become personally and emotionally involved in the events of the day. The activist reporter believes he should proclaim his beliefs if he wishes, and that it is not only permissible but desirable for him to cover the news from the viewpoint of his own intellectual commitment." In many respects, Dr. Hvistendahl's suggestions sound reminiscent of interpretive reporting but he denies this and considers activist reporting an important, supplementary adjunct to contemporary standards of objective news reporting and interpretive writing.

The other article, by Dr. Nathan Blumberg, is a condensation of a long analysis of the part played by the establishment media during the Democratic National Convention in 1968. It is a cry for "relevancy" in that the double standards and hypocrisy of some leading newspapers are exposed. It is no wonder, Dr. Blumberg observes, that about sixty-five Chicago daily newsmen organized to publish the *Chicago Journalism Review* "soon after the battle of Chicago." Today, of course, there are journalism reviews in many major cities.

While these are not all of the new concepts shaking the mass media, we feel they are the major concepts which need increased discussion by people interested in the future of our style of communication. What we are as a nation in the eighties may well be determined by what we undertake—or neglect to undertake—during the remainder of these seventies.

Chapter I

INCREASING ACCESS TO THE MASS MEDIA

MULTIPLYING MEDIA VOICES

Edwin Diamond

Every day at 8 a.m. President Richard M. Nixon finds a loose-leaf briefing book on his desk with the label FOR THE PRESIDENT'S EYES ONLY. Inside, neatly typed on the loose-leaf sheets, is a summary of news and comment from scores of daily newspapers, a dozen columnists and magazines, the three networks, and a scattering of journals and newsletters—a digest representing the combined rewriting and editing efforts of five White House staff assistants. The briefing book is a highly professional newspaper with a readership of one—one important way the chief executive of the United States tries to keep informed about what voices outside the Administration are saying about him, his policies, the nation he leads, and the parlous times. Though the book's contents are secret, fears that the President's briefing experts supply only a roseate Republican view of the world are apparently unfounded; staff men assure inquirers that the President gets Mary McGrory as well as Stanton Evans—the bitter along with the better, as Jane Ace used to say.

Yet the limits of the briefing book's perspective inevitably match the limits of the American mainstream media themselves. The voices the President hears in his briefing book are:

—Overwhelmingly white, mostly middle-aged, and usually affluent—a fair representation of the "non-black, non-young, non-poor" American electorate that public opinion analyst Richard Scammon says put Mr. Nixon in office and will decide who the next President is in 1972.

Edwin Diamond, member of the political science faculty at MIT and former senior editor at *Newsweek*, is an established media critic. This article is reprinted with permission of *Columbia Journalism Review*, where it originally appeared in the Winter, 1969-70 issue.

—Reflexively Establishment in thought patterns, life style, and outlook. To be sure, the owners of the newspapers, magazines, and radio-TV stations included in the briefing book may be regarded as Republican while a majority of their writers and reporters may be Democrats; but both are generally committed to the commonly received political structures and goals of the present system.

Mr. Nixon, in effect, is unlikely to hear the gravelly, hip voice of Putney Swope, the black advertising man who took over a Madison Avenue agency in Robert Downey's black comedy and announced: "I'm not here to rock the boat. I'm here to sink it." And the limits of the Presidential view are also shared by ordinary citizens; by inclination, it is their understandable nature to avoid the boat-rockers and the boat-sinkers in order to stay dry and comfortable. Wise editors and advertising men know that people tend to read what reinforces their beliefs; that the ads for Ford cars, for example, are read mostly by people who already own Ford cars and are reminding themselves why they were so wise in their purchase of their car.

But suppose there are some responsible citizens who have a desire to hear something more than the captain's reassuring voice— whether it is a captain of state, industry, education, or labor? He must work to dig out this information. Newspapers, magazines, and radio-TV stations don't come cheap: the Los Angeles *Times* recently paid some $90 million for the Dallas *Times Herald* and its TV-radio station, a CBS affiliate; *Newsweek*, perhaps the last major magazine bargain, was bought for $9 million in 1961. Today the boat-rockers and boat-sinkers can't afford such prices. Nor does the interlocking ownership of newspapers, magazines, and radio-TV outlets do much to increase access to fresh, new, and different voices.

Many media barons realize this. They have seen the disenchanted readers and viewers vote with their feet—drop out of the mainstream audience or refuse to take the mass media seriously, and subscribe to the *New York Review of Books* or, among the young in San Francisco, the *Bay Guardian*. And the most enlightened owners also know all the strong ideological arguments against the concentration of major news outlets in fewer private hands.

Not surprisingly, then, there were intense cries of pain when Spiro T. Agnew, like a dentist drilling without novocaine, recently touched this most sensitive media nerve end. His approach was hamhanded, but he knew where the sore point was. Fortunately, there is a remedy for the trouble, and interestingly, the fate of steps to increase the diversity of media voices rests in good part in the hands of the Administration in Washington.

Of course, media with alternative, independent, and sometimes ornery views have existed for decades with no need of government help. Among them are the venerable *New Republic*, the *Nation* on the left and, more recently on the right, the *National Review*. In Washington, I.F. Stone publishes a biweekly which ferrets out stories that the straight press with its twenty-three-man capital news bureaus often overlook. One of the most significant and largely under-reported media phenomena is the success of regional gadflies such as the biweekly *Texas Observer* published in Austin. The *Observer* broke the lugubrious story of the Lyndon Johnson appointee to the U.S. Office of Education who had plagarized his Ph.D. thesis and for a decade passed himself off as a "Doctor." In Philadelphia, the monthly *Philadelphia* magazine exposed venality on the *Inquirer* and also did a telling portrait of publisher Walter Annenberg, now Ambassador to Great Britain. In Boston, Louis Lyons, former curator of the Nieman Fellowship program, delivers a nightly newscast which usually provides a perspective other newsmen ignore. In Denver, Eugene Cervi regularly takes on the Denver establishment—including its newspapers—in his weekly *Cervi's Journal*.

More recently, major cities and many smaller ones, too, have spawned a counter-culture press for blacks and the dissident or alienated youth; an estimated 150,000 readers throughout the U.S. now read such sheets as the Los Angeles *Free Press*, the *Fifth Estate* in Detroit, the *East Village Other* and the *Village Voice* in New York, the *Berkeley Barb* and the *Black Panther* in the San Francisco area, the *North Carolina Anvil* in Chapel Hill, the *Mississippi Freelance* in Greenville, Miss., the *Florida Observer* in Tallahassee, the *Great Speckled Bird* in Atlanta, and the *Old Mole* in Boston. Only a year ago such papers could be put down as underground efforts, too crude in production and thought to be considered more than the passing scatology of sophomores; today some are so successful that the above-ground press can learn basic journalistic lessons from them. The *Berkeley Barb's* popular Dr. Hip, for instance, gives advice on the medical problems that are really on the minds of young readers—questions about abortion and birth control, the effect of drugs on intercourse, techniques for a better sex life—that don't find their way into Dr. Alvarez's columns for the Geritol crowd. And in Atlanta, the *Bird* dug out, long before the established papers, stories of bus fare increases and the cozy relationship between the Georgia utilities and the State Public Service Commission.

Nothing, in fact, points up the national journalistic flabbiness throughout the 1960s as much as the long list of major news breaks achieved by nonjournalists or writers outside the media mainstream, from Ralph Nader's auto safety exposes to the surfacing of the Songmy atrocity charges by Seymour Hersh, free-lance former AP man.

Broadcasting, unlike the press, is subject to the laws of physics and of the U.S. Government. Both have conspired to open up a whole new territory within television—the ultra-high frequency (UHF) band that lies between channels 14 and 83 on all late-model TV sets. In 1964, TV sets were equipped only to pick up signals within the very high frequency (VHF) band—channels 2 through 13. [That year] a federal law required set manufacturers to add the special UHF receivers and antenna. An estimated 60 percent of all U.S. sets now have the UHF gear. The UHF dials do not click into place and must be fine-tuned; but those viewers who take the time to fiddle are often rewarded with minority-taste programming not found on the 2-13 band. Today there are some 265 UHF'ers in the U.S., about 120 of them commercial stations such as KKOG-TV in Ventura, Calif., which disdains syndicated reruns and daytime Hollywood talk shows for such fare as a bilingual Mexican-American variety program and discussion panels that Venturans can appear on simply by dropping in at the KKOG studio across from the Greyhound bus depot. Independent KKOG, boosted by local advertisers, went into the black in its first year.

In other cities, UHF outlets often point their programming at commercial TV dropouts or the ethnic market. Philadelphia's WPHL presented an eighteen-part Ingmar Bergman film festival, and KMEX in Los Angeles offers only Spanish language programs to the estimated 1.7 million Latin Americans living in Southern California. The general manager of KMEX likens his operation to "being the only TV station in the seventh-largest city in the country."

The UHF band as a whole still does not compete with VHF stations in quality of news coverage, most typically because of financial anemia. But an example of what a municipal UHF station can do for overlooked audiences is provided by WNYC, Channel 31, in New York: parents have been told how to recognize symptoms of drug addiction in their children, and there is a valuable course called "English for Americans." With another push from Washington, click-type UHF dials would be possible. Then progress would be up to such groups as the Kaiser Broadcasting Corporation, which operates WKBS (Channel 48) in Philadelphia with a twenty-three-man staff and a $500,000 annual news budget. Kaiser owns five other UHF stations, the possible nucleus of a new TV "network."

Almost all Americans, however, get their news from commercial television, in particular NBC and CBS. A Louis Harris Poll, taken in late 1969 for *Time*, shows that nine out of ten citizens regularly watch TV news. CBS and NBC split 70 per cent of this regular viewing public; ABC gets 12 per cent; non-network stations the remainder. Such TV habits impose a social homogeneity on the country that has been much lamented.

Those who want a true fourth network that could be an alternative to the sameness of news and public affairs on the three major commercial networks have rested their hopes for the past decade on National Educational Television. But NET also suffers from money problems—as well as from organizational rivalries between the New York-based headquarters and the individual stations that would require a Niccolo Machiavelli to explicate. Now the noncommercial TV effort has a new name—it is officially called public television rather than the musty, library-sounding educational television—and a new structure. In 1967 Congress established the Corporation for Public Broadcasting to organize public TV on a national basis. Congress, however, failed to provide any permanent funding for the Corporation, and each year CPB will have to ask for new funds. Because of this dependence, some critics—and some staff members within public television—fear that CPB will dance to the piper's tune of Congressional review, eschewing hard-hitting commentary.

These critics see *The Advocates*, the Corporation's first big entry of the 1969-70 season, as an example of the kind of "balanced format" to be expected when the Government is a co-sponsor. *The Advocates* is nothing if not even-handed. Each week it explores a specific proposal being offered as a solution for one of the nation's major problems. In a live "mock trial" two "advocates" use dialogue, witnesses, and exhibits in an attempt to persuade a "decision-maker," who is usually a legislator involved with the issue being discussed. The underlying idea, according to the show's originator, Roger Fisher—a forty-eight-year-old professor on leave from Harvard Law School—is that TV viewers should be "citizens, not spectators." The Ford Foundation helps pick up the $3.2 million tab for *The Advocates*.

The first dozen programs suggest that the even-handed format at least does not prevent *The Advocates* from debating issues that affect the sponsors; the premiere took up anti-smog legislation in California and two other early shows argued Vietnam and the SST project. On this record, CPB deserves strong governmental support, especially from those who say they are concerned about the monopoly of the media by small "self-elected" bands.

The reach of government most directly affects national commercial television. Under present FCC regulations, a broadcast license must be renewed every three years upon application to the FCC. The theory behind the law was to utilize review to make sure that station programming served at least modestly "the public interest"; i.e., offered a modicum of local news, public affairs, and cultural programs in addition to sold commercial time. In practice, the FCC has been a blindfolded monitor: no license has ever been withdrawn, though WHDH-TV in Boston (owned by the Boston Herald Traveler Corporation) may be transferred to a competing group if an unprecedented FCC transfer order of last January is upheld in court; and WLBT in Jackson, Miss., also may lose its license as a result of a challenge by a group of blacks and the United Church of Christ. [Editor's Note: Both lost licenses.]

In recent months, the Jackson, Miss., challenge has been emulated in other cities. Black leaders, including a group called Black Efforts for Soul in Television, have argued that white-owned media cannot express black consciousness and culture.

The efforts to get "soul" on TV already have achieved some uncredited victories: WPIX in New York, owned and operated by the New York *Daily News*, had a deserved reputation as one of the country's least distinguished stations, notable for its skeleton news staff and *I Love Lucy* reruns. Then blacks organized in New York to challenge its broadcast license; in the months since, WPIX has turned its cameras more on the real problems and lives of the city's minorities.

The other force now loosed upon the FCC licensing procedures is Senator John O. Pastore, the diminutive Rhode Islander who wields enormous power in the broadcast industry through the Senate Communications Subcommittee. The Pastore committee's public hearings on sex and violence had a galvanic influence on the network executives who put together the TV entertainment schedule. The 1969-70 season, by any standard, has been Pastore-ized. Now Pastore is the author of the pending bill that would ban competition for broadcast licenses, and his arguments and the blandishments of the broadcast lobby in Washington have won for the bill twenty-five Senate co-sponsors (some of them up for reelection in 1970 and in need of friends). In the House, co-sponsors number 100 Representatives, whose two-year terms—only one year less than the duration of a broadcast license—apparently are no bar to their ability to run their affairs.

There is nothing inherently virtuous in blackness or in whiteness, in bigness or in smallness. And the UHF station in Washington may be a grind house getting by with three old movies a day while at the same time VHF commercial WTOP is offering the case against Judge Clement Haynsworth (WTOP's sister medium, the Washington *Post*, was supporting Haynsworth editorially). But there is a virtue in diversity—in sharpened news coverage and in widened access to print and to the cameras. A number of ideas and techniques have been advanced to achieve these goals:

1. Ben Bagdikian has proposed that newspapers devote a full page to the letters column. *Newsday* publisher Bill D. Moyers once ordered his editorial page editors to concentrate on letters that answer or criticize the paper's editorials. It is interesting that editors are rediscovering this principle of the open forum; in the Soviet Union newspaper editors—particularly editors of youth papers such as *Komsomoskaya Pravda* —regard their letters not just as a means of learning what is on their readers' minds but as the prime way of conducting debates and airing discussions about life on the farm or in the city. The paper claims that it receives no fewer than 3 million such letters a year. In the U.S., a letters page represents only a modest opening wedge; the Detroit *News* had a better idea. Its editors have cleared a whole section, a weekly supplement called The Other Section, to let college editors and other outsiders under the age of thirty-five state their views on music, fashions, and, of course, on the failings of the Establishment press.

2. TV news could reexamine its "show biz" style and sports-weather-news approach. A good example of a program that has done this is the well known KQED *Newsroom* on public TV in San Francisco. KQED concentrates on interpretive reporting of basic "hard news"; there is no compartmentalized crime news, sports, or weather; no frivolous features. It covers the material in considerable depth, doing as few as ten stories in sixty minutes. *Newsroom* looks like a newsroom—a rim around which various beat men tell their stories. The education man, Joe Russin, Harvard-trained and wearing a handlebar moustache, brings a knowledge of what the Board of Regents of the University of California is doing that can't be paralleled on any commercial station in the area.

Not long ago ABC tried bringing in outsiders—thirty of them, in fact, including Joseph Alsop, Bill D. Moyers, I.F. Stone, Ralph Nader, and James Kilpatrick—for comment pieces on its evening network news. According to ABC News vice president William Sheehan, "the show laid an egg," a failure he attributes in part to the fact that the commentators went on at the end of the program when people apparently had had enough of the news. But the argument that ratings will inevitably suffer if there is any tinkering with present holy formulas doesn't hold—KQED is doing so well that the idea is being exported to other cities.

3. TV can be made into true two-way communication. The potential of cable TV—the "wired city"—is only now being explored. Already, Editor Robert M. White II of the Mexico, Mo., *Ledger*, has turned the cable channel his paper owns into a New England town meeting; three or four times a night during the winter months the cameras show various city politicians, newly arrived teachers, county officials, and in one case a returned Vietnam veteran, who appear in the studio, make a presentation, and then answer live telephone calls from city residents. "The only limit to what we can do on cable TV is our own imagination," says White.

Beyond that, electronics engineer Eugene Leonard, president of Systems Resources Corporation in New York, visualizes the day when every home will have its own computer terminal spliced into a telephone line. Leonard thinks the principle of computer time-sharing now being used in industry could be combined with the philosophy of *The Advocates.* In this way TV debates could be joined by thousands of viewers-voters far beyond the studio—true participatory democracy.

4. The principle of civilian review of the media could be established. Lee Smith, associate editor of *Newsweek*, recently looked into the idea in connection with his work for the Press Section, and found much support for the idea. "There is something very hypocritical and arrogant about us newsmen," he says. "We freely criticize policemen who object to any kind of outside examination of what they are doing and we chide teachers who believe that only they know what should be taught. But then we automatically dismiss civilian review of our news judgment as unprofessional and simply meddlesome. The record shows that we don't always know what news is or how it should be handled."

How do you get civilian reviews? An ombudsman is one way. The Louisville *Courier-Journal* two years ago appointed former city editor John Herchenroeder to look into reader complaints against the newspaper. In his first year he checked 400 complaints and in his second year 500, most of them mistakes arising from carelessness rather than bias. The system has not made Herchenroeder popular with the staff. "Going into the cityroom," he says, "I now know how a policeman feels going into the ghetto."

In 1947 a twelve-member commission named by Robert M. Hutchins, then chancellor of the University of Chicago, analyzed the failings of the press and also proposed some sort of ombudsman—an independent agency to appraise and report annually on media performance. The English set up such an agency fifteen years ago to investigate complaints against the British press. Recently, for example, the press council looked into a complaint against the *News of the World* for publishing the memoirs of Christine Keeler (the allegation: it raked up an old scandal and thus invaded the privacy of people such as John Profumo who have tried to live down their pasts). The council also handles such complaints as staged pictures, fabricated interviews, racial slurs, and the use of subterfuge in getting a story. The council has no legal power, but a reprimand—particularly when published in rival newspapers—has made the British press more conscious of its responsibilities.

The Mellettt Fund has helped establish at least six functioning local press councils in the United States: in Bend, Ore.; Seattle; Redwood City, Calif.; Cairo and Sparta, Ill.; and St. Louis. Others also have been established by newspapers, including the Newark *Evening News*, Littleton, Colo., *Independent;* and an Indian biweekly in Rosebud, S.D.

5. Finally, the media can engage in some mutual criticism and self-examination. There has been no successor to the late A.J. Liebling's column, "The Wayward Press," at the *New Yorker*, and, says editor William Shawn, he has no plans for a successor until he finds "someone who can come up with the standard Liebling set." A.M. Rosenthal, managing editor of the New York *Times*, says he has considered a column of criticism of the news media but has not moved on it because "we feel that we have a lot more to do to improve ourselves before we start on others." And Reuven Frank, president of NBC News, offers a familiar industry reason for his network's lack of a program of press criticism: "I can't afford to have people switch off, and I don't think people are interested in knowing about the American press."

But if media chiefs will not assume the role, then impatient Indians will. After the battle between the police and the demonstrators in Chicago in 1968, a group of young reporters—angered by their papers' reluctance to criticize Mayor Daley and the police—started the *Chicago Journalism Review*, a monthly catalogue of oversights and, some say, distortions by Chicago newspapers and TV stations. Recently *Review* staff members branched out into a weekly FM radio program of press criticism. Young reporters also are trying to start reviews in New York, Detroit, Albany, and elsewhere. The

Antioch Review, in its Fall, 1969, issue, initiated a new column of press criticism by veteran newsman James Aronson. Freedom House announced in New York City a plan for "a continuing analysis of news media performance." And in Washington, the *Post* has not waited on either the young or an enterprising nonprofit organization: the *Post* recently organized a panel of 800 readers the editors can query in detail once a month and ask for periodic evaluations of the paper's performance. Its editors are also contemplating a column, in the tradition of A.J. Liebling, monitoring how the paper is doing its editorial job. [Editor's Note: The column was tried and it worked, according to Katharine Graham, publisher.]

One of the major stories the *Post* surely must cover—whether or not a "Wayward *Post*" column is looking over its shoulder—is how the Administration and Congress respond to the opportunities they now have to increase the number and diversity of voices heard throughout the country. Technical help for a UHF band that is only beginning to strike up, aid to cable and pay TV, no-strings support for the Corporation for Public Broadcasting, and defeat of the Pastore Bill and Newspaper Preservation Act would be of immense help in broadening the speaker's platform. If now is not the time, when?

PRINT MEDIA: ACCESS AND REPLY

ACCESS TO THE PRESS: A NEW CONCEPT OF THE FIRST AMENDMENT

Jerome A. Barron

In American law the classic question of free expression has always been whether something already said or published can be the subject of legal sanction. It has been the stated purpose, not always accomplished, of our constitutional law to try to keep as much as

Jerome A. Barron, law professor at George Washington University, originally published "Access to the Press—a New First Amendment Right," in the June, 1967 *Harvard Law Review.* This edited text appeared in March, 1969 *Seminar Quarterly* and is reprinted with Professor Barron's permission.

possible of what is said and published out of the reach of legal sanction. Therefore, for those who are able to obtain access to the media our law is a source of considerable strength. But what about those whose ideas are too unacceptable to gain entrance to the media? Is it time to focus our attention not only on the protection of ideas already published but on making sure that divergent opinions are actually able to secure expression in the first place?

The failure of existing media in this regard is revealed paradoxically by the advent of the sit-in and now the riot. These are really an inadequate underground press which bear tragic witness to the unwillingness of existing mass communications to present unpopular and controversial ideas. If southern newspapers had given voice to the Negro community's real feelings about segregation during the past 50 years a whole society would not have been so startled by the sit-in. If the northern press had given some space to the feelings of the Negro community about discrimination in housing and slum living in general, they would not have been so startled by the riots in Detroit, Newark and New Haven. Recently stories appeared in the press about a newspaper in Lynchburg, Virginia, which would only publish obituaries of Negroes if they were purchased as commercial advertisements. But this was just a particularly unattractive symptom of a basic problem—the horror of upsetting the community applecart—which dominates the press in this country. The dissenter is thus driven to look for novel, even violent, techniques to capture the attention of the public. Paradoxically, when he does this he reaches instantly the network coverage, the front-page story, which otherwise he could never have obtained. For now the trappings of violence and shock have a claim both to "news" and, less avowedly, to entertainment which the commercial bias of the media instantly picks up for immediate coverage.

The grand language of the First Amendment has been used by the media to say that government may impose no responsibilities on them. But constitutional protection is given not to the "press" but to "freedom of the press." What was desired was assurance for the interchange of ideas. But the present structure of the mass media is away from rather than toward ideas. Ideas suggest disagreement and disagreement is not good for business. As V.O. Key wrote in his "Public Opinion and American Democracy": "Newspaper publishers are essentially people who sell white space on newsprint to advertisers." In the light of this, the present constitutional status of the American press is a romantic one. The theory is that the "marketplace of ideas" is self-executing and that according to some Darwinian principle the best ideas will secure primacy over all competing ones.

A more mundane but more candid approach to the First Amendment ought to lead to the realization that a right of expression which is dependent on the sufferance of the managers of the mass media is pitifully anemic.

The difficulty with doing anything about this situation is that the First Amendment has conventionally been thought of as prohibiting *governmental* restraints on expression. But what of private restraints on expression?

Suppose a monopoly newspaper publisher decides that a certain cause or person shall simply receive no space in its pages? What remedy does such a person have? Presently the answer to this question is simple: none. What would seem necessary would be an approach to free speech and free press—the area which constitutional lawyers describe as First Amendment problems—which would recognize that forbidding governmental restrictions on expression is quite useless if the power to prevent access to the channels of communication may be exercised at the pleasure of those who control them. The mandate for a free press is not a constitutional gift to publishers alone. The reader, the public, and in a larger intellectual sense, the world of ideas, all have a stake in the press. That indeed is the reason for the special status of the press in the United States.

The lack of any obligation on newspapers to publish minority viewpoints is particularly aggravated by the rise of the one-newspaper city. Little attention has been given to the problems raised by the vanishing numbers and the general blandness of the American press. In New York City where 14 English language newspapers were published in 1900, only two morning papers and one afternoon paper survive. Nor is this a big-city phenomenon. In a book significantly entitled "Freedom or Secrecy," J. Russell Wiggins of the *Washington Post* offered these statistics on the lack of competition in the American press:

> "The number of newspapers in the United States declined from 2202 in 1909-10 to 1760 in 1953-4. The number of cities with competing daily newspapers declined from 689 to only 87. The number of cities with non-competing dailies increased from 518 to 1301. Eighteen states are now without any locally competing daily newspapers."

The goal of informing the public is the reason that the American Constitution has a First Amendment which says that "Congress shall make no law . . . abridging the freedom of speech, or of the press," in the first place. As Mr. Justice Brandeis put it 40 years ago, the First Amendment rests on the premise that free expression is indispensable to the "discovery and spread of political truth" and that "the greatest menace to freedom is an inert people." It might be said that the decline in the number of newspapers and the rise of monopoly situations is offset by the fact that newspapers not only compete with each other but with radio and televison as well. But what is the effectiveness of radio and television competition in terms of informing the public?

Marshall McLuhan's singular insight into the electronic media is that the attraction they have for us is in their form, rather than in what they have to say. What intrigues us is the television screen itself. The implication from this would appear to be that the electronic media are not very well suited to making public issues meaningful. The question then arises: perhaps on balance the existing press *is* doing this informing job well enough. The fact that the press is in fewer hands than ever has not resulted in a desire on the part of its controllers to bend us, Orwellian fashion, to their political will. The problem is that the media, print and electronic, share a common blandness, a pervasive aversion for the novel and the heretical. The reason for this is that the controllers of the media have no political wish to dominate. They are business men and their stance is essentially one of political neutrality. It is simply not good business to espouse or even give space to heresy and controversy.

Despite the foregoing, there appears to be no change in the approach to the First Amendment and to the press from the romantic view which has thus far prevailed. Judicial indifference to the problem of access to the press was vividly underscored by a case decided by the Supreme Court in 1964. There the Supreme Court reversed a $500,000 libel suit which Commissioner Sullivan of Montgomery, Alabama, had won against *The New York Times* in the state courts of Alabama. Among other things, Commissioner Sullivan charged that he was libelled by a political advertisement appearing in the *Times* on March 29, 1960, entitled "Heed Their Rising Voices," which protested the handling of a civil rights demonstration by Birmingham, Alabama, police. Mr. Sullivan was the Birmingham City Commissioner in charge of the Police Department. The Supreme Court of the United States created a new privilege for newspapers sued by public officials for libel: no damages would be allowed unless the official suing could show that the newspaper acted in "actual malice." As a legal matter, "actual malice" is most difficult to prove. Therefore the decision in *New York Times v. Sullivan* amounted to a grant to the press of a new and relatively complete freedom, where articles about public officials are concerned, from the libel laws. The rationale of the decision, as Mr. Justice Brennan put it, rested on the "principle that debate on public issues should be uninhibited, robust, and wide-open, and that it may well include vehement, caustic and sometimes unpleasantly sharp attacks on government and public officials."

But the disturbing aspect of the *New York Times* decision is its romantic and unexamined assumption that limiting newspaper exposure to libel suits will automatically result in removing restraints on expression and thus lead to the "informed society." Although the Supreme Court changed the law of libel for the benefit of newspapers, the court did nothing in the way of demanding something in exchange from the press such as a requirement to provide space for reply by the public officials which newspapers choose to attack.

What is particularly disturbing is that the newspaper freedom from libel litigation begun in the Supreme Court is being extended by the lower courts to attacks in the press on non-elected persons, so-called "public figures," as well as public officials. Thus when Linus Pauling was attacked by the *National Review* he sued for libel; the New York Court took the position that Pauling was equivalent to a public official in that like such an official he had voluntarily entered public life and debate and therefore that newspapers and magazines should have the same freedom to attack him, without fear of libel suit, in the interest of "uninhibited and robust" public discussion.

One would not quarrel with this approach if some awareness were also displayed that as the law presently stands if someone in the public eye becomes a source of irritation to a publisher, he may attack such a person both without too much concern for the libel laws and with no duty to provide such a person an outlet for his views. How much does this contribute to "wide-open" public discussion?" Probably very little. One can rationalize and say that the *New York Times* case is a victory for the left and the Pauling case a victory for the right. But both represent a defeat for the goal of providing the public with a balanced presentation of controversial public issues.

Nevertheless the legal horizon is not entirely bleak. A case offering very encouraging possibilities for the future was decided by the United States Court of Appeals for the District of Columbia in 1966. In that case, various Negro churches and organizations brought suit against the Federal Communications Commission for renewing the license of the owner of a Broadcast station in Jackson, Mississippi.

The Negro organizations, claiming to speak for the 45% of Jackson which is Negro, claimed that the station had failed to provide effective opportunity for the expression of views in favor of integration although the station gave very effective opportunity for expression of segregationist views. The Federal Communications Commission took a narrowly technical position and said that the Negro organizations were not the appropriate persons to challenge renewal. Only those could challenge renewal who were in the broadcast business: in other words in direct competition with the station.

The Court held that the interests of community groups in broadcast programming was sufficient to entitle the Negro organizations to demand a full hearing on whether the Jackson station ought to have its license renewed. The Jackson, Mississippi, broadcast case marks the beginning hopefully of a new judicial awareness that our legal system must protect not only the broadcaster's right to speak but also public rights in broadcasting. It amounts to recognition that there is a community or public interest involved in the media as well as the interest represented by management. The Court put the matter with stark simplicity: "(T)he freedom of speech protected against government licensees of means of public communication to exclude the expression of opinions and ideas with which they are in disagreement." *(sic)* Furthermore, the Court said that requiring broadcast licensees to use their license so that the listening public may be assured of "hearing varying opinions on the paramount issues facing the American people is within both the spirit and letter of the first amendment."

That such a decision comes out of a broadcasting context is not too surprising for the FCC has long had a rule, the so-called "fairness" doctrine, that broadcasters have an obligation to provide balanced presentation of a constitutional issue of public importance. It is a kind of "equal time" for ideas requirement. The rule has not been a great success. The path of evasion is too obvious: avoid controversy and you won't have to give time to viewpoints you don't like. On the other hand, failure to provide balanced presentation of controversial issues might result in a refusal to grant a broadcast licensee, who only has his license for three years, renewal. Such decisions are now more likely since it has been held as a result of the Jackson, Mississippi, case that groups in the community as well as other broadcast stations and applicants have a right to call the station to account.

The new development in broadcasting is in sad contrast to the situation of the press. In this area, not only has there been no new ground broken but, indeed, as we have seen, developments are if anything retrogressive. Thus the Court in passing in the Jackson, Mississippi, case remarked: "A newspaper can be operated at the whim or caprice of its owners; a broadcast station cannot." Is it not time to rethink whether mass circulation newspapers, many of which are monopoly situations, ought to continue to be operated entirely "at the whim or caprice" of the owner?

I would hope that the new awareness of the listener's stake in broadcasting would lead to a similar concern for the reader's stake in the press. Obviously the daily press cannot be at the disposal of the vanity of the public. Everyone cannot be written about and every idea cannot be given space. In the *United Church of Christ* case, the Jackson, Mississippi, Negro organizations were allowed to contest the station's license although this certainly did not mean that in the future just any listener could contest a licensee's renewal application. The basic test is whether the material for which access is desired is in fact suppressed or undercovered. If it is, it is still not necessary to give space to every group associated with the suppressed viewpoint as long as one such group is allowed to present its case. The machinery for implementing some guarantee of confrontation of ideas could be achieved independently of legislation through the courts themselves by decision. In the *New York Times* case the Supreme Court created a new relative freedom from libel for newspapers by the method of "interpreting" the First Amendment. Similarly, techniques could be used to fashion a right of access to the press for the public. If this approach does not work, then a carefully worded right of access statute which would aim at achieving a meaningful expression of divergent opinions should be attempted. The point is that we must realize that private restraints on free expression have become so powerful that the belief that there is a free marketplace where ideas will naturally compete is as hopelessly outmoded as the theory of perfect competition has generally become in most other spheres of modern life.

RIGHTS OF ACCESS AND REPLY

Clifton Daniel

So far as I am concerned, we can begin with a stipulation. I am perfectly prepared to concede that there is a problem of access to the press in this country. However, the dimensions of the problem have been greatly exaggerated, and the proposed legal remedies are either improper or impractical.

My contention is that the remedies should be left largely to the press itself and to the reading public, and that adequate remedies are available.

About the dimensions of the problem: I suppose there *are* some publishers and editors who capriciously and arbitrarily refuse to print material with which they disagree. But I don't know them.

In an adjudication made two years ago, the British Press Council, which is the official British forum for complaints against the press, had this to say: "We are finding more and more that even quite large localities cannot support more than one newspaper. We are satisfied, however, that most editors of such newspapers are now accepting it as a duty to see, as far as possible, that events and views of interest to all shades of opinion are impartially reported while reserving the editorial right to come down on one side or the other."

Exactly the same thing could be said—and truthfully said—about the press in this country. More than thirty years ago, Eugene Meyer, who had quarreled with the New Deal, resigned from the Federal Reserve Board, and bought *The Washington Post*, set out deliberately to find a New Deal columnist for his newspaper. He thought his readers were entitled to get the New Deal point of view as well as his own.

Hundreds of American publishers and editors take the same attitude today. They go out of their way to find columnists and commentators who are opposed to their own editorial policies.

New ideas are not being suppressed. On the contrary, a hurricane of dissent is blowing through the world. It is shaking the foundations of all our institutions. Can anyone here doubt the truth of that statement?

Clifton Daniel, associate editor of the *New York Times*, was a member of a six-man panel before the Section on Individual Rights and Responsibilities, 1969 American Bar Association Convention. The text was reprinted in the December, 1969 *Seminar Quarterly* along with Commissioner Cox's statements and is used with Mr. Daniel's permission.

When and where has it ever before been possible for a man like the Rev. Ralph D. Abernathy to reach an audience of millions by simply painting a few signs, assembling 150 poor people, and appearing before the television cameras at the gates of Cape Kennedy?

The great guru of the right of access, Prof. Jerome Barron of the George Washington Law School . . . speaks of insuring "access to the mass media for unorthodox ideas."

I thought until I got into this argument that the main complaint against the press was that we were giving too much access to the unorthodox—hippies, draft-card burners, student rioters, black militants, and the people who make dirty movies and write dirty books. At least, that's the message I get from the mail that comes across my desk.

In spite of the mail, I still concede that there is a problem of access to the press. But its dimensions are not great and the solutions proposed are not practical.

Advocates of the right of access blandly ignore the problems and techniques of editing a newspaper. Prof. Barron speaks of the press as having "an obligation to provide space on a non-discriminatory basis for representative groups in the community."

Note the key words: Space. Non-discriminatory. Representative groups.

First: Space! How much space?

The New York Times received 37,719 letters to the editor in 1968. At least 85 to 90 per cent of these letters, in the words of our slogan, were "fit to print." However, we were able to accommodate only six per cent. If we had printed them all—all 18 million words of them—they would have filled up at least 135 complete weekday issues of *The New York Times.* Yet, every letter-writer probably felt that he had some right of access to our columns.

Some letter-writers and readers have been aggressively trying to enforce that presumed right. For many months the adherents of an artistic movement called Aesthetic Realism have been petitioning and picketing *The New York Times*, demanding reviews for books and paintings produced by members of the movement. Criticism, incidentally, would be meaningless if critics were required to give space to artistic endeavors they consider unworthy of it.

Art galleries in New York plead for reviews. They contend that it is impossible to succeed in business without a critical notice in *The Times.* That is probably true. But no one, surely, is entitled to a free ad in the newspapers. No artist has a *right* to a clientele. He has to earn his audience by the forcefulness of his art, the persuasiveness of his talent. How much more cogently does this apply to political ideas!

Non-discriminatory! Discrimination is the very essence of the editing process. You must discriminate or drown.

Every day of the year *The New York Times* receives an average of a million and a quarter to a million and a half words of news material. At best, we can print only a tenth of it. A highly skilled, high-speed process of selection is involved—a massive act of discrimination, if you like—discrimination between the relevant and the irrelevant, the important and the unimportant.

When I was preparing these remarks, I suggested to my secretary that she buy a bushel basket, and fill it with press releases, petitions, pamphlets, telegrams, letters and manuscripts. I wanted to empty the basket here on this platform just to show you how many scoundrels, scroungers and screwballs, in addition to respectable citizens and worthy causes, are seeking access to the columns of our newspaper.

Actually, 168 bushels of wastepaper, most of it rejected news, are collected and thrown away every day in the editorial departments of *The New York Times.* Do you imagine that the courts have the time to sort it all out? Do they have the time and, indeed, do they have the wisdom? Even if judges do have the time to do my job as well as their own, I think Ben Bagdikian, the leading critic of the American press, is right when he says that "judges make bad newspaper editors."

Representative groups! What constitutes a representative group? Who is to decide? I would say that representative groups already have access to the press. It's the unrepresentative ones we have to worry about.

I am not prepared to argue that it's easy for anybody with a cause or a grievance to get space in the newspapers. Indeed, it isn't easy. In my opinion, it shouldn't be. When you begin editing by statute or court order, your newspaper will no longer be a newspaper. It will be "little more than a bulletin board," as Mr. Jencks has said, [Richard W. Jencks, President, Columbia Broadcasting System Broadcast Group] "—a bulletin board for the expression of hateful or immature views."

Nowhere in the literature on access to the press do I find any conspicuous mention of the hate groups. Does this newfangled interpretation of freedom of the press mean that an editor would be obliged to give space to ideas that are hateful to him? Must he give space to advertisements that are offensive to his particular readers? Must a Jewish editor be forced to publish anti-Semitism? Must a Negro editor give space to the Ku Klux Klan?

Prof. Barron, it seems to me, looks at these problems in a very simplistic way, and defines them in parochial terms. All but the most localized media have national connections of some sort: They broadcast network television programs. They buy syndicated columnists. They subscribe to the services of the great national news agencies. An idea that originates in New York is, within a matter of minutes, reverberating in California.

In determining who is to have access to the press, who would decide how widely an idea should be disseminated? Must it be broadcast in prime time on the national networks? Must it be distributed by the Associated Press and United Press to all their clients? And must all the clients be required to publish or broadcast it? Just asking these questions shows how impractical it is to enforce access to the press by law or judicial fiat.

It is impractical in another sense. In contested cases, it might take a year or more to gain access to the press for a given idea or item of news. And if there is anything deader than yesterday's news, it's news a year old.

Not only is it impractical to edit newspapers by statute and judicial interpretation, but it would, in my view, be improper—that is to say, unconstitutional.

My position on that point is a very simple one: Freedom of the press, as defined by the First Amendment, means freedom of the press. It doesn't mean freedom *if*, or freedom *but*. It means freedom *period*. Prof. Barron's proposition, however exhaustively elaborated, cannot disguise the fact that it involves regulation of the press— freedom *but*.

I cannot guess what the makers of our Constitution would have said about television, but I have a pretty good idea of what they meant by freedom of the printed word, and they certainly did not mean that it should be controlled, regulated, restricted or dictated by government officials, legislators or judges. Indeed, the makers of the Constitution meant exactly the opposite—that officialdom, constituted authority, should keep its hands off the press, that it should not tell newspapers what to print or what not to print.

To repeat: My proposition does not mean that there is no need for greater access to the press. It simply means that legislators and judges should not be—indeed cannot be—the ones to decide how much access there should be. Editors should decide, under the pressure of public and official opinion, constantly and conscientiously exercised.

There are effective devices that the newspapers and their readers could employ. Mr. Bagdikian mentions some of them in the *Columbia Journalism Review:*

1. Start a new journalistic form: an occasional full page of ideas from the most thoughtful experts on specific public problems.
2. Devote a full page a day to letter-to-the-editor.
3. Appoint a fulltime ombudsman on the paper or broadcasting station to track down complaints about the organization's judgment and performance.
4. Organize a local press council of community representatives to sit down every month with the publisher.

Press councils have already been tried in several small cities. They work well. A press council for New York City—or perhaps a media council, taking in broadcasters as well as newspapers and magazines—is under consideration by the Twentieth Century Fund. In September, 1969 the Board of Directors of the American Society of Newspaper Editors went to London to make a study of the British Press Council.

There are also other ways, as Mr. Bagdikian says, "of keeping the press a relevant institution close to the lives of its constituents."

One way is hiring reporters from minority groups, as the newspapers are now doing. Not only is opportunity given to the minorities, but also they bring into the city room the special attitudes of their communities.

In New York the communities themselves, with outside help, are bringing their problems to the attention of the press. Community representatives have been meeting with newspaper editors and broadcasting executives under the auspices of the Urban Reporting Project. A news service is being organized by the Project to provide continuous reporting from the neglected neighborhoods to the communications media.

In one of the neighborhoods—Harlem—a new community newspaper, the *Manhattan Tribune,* has been established to train Negro and Puerto Rican journalists.

I am aware that not everybody with a cause can afford a newspaper to promote it. It is not as difficult, however, to launch a new newspaper as some people would have you believe.

In 1896 a small-town publisher, Adolph S. Ochs, came to New York from Chattanooga, Tenn., borrowed $75,000, bought the moribund *New York Times,* and converted it into an enterprise that is now worth $400 million on the American Stock Exchange.

They say nobody will ever be able to do that again. But I wonder.

Fourteen years ago, Norman Mailer, the novelist, and Edwin Fancher put up $5,000 apiece to start an offbeat, neighborhood weekly in Greenwich Village. Altogether, only $70,000—less than Adolph Ochs needed to gain control of *The New York Times*—had to be invested in the *Village Voice* before it turned a profit. Its circulation is now more than 127,000—greater than the circulation of 95 per cent of United States dailies. Its annual profit is considerably more than the capital that was required to launch it.

From the beginning, the *Village Voice* has been a forum for those unorthodox opinions that are said to be seeking access to the press.

It was the *Village Voice* that blazed the trail for the underground press. While you may think that the underground press is scatological and scurrilous, its existence is nevertheless welcome proof that our press is indeed free, and that the First Amendment does not have to be reinterpreted, rewritten or wrenched out of context to give expression to unorthodox ideas.

I had not intended in these remarks to discuss the right of reply. But I think I should respond to Commissioner Cox, [FCC Commissioner Kenneth A. Cox] who says that Congress could constitutionally apply equal time and right-of-reply obligations to newspapers.

I don't agree with him. The First Amendment very plainly says—it couldn't be plainer—that Congress shall make *no law—no law*—abridging freedom of the press.

However, the right of reply does not provide as much of a problem for newspapers as enforced access to the press. Indeed, the right of reply is widely recognized and accepted. In practice, most newspapers recognize a prior-to-publication right of reply when dealing with controversial matters.

On *The New York Times*, we have a standing rule that anyone who is accused or criticized in a controversial or adversary situation should be given an opportunity to comment before publication. The rule is sometimes overlooked in the haste of going to press. It is often not possible to obtain comment from all interested parties, but the principle is there and the effort is required. More importantly, the same is true of the news agencies which serve practically every daily paper and broadcasting station in the United States.

The right of reply after publication is also widely accepted. However, I would caution against creating an absolute right of reply or trying to enshrine such a right in law. Newspapers, it seems to me, *must* have the right to refuse to publish a reply, provided they are willing to accept the consequences of doing so—a suit for damages, for example.

ELECTRONIC MEDIA: INCREASING AND PROTECTING ACCESS

WHAT THE FCC MUST DO

Nicholas Johnson

Virtually every country in the world treats broadcasting as an activity possessed of unique public responsibilities. In many countries—Scandinavia among them—all stations are owned and programmed by an agency of government or a public corporation. Other nations have recently supplemented their public broadcasting facilities with the competition of privately owned, commercial stations—subject to government regulation. Japan is an example. When England supplemented its world-famous BBC with a commercial "independent television service" the new stations continued to be publicly owned. They are merely programmed, during portions of the week, by various programming companies licensed for fixed terms by the Independent Television Authority (ITA). (Unlike the FCC, the ITA has been quite freely encouraging competition by refusing to renew some companies' authority.)

During the debates on the Radio Act of 1927 and the Communications Act of 1934, Senators and Congressmen repeatedly expressed their awareness of the potential economic and political power of this industry, its great opportunity and responsibility, and the need for a close public check upon it. As early as November,

Nicholas Johnson, an outspoken member and critic of the Federal Communications Commission, is the author of *How to Talk Back to Your Television Set.* These ideas are based on his testimony to the Senate Subcommittee on communications regarding the "Pastore Bill" and are used with Mr. Johnson's permission. Reprinted also with the permission of *Columbia Journalism Review* (Winter, 1969-70).

1927, Secretary of Commerce Herbert Hoover urged at the Fourth National Radio Conference that each applicant for a broadcast license be required to prove "that there is something more than naked commercial selfishness in his purpose. . . . [W]e should not freeze the present users of wave lengths permanently in their favored position, irrespective of their service." In 1927 and 1934 Congress purposefully provided that an FCC license would be only "for the use . . . but not the ownership" of the assigned frequency. A six-month license term was originally specified. Later, as the industry gained political power, this term was extended to one year and then to three years. (Recently the industry has been urging a *five*-year term!)

After the original term the FCC must make *an affirmative finding*, every three years, that a renewal of the license will serve the public interest; it is not, like a license to practice law, something that lasts for life unless revoked. The FCC may refuse to renew, and grant the license to another party. Thus the licensee's relationship to the Government is very much like that of a highway contractor—he is free to bid against others for an extension of the profitable relationship, but he is not entitled to an additional term as a right. As Judge Warren Burger said for the U.S. Court of Appeals, "after nearly five decades of operation the broadcast industry does not seem to have grasped the simple fact that a broadcast license is a public trust subject to termination for breach of duty."

For a variety of reasons, the system simply hasn't worked as intended. As in so many other instances of "regulation" of an industry, the FCC has permitted irresponsibility to run rampant—under its imprimatur and protection. Lest there be any doubt about the drubbing the public has taken under its leadership, consider these cases:

—The FCC once decided that a radio station proposing thirty-three minutes of commercials per hour would be serving the public interest. *(Accomack-North Hampton Broadcasting Co., 1967.)*

—It permitted the wholesale transfer of construction permits from one licensee to another, prompting the Special Investigations Subcommittee of the House Interstate and Foreign Commerce Committee to conclude in 1969: "The Commission apparently confused its role as guardian of the public interest with that of guardian of the private interest."

—The FCC approved a license transfer application for a station that quite candidly conceded it proposed to program no news and no public affairs at all. *(Herman C. Hall, 1968.)*

—When presented with charges that a Southern station was engaged in racist programming, the FCC first refused to let the complainants participate in the case, then found that the station's performance entitled it to a license renewal. *(Lamar Life Broadcasting Co., [WLBT], 1965; 1968.)* Even technical violations get little attention. Recently the Commission refused to consider revoking the license of a station whose owner, it was charged, had ordered his engineer to make fraudulent entries in the station's log book, operated with an improperly licensed engineer, and whose three stations had amassed eighty-seven other technical violations over a three-year period.

Violations of the most elementary principles of good business practice don't arouse the Commission to action. Recently the FCC examined the record of a station guilty of bilking advertisers out of $6,000 in fraudulent transactions. The local Better Business Bureau had complained. The station was already on a one-year "probationary" license status for similar offenses earlier. The result? The majority had no difficulty finding the station had "minimally met the public interest standard," and it therefore renewed the license. *Star Stations of Indiana, Inc. [WIFE], 1969.)*

Every industry requires *some* minimal standards—in this instance, of programming, advertising, ownership patterns, technical performance, and business practices. The FCC is not providing them. Nor is the industry doing any better with "self regulation." The New York Code manager of the National Association of Broadcasters Code of Good Practice, Warren Braren, recently resigned rather than continue to work with an organization so little concerned about its own standards. When the Eisenhower Commission on violence addressed the matter of the industry's "self regulation" of violence, it concluded, "The television industry has consistently argued that its standards for the portrayal of violence and its machinery for enforcement of these standards are adequate to protect the public interest. We do not agree."

If FCC regulation hasn't worked, and industry self-regulation is even weaker, what alternatives are there?

There are two principles to which we are deeply committed in America: competition and democracy. Institutions spring up from time to time that deviate from these principles, but we eventually bring them into conformity. And if we cannot create pure "competition" or "democracy" in a situation we try to simulate them; to make the institutions work *as if* competition and popular control were a check upon them. So it has been with broadcasting.

We want the American people to have "the best"—the best cameras, copying machines, television programming. Every business-man takes a risk of losing his position in the market. A multimillion-dollar plant can become worthless overnight. Bankruptcy rates are high. Those are risks the American people, and their government, are willing to take; those are risks the American businessman is willing to exchange for the opportunity to make great profits. When the Polar-oid camera came on the market, no one concerned himself about providing protection to conventional camera makers and their "right" to continue in business. No one thought of requiring Xerox first to prove that conventional copying machines were not serving the public interest, before displacing other manufacturers' positions in the market. What we do as a people, in effect, is to subject the products offered for sale to a "comparative hearing"; the one that wins is rewarded with handsome profits, the one that loses may suffer losses in the millions.

This kind of pure competition cannot work in TV program-ming. There are only a limited number of available frequencies; the demand exceeds the supply. There is no way that the new program-ming idea can find its way into the marketplace. Our typically Amer-ican solution has been to try to stimulate that market process. Con-gress has provided that no one has a "right" to have his station license extended beyond its original term, that competing applica-tions can be filed, that they must be considered by the people's representatives (the FCC), that programming proposals will be com-pared, and that the people will thus be assured "the best" in tele-vision programming as in other areas of their lives.

To select "the best" is a pragmatic approach. The best may not be very good. It may be an unexpected deviation from our previous standards. But standards tend, by their nature, to be minimal and conventional. One of the beauties of competition is that it is innova-tive. You cannot "predict" a Polaroid, a Xerox, or a transistor; but you want a system that makes them available to the people when they come along. It is impossible to define the "perfect note." But it is possible for us to determine which of two notes is the higher. That is what the FCC must do when comparing programming proposals.

Not only does competition lead to innovation from newcomers to an industry; it also offers a spur to improve performance on the part of those already in the business. The broadcasters have com-plained that unless competing applications are curtailed, those in the business will have to cut back on investment in programming. In fact, the broadcasters' response to competitive challenges has not been to cut back upon programming; they have responded to competition like any other industry. *Variety* reports:

> The recent wave of license challenges . . . has without question raised the level of program aspiration in most major markets, and particularly in those where the jump applications were filed. There is on the whole discernably more local involvement, more community affairs and educational programming, more news and discussion and more showcasing of minority talent since the license challenges than there were before.

This is healthy; it's American; it benefits everyone.

The argument is made by some broadcasters that they cannot fight "blue sky" promises from a fly-by-night applicant for their license. Of course, this could be a theoretical problem. But the FCC has had more than forty years' experience in evaluating programming proposals—and the financial and professional ability of applicants to deliver on them. Its record is pretty good. It can be expected to continue to be biased in favor of the existing operator, and to take a very realistic look at competing proposals. Moreover, the incumbent operator is in the very best position to reply to impractical proposals. He may have tried some of them, and can explain why they didn't work. The "blue sky" objection to competing applications simply cannot withstand close analysis.

The benefits of competition are not limited to comparative evaluation of programming proposals. Ownership is also a legitimate consideration. In many communities the FCC has permitted the owner of the only AM station to acquire the only FM because there were no competing applications for the FM. The public is better off, the majority has reasoned, with the additional service run by a monopolist than without it at all. If there is only one man in town who wants to run the morning and evening newspaper, TV station, and AM-FM radio stations, there's not much the FCC can do about it short of shutting down some of these facilities. When a potential new operator comes along there is.

Nor is competitive ownership limited to considering the number of commercial operators. Blacks, who now own less than ten of the 7,500 operating stations and none of the nation's TV stations, believe themselves even further excluded from participation in the ownership of the most valuable stations by the "Pastore Bill." It is no solution to argue that minority groups should be satisfied with access to ownership of the most undesirable properties—those which at best

promise short-term losses and a minimal possibility for long-run via-
bility. Nor can we expect that blacks will be able in the near future
to acquire the most desirable properties by bidding in the virtually
free market for broadcast licenses. This bill will cut off the only
avenue to responsible minority participation in the ownership and
operation of broadcast stations. And "minority groups" change.
That's why ownership should remain as flexible ten years from now
as today. Mexican-Americans and the American Indians are beginning
to get organized. Senior citizens, the young (a major portion of the
radio audience), and the new-found "Middle America" are also
"minority groups."

There are other alternatives to station ownership by white businessmen. Congress and the FCC have provided a great deal of encouragement to the competition known as "educational broadcasting."
Hopefully, we both intend to provide it even more support. But
many communities are now without VHF educational TV stations,
or AM educational radio stations. Should competing applications for
these facilities from public broadcasting stations be forever prohibited in these communities? There are now audience-supported
radio stations in the area of New York, Los Angeles, San Francisco,
Houston, Seattle, and St. Louis. These stations provide a noncommercial service so valued by the audience that it is willing to sustain
the programming with voluntary contributions. This is yet another
pattern of alternative ownership and competition.

What if a community group offered to operate a local commercial station on a nonprofit basis, plowing the money from commercials back into programming and other broadcast-related activities?
Should the community be denied this service? Should consideration
of this "competing application" be refused until the FCC has first
found that one of the local stations is not serving the public interest
(or, in Chairman Burch's proposed language, that it is not "substantially . . . attuned to meeting the needs and interests of its area")?

The practical advantages of competition aside, there is even
some question as to whether the "Pastore Bill" is Constitutional. The
First Amendment flatly bars Congress from enacting laws abridging
the freedoms of speech and the press. If Congress were to state that
only one, two, or three persons would be permitted to operate newspapers in any one community, such a law would clearly violate the
Constitution. And if Congress were to state that no more than three
named persons could use "soap boxes" to speak in a public park at a
time, such a law would also violate the Constitution. Free speech is
not truly "free" if one is forced to speak in a closet. The First

Amendment sanctions, not just "speech," but "effective speech" [*Edwards v. South Carolina, 1963; Saia v. New York, 1948*]; the effectiveness of this speech depends on the existence and nature of an appropriate forum. There is no more appropriate "public forum" today than the radio and television media. It does no good to say that citizens have the rights of free speech and press, and then deny them access to the most important methods of communication to modern man: the broadcast media.

So much for "competition." The other basic principle is "democracy," or as the redundant expression has it, "participatory democracy." Our country is caught up in a wave of citizen and consumer participation. We have suddenly become aware of just how unrepresentative and unresponsive our major institutions are. We are reforming our national party structure and procedures. Citizen panels are being established to review complaints against the police, and to participate in local educational policy. Increasing amounts of education, leisure time, and disposable income are creating an exponential growth in the number of people who want, and know how to get, "a piece of the action."

Broadcasting cannot expect to be immune. During the 1968 Presidential campaign each candidate made participatory democracy a part of his program. President Nixon talked of listening posts to hear directly from the people; George Wallace urged the return of more power from Washington to local communities; Robert Kennedy spoke of "participatory democracy"; and Eugene McCarthy, of "the new politics." Hubert Humphrey used similar rhetoric. The challenge is to devise systems that leave the people as much opportunity as possible for participating in the decisions that affect their lives. In a densely populated, highly industrialized nation there will be a need for a great many national decisions.

In broadcasting, we must arrive at some national plan for the allocation of TV channels across the country. But who operates those stations, and what they program, need not be determined nationally. There is a balance between popular control and federal regulation. When we can devise ways meaningfully to involve the public in the regulatory process we thereby reduce the need for government-initiated regulation.

What can we do? FCC Commissioner Kenneth Cox and I have set forth our modest efforts at programming evaluation and standards in opinions dealing with renewals in Oklahoma, New York, and the Washington, D.C., area. These studies—especially the latter two—represent an effort to rank stations by common criteria. It is an effort to stimulate competition, or the comparative hearing process. It provides a means whereby the Commission could, if it so chose, undertake a more thorough review of the performance of those stations that rank in the bottom 25 per cent or 10 per cent. So far, as Professor Louis L. Jaffee has noted, "The Commission has not seen its way clear even to respond on the merits" to this suggestion.

Congressman John Moss of the House Interstate and Foreign Commerce Committee has urged that public renewal hearings be held in the communities where the stations are located. Local hearings might prove impractical for all communities, but encompassing the top hundred markets would require less than three additional hearings a month for FCC examiners.

There are other ways of telling the public of its rights in the license renewal process. Full-page ads and repeated, intelligible radio and TV announcements could be used—instead of the present small-print legal notices and rare and perfunctory broadcast announcements. The FCC could provide the same kind of information and assistance to public groups interested in the renewal process that it now provides broadcasters when its top staff travels about, speaking, answering questions, and distributing literature and helpful hints to licensees about to fill out renewal forms. Most important, if public participation is to work effectively, Congress and the Commission must recognize the tremendous handicap in financial and professional resources that any public group confronts when competing against a well established broadcaster. There must be some economic incentive for the protesting group. The possibility of competing applications, with the ultimate reward of obtaining the license, is such an incentive—and another reason why competing applications should not be discouraged.

The law has often recognized the need for such incentives. Treble damages are awarded in some antitrust cases, as an incentive to private policing rather than the alternative of more government action. Statutes provide the award of attorneys' fees in some instances. Other agencies—like the National Labor Relations Board or the Neighborhood Legal Services Project of the Office of Economic Opportunity—provide lawyers directly to complaining parties.

There are 7,500 stations in this country. All the licenses in a given state come up for renewal at the same time. With three-year terms, this means roughly 2,500 a year. Even if the FCC were to take away two or three licenses a year—something it has yet to do during its forty-two-year history—we would still be providing rubber stamp renewals to 99.9 per cent of the stations. Professor Jaffe has posed the question "whether a communication industry financed by private capital can be run on a three-year basis." Given an industrywide average 100 per cent rate of return annually on depreciated tangible investment, and a 99.9 per cent (or better) probability of license renewal, I would agree with Professor Jaffe that "once the question is asked it appears to be almost rhetorical."

The really outstanding broadcaster has little to fear. He knows the people of his community and they know him. He heads off legitimate complaints before they become serious. He seeks out representatives from all segments of his audience, including potential protestors, even before they look for him. He knows such an approach is good, audience-building business—as well as public service. Any group seriously looking for a license to challenge is going to go after the station with the worst record in town, not his station.

Further, there is no reason why the FCC need hold long, useless, harassing hearings. Administrative practice is flexible enough to permit the FCC to draft hearing issues tightly, and to use informal pre-hearing procedures, to dispose of the frivolous cases quickly. (In fact, the most innovative current development has been the negotiated "settlements" in Texarkana and Rochester between outraged citizens and local broadcasters; renewal hearings were contemplated, then dropped, in exchange for concessions.)

Finally, if anyone in or out of the industry is seriously interested in helping to draft standards for the comparative evaluation of stations' license renewal, their contribution will be most welcome. In our renewal opinions, Commissioner Cox and I have called on the academic community to devote some of its intellectual resources to this problem. So far there has been no response.

It is significant, I believe, that the FCC is officially on record as opposing the "Pastore Bill." Its members feel deeply enough about it to have presented an unusual number of personally prepared statements. Some believe the present procedure—if made to work—is best. Others have attempted to fashion compromise positions that give away less than the bill. None, however, on the old Commission, offered the bill their enthusiastic support. Only one Commissioner does so now, in a most summary and general statement.

The issue before us ought to be stated starkly. It is, quite simply, who is to retain the potential to rule America. We know, if we are honest with ourselves, which segments of the economic and social structure have the loudest voices in the decision-making process in Washington. But the *potential* for popular check remains. It remains, however, only so long as the people can obtain education and information, only so long as they can communicate with each other, only so long as they can retain potential control over the mass media of this country. So long as we preserve the people's *potential* to rule— their *potential* opportunity to participate in the operation of their mass media—there is some hope, however small, that some future generation—perhaps the next—will use this potential to rebuild America.

WHAT CAN WE DO ABOUT TELEVISON?

Nicholas Johnson

Television is more than just another great public resource—like air and water—ruined by private greed and public inattention. It is the greatest communications mechanism ever designed and operated by man. It pumps into the human brain an unending stream of information, opinion, moral values, and esthetic taste. It cannot be a neutral influence. Every minute of television programing—commercials, entertainment, news—teaches us something.

Most Americans tell pollsters that television constitutes their principal source of information. Many of our senior citizens are tied to their television sets for intellectual stimulation. And children now spend more time learning from television than from church and school combined. By the time they enter first grade they will have received more hours of instruction from television networks than they will later receive from college professors while earning a bachelor's degree. Whether they like it or not, the television networks are playing the roles of teacher, preacher, parent, public official, doctor, psychiatrist, family counselor, and friend for tens of millions of Americans each day of their lives.

TV programing can be creative, educational, uplifting, and refreshing without being tedious. But the current television product that drains away lifetimes of leisure energy is none of these. It leaves its addicts waterlogged. Only rarely does it contribute anything meaningful to their lives. No wonder so many Americans express to me a deep-seated hostility toward television. Too many realize, perhaps unconsciously but certainly with utter disgust, that television is

Nicholas Johnson, FCC commissioner, is a frequent contributor to the mass media. This, his second article of the book, originally appeared in *Saturday Review* (July 11, 1970) and is reprinted with both his permission and that of *Saturday Review*, copyright 1970.

itself a drug, constantly offering the allure of a satisfying fulfillment for otherwise empty and meaningless lives that it seldom, if ever, delivers.

Well, what do we do about it? Here are a few suggestions:

STEP ONE: *Turn on.* I don't mean rush to your sets and turn the on-knob. What I do mean is that we had all better "turn on" to television—wake up to the fact that it is no longer intellectually smart to ignore it. Everything we do, or are, or worry about is affected by television. How and when issues are resolved in this country—the Indochina War, air pollution, race relations—depend as much as anything else on how (and whether) they're treated by the television networks in "entertainment" as well as news and public affairs programing.

Dr. S.I. Hayakawa has said that man is no more conscious of communication than a fish would be conscious of the waters of the sea. The analogy is apt. A tidal wave of television programing has covered our land during the past twenty years. The vast majority of Americans have begun to breathe through gills. Yet, we have scarcely noticed the change, let alone wondered what it is doing to us. A few examples may start us thinking.

The entire medical profession, as well as the federal government, had little impact upon cigarette consumption in this country until a single young man, John Banzhaf, convinced the Federal Communications Commission that its Fairness Doctrine required TV and radio stations to broadcast $100-million worth of "anti-smoking commercials." Cigarette consumption has now declined for one of the few times in history.

What the American people think about government and politics in general—as well as a favorite candidate in particular—is almost exclusively influenced by television. The candidates and their advertising agencies, which invest 75 per cent or more of their campaign funds in broadcast time, believe this: to the tune of $58-million in 1968.

There's been a lot of talk recently about malnutrition in America. Yet, people could let their television sets run for twenty-four hours a day and never discover that diets of starch and soda pop can be fatal.

If people lack rudimentary information about jobs, community services for the poor, alcoholism, and so forth, it is because occasional tidbits of information of this kind in soap operas, game shows, commercials, and primetime series are either inaccurate or missing.

In short, whatever your job or interests may be, the odds are very good that you could multiply your effectiveness tremendously by "turning on" to the impact of television on your activities and on our society as a whole—an impact that exceeds that of any other existing institution.

STEP TWO: *Tune in.* There are people all over the country with something vitally important to say: the people who knew "cyclamates" were dangerous decades ago, the people who warned us against the Vietnam War in the early Sixties, the people who sounded the alarm against industrial pollution when the word "smog" hadn't been invented. Why didn't we hear their warnings over the broadcast media?

In part it is the media's fault, the product of "corporate censorship." But in large part it's the fault of the very people with something to say who never stopped to consider how they might best say it. They simply haven't "tuned in" to television.

Obviously, I'm not suggesting you run out and buy up the nearest network. What I am suggesting is that we stop thinking that televison programing somehow materializes out of thin air, or that it's manufactured by hidden forces or anonymous men. It is not. There is a new generation coming along that is substantially less frightened by a 16mm camera than by a pencil. You may be a part of it. Even those of us who are not, however, had better tune in to television ourselves.

Here is an example of someone who *did*. The summer of 1969, CBS aired an hour-long show on Japan, assisted in large part by former Ambassador Edwin Reischauer. No one, including Ambassador Reischauer and CBS, would claim the show perfectly packaged all that Americans want or need to know about our 100 million neighbors across the Pacific. But many who watched felt it was one of the finest bits of educational entertainment about Japan ever offered to the American people by a commercial network.

Ambassador Reischauer has spent his lifetime studying Japan, yet his was not an easy assignment. An hour is not very long for a man who is used to writing books and teaching forty-five-hour semester courses, and there were those who wanted to turn the show into an hour-long geisha party. He could have refused to do the show at all, or walked away from the project when it seemed to be getting out of control. But he didn't. And as a result, the nation, the CBS network, and Mr. Reischauer all benefited. (And the show was honored by an Emmy award.)

There are other Ed Reischauers in this country: men who don't know much about "television," but who know more than anyone else about a subject that is important and potentially entertaining. If these men can team their knowledge with the professional television talent of others (and a network's financial commitment), they can make a television program happen. Not only ought they to accept such assignments when asked, I would urge them to come forward and volunteer their assistance to the networks and their local station managers or to the local cable television system. Of course, these offers won't always, or even often, be accepted—for many reasons. But sooner or later the dialogue has to begin.

There are many ways you can contribute to a television program without knowing anything about lighting or electronics. Broadcasters in many large communities (especially those with universities) are cashing in on local expertise for quick background when an important news story breaks, occasional on-camera interviews, suggestions for news items or entire shows, participation as panel members or even hosts, writers for programs, citizen advisory committees, and so forth. Everyone benefits. The broadcaster puts out higher-quality programing, the community builds greater citizen involvement and identification, and the television audience profits.

Whoever you are, whatever you're doing, ask yourself this simple question: What do I know or what do I have to know or might find interesting? If you're a Department of Health, Education and Welfare official charged with communicating vital information about malnutrition to the poor, you might be better off putting your information into the plot-line of a daytime television soap opera than spending a lifetime writing pamphlets. If you're a law enforcement officer and want to inform people how to secure their homes against illegal entry, you might do better by talking to the writers and producers of *Dragnet*, *I Spy*, or *Mission: Impossible* than by making slide presentations.

STEP THREE: *Drop out.* The next step is to throw away most of what you've learned about communication. Don't make the mistake of writing "TV essays"—sitting in front of a camera reading, or saying, what might otherwise have been expressed in print. "Talking heads" make for poor television communication, as educational and commercial television professionals are discovering. Intellectuals and other thinking creative people first have to "drop out" of the traditional modes of communicating thoughts, and learn to swim through the new medium of television.

Marshall McLuhan has made much of this clear. If the print medium is linear, television is not. McLuhan's message is as simple as one in a Chinese fortune cookie: "One picture worth thousand words"—particularly when the picture is in color and motion, is accompanied by sound (words and music), and is not tied to an orderly time sequence.

Mason Williams, multitalented onetime writer for the Smothers Brothers, is one of the few to see this new dimension in communication. He describes one of his techniques as "verbal snapshots"—short bursts of thought, or poetry, or sound that penetrate the mind in an instant, then linger. Here are some that happen to be about television itself: "I am qualified to criticize television because I have two eyes and a mind, which is one more eye and one more mind than television has." "Television doesn't have a job; it just goofs off all day." "Television is doing to your mind what industry is doing to the land. Some people already think like New York City looks." No one "snapshot" gives the whole picture. But read in rapid succession, they leave a vivid and highly distinctive after-image.

Others have dropped out of the older communications techniques and have adapted to the new media. Those students who are seen on television—sitting in, protesting, assembling—are developing a new medium of communication: the demonstration. Denied traditional access to the network news shows and panel discussions, students in this country now communicate with the American people via loud, "news-worthy," media-attractive aggregations of sound and color and people. Demonstrations are happenings, and the news media—like moths to a flame—run to cover them. Yippie Abbie Hoffman sees this clearer than most:

> So what the hell are we doing, you ask? We are dynamiting brain cells. We are putting people through changes. . . . We are theater in the streets: total and committed. We aim to involve people and use . . . any weapon (prop) we can find. All is relevant, only "the play's the thing." . . . The media is the message. Use it! No fund raising, no full-page ads in *The New York Times*, no press releases. Just do your thing; the press eats it up. Media is free. *Make news.*

Dr. Martin Luther King told us very much the same thing. "Lacking sufficient access to television, publications, and broad forums, Negroes have had to write their most persuasive essays with the blunt pen of marching ranks."

Mason Williams, Abbie Hoffman, Dr. Martin Luther King, and many others have set the stage for the new communicators, the new media experts. All dropped out of the traditional communications bag of speeches, round-table discussions, panels, symposia, and filmed essays. And they reached the people.

STEP FOUR: *Make the legal scene.* Shakespeare's Henry VI threatened: "The first thing we do, let's kill all the lawyers." Good advice in the fifteenth century perhaps. But bad advice today. We need lawyers. And they can help you improve television.

Examples are legion. The United Church of Christ successfully fought *two* legal appeals to the United States Court of Appeals for the District of Columbia, one establishing the right of local citizens groups to participate in FCC proceedings, and one revoking the license of WLBT-TV in Jackson, Mississippi, for systematic segregationist practices. In Media, Pennsylvania, nineteen local organizations hired a Washington lawyer to protest radio station WXUR's alleged policy of broadcasting primarily right-wing political programing. In Los Angeles, a group of local businessmen challenged the license of KHJ-TV, and the FCC's hearing examiner awarded them the channel. [Editor's Note: The challenge was rebuffed by the Commission.] There are dozens of other examples of the imaginative use of rusty old legal remedies to improve the contribution of television to our national life.

For all their drawbacks, lawyers understand what I call "the law of effective reform"; that is, to get reform from legal institutions (Congress, courts, agencies), one must assert, first, the factual basis for the grievance; second, the specific legal principle involved (Constitutional provision, statute, regulation, judicial or agency decision); and third, the precise remedy sought (legislation, fine, license revocation). Turn on a lawyer, and you'll turn on an awful lot of legal energy, talent, and skill. You will be astonished at just how much legal power you actually have over a seemingly intractable Establishment.

STEP FIVE: *Try do-it-yourself justice.* Find out what you can do without a lawyer. You ought to know, for example, that every three years *all* the radio and television station licenses come up for renewal in your state. You ought to know when that date is. It is an "election day" of sorts, and you have a right and obligation to "vote." Not surprisingly, many individuals have never even been told there's an election. [Editor's Note: The renewal schedule is given on page 45.]

Learn something about the grand design of communications in this country. For example, no one "owns" a radio or television station in the sense that you can own a home or the corner drugstore.

It's more like leasing public land to graze sheep, or obtaining a contract to build a stretch of highway for the state. Congress has provided that the airwaves are public property. The user must be licensed, and, in the case of commercial broadcasters, that license term is for three years. There is no "right" to have the license renewed. It is renewed only if past performance, and promises of future performance, are found by the FCC to serve "the public interest." In making this finding, the views of local individuals and groups are, of course, given great weight. In extreme cases, license revocation or license renewal contest proceedings may be instituted by local groups.

You should understand the basic policy underlying the Communications Act of 1934, which set up the FCC and gave it its regulatory powers. "Spectrum space" (radio and television frequencies) in this country is limited. It must be shared by taxicabs, police cars, the Defense Department, and other business users. In many ways it would be more efficient to have a small number of extremely high-powered stations blanket the country, leaving the remaining spectrum space for other users. But Congress felt in 1934 that it was essential for the new technology of radio to serve needs, tastes, and interests at the local level—to provide community identification, cohesion, and outlets for local talent and expression. For this reason, roughly 95 per cent of the most valuable spectrum space has been handed out to some 7,500 radio and television stations in communities throughout the country. Unfortunately, the theory is not working. Most programing consists of nationally distributed records, movies, newswire copy, commercials, and network shows. Most stations broadcast very little in the way of locally oriented community service. It's up to you to make them change.

You have only to exercise your imagination to improve the programing service of your local station. Student groups, civic luncheon clubs, unions, PTAs, the League of Women Voters, and so forth are in an ideal position to accomplish change. They can contact national organizations, write for literature, and generally inform themselves of their broadcasting rights. Members can monitor what is now broadcast and draw up statements of programing standards, indicating what they would like to see with as much specificity as possible. They can set up Citizens Television Advisory Councils to issue reports on broadcasters' performance. They can send delegations to visit with local managers and owners. They can, when negotiation fails, take whatever legal steps are necessary with the FCC. They can complain to sponsors, networks, and local television stations when they find commercials excessively loud or obnoxious. If you think this is dreamy, pie-in-the-sky thinking, look what local groups did in 1969.

Up for Renewal?

All licenses within a given state expire on the same date. Stations must file for license renewal with the FCC ninety days *prior* to the expiration date. Petitions to deny a station's license renewal application must be filed between ninety and thirty days *prior* to the expiration date. Forthcoming expiration dates* for stations located in the following states include:

- Florida, Puerto Rico, and the Virgin Islands: February 1, 1973; 1976; and 1979.
- Alabama and Georgia: April 1, 1973; 1976; and 1979.
- Arkansas, Louisiana, and Mississippi: June 1, 1973; 1976; and 1979.
- Tennessee, Kentucky, and Indiana: August 1, 1973; 1976; and 1979.
- Ohio and Michigan: October 1, 1973; 1976; and 1979.
- Illinois and Wisconsin: December 1, 1973; 1976; and 1979.
- Iowa and Missouri: February 1, 1974; 1977; and 1980.
- Minnesota, North Dakota, South Dakota, Montana, and Colorado: April 1, 1974; 1977; and 1980.
- Kansas, Oklahoma, and Nebraska: June 1, 1974; 1977; and 1980.
- Texas: August 1, 1974; 1977; and 1980.
- Wyoming, Nevada, Arizona, Utah, New Mexico, and Idaho: October 1, 1974; 1977; and 1980.
- California: December 1, 1974; 1977; and 1980.
- Washington, Oregon, Alaska, Guam, and Hawaii: February 1, 1972; 1975; 1978; and 1981.
- Connecticut, Maine, Massachusetts, New Hampshire, Rhode Island, and Vermont: April 1, 1972; 1975; 1978; and 1981.
- New Jersey and New York: June 1, 1972; 1975; 1978; and 1981.
- Delaware and Pennsylvania: August 1, 1972; 1975; 1978; and 1981.
- Maryland, the District of Columbia, Virginia, and West Virginia: October 1, 1972; 1975; 1978; and 1981.
- North Carolina and South Carolina: December 1, 1972; 1975; 1978; and 1981.

---

*Dates subject to change.

Texarkana was given national attention last year when a large magazine reported that the city's population of rats was virtually taking over the city. Of lesser notoriety, but perhaps of greater long-run significance, was an agreement hammered out between a citizens group and KTAL-TV, the local television station. In January 1969, the Texarkana Junior Chamber of Commerce and twelve local unincorporated associations—with the assistance of the Office of Communications of the United Church of Christ—filed complaints with the FCC, and alleged that KTAL-TV had failed to survey the needs of its community, had systematically refused to serve the tastes, needs, and desires of Texarkana's 26 per cent Negro population, and had maintained no color origination equipment in its Texarkana studio (although it had such equipment in the wealthier community of Shreveport, Louisiana). But they didn't stop there. Armed with the threat of a license renewal hearing, they went directly to the station's management and hammered out *an agreement* in which the station promised it would make a number of reforms, or forfeit its license. Among other provisions, KTAL-TV promised to recruit and train a staff broadly representative of all minority groups in the community; employ a minimum of two full-time Negro reporters; set up a toll-free telephone line for news and public service announcements and inquiries; present discussion programs of controversial issues, including both black and white participants; publicize the rights of the poor to obtain needed services; regularly televise announcements of the public's rights and periodically consult with all substantial groups in the community regarding their programing tastes and needs.

The seeds of citizen participation sown in Texarkana have since come to fruition elsewhere. Just recently five citizens groups negotiated agreements with twenty-two stations in Atlanta, Georgia, and similar attempts have been made in Shreveport, Louisiana; Sandersville, Georgia; Mobile, Alabama; and Jackson, Mississippi.

In Washington, D.C., . . . a group of students under the supervision of the Institute for Policy Studies undertook a massive systematic review of the license applications of all television stations in the area of Washington, D.C., Virginia, West Virginia, and Maryland. They used a number of "performance charts" by which they evaluated and ranked the stations in amounts of news broadcast, news employees hired, commercials, public service announcements, and other factors. The result was a book that may become a working model for the comparative evaluation of television stations' performances.* Citizens groups all over the country can easily follow their example.

I have felt for some time that it would be useful to have detailed reviews and periodic reports about the implications of specific television commercials and entertainment shows by groups of professional psychiatrists, child psychologists, educators, doctors, ministers, social scientists, and so forth. They could pick a show in the evening—any show—and discuss its esthetic quality, its accuracy, and its potential national impact upon moral values, constructive opinion, mental health, and so forth. It would be especially exciting if this critical analysis could be shown on television. Such professional comment would be bound to have *some* impact upon the networks' performance. (The 1969 *Violence Commission Report* did.) It would be a high service indeed to our nation, with rewards as well for the professional groups and individuals involved—including the broadcasting industry. It is not without precedent. The BBC formerly aired a critique of evening shows following prime-time entertainment. It would be refreshing to have a television producer's sense of status and satisfaction depend more upon the enthusiasm of the critics and audience than upon the number of cans of "feminine deodorant spray" he can sell.

These examples are only the beginning. Television could become our most exciting medium if the creative people in this country would use a fraction of their talent to figure out ways of improving it.

STEP SIX: *Get high (with a little help from your friends).* Have you ever made a film, or produced a TV documentary, or written a radio script? That's a real high. But if you're like me, you'll need help—lots of it—from your friends. If you've got something to say, find someone who's expert in communication: high school or college filmmakers, drama students, off-time TV reporters, or local CATV outlets with program origination equipment. Bring the thinkers in the community together with the media creators. CBS did it with Ed Reischauer and its one-hour special on Japan. You can do it too. Get others interested in television.†

---

*(IPS, *Television Today: The End of Communication and the Death of Community*, $10 from the Institute for Policy Studies, 1540 New Hampshire Avenue, N.W., Washington, D.C.) Citizens groups all over the country can easily follow their example.

†A free pamphlet, "Clearing the Air," has been published by Media Ithaca, Department of Sociology, Cornell University, Ithaca, New York 14850. It explains how average citizens can obtain free air time over radio, television, and CATV.

STEP SEVEN: *Expand your media mind.* Everyone can work for policies that increase the number of radio and television outlets, and provide individuals with access to existing outlets to express their talent or point of view. Those outlets are already numerous. There are now nearly ten times as many radio and television stations as there were thirty-five years ago. There are many more AM radio stations, including the "daytime only" stations. There is the new FM radio service. There is VHF television. And, since Congress passed the all-channel receiver law in 1962, UHF television (channels 14-83) has come alive. There are educational radio and television stations all over the country. There are "listener-supported" community radio stations (such as the Pacifica stations in New York, Los Angeles, Houston, and Berkeley). This increase in outlets has necessarily broadened the diversity of programing. However, since the system is virtually all "commercial" broadcasting, this diversity too often means simply that there are now five stations to play the "top forty" records in your city instead of two. In the past couple years, however, educational broadcasting has gained in strength with the Public Broadcasting Corporation (potentially America's answer to the BBC). Owners of groups of profitable television stations (such as Westinghouse and Metromedia) have begun syndicating more shows—some of which subsequently get picked up by the networks.

Cable television (CATV) offers a potentially unlimited number of channels. (The present over-the-air system is physically limited to from five to ten television stations even in the largest communities.) Twelve-channel cable systems are quite common, twenty-channel systems are being installed, and more channels will undoubtedly come in the future. Your telephone, for example, is a "100-million-channel receiver" in that it can call, or be called by, any one of 100 million other instruments in this country.

Cable television offers greater diversity among commercial television programs—at the moment, mostly movies, sports, and reruns—but it can also offer another advantage: públic access. The FCC has indicated that cable systems should be encouraged and perhaps ultimately required to offer channels for lease to any person willing to pay the going rate. In the *Red Lion* case, the Supreme Court upheld the FCC's fairness doctrine and, noting the monopolistic position most broadcasters hold, suggested that "free speech" rights belong principally to the audience and those who wish to use the station, not the station owner. This concept—which might raise administrative problems for single stations—is easily adaptable to cable television.

If someone wants to place a show on a single over-the-air broadcast station, some other (generally more profitable) program must be canceled. A cable system, by contrast, can theoretically carry an unlimited number of programs at the same time. We therefore have the opportunity to require cable systems to carry whatever programs are offered on a leased-channel basis (sustained either by advertising or by subscription fee). Time might even be made available free to organizations, young film-makers, and others who could not afford the leasing fee and do not advertise or profit from their programing. Now is the time to guarantee such rights for your community. City councils all across the nation are in the process of drafting the terms for cable television franchises. If your community is at present considering a cable television ordinance, it is your opportunity to work for free and common-carrier "citizens' access" to the cables that will one day connect your home with the rest of the world.

Television is here to stay. It's the single most significant force in our society. It is now long past time that the professional and intellectual community—indeed, anyone who reads magazines and cares where this country is going—turn on to television.

BROADCAST REGULATION BY CONTRACT: SOME OBSERVATIONS ON "COMMUNITY CONTROL" OF BROADCASTING

Richard Jencks

As America enters the second year of the decade of the Seventies, its most characteristic protest movement is no longer the Civil Rights Movement—or the Peace Movement—or the revolt of youth.

Instead, it is that combination of causes which has been summarized by the awkward word "consumerism." . . .

The consumerism movement is in many ways typically American. It is reformist in its objectives, populist in its rhetoric, intensely pragmatic in its methods. . . .

On issues ranging from the ecological impact of pesticides to the urgent need for automobile safety, and from thermal pollution to the

Richard W. Jencks, Vice President, CBS Washington, delivered these remarks on "Broadcast Regulation by Private Contract: Some Observations on 'Community Control' of Broadcasting" at the 1971 Broadcasting Industry Symposium, Washington, D.C. This edited version is used with his permission.

SST, consumerism is persuading the public to demand of government that it reorder its priorities, and that it pay less attention to conventional notions of progress.

In all of these activities the aim of consumerism was to induce government action, whether by the executive branch, by the Congress, or by regulatory agencies.

In broadcasting, consumerism has stimulated regulatory action in a number of areas, of which one of the most notable was in connection with the broadcast advertising of cigarettes.

Consumerism is responsible for another development in the broadcast field in which its role is quite different—in which it seeks not so much to encourage regulatory action as to *substitute* for government regulation a novel kind of private regulation.

That development is a trend toward regulation of broadcasting through contracts entered into by broadcast licensees with private groups—contracts entered into in consideration of the settlement of license challenges. This form of regulation has been called the "community control" of broadcasting. It begins with the monitoring and surveillance of a broadcast station by the group. It ends with the group's use of the license renewal process in such a way as to achieve a greater or lesser degree of change in—and in some cases continuing supervision of—a broadcast station's policies, personnel and programming. . . .

A strategy was developed in which a community group would, prior to the deadline for a station's renewal application, make demands for changes in a station's policies. If a station granted these demands they would be embodied in a contract and embodied, as well, in the station's renewal application. If a station refused to grant these demands the group would file a petition to deny renewal of the station's license. Such a petition, if alleging significant failures by the licensee to perform his obligations, can be expected to bring about a full-scale FCC hearing. As a result, there is obviously a powerful incentive in these situations, even for the best of stations, to try to avoid a lengthy, costly and burdensome hearing by attempting to reach an agreement with such a group. . . .

Probably the most fundamental demand made in recent license challenges is that a large percentage of the station's weekly schedule be programmed with material defined as "relevant" to the particular community group—usually an ethnic group—making the demand. . . . The demands I am referring to here go far beyond even what the most responsive broadcast stations have done in the way of local public service programming or what the FCC has expected of them.

In one recent case it amounted to a demand that more than 40 percent of a station's total programming schedule must be programmed with material defined as "relevant" to the minority group. . . .

Philosophically, this kind of demand raises a basic question as to the purpose of a mass medium in a democratic society. Should the broadcast medium be used as a way of binding its audience together through programming which cuts across racial and cultural lines? Or should it be used as a means of communicating separately with differentiated segments of its audience? . . .

It seems possible that there is a strong thread of racial separatism in the demand for relevance. Like the demand of some black college students for segregated dormitories, it may be regarded in large part as a demand for segregated programming. . . .

Connected with the notion of relevance is the interesting idea that programming done as part of a requirement of "relevance" must be an accurate reflection of the "life-style" of the particular minority community.

The director of a national organization whose purpose is to encourage license challenges by local groups recently spelled out what he meant by the idea of the truthful portrayal of a life-style. On his arrival in Dayton, Ohio, to organize license challenges by local groups there *Variety* described his views as follows: "If one third of Dayton's population is black, then one third of radio and TV programming should be beamed to the black community. And this should be produced, directed and presented by blacks." Referring to JULIA, the NBC situation comedy, he was then quoted by *Variety* as saying: "How many black women really live like JULIA? I'd like to see her get pregnant—with no husband. That would be a real life situation."

Now, I think that was meant seriously and it is worth taking seriously. . . .

Considerations like these go directly to the heart of what a mass medium is, and how it should be used. We live in an era in which the mass media have been dying off one by one. Theatrical motion pictures are no longer a mass medium and less and less a popular art form. They now reach relatively small and diverse social groups—not infrequently, I might add, with strong depictions of social realism. They no longer reach the population at large. Magazines, once our most potent mass medium, are almost extinct as such. There are plenty of magazines to be sure, but almost all serve narrow audiences. . . . Central city newspapers, as suburbanization continues, find their ability to reach megalopolitan areas steadily decreasing. . . .

Television can be said to be the only remaining mass medium which is capable of reaching most of the people most of the time. Is it important to preserve television as a mass medium? I think so. I think so particularly when I consider the racial problem in this country.

For the importance of television as a mass medium has not been in what has been communicated *to* minorities as such—or what has been communicated *between* minority group leaders and their followers—but in what has been communicated *about* minorities *to the general public.* . . .

Such communication occurs when programs are produced for dissemination to a mass audience for the purpose of *uniting* that audience in the knowledge of a problem, or in the exposure to an experience, not for the purpose of fragmenting that audience by aiming only at what is deemed "relevant" by leaders of a single minority group. . . .

I referred earlier to the excoriation by some black leaders of NBC's JULIA, the first situation comedy to star a black woman. The question may well be asked whether the shift for the better in white American attitudes about black people is not more likely to have been caused by programs like JULIA—and by the startling increase in the number of black faces on other television entertainment programs which began in the mid-60s—as it is to any other single cause.

No one should doubt that racial attitudes *have* changed, even though much remains to be done. A Gallup poll, published last May, asked white parents in the South whether they would object to sending their children to school where any Negroes were enrolled. In 1963, in answer to the same question, *six* out of every *ten* white parents in the South had told Gallup pollers that they would object to sending their children to schools where any Negroes were enrolled. In 1970, seven years later, according to Gallup, only *one* parent in *six* offered such an objection. Other recent public opinion polls show similar gains in white attitude toward blacks. . . .

These advances in the direction of an integrated society were made possible in part, I suggest, by a mass medium which, with all its faults, increasingly *depicted* an integrated society. . . . Americans who in their daily lives seldom or rarely deal on terms of social intimacy with black people have been seeing them on the television screen night after night for some years now. . . .

If audience fragmentation to meet the special requirements of minority groups would destroy television as a *local* mass medium it would, by the same token, of course, make impossible the continuance of network television as a *national* mass medium. Again, some might welcome this. Some think it might happen anyway. John Tebbel, writing recently in *The Saturday Review,* observed: "There is no reason to suppose that network television is immune to the forces that are gradually breaking up other national media." He does not, however, celebrate that possibility. "It is seldom realized," writes Tebbel, "how much network television binds the nation together... To fragment television coverage into local interests might better serve the communities, as the egalitarians fashionably argue, but it would hardly serve the national interest which in the end is everyone's interest."

I have discussed what seems to me to be the basic objective of community group demands upon the media—the fragmentation of programming to serve what are perceived as ethnically relevant interests.

The *means* used by the community groups may have an important impact on the nature of American broadcast regulation, and in particular upon the FCC. Commissioner Johnson often has provocative insights and this instance is no exception. He has praised the idea of regulation by community groups and has called upon his colleagues on the Commission to, in his words, "set a powerful precedent to encourage local public interest groups to fight as 'private attorney generals' in forcing stations to do what the FCC is unable or unwilling to do: improve licensee performance."

This puts the question quite precisely. *Should* private groups be encouraged to do what official law enforcement bodies are "unable or unwilling to do"? In particular, should they police a licensee by means of exploiting the power of that very regulatory agency which is said to be "unable or unwilling" to do so?

It would seem that to ask the question is to answer it. Despite the trend of vigilantism in the Old West, it is not a theory of law enforcement which has found many supporters in recent times.

In the first place, private enforcement is unequal. Although Commissioner Johnson may refer to the role of these groups as that of "private attorney generals," they do not act as a *public* attorney general has to act; the demands they make on a television or radio station are rarely if ever concerned with any constituents other than their own.

In the second place, private law enforcement is hard to control. Whenever law enforcement depends on the action of private groups, the question of private power is apt to become all too important. A medium which can be coerced by threat of license contest into making such concessions to black or Spanish-speaking groups can as readily be coerced by a coalition of white ethnic groups. More so, in fact, since in most American cities there is, and will continue to be for some time, a white majority. To expect a situation to exist for long in which tiny minority groups can coerce stations into providing special treatment, and not to expect the majority to seek the same power over the station, is to expect, in Jefferson's famous phrase, "what never was and never will be."

Clearly there is at the heart of this matter a broad question of public policy—namely, whether public control of licensee conduct should be supplemented by any form of private control. It is plain that the encouragement of "private attorney generals" will result to some degree in the evasion of the legal and constitutional restraints which have been placed upon the regulation of broadcasting in this country. . . .

For a weak broadcaster, if not a strong one, will doubtless be found agreeable to entering into a contract under which he will be required to do many things which the Commission itself either *cannot do*, *does not wish to do* or *has not yet decided to do*. . . .

All this might be questionable enough if community group leaders were clearly representative, under some democratically controlled process, of the individuals for whom they speak. However public spirited or *bona fide* their leadership, however, this is rarely the case. The groups making these challenges are loosely organized and tiny in membership. Not infrequently, the active members of a group seeking to contract with stations in a city of several million number scarcely more than a few dozen.

So far the effectiveness of community group strategy has rested upon the paradoxical willingness of the Commission to tacitly support these groups and their objectives. . . . Many of those who believe that the Commission is a "do-nothing" agency may not be concerned with where regulation by private contract is likely to lead. Others may feel that to weaken duly constituted regulatory authority by condoning such private action is, in the long run, to make the performance of broadcast stations subject to undue local community pressures. These pressures may not always be exerted in socially desirable ways.

Not long ago the Commission held that it was wrong for a broadcast licensee to settle claims made against it by a community group by the payment of a sum of money to the group even for the group's legal expenses. The Commission felt that this would open the way to possibility of abuse, to the detriment of the public interest.

But nonmonetary considerations which flow from the station to a community group can be just as detrimental. Suppose, for example, a weak or unwise station were to give a community group special opportunities to influence the coverage of news. Is such a concession less damaging to the public interest than the payment of money? . . . I mentioned early in this talk that the consumerism movement, at its best, is in many ways fully within the American tradition. . . . But it must be added that the movement is also typically American in its excesses. It is sometimes puritanical, usually self-righteous and often, in its concern with ends, careless about means.

The American system of broadcasting, while not perfect, has made real contributions to the public good and social unity. It has done this through the interaction of private licensees, in their role as trustees of the public interest, on the one hand, and the authority of government through an independent nonpartisan regulatory agency. Heretofore in this country when we have spoken about the community, we have generally meant the community as a whole, acting through democratic and representative processes.

I suggest that those who are interested in the quality of life in this country—as it pertains to the preservation of a vigorous and independent broadcast press—should wish to see that private community groups do not supplant the role either of the broadcaster or of the Commission.

ASLEEP AT THE SWITCH OF THE WIRED CITY

Fred W. Friendly

When such diverse voices as William Fulbright, Paul O'Dwyer, Nicholas Johnson, Spiro Agnew, and Harry Belafonte are raised against the state of broadcast journalism and the limited access to the media, they are partly right. But they are right for the wrong reasons. Like most of us, they have been asleep at the switch—and often at the wrong switch.

Fred W. Friendly, member of the faculty of Columbia University's Graduate School of Journalism, teamed with Edward R. Murrow at CBS to give television audiences their first taste of tough public affairs reporting. Mr. Friendly's concerns about the future of the industry he helped develop are used with his permission. They first appeared in *Saturday Review* (October 10, 1970), copyright 1970.

Senator Fulbright complains that "exclusive access" of the administration to television with no automatic right of reply for members of Congress "is a dangerous, unchecked power. . . ."

Vice President Agnew castigates the network news organizations as "a tiny enclosed fraternity of privileged men, elected by no one and enjoying a monopoly. . . ."

Paul O'Dwyer and Newton Minow, as defeated candidate and former regulator respectively, condemn the high cost of political air time which, in effect, permits some rich candidates to buy an election. . . .

Harry Belafonte and the applicants for KNBC-TV, Los Angeles, protest the absence of television channels for minority use. . . .

John Macy, Joan Cooney, and the Ford Foundation view with alarm the reality that public broadcasting has no VHF transmitters in Washington, Los Angeles, Detroit, and fifty other major American cities. . . .

All have identified the disease, but they are misled by the side effects of the temporary remedies improvised for the original ailment, what physicians call iatrogenic disease.

What ails us is not too many Brinkleys and Cronkites, not the broadcast executives who favor President Nixon at the expense of Senators Fulbright and McGovern, not a conspiracy of white supremacist station owners who will not give minority groups the prime time of day (although there are a few of these). Rather, the major restrictive and malevolent force is the absurd shortage of air time. Exclusive access for the President, or the broadcaster you dislike, or the millionaire candidate is "dangerous power," as Fulbright calls it, only because the limited number of channels artificially swells the audience and inflates the price.

To restrict Louisville to two major VHF channels, and the nation's capital to four, to allow an electronic cartel in New York and Los Angeles to be monopolized by the seven early license holders, is to create an autocracy where a very few citizens are more equal than all the others. At stake is not the First Amendment or the right of free speech, but the exclusive custody of the master switch.

What is wrong is that a single organization, no matter how responsible, should be the gatekeeper, principal user, rate-maker, and adjudicator of who shall ride. Far from limiting the three major news networks' right to the air or right to report, I would increase the channels available to all users, including the networks. The present system necessarily limits that freedom of speech the broadcasters so eloquently demand and so seldom fully exercise. Eric Sevareid and

Howard Smith simply do not have the latitude of a Tom Wicker and a William Buckley, not because they are any less bold or any less wise, but because the exclusive nature of the electronic printing press requires caution in interpretative reporting and news analysis.

Walter Lippmann once said that this situation was like having just three printing presses, and, in fact, it is this seller's market which prevents the highly skilled network news organizations from getting the air time their assignment requires. The concern over news programs is shared by the network producers, who are constantly aware of that unbearable nightly attempt to shoehorn a daily news budget into twenty-two minutes, causing oversimplification in the interest of time, overdramatization in the interest of impact. The three major networks would at once expand their nightly news to an hour if they could just get the air time from the affiliated stations. But, once again, it is a shortage of air space and, therefore, the bloated value of air time.

For the politician, Lippmann's analogy of three printing presses should be projected to three electronic soapboxes. A half-hour on that soapbox now costs a national candidate more than $100,000, a local politician as much as $6,000 to $8,000 a minute. Television has become such a political necessity that Kenneth Gibson or Hugh Addonizio, running for mayor of Newark, a city of 400,000, is forced to buy a market of twenty million, extending from Princeton, New Jersey, to Danbury, Connecticut, to Queens, New York. It has made the high cost of campaigning an aberration of democracy.

It is not my purpose here merely to curse the darkness, but also to state that this age of short supply could be coming to an end. The phenomenon of a thick strand of tensiled copper wire encased in plastic may change television as much as television changed wireless radio, for the miracle of the wireless is about to be replaced by the practical necessity of the wired city. The old line-of-sight transmitter that made the highest point in town a landmark may soon become the relic of another age, like trolley tracks or the towpath along the Erie Canal.

It is ironic that the cable, which came unceremoniously as an improvised method of relaying television reception into rural areas, may now be coming to revolutionize the big cities. This ordinary-looking shaft of copper is a true turnpike, as geometrically enlarged in capacity as a sixty-lane thruway would be over the old unpaved Boston Post Road. Comparing this coaxial cable to a telephone wire, says FCC Commissioner Nicholas Johnson, is like "comparing Niagara Falls to a garden hose." With it, every home could have the capacity to receive forty picture channels, several digital display screens, virtually unlimited stereo music positions, a facsimile newspaper or daily news magazine, and facilities for reading the gas meter and keeping watch for fire and intruders. The possibility for such a two-way, feedback system linked to our schools, hospitals, libraries, and businesses is a clear and present dream. And its potential impact on news and public affairs, on the print and broadcast media, on the way we entertain ourselves and teach our children is what the challenge of '76 is all about. When one's imagination adds to this the opportunity for combining it with cassette storage and retrieval libraries, and all of it with synchronous satellites to interconnect the major cities and eventually the continents, the mind may well boggle.

We had better not let it boggle us. If we again permit the wizardry and razzle-dazzle of technology to cause us to marvel at cable's short-term luxuries, we may find ourselves, as we did with radio and television, trapped in a thicket. Because these miracles sneak up on us, because we come by them more easily than we seem able to manage them, we permit new layers of the status quo to limit and often exclude decision-making that future opportunities demand.

Currently, the wired cities of America are being laid out by the same kind of rugged individualist and venture capital that in another age built our railroads and then permitted them to lapse into extinction. For the most part, the charters and regulations for the wired city are being drafted by the same mentality that plotted the interstate highway system at the sacrifice of a series of rapid transit systems. There is nothing venal or dishonest about these city managers and entrepreneurs. They are simply trying to make a buck for their city, a million for their investors, or to insure a dominant place for their company in the system by which pay television will operate.

Although the wired city could be a blessing, could eliminate the questions raised by the Agnews, Fulbrights, Johnsons, and many broadcast journalists, the truth is that without better planning and more regulation than we have presently in broadcasting, the new CATV system could be a debilitating and decaying force that could one day make us look back on the Sixties as the Golden Age. The wired city will not be an improvement just because it is there. Sixty channels will not stop the decay simply through diversity. The current monopoly could give way to a new Tower of Babel, in which a half-hundred voices scream in a cacophonous attempt to attract the largest audience. Somewhere between the monopoly of television and the nickelodeon of radio must come a free, but not reckless, plan for the wired nation.

There are, of course, lavish expectations of the fortunes to be made in CATV, and the bankers and financial analysts have studied it more than have most broadcasters or public representatives. What CATV can do for the nation is a blurred picture with ghosts of promises past. What CATV can do for the investor is becoming clear. If forty to sixty million homes are wired at $5 a month, it could become a $3-billion industry, and the private sector is asking the right questions to determine whether it will work: Will urban residents who do not live in cable country pay $5 a month for better pictures, and will the squabbles for jurisdiction among city, state, and federal authorities be worked out?

The tragedy is that the public sector has not yet determined the question it must ask to save itself. All the obvious questions about right of access, community participation, and protection of current broadcasters are rhetorical ones with unsecured promissory notes as answers; and they will remain so until America gets down to the bitter reality that none of the pledges can be redeemed unless a guaranteed method is found to recycle some of the profits into quality programing.

You can give channels to Leonard Bernstein, Sol Hurok, the Smithsonian Institution, Walter Cronkite, Robert Saudek, Mike Nichols, and Joan Cooney, but if you don't also provide them with a respectable budget, even they cannot deliver. Advertising money is going to continue to go where it now goes. Pay television may provide for some channels, but the box office is not likely to do any more for "the box" than it did for Times Square. If the new technology is permitted to reap the highest potential for the owners, the public interest will again be forfeited. Television promises, without solid guarantees, are only illusions.

The traditional remedy is to call for some well-defined regulations that would lay out the public requirements. Begin by clearing up the present jurisdictional morass of harried city officials, technically unsophisticated judges, and an overworked, understaffed, underfinanced FCC. Then adopt specific rules for the highest technical quality. Finally, it could be required that CATV be placed on a strict common-carrier basis with well-defined rules for access and number of channels available for public-interest programing.

But even assuming that you could accomplish all that by carrying the torch through a maze of powerful, conflicting political and economic interests, our past experience gives no assurance that regulation alone will enable the people to benefit from this new tool. The regulatory pattern developed by the Federal Communications Act of

1934 recognized the potential dangers of total commercial use of the new technology and called for regulation that had as its standard "the public interest, convenience, and necessity." Thirty-five years of experience teaches us that to impose that kind of regulatory pattern on cable television would be to confuse responsibility for loopholes. For instance, while today's technology makes possible twenty to forty-odd channels, cable operators continue to build their systems with the smallest investment possible. As a result, of 2,300 cable systems in the United States operating in 1969, only twenty-six had more than twelve channels. A survey of ownership reveals an almost mirror image of the broadcast industry—with the emphasis on the largest profit based on the smallest investment. In March of 1970, broadcasting interests already had controlling interest in 36.5 per cent of the cable systems operating. Most important is that nearly all the short-term community potential is being neglected, as no regulation has been developed to assure access to the system by all groups. Again, rules of access without guaranteed sources for programing on nonadvertiser channels are an exercise in futility, much like giving every orphan the legal right to attend college but without providing scholarships. The biggest loophole would be to insist on a minimum of public-service programing and then leave the definition and budget for such broadcasts to the franchise owners. That would be but a license for another electronic ghetto.

What is needed in the traditional structure are new elements of public enterprise that, by the sheer economic and political force of their position, will emerge as powerful contenders for cable franchises. In this way, the public can realize its fair rate of return by entering the sweepstakes where it counts—as a majority stockholder who can assure that sufficient revenue is recycled for serious community programing.

Public ownership in the power industry, such as the TVA, not only has been a useful benchmark, but it has helped to keep the rates down and the services up. We may already have a miniature Muscle Shoals demonstration of this possibility in Vincennes, Indiana, where the university floated two bond issues and was awarded cable franchises in four communities in Indiana and Illinois. The estimated income for 1971 may approach $350,000, most of which will go into programing for instructional and public television in the Vincennes area.

Most urban centers are still a blank page as far as the wired city concept goes. There is no status quo to bind us to the past, to obscure this new visibility. A new land rush to public enterprise could be opened to the public broadcasting center, the regional university or library, or a consortium of all of them. Under such a plan they might operate the system, but be just another user with limited access to some of the sixty channels. All others, including the commercial broadcasting stations, the city government and newspapers, would have expanded access, and revenue from the cable system would be used for improved programing. Only in this way will the public interest acquire a piece of the action and the benefits.

Tragically, even this option may have been denied the public sector by a little-reported FCC rule, curiously championed by well-meaning liberals on the commission. Attempting to untangle the threads of distant signal importation and copyright that are directly related to the growth of cable, the FCC acted to restrict local broadcasters from owning cable systems in their own areas. While no one can argue with the basic philosophy underlying that rule, the commission has also sought to exclude all of the public broadcasting stations. What they seem to be saying is that the commercial stations will be too dominant and the public ones too passive.

I would be the first to agree that public broadcasting has not always acted with the verve, intelligence and excitement that many of its supporters have claimed. However, I would argue that to take this shotgun approach in targeting public broadcasting in the cross-ownership rule is precipitous action that can only play into the hands of the people who most want to exploit this system.

This is the time to keep all options open. For if some method is not found to regenerate the revenues for quality programing, this new rocket will fly off in its own mercantile orbit beyond everyone's control. If we were redesigning the streets of our city, rezoning our parks, changing the location of our bridges, everyone would demand to be heard. Simply because the concept of the wired city is currently beyond most people's vision does not mean that we can afford to let it slip beyond our grasp.

Chapter II

INCREASING CONTROL OF THE MASS MEDIA

EXTERNAL CONTROLS: CITIZEN REVIEW

NATIONAL CENTER FOR STUDY OF THE MEDIA

The public should be able to ask the media to improve when they falter, but responsible criticism, like responsible media operation, requires information about the subject matter in order to be accurate and effective. Until now, the media have not been quick to divulge information about their practices. As a result, review and criticism of the media are based on little information or misinformation. One solution, we believe, is to provide for continuing systematic collection of data about media performance, practices, values, and effects.

TASK-FORCE PROPOSAL

The report and proposal of the Hutchins commission were received with widespread public scorn and bitter media indignation. That scorn has not abated, for the critical needs which gave rise to that commission's proposal remain substantially unsatisfied.

We believe that there is a clear need for a national center for media study, independent of both media and government, and responsible to the people. We also recommend the immediate establishment of the center to bring to life the proposals made by the many astute and concerned observers of the media.

The case for an independent agency rests upon two basic judgments: (1) that the recurring conflict between media commercial in-

Quoted in the January 21, 1970 *Christian Science Monitor,* this excerpt is from the task force report of the National Commission on the Causes and Prevention of Violence. (The Appendix to this book carries another important summary of suggestions deserving more study.)

terest and the public interest distorts both the performance of the media and their capacity for self-evaluation and self-criticism; and (2) that the media, through industry self-regulation, are capable of improving their performance under the stimulus of responsible criticism.

OUTSIDE AGENCY DESCRIBED

The harsh responses to the Hutchins commission's and comparable later proposals were based on a perceived threat to freedom of the press which many journalists see as inherent in any form of external observation of media performance.

Yet the "independent agency" was conceived and articulated as a discreet alternative to governmental surveillance; it would be as independent of political influence as any private institution, and would be completely devoid of any regulatory authority. These conditions are of paramount importance.

Nevertheless, we do not believe that the financing of the operations of an organization so basic to our society should be left to the willingness of a foundation to underwrite its substantial costs, nor the ability of a university, sufficiently free of economic pressures, to undertake so strenuous a responsibility. No university or foundation has undertaken such a program in the years since the Hutchins commission's proposal was advanced. We think the known and potential effects of the media are so critical that we cannot wait another quarter-century.

In our judgment, the requisite permanence, independence, and status for an organization capable of constructive impact upon media performance can best come from a nonprofit corporation, organized under the laws of the District of Columbia. This organization should be granted such additional powers as may be required (provided by legislation on the pattern of the Public Broadcast Corporation); without any continuing responsibility to report to Congress or other government agency or official; with a financing mechanism independent of the political processes; and with clearly delineated powers of monitorship, evaluation, and publication, but without sanction.

The center for media study would be independently administered, maintained, and financed, and should have the requisite national standing and absolutely essential independence to ensure that its findings and judgments would be subject to minimum influence by the media or government.

We suggest that the operations of the center be governed by three distinct boards: a governing board with overall supervisory responsibility and policymaking powers; a research board to devise and execute continuing research and analysis of media practices and effects; and a media advisory board. To provide the impetus necessary to begin the center, we suggest that initial three-year appointments to the center's governing boards be made by the President of the United States.

To ensure the political as well as the economic independence of the center, the President should select a governing board of prominent nonpolitical and nonmedia public figures, with significant social and economic minority representation. To ensure that the center has access to the specialized knowledge and competence available in the media, the President should also select a media advisory board from nominees submitted directly by the media themselves.

Finally, the President should appoint a research board from among distinguished academic specialists in such diverse but relevant disciplines as communications research, social psychology, sociology, cultural anthropology, communications technology, law, psychiatry, economics, and management.

We have considered numerous possible methods of funding the operations of the center. Our primary concern has been to ensure that the center will be subject neither to government nor media pressures. We also have sought methods of financing which would involve individual participation across the widest possible spectrum of the public.

If the media are to be responsible directly to the people, as Dr. [Frank] Stanton of CBS and others have suggested, we believe it appropriate for the people to be asked to participate directly in a proposal to examine how well the media discharge that responsibility. We suggest that individual contributions be solicited through a nationwide advertising campaign, planned as a public service by the Advertising Council, and carried as public service advertising in all of the mass media. Supplemental advertising space or time could be purchased either from funds provided initially by a foundation or from contributions received from the public.

As an incentive for individual contributions, there would be the usual federal income-tax deduction. A more viable alternative, however, would be a direct federal tax credit of up to $5 per person.

If contributions exceed the amounts needed to operate the center, the excess funds could be invested in government securities, with a set percentage of the proceeds used, for example to endow additional scholarships, to supplement mid-career training programs, or to be added to the center's endowment.

Supplemental means of financing would include a dedicated tax on advertising or on the sale of radio and television receivers, on gross receipts of the media, or on foundations. One disadvantage of the dedicated tax is that the money passes through government control. The objection could be partially met by placing the funds in a trust account, free from the annual appropriations process.

Still other funding sources could include contributions from universities or corporations. Grants from the media industry would also be accepted. Within broad categories, funds provided by the industry would be employed wholly at the discretion of the center's governing board.

HOW COMMUNITY PRESS COUNCILS WORK

Donald E. Brignolo

Twenty-two years after the Commission on Freedom of the Press suggested the establishment of an evaluative agency for the mass media, pilot community press councils were operating in Bend, Ore., Redwood City, Calif., and Cairo and Sparta, Ill., under the auspices of the Mellett Fund for a Free and Responsible Press, a non-profit corporation. The objective was to demonstrate the utility of press councils as a two-way communicative link between the press and the public and to encourage more responsible press performance without infringing upon established freedoms.

These new press councils are best described by one editor as voluntary, private, non-governmental, lay citizen groups meeting in unfettered, uninhibited, objective and responsible criticism of the press with a view to forcing upon the proprietors of the media a measure of self-discipline.

Although the Mellett Fund experiments have ended, all but the Redwood City press council have been restarted on a permanent basis. Co-existing with the Mellett demonstration projects has been the privately financed Littleton (Colorado) Press Council, which was organized in 1967 as the first contemporary community press council to be started on a permanent basis.

Donald E. Brignolo received his M.A. at the University of Missouri. He compiled this report for Freedom of Information Center Reports (No. 217, March, 1969). It was reprinted in December, 1969 *Seminar Quarterly* and is used with permission of the FOI Center.

Internationally, press councils are not a new phenomenon. As early as 1916, Sweden formed the Press Fair Practices Commission to serve as a mediary between the press and the public. Since that time about fifteen countries have set up press councils or courts of honor. In most nations, the press council is seen as a protector of freedom of the press and as a means of establishing a dialogue between the newspaper and the readers.

J. Edward Gerald of the University of Minnesota described the characteristics of the effective overseas press council:

1. It is a private body designed to ward off government pressure upon the press.
2. It operates as a buffer between the press and the public and between the press and government.
3. Its membership is composed of balanced representation of the community and media.
4. It has no statutory power and relies on public support after reporting its deliberations and decisions.
5. It appears to function best in nations where newsmen avoid all forms of extremism.

Proponents of the press council idea in this country usually point to the successful European councils as a model. They say that a press council induces a sense of responsibility in the newspaper publisher; allows the newspaper to explain *why* it operates as it does; permits the public to make their complaints, desires and needs known to the publisher; and increases understanding of the newspaper.

Meanwhile, opponents of the press council idea argue that newspapers are already engaging in self-criticism and self-discipline, thus a council is unnecessary; the press council may fall into the "wrong" hands, such as those of politicians or government; and the council idea would infringe on freedom of the press.

In the United States, the vast contemporary dialogue about press councils is rooted in the 1947 report of the Commission on Freedom of the Press, also known as the Hutchins Commission, named after its chairman, Robert Hutchins, then chancellor of the University of Chicago. The 133-page document, highly critical of the press, contained a recommendation for the creation of an independent agency "to appraise and report annually upon the performance of the press."

The Hutchins Commission recommended a national continuing commission, but none has been established to date. This report may have sparked the press, more than twenty years later, to awaken to its responsibilities and set up local press councils in the United States.

Adherents of the local press council say there is no way to make a national press council function effectively in the United States because of the preponderance of local newspapers. "Even state and regional press associations have their difficulties," Richard Tobin has said.

William L. Rivers of Stanford University stated in an interview: "There is still a yearning for a national press council, but a local case would have to be a big one for a national council to deal with it." In effect, a national council would be compelled to examine some 1,750 newspapers or a large sample of them.

The community press council, composed of local citizens and media representatives, has been advanced many times since the Hutchins report, with varying degrees of longevity and success.

The first local press council on record is the Colorado Editorial Advisory Board, set up in 1946 by Houstoun Waring of the Littleton (Colo.) *Independent.* For six years, eight newspaper editors met with eight critics, each representing a different field: sociology, journalism teaching, economics, psychology, political science, public opinion polling, race relations and international relations. Since that time, the media executives have sponsored an annual Critics Dinner, attended by ten leading citizens "to tell us what they would do if they were editor," Waring said. The Colorado Editorial Advisory Board, as we shall see later, was restarted in 1967 as a permanent press council.

In 1958, another pioneer press council was established for a brief time in Santa Rose, Calif., by Dr. Chilton R. Bush of Stanford University. The Citizens Advisory Council, as it was called, was composed of community leaders who were to meet quarterly to evaluate the performance of the *Press Democrat*, the local newspaper.

The press council idea circulated spasmodically during the 1950's and early 1960's. In 1963 Barry Bingham, president and editor of the Louisville *Courier-Journal* and *Times*, proposed the creation of a local press council to act as a public forum for the newspaper and the readers. Bingham did not set up a local press council but established the nation's first fulltime "ombudsman" for a newspaper. This is an official to whom the [public] can complain and who has power, though an employe of the newspaper, to request change or addition.

The Association for Education in Journalism (AEJ), which met in Boulder, Colorado, in the summer of 1967, energetically revived the press council idea. The dialogue generated at that convention gave impetus to Houstoun Waring and Garrett Ray of the Littleton (Colo.) *Independent* to restart the Colorado Editorial Advisory Board, this time as a permanent community press council.

The Littleton Press Council was established on Nov. 16, 1967, as the first contemporary community press council to be operated from the start on a permanent basis. Since that time, the ten-member group has met quarterly with newspaper representatives to criticize and advise on newspaper performance. For example, the council has criticized the newspaper for inferior typography and for placing obituaries on the front page. On another occasion, the council requested the need for more student reporters "to keep the community aware of what students are doing." The Press Council has also urged the newspaper to crusade for better vocational training on the high school level and to foster more community beautification.

The Littleton Press Council is a non-experimental venture, thus no tests have been made to determine the effect, if any, of the council on the newspaper. Two of the obvious effects are: (1) the introduction of youth news and elimination of column rules; and (2) the creation of a Youth Advisory Council, an outgrowth of the press council. According to publisher Garrett Ray, the youth council helps the newspaper "to keep in touch with what young people are doing and thinking."

The press council movement in this country was given a forward thrust by the Mellett Fund for a Free and Responsible Press, an independent, non-profit corporation which, from Sept. 1967 through Oct. 1968, financed experimental community press councils in selected cities. General councils were supported in Bend, Ore., and Redwood City, Calif., administered by Stanford University; other press councils were set up in Cairo and Sparta, Ill., directed by Southern Illinois University. The objective was to promote a continuous dialogue between the representatives of the community and press, without infringing on press freedom, and to demonstrate the overall usefulness of a press council.

In addition to the community press councils, the Mellett Fund also financed summer racial councils in 1968 in Seattle and St. Louis, to contribute to the need for "communication across racial lines" called for by the National Advisory Commission on Civil Disorders. The Seattle Communications Council, composed of both print and broadcasting representatives, was administered by the University of Washington School of Communications. The University of Missouri Center for Community and Metropolitan Studies administered the St. Louis summer council. The final results of the racial councils and the year-long experiments are forthcoming from the Mellett Fund. Undoubtedly, the Mellett councils represent the first systematic attempt in this country to demonstrate the utility of the community press council.

The Mellett Fund for a Free and Responsible Press was created through a bequest of about $40,000 from Lowell Mellett, newspaper editor and columnist, to the American Newspaper Guild to be used to encourage responsible press performance without infringing on press freedom. In turn, the Guild set up the Fund as an independent corporation to further the aims of the bequest. Press critic Ben H. Bagdikian was named president of the organization, which is located in Washington, D.C.

On Sept. 24, 1966, the Mellett Fund officers adopted the press council idea and established some basic ground rules for the proposed experimental councils. One rule was that the council could have no power to effect change in the local newspaper. Bagdikian said the council "could study, discuss or vote, always with the publisher as a member of the group. But the paper retained discretion over its own contents." Another rule was that the administration of each council—its design, implementation and final report—would be in the sole hands of a university journalism professor who had a strong practical newspaper background.

On July 21, 1967, the Mellett Fund announced a grant of $16,250 to Dr. William L. Rivers of the Stanford University Department of Communication to administer year-long pilot press councils in two cities. Rivers is the author of two journalism textbooks and *The Opinionmakers*, a book on Washington journalism.

Rivers decided ("The West Coast Councils: An Interim Report") to try two different formats in order to test different principles. In one city the proceedings would be publicized, but not in the other. And in one city the membership would be composed mainly of civic leaders; in the other the council would be a cross-section chosen by occupation. . . .

Rivers wanted cities of moderate size. So he isolated the town of Bend, Ore., (population 12,000) and a suburban city, Redwood City, Calif. (population 60,000). He also obtained the cooperation of Robert W. Chandler, president and editor of the Bend *Bulletin*, a newspaper with a daily (except Sunday) circulation of 7,800, and Raymond L. Spangler, publisher of the Redwood City *Tribune*, a daily with a circulation of 21,000. Both are Stanford University graduates and are active in professional associations. Both are past presidents of Sigma Delta Chi, a professional journalism society.

Three women and six men were selected for nine-member councils in both cities. In Bend, Rivers asked the publisher for nominees. He chose seven and recruited two more on his own. The press council was composed of civic leaders who criticized the newspaper on the basis of social issues. In Redwood City, Rivers chose a cross-sectional membership whose names were gleaned from lists of organizations and institutions. "This kind of council serves as a consumer panel," Rivers said "and is the best kind to answer specific questions about the newspaper itself, such as the society and sports pages."

The press councils met monthly from September 1967 to May 1968, with the Bend group receiving maximum publicity and Redwood City minimum publicity. The members deliberated for about one-and-one-half hours each time in a restaurant's private dining room.

Rivers chose to moderate the sessions and [William B.] Blankenburg served as secretary. An experiment was tried in which one meeting in each city was conducted without newspaper representatives present. "These were frustrating sessions," Rivers said. "In effect, the council members were talking to the walls." He said a council meeting is "valueless" and "counter-productive" without newspaper participation.

At the early council meetings, most members were largely concerned with information-seeking about journalism. Rivers commented that most members were "surprisingly innocent of knowledge of the press."

The results of "newsmaker" (accuracy) surveys conducted by Rivers provided about half the agenda topics for council meetings in both cities. These consisted of mailing clippings and questionnaires to the persons mentioned in the local stories. The respondents were asked to evaluate the news items from the standpoint of accuracy, adequacy and fairness. Other discussion topics ran the spectrum from whether juveniles' names should be printed to territorial rights for syndicated columns, from ink that smudges on the hands to balance on the editorial page. Racial issues were also discussed in Redwood City.

On Sept. 15, 1967, the Mellett Fund made a second grant, this time for $8,786, to Dr. Howard R. Long, chairman of the Southern Illinois University Department of Journalism, to administer two more experimental press councils. Dr. Long, who is editor of the quarterly, *Grassroots Editor*, was assisted in the project by an SIU faculty member, Dr. Kenneth Starck, who served as field director and moderator of the council meetings. The University later provided an additional $5,123 to support the pilot projects.

Long and Starck wanted press councils to function in cities representing different social and economic settings. One choice was Cairo, Ill., (population 9,348), a racially tense community which has just begun to climb out of an economic decline. About 38 per cent of the population is black. By contrast, Sparta (population 3,452), the other study site, is only 10 per cent black and has a teeming economy based on a mixture of agriculture, railroad and small industries.

Another reason for selecting the communities: both daily and weekly newspaper operations are represented and the publishers pledged their full cooperation. The Cairo *Evening-Citizen*, a five-day-a-week newspaper with a circulation of 6,600, is published by Martin Brown. The other publisher is William H. Morgan, who puts out the Sparta *News-Plaindealer*, a weekly with a circulation of 5,381.

Long and Starck decided to vary the formats of the press councils to determine whether different procedures have any effect on the operation of a newspaper. In Cairo, the council was "directed" that is, it functioned with minimum local publicity. At the first meetings the members were given background information about the role of the press in society. Later a system was devised by which members could vote by secret ballot to reflect their sentiments on the performance of the newspaper. In Sparta, the press council was "non-directed," that is, members were encouraged to search on their own for the role of the newspaper in society and the proceedings received maximum publicity.

The criteria for membership were that persons should be active in the city or represent a wide variety of community interests. Starck recruited members following interviews with persons whose names had been suggested by various community citizens. Each council consisted of fifteen persons. Starck said: "Individuals with extremely militant racial positions were avoided." The active council members in both cities included housewives, school officials and business and professional people. Five Negroes were represented on the Cairo council; three served on the Sparta council.

The community press councils met monthly in both cities, from Dec. 1967 to Sept. 1968 in Cairo, and from Feb. through Oct. 1968 in Sparta. Council members deliberated for an average of about two-and-a-half hours at each meeting.

The discussion topics came in two bundles: (1) those dealing with the newspaper, such as its function in the community and questions pertaining to production and policy; and (2) issues dealing with the whole community, such as water pollution or race relations. "Most of the time these issues were intermingled," Starck said, "the only difference being whether the newspaper or the entire community served as the discussion base." Some of the questions asked by

Council members were: "What is the policy in printing names of juveniles in stories?" and "Exactly what is—or should be—the newspaper's role in our community?"

Various methods were employed by the administrators of the Mellett Fund press councils to evaluate the possible effects of the experiments. At Stanford, Rivers and Blankenburg used similar procedures in both cities. They employed the questionnaire in the "newsmaker" surveys mentioned earlier. The items asked for the respondent's evaluation of the story, the degree of "seriousness" of any error noticed, and how well he was acquainted with newspaper staff members.

The administrators also measured all council members early and late on their attitudes toward the newspapers, using a modification of the Brinton-Bush-Newell questionnaire which measured 12 dimensions of newspaper quality such as racial and religious fairness and the general area of satisfaction.

"These tests made it clear," Rivers said, "that the members ran across the spectrum in both cities, from an acidly critical stance toward the papers to welcoming acceptance of almost anything the editors chose to present."

At Southern Illinois University, Long and Starck used different procedures in each city. In Cairo, a content analysis of news, editorials and photographs was used to determine the effects of the press council on the Cairo *Evening-Citizen*. In Sparta, the researchers used the Brinton-Bush-Newell questionnaire to obtain normative data about readers' attitudes toward the newspaper. Two surveys were made, one before public announcement of the formation of the council and the other in the month of the final meeting, to study audience attitude change, if any, toward the *News-Plaindealer* during the life of the press council.

What resulted from the press council experiments? The results of the tests and a perusal of commentary from the participants indicates that a press council can have three intermingling effects: it can make the publisher more aware of the need for responsible press performance; it can serve a valuable public relations function by acting as a two-way communicative link between the press and public; and, it can enhance the esteem and understanding of the newspaper in the eyes of the public.

1. *The community press council tends to lead the newspaper publisher to a greater awareness of the need for responsible press performance.*

Sparta publisher William H. Morgan said, "The council certainly gave me a much better idea of what my readers notice and don't notice in the *News-Plaindealer.*" He also said, "We now know more what the community expects from the newspaper, and we've made some changes"—one of which was a more thorough coverage of local government.

Press council criticism in Cairo regarding the scarcity of front-page local news and local editorials "put management on its toes," said Martin Brown, publisher of the *Evening Citizen.* A content analysis of that paper revealed a tendency to devote more page-one space to local news at the end of the experiment than at the start. The findings also disclosed a significant increase in the number of local editorials during the last quarter of the council's existence.

On the West Coast, both publishers said that more than half of the council suggestions were "valuable." The publishers made some changes, but these were modest; for example, they made certain that page numbers are at the tops of pages and used more maps and diagrams.

Generally, Blankenburg found most West Coast council members reticent to engage in sharp criticism of the performance of the newspaper. He cited four reasons: (1) The members were ignorant of journalistic norms and techniques; they spent a good deal of time educating themselves. (2) They felt constrained to be responsible, and not to lash out without data, but they felt little need to gather data. (3) The publishers had good answers for most criticisms. (4) Neither was a bad newspaper.

Bend publisher Robert W. Chandler said: "I cannot point to anything we have done to improve our practices, and I think we were doing pretty well prior to the start of the council."

The "newsmaker" (accuracy) surveys conducted on the West Coast in Nov. 1967 and May 1968 provided a measure of public attitude toward the newspaper as well as a way of detecting changes in newspaper accuracy. The results of the surveys indicated that both newspapers tended to slip downward in accuracy during the life of the council, with the greatest change occurring in Bend. After the experiment had ended, Chandler said: "I would guess we are more aware of the need for accuracy and fairness than we were before the press council started."

Redwood City publisher Ray Spangler commented that the sheer presence of a community press council induces a publisher to reflect more carefully upon his journalistic performance. He said:

Another valuable by-product is a sense of responsibility one enjoys when he knows a problem cannot merely be swept into a newspaper wastebasket if a press council is sitting nearby to ask questions about the ultimate disposition of a problem. Not that the editor would be less responsible without a press council—but with one he might be more certain and immediate.

2. The community press council serves a valuable public relations function: it allows the publisher to explain newspaper policy and practice to the readers and, at the same time, affords citizens the opportunity to make their needs known to the newspaper.

Sparta publisher William H. Morgan cited the value of a press council in affording him "an opportunity to explain" to the members some of the difficulties of production problems. William Rivers noted, "One value for the newspaper is obvious: The opportunity to explain to a group of interested citizens *why* a newspaper operates as it does."

All four community press councils engaged in some discussion of community needs but, particularly on the West Coast, many of the suggestions were "trivial." Blankenburg explained: "Our councils did not do as much of this as they might, because from the start they aimed at criticism."

3. The sheer presence of the community press council increases the esteem and understanding of the newspaper in the eyes of the council members and the readers.

The results of the pre- and post-press-council attitude surveys in Sparta, using the Brinton-Bush-Newell test, indicated that readers placed more confidence in the newspaper's leadership . . . at the end of the council experience than previously.

Similarly, West Coast press council members thought more highly of their newspaper at the end of the experience. Results of the Brinton-Bush-Newell attitude tests done there showed greater change for Redwood City council members. But Robert Chandler of Bend said:

> From the newspaper's standpoint, I suspect (the press council) should help us by making our readers aware of the fact that unbiased persons in the community generally feel we are both accurate and fair within the limitations of time, money. . . . I am not sure we achieved such a result, at least as yet.

The experimental press councils supported by the Mellett Fund were advisory bodies, having no power to impose suggestions on the proprietors of the media. At the end of the pilot projects, none of the publishers felt that his journalistic freedom had been controlled in any way. For example, Martin Brown of Cairo assured others who might adopt a similar press council "not to worry about the loss of control or any inroads on the management's decisions which a press council might make."

In Redwood City, Ray Spangler adopted an unpublicized format because he did not want even the *appearance* that he was giving up some managerial control. He said:

> I do not believe that an unpublicized press council such as we had involves an abdication of authority by a newspaper. To the contrary, it establishes a communications link with the public, valid to the extent that the council is a cross section of the community.

The last of the four major Mellett Fund experimental press councils ended operations in Oct., 1968. Probably the most noteworthy achievement of the projects is that three of the four community press councils have been restarted voluntarily on a permanent basis. The only dropout is Ray Spangler of the Redwood City *Tribune.* "We have not restarted the council," he said, "and would probably do so only for a special project." Spangler, incidentally, has relinquished his post as *Tribune* publisher.

On Nov. 8, 1968, Robert Chandler restarted the Bend Press Council "to see how such an operation can run without the financial hand of a foundation or the guidance of a college professor." Chandler made the following changes: (1) Membership is set up on a revolving, three-year basis; (2) The council will meet four or five times a year instead of eight; and (3) the council will meet, without dinner, in the offices of a law firm.

In southern Illinois, both press councils have been restarted as permanent advisory bodies. William H. Morgan said: "Members of the council have indicated that they would like to make the press council in Sparta a permanent thing, and I heartily agree."

William Blankenburg envisions a variety of kinds of press councils: (1) one-medium; (2) multi-medium; (3) local; (4) regional; (5) lay; (6) professional; (7) short-term; (8) one-problem (e.g., election coverage) and (9) general councils.

Suggestions have been made for those who wish to set up press councils in their communities: (1) An outside resource person with a knowledge of journalism is necessary in organizing a council, one publisher said; (2) "The important factor is the attitude of the publisher," William Rivers said. "A press council is useful if the publisher is open to current and changing experiences;" and (3) The initial focus of the council should be on the information needs of the community; criticism should be secondary and come naturally.

What does the future hold for the community press council? At this point in time it is difficult to determine whether the opinions of newspaper publishers will jell in favor or disfavor of the concept. But the fact that Ray Spangler has chosen not to restart his council indicates, perhaps, that all is not well with community press councils.

Spangler mentioned a "considerable anti-press-council opinion" in the United States, although he did not indicate the criticisms or identify the critics. He said there appears to be "considerable alarm" that some Canadian precedents might be followed here. He was presumably referring to the press council ideas that have been discussed during the past two years in Ontario and Quebec. These councils will be modeled after the British Press Council, which handles complaints against the press, issues formal censures and exerts influence through the power of publicity.

Should press councils be the wave of the future? William Rivers said that "a press council is not a necessity in every city. It would have its greatest utility in big cities where a significant portion of the population is at odds with the community power structure."

Mellett Fund president Ben H. Bagdikian warned, to the contrary, that the press must set up a mechanism to judge professional performance or face some sort of accountability. He says that unless *all* newspapers in the country adopt local press councils, there will result some kind of forced intervention similar to that in trial coverage proceedings.

The Mellett Fund apparently has demonstrated that a community press council can function effectively in this country without infringing upon the publisher's freedom. The utility of the press council is seen in alerting the publisher to his responsibilities in areas such as racial coverage and in helping to close the growing "credibility gap" between the newspaper and its readers.

The permanent community press councils that were operating in 1969 represented inchings in the direction of acceptance of the idea that an advisory body, set up to evaluate newspaper performance, can be beneficial to both the public and the press. [Editor's Note: Minnesota started a *statewide* press council in September 1971. See Alfred Balk, "Minnesota Launches a Press Council," *Columbia Journalism Review*, December, 1971.]

INTERNAL CONTROLS: PROFESSIONAL REVIEW

THE CREDIBILITY GAP AND THE OMBUDSMAN

Norman E. Isaacs

American journalism—print and electronic—is in an unhappy period.

Despite great gains in all forms of coverage, in scope, in techniques, and general expertise, public and governmental attacks on how we practice our craft rise steadily in intensity.

Lacking a better term, some of us have borrowed our own description of the key political headache of the Johnson Administration. We call it the "credibility gap" existing between press and public.

In mid-December, I (among others) testified before the National Commission on the Causes and Prevention of Violence. The main thrust of my complaint was that all the forms of journalism are exhibiting a defensiveness that is almost paranoid; that there are many things which we do wrong, things we admit to each other when gathered privately in the bar, but which we stubbornly refuse to concede in public.

I did not know at the time that the word had spread beyond our circles, but at year's end there was a report from the International Press Institute saying that the American press may be harder put to regain the readers' trust than to overcome all the other problems bedeviling us.

Journalism in the print form has been under attack from its birth. Early in this century reputations were destroyed (Frank Munsey's for example) and made (by those like Adolph Ochs and Carr Van Anda) on the simple basis of press responsibility.

Public criticism was intense during the "yellow journalism" period at the turn of the century; and during the "jazz journalism" decade of the 1920's. But we had climbed out of that mudhole.

Norman Isaacs, longtime voice for improvement of the press within American Society of Newspaper Editors (ASNE) circles, is the distinguished former editor of the *Louisville Courier-Journal.* The February, 1969 *ASNE Bulletin* carried his thoughts, used with permission of the *Bulletin.*

From what I have been able to gather, television is still in a state of shock over the public response to its coverage of the confrontations and the convention scenes in Chicago. I understand that thousands of letters, wires and calls flooded the TV networks from citizens who saw and didn't believe. The protests can be summed up as saying: "You're damned liars!"

The electronic media news people are getting a bitter taste of what newspapers have been getting—and asking for, too—for decades.

The "credibility gap" was showing in the 1930's. Writing about that period in their excellent history, "The Press and America," Edwin Emery and Henry Ladd Smith wrote:

> "The press as an institution thus came under challenge more directly than at any time since the Federalist attack upon press freedom in the 1790's."

Our best friends were telling us the unpleasant truths, but the majority wouldn't listen then nor listen in the 1950's when the "one-party press" charge took on such currency. Some of the lapses in fairness then were horrendous. One big newspaper used its page one as a billboard for the Republican nominee's visit to town.

Sigma Delta Chi voted for a major national study of the press's performance. Every important university professor then engaged in journalistic research took part in drawing up a plan. I happened to be chairman of the project and remember, sadly, that it was rejected by the nation's publishers by an overwhelming vote. Sadly, because the people in charge of the communications industry were once again granting themselves the right to criticize anyone and anything, but insisting in insulating themselves against even the fairest kind of in-house research.

Yes, an argument can be made that over the years our own shortcomings were magnified out of proportion by the exaggerations of others. Certainly, Time Magazine's opinionated style had its effect on public attitudes. Many editors protested the tendency to equate Time's slanting with their own inadvertent coverage errors. Whether it made any difference to the public is highly questionable.

To my mind, the public view of television reporters at work has been devastating for the American newspaperman. In Washington, I did a mimicry of a TV reporter harassing, badgering, twisting out of context the evasive comments of Senator Philip Hart. (I was using him and Congressman Hale Boggs as examples only because they were facing me.)

It wasn't far-fetched mimicry. I was trying to illustrate the TV reporting techniques on a story like the one the networks tried to float of Senator Ted Kennedy for the Democratic nomination. So I went through the act, which was good enough to draw approving laughter from those present.

"Were you in Chicago?" asked Senator Hart.

"No, I wasn't, Senator."

"But it happened to me!" he exclaimed.

Whether one accepts these as contributing factors or not, there can be no question that newspapers everywhere in the country are under public attack. In some cities, public officeholders have cynically adopted the technique of putting the local press under a constant barrage of accusations of unfairness. That many of these statements are patently self-serving and unworthy is shrugged off by the officeholders. They crave office more than they honor truth and to them the newspapers are convenient "whipping boys."

The strange part is that newspapers, other than protesting, have done little to counteract the pressures. And it seems to many of us that we must act, or else see still further erosion of our public position.

Vincent S. Jones, executive editor of the Gannett Newspapers, and ASNE president, has challenged several newspaper organizations this past year about our smug views.

He has shuddered publicly over the industry's acceptance of the incredible number of typographical errors which happen in so many newspapers.

"Any stenographer in our offices," he has said, "who would make one fraction of these punching mistakes would be fired tomorrow."

He has called sharp attention to the many errors in fact which appear, the unanswered questions in sloppily written stories, the underplays and overplays which mark so much of our daily erratic follow-through on stories. He has been critical of journalism's willingness to accept so much "over-the-transom" material from p.r. agencies and governmental flaks. "Do we go after comparable material on our own?" he has demanded to know.

He has been publicly critical of reporters who lecture news sources instead of interviewing them.

"Our interpretives," he has said, "are often far from objective or complete."

Vin maintains that the distrust of the communications media can be traced to the number of things we don't cover or cover shabbily and woodenly. "How many of us," he asks, "have witnessed events or attended events and been staggered by the published reports?"

Here he is emphasizing what I believe is a weakness on all news-papers—of basic accuracy. It is traditional with an older generation to look with concern on a newer one, and there are many veteran newspapermen who express bewilderment over what they consider a serious impairment in the young reporter's concepts about accuracy.

Many of us attribute this to the breakdown in the educational process which has resulted in so many of the new generation not being able to spell properly.

To check on myself, I put it up to a member of the younger generation—Steve Isaacs, metropolitan editor of the Washington Post. He was partly scornful of my reaction.

"You older fellows are just being crotchety," he retorted. "I'll put my younger reporters' spelling up against the older ones' any day. And I'll put my spelling up against yours."

"What you're missing," my son said, "is that we have a new breed of newspapermen. To them the concept is more important than the details. The unfortunate part is that they don't realize the wrong details destroy the concept."

He has a point. It matches that of Vin Jones and blends with the tale I related to the Commission on Violence about my own discomfiture over the standards of our Louisville newspapers (which we like to think try extraordinarily hard to do a good and honorable job). I was fielding questions of teachers at a Newspaper in the Classroom seminar. One teacher paid the customary tribute to our newspaper's standing, then said:

"One thing worries me, though. I haven't had a lot of personal experience with the newspapers—maybe five or six articles. But every one of them has been wrong."

"In what way?" she was asked.

"Well," she replied, "in the name of the organization being wrong, or the date of the meeting, or the time, or the place, and even the names of the people being spelled wrong. I know they're not big things, but they're wrong and it makes me worry about the rest of what I read."

There was a long pause while I stared out the window and tried to tick off the episodes. Finally, I had to say: "You know, it's happened to me, too. Those are the things that drive us wild."

So it was that A.H. Raskin of the Editorial Board of The New York Times struck a responsive nerve in June 1966 with his article in The Times' Magazine, "What's Wrong With American Newspapers?"

Mr. Raskin proposed that "newspapers establish their own De-partments of Internal Criticism to check on the fairness and adequacy of their coverage and comment. The department ought to be given enough independence in the paper to serve as an ombudsman for the readers, armed with authority to get something done about valid complaints and to propose methods for more effective performance. . . ."

Some years earlier, Barry Bingham had proposed local press councils. When it wasn't taken up, we even tried to prompt some university executives here to get one going, but it was in vain.

Hence, it was understandable that we would jump at Abe Raskin's idea and create our own ombudsman. The word is difficult. It's Scandinavian for the official in charge of public complaints and with power to do something about them. A number of people adept with words have tried to arrive at some Anglo-American definition, but they have not yet succeeded.

At any rate, in our area the ombudsman idea has caught the imagination of many in the general public. Many people joke about the word, but it is clear they know the intent—and they seem to respect it. It has been successful enough so that we now list it in the phone book.

It has to be conceded that the idea contains grave backfire possibilities for a newspaper that would look on the function as a public relations gimmick. A newspaper has to be deeply earnest about the whole thing—and to give the assignment to someone good enough and important enough to make it work.

In our case, it is a man who was city editor for almost a quarter of a century, who is widely respected, who has a deep devotion to the calling and who, oddly enough, happens to have a different political party affiliation than any of the rest of us in management.

Some reporters and deskmen still seem to resent the ombudsman idea. This may be part hangover from its inception. Our ombudsman, John Herchenroeder, insists on prompt and proper corrections. For a while we had a steady run of such corrections, and everyone was uneasy. That we have fewer of them today is proof of the usefulness of this policing arm.

Most of the complaints have been about minor errors. But there also have been a few major ones. The great gain has been in establishing a line of contact. The average reader doesn't just call John to complain; he calls to talk it out.

From this, we have been getting a flow of information that has been invaluable. One conversation about an oversight resulted in a major watershed story that took a full page of the newspaper.

Complaints about the way we do some things have brought on reviews by our news executives—and changes in news policy. We have begun periodic explanations in the Sunday paper about our short-comings, why some mistakes happened and what steps we've taken to prevent repetition. The public response has been extraordinarily good. But as said earlier, it isn't a gimmick and it can't be treated as one.

We also have felt strongly enough about the general problem of news responsibility to set ourselves up as watchdog for the entire process of news coverage in the area we serve. On two occasions, when the standard wire services and the electronic media acted with unwise haste in covering stories of conflict (they were non-stories), we researched the episodes from beginning to end and published the reports, naming names, news services and stations involved (including our own affiliate). It can be demonstrated that there is currently more responsibility being shown in this phase of news coverage.

When all is said, however, what we face is a massive problem about our standing for which no one has any sure answers. What I have outlined is simply one newspaper operation's honest pursuit of answers, and of its efforts to make its record an open one, subject to criticism, just as we criticize all others in the American society. There are others, like Bob Chandler's experiment with a local press council in Bend, Ore., as well as Ray Spangler's in Redwood City, Calif., and another involving the Cairo (Ill.) Citizen.

The young newspaper people tend to hold that much of our poor standing with the public can be traced to our image (dreadful word, but pertinent here) as a key part of the national, state and local establishments.

There is no sense in denying this, or in decrying it. It is true. In some instances, it is even useful. If newspapers were not part of the establishment, they would have little leverage to use when it becomes necessary to take private action in the public good. That the estab-lishment connection has been misused often is hardly a secret. My point is that it can be good, and often is. But whether the connection be used for good effect or bad, it is a fact.

The real difficulty may lie in the fact that we have become remote. We are no longer in close touch with the public we serve. Today's journalist is a member of the upper intelligentsia. He reads serious books, is a member of Foreign Relations committees, is a concerned critic of the socio-economic problems in his area and in the nation. There is, indeed, a gap between newspapermen and reader.

Those of us who for years have been appearing at the police training institutes should have anticipated (although we didn't!) the reaction of the Chicago police to reporters and photographers. Each time we have participated in such sessions, we have been shocked by the amount of police hostility to newspapers. The police bluntly express a lack of regard for the reporters who cover the beats and they consider newspaper editors not merely unapproachable and un-interested overseers, but enemies.

I am among those who believe that our defensiveness led to the creation of the Reardon Committee. Indeed, I can produce a note from Judge Reardon saying just that. Those editors who were seri-ously appraising the coverage of crime years ago were the ones who were making sensible adjustments in their news philosophies and creating the basis for quiet, informal but effective guidelines with the local and state bar associations.

The business of running nationally prepared advertisements about the virtues of journalism won't do any more. They are obso-lete in this day of protest and challenge. We have to prove our virtues.

We're caught in a vicious circle. The TV viewer who gets soured by the abrasive performance of a network reporter in a political convention doesn't let it end there. When he picks up our news-papers, he doesn't give our own experienced and responsibly accurate reporters credit for diligence, manners or competence.

It is my contention that by our ineptitudes and astonishing defensiveness we not only have dug our own holier-than-thou pit but we also continue to dig it deeper by our failure to address ourselves to the public, even on simple things like making clear our regret for inadvertent error or negligence.

The basic question probably is whether American journalism is willing to undergo some private examination of its own to see if there are some constructive steps that can be taken to convince the citizenry of our essential fairness, of our dedication to accuracy and of our willingness to listen.

'REPORTER POWER' TAKES ROOT

Edwin Diamond

One of the most significant and underreported social experiments of 1969 took place in the small northern California community of Willits. There, forty-three-year-old George Davis, a football coach who describes himself as "a small man with nothing to lose," fielded a football team each Saturday using the principle of participatory democracy; the players themselves voted on who should be in the starting lineup. The team lost its first four games of the season but rallied and ended in a tie for the league championship. This record, of course, might have been as much due to talent as to democracy. Still, the implications of the Davis experiment are clear; in an era marked by the pervasive and passionate questioning of all authority, even the football coach—that traditionally rigid hierarchical figure—is trying to bend with the times.

In American news media most communications caliphates are more like Vince Lombardi than George Davis—they are big men with a lot to lose, so to speak—and so the principle of electing editors or announcers has not yet been established. But a sampling of attitudes in a number of city-rooms, magazine offices, and broadcast studios indicates that day may not be far off. In various cities journalists have banded together to impress their professional beliefs and occupational misgivings upon management.

At the Gannett papers in Rochester, N.Y., editorial staff members have begun sitting in with the papers' editorial board on a rotating basis. In Denver, a new Newspaper Guild contract signed in mid-March 1970 establishes an ethics committee and a human rights committee that will meet regularly with management. The human rights committee plans to take up the question of minority employment (women as well as blacks) at the *Post;* the three-member ethics committee, which will meet with three representatives of management, wants to discuss such hoary *Post* practices as trade-outs— editorial puffs written about an advertiser to fill out a special section. And in Providence, R.I., a Journalists Committee has held several meetings with management about specific staffing and policy changes

Edwin Diamond, also author of the book's opening chapter, contributes to leading magazines on a regular basis. His observations on "Reporter Power" were published in the Summer, 1970 *Columbia Journalism Review* **issue on "The Coming Newsroom Revolution." They are reprinted here with the permission of** *Columbia Journalism Review.*

on the *Journal* and *Bulletin*. The Committee acted after surveying a sizable portion of the editorial staff, then compiling the survey and mimeographing it for distribution.

Guild contract negotiations are still grimly contested in the news media, as are labor contracts in most business enterprises. But the new benefits that journalists have begun to seek go far beyond the usual guild bargaining points of wages and hours. The new grievances involve, first of all, moral—almost theological—concerns. When the Association of *Tribune* Journalists was formed by reporters at the Minneapolis *Tribune* in February 1970, for example, it carefully stated that the group was not a collective bargaining unit but an agent for bringing "our best thoughts into a dialogue with management." There had been the usual grumbling at the *Trib* about shortages of staff and space, but there was a new element in the talk. As an association member later explained, "There was a feeling on our part of loss of respect. We were being treated like army privates and the editors were officers; we were to do what we were told and like it and no one gave a damn if we thought our orders were sane or insane."

The *Tribune's* enlisted men and women moved decisively to assert "rights of participation" in the choice of their junior officers: when two *Trib* assistant city editors announced that they planned to leave the paper, the local Guild unit adopted a resolution stating that "reporters, photographers, and copydesk editors should advise and consent to management's nominations." The next day management met with the Guild and said that while it was not giving up its prerogatives it was willing to take the staff's nominations into account. It is a small step for the *Trib*, but a giant leap for American journalism—which more and more is moving toward the model of *Le Monde* and other European publications.

Similarly, the men and women who produce programs for public television have formed an association concerned not with residuals but with, among other subjects, the social content of programs and the racial hiring practices of their industry. And reporters in several cities have founded journalism reviews.

The concerns that have stimulated these various activities are immediately recognizable as the concerns that have dominated much of the news covered by media men and women in recent years. Journalists who have followed the fight of parents to decentralize schools, the demands of students to have a say in the investment policies of the universities, and the blacks' and radical whites' challenge to the established institutions of society, have now begun to think about applying to their own lives principles of community control, participatory democracy, and collective action.

The development of this new consciousness is fairly recent. Ten or fifteen years ago, unions battled to win wage increases and to protest mergers, but the way a publication or station was run—from the color scheme of the newsroom walls to the overall editorial policies—remained the prerogative of the owner. The journalist's attitude was, typically, acquiescent; after all, was it not management's bat and ball—and ball park (although in broadcasting, the air *does* belong to the public and the station owner has only the loan of it)?

With affluence, the new temper of times, and the seller's market for young talent, this attitude has changed. Media executives now know (and graduate school studies show) that the brightest young people, on the whole, are not going into journalism, and that even those who are graduated from journalism schools often choose public relations work over reporting jobs. Even more alarming to an editor or news director with proper regard for talent is the attrition rate of good young newsmen and women after two or three years in the business. Money and bylines alone are no longer sufficient inducements; if executives want to attract and keep good young people, they must be attentive to or at least aware of their opinions. As often as not, a good university-trained reporter who is now in his or her late twenties picketed for civil rights while in high school, spent a freshman summer in Mississippi or Appalachia, and sat in at the Dean's office during senior year—or covered these events for the school paper. Now they are turning reformist toward their own profession.

Recent unrest at the *Wall Street Journal* is a case in point. The *Journal* reached its present eminence in part by hiring good young people right out of college, training them, and giving them the time and the space to develop long, informative reports and trend stories. Now, says an older hand at the paper, "these younger people are much more activist-minded and more willing to needle management." During the Vietnam Moratorium Day in October 1969, several younger reporters wanted to march on Broad street, a block from Wall, with at least one sign saying WALL STREET JOURNALIST FOR THE MORATORIUM. Management's position was that it didn't mind the marching but didn't think the wording of that one sign was proper because it might "raise questions about the *Journal's* objectivity in the reader's mind."

A confrontation on Moratorium Day was avoided—according to one witness, the sign was carried but not held up. But the young activists then dispatched a petition to management asking for a clarification of the *Journal's* "position" on what they could do with their private lives. In response, executives Warren Phillips and Ed Cony issued a memorandum noting that "we must be concerned not only with avoiding bias in our news columns but also with avoiding the appearance of bias." They concluded: "It is the individual's obligation to exercise sufficient judgment to avoid such embarrassment." The younger reporters also have expressed their concern about what the *Journal* does on the editorial page; when the *Journal* ran an editorial that seemed to blame New York City's telephone troubles on allegedly slow-witted welfare mothers hired to operate switchboards, a newsroom caucus told management that reporters didn't want to be associated with a paper that had such mossback views.

The *Journal's* radical "cell" remains largely an *ad hoc* group springing to life when an issue presents itself. At the Minneapolis *Tribune*, however, the new consciousness of younger journalists has manifested itself in a formal organization. During the Fall of 1969, by all accounts, the *Tribune* had a morale problem compounded by a high turnover and some admitted paranoia on the part of the staff. A group of reporters began meeting on Sunday mornings—for a while they were known as the Underground Church—to see if anything beside complaining could be done. The Underground Church members repeated the usual litany of city-room complaints—the need for more phones, better files, more out-of-town exchanges—but they also were concerned with such traditional domains of management as the size of the travel allowance, the company's fiscal and budgetary procedures, and the circulation breakdown by area. More important, the Underground Church challenged the *Tribune's* news judgment, most particularly on those issues that have polarized so much of the country. One young reporter drew up the following indictment:

> The *Trib's* sins tend to be those of omission, rather than commission. We sent no one to the Chicago Conspiracy trial despite repeated requests from staffers who wanted to go. We sent no one to Washington last November with the thousands of Minnesotans who participated in the Vietnam Moratorium. We do have a D.C. bureau which handled Moratorium coverage but we did not, like our rival paper, the *Star*, see fit to send anyone on the buses of demonstrators from our state. . . . The November Moratorium was our right-hand, front-page lead story, with a front-page picture of masses of marchers going along peaceably. The story by Chuck Bailey of our D.C. bureau devoted the first five paragraphs to general comments on the demonstration. The next six paragraphs were on the violence that occurred there. Then followed twelve paragraphs on the speeches, color, etc. We used only the official 250,000 figure for the number of participants and did not mention any higher estimates.

On the second front page only one of the five pictures showed a peaceful scene (Coretta King marching). One was rioters getting tear-gassed, another a draft-card burning, another an American flag being carried upside down, and the fourth a flag-burning which turned out, on close inspection, to be counter-demonstrators burning a Vietcong flag. According to our own figures, one-250th of the people at that demonstration got at least three-fifths of the pictures on the second front page and about one-fourth of the main story. . . .

We do, of course, often do a good job breaking a story. Give us a cyclone or a postal strike or the Governor saying he won't run again, and we're all over it. We get the sidebars and the reactions and the whole thing. But in trying to explain what the hell is happening in this society in any larger way—perspective, context, whatever you want to call it—the *Trib* just ain't there."

The Underground Church soon realized it could go in two possible directions: the reporters could start a publication modeled after the *Chicago Journalism Review* which would regularly monitor the local press' performance on stories like the November Moratorium, or they could try to work within the organization by establishing a "dialogue" with management. The Church chose the [latter] course, and plans for a *Twin Cities Journalism Review* were put on the back burner. Early this year, John Cowles, Jr., president of the Minneapolis Star and Tribune Co. (and also the majority owner of *Harper's* magazine), and Bower Hawthorne, vice president and editor of the *Tribune*, were invited to meet with some of the staff and discuss the paper's direction. Hawthorne, meanwhile, had invited all staff members to his own meeting to discuss the paper—the two invitations apparently crossed in the interoffice mail. The meetings took place—"by this time we were communicating like hell," one reporter recalls wryly—and the dissidents formally organized into the Association of *Tribune* Journalists.

The managing editor, Wallace Allen, drew up an extensive questionnaire which was distributed to some 100 staff members; forty-seven returned their forms. Allen's own summary of the responses reflects the low opinion the workers had for the paper and the management. Five of the nineteen "impressions and conclusions" he drew from the replies are especially noteworthy:

—You want a great deal more information about company direction, through direct and personal communication with management up to the highest level.

—Some of you feel strongly that staff members should play a part in policymaking and decision-making. You do not wish to run the newspaper but you would like to be consulted on what is done and informed in advance of both major and minor decisions.

—You feel that news policy and direction are not being handed down fully or clearly. You have only a vague idea—or no idea—of what we are trying to do and where we are trying to go.

—You feel that our approaches to covering the news and the ways we present it are not up to date. You want to see change and progress in an orderly, responsible but exciting way.

—Many of you feel that the *Tribune* was a progressive and exciting newspaper until about six months or so ago. You indicate that the letdown may have come from confusion in management's mind about news direction when it discovered the silent majority. You feel management switched direction in an attempt to respond to changing social conditions but switched in ways that revealed ignorance of basic issues.

Allen's efforts at communications apparently had a calming effect on the staff, which by and large adopted a "wait and see" attitude. As of late Spring 1970, the Association continued to meet every other week or so and was reviving plans for the *Twin Cities Journalism Review*.

The Association of Public Television Producers, another group of journalists who went "above ground" out of a deep concern about their professional lives, has also become engaged in management matters. Men and women on every level in public television are worried about the continued unfettered operation of noncommercial TV in the United States, especially because the new Corporation for Public Broadcasting has to go to Congress each year for funds. The Association came forward during Congressional hearings last year to discuss alternative plans for financing public TV; its spokesman, Alvin Perlmutter, a National Educational Television producer, told the Pastore Committee that he personally favored financing PTV by a tax on the profits of the commercial networks rather than the present arrangement in which public TV is dependent on the goodwill of 535 Congressmen. Perlmutter was rewarded with a lecture from Senator Pastore, advising him not to bite the hand that is feeding him. More recently, the Association publicly protested the decision of some local public TV stations not to show the NET documentary *Who Invited US?* a highly critical study of U.S. foreign policy. Like the reporters at the Minneapolis *Tribune*, the public TV producers want to see certain stories run—and they are prepared to challenge past assumptions about whether the people who have the bat and ball can make all the rules of the game.

The women's movement at *Newsweek* also has been willing to try its case in public. The conditions that the *Newsweek* women found objectionable—segregation of women into the scut work of research, the lack of writing opportunities (fifty male writers to one woman), and the general atmosphere of exclusion—had for years

The Providence journalists committee

One day in July 1969, Nick Mottern, thirty-one-year-old labor reporter for the Providence *Journal,* was sitting at his typewriter pondering the number of newsmen who had left the paper and the dissatisfaction that many colleagues had voiced about their work. He turned to a colleague at the desk behind him and said, "Why don't we do something about things here?" They invited other reporters for the morning *Journal* and its sister paper, the evening *Bulletin,* to meet in a cafeteria downstairs. Out of that meeting came a Journalists Committee, which surveyed staff concerns and began meeting with editors. It also compiled a twenty-one-page mimeographed pamphlet titled "Proposals for the Improvement of the Providence *Journal* and the evening *Bulletin.*" Among its points:

> The Providence *Journal* has held a relatively high reputation for competent journalism, but the . . . Committee believes that it is not doing enough to meet the needs of its readers, that it is not living up to its reputation . . .; the size and organization of the news staffs do not allow the newspapers to go far enough beyond the reporting of events and reaction to events to tell the people of Rhode Island what they need to know to improve their lives and their state. . . .
>
> In our talks with the editors, it became apparent that they believe the staple of the newspapers to be their coverage of major and minor events, governmental activity, public statements, and social news. We recognize the importance of this type of coverage, and we do not recommend that it be abandoned. We do believe that changes must be made to permit more in-depth and investigative reporting. . . .
>
> Rhode Island is a stronghold for the Mafia. To think that its ability to flourish here is not made possible by the cooperation of government and business is naive. It is also naive to believe that the Mafia does not make the state more susceptible to forms of corruption not directly related to organized crime. . . . We believe there are sufficient projects to keep an investigative reporting team busy indefinitely. Some are:
>
> —Conflict of interest in the General Assembly.
>
> —The Providence Police Department.
>
> —The financial affairs of Progress for Providence.
>
> —The structure of state political parties and where they get their money.
>
> —The relationships of prominent persons to the underworld.
>
> —The underworld influence at Rhode Island race tracks.
>
> —A study of the credentials and activities of judges and an examination of their decisions for evidence of conflicts of interest.
>
> —Interlocking business directorates.
>
> —The operation of credit unions in the state.
>
> —The connections of unions to the underworld.
>
> —An examination of governmental construction contract awards that would include an investigation of bidding and dead-line enforcement procedures. . . .

Consumer affairs receives spotty coverage, but it is a subject of high interest to every reader. Government has begun to recognize the political necessity and advantage of working for the consumer, and we believe it is in line with the newspapers' interest and responsibility to do likewise. . . . A recent *Journal* story with extremely high reader interest was Michael Madden's dissection of the local funeral business. Stories that might be developed include:

—The varying costs of auto repair and body work.

—Safety of appliances.

—Costs of medicine.

—Food preparation and handling in restaurants.

—Food clubs and group buying.

—Utility costs.

—Analysis and comparison of insurance plans.

—Health, reducing and physical fitness clubs.

—Service costs on appliance repair.

—Costs of basic legal services. . . .

We propose that a post be established on the *Bulletin* for a consumer affairs reporter and that a *Journal* reporter or reporters be assigned on a continuing basis to stories in this area. . . .

In order to give the city editor more time for planning and working with reporters, we suggest that the bulk of the reading of advance copy be done by the assistant city editor and that the review of press releases and related work be done by a reporter or copy editor. . . .

The committee requests that members of various staffs be allowed to attend meetings held between the editors and the publisher in order to understand better the operation of the newspapers and to offer the viewpoint of the staffs in discussions of news policy. These representatives would be selected by their fellow staff members for a specified period. . . .

Some changes have resulted from Committee activities, says Charles H. Spilman, *Journal* managing editor. They include more stories with bylines, modifications in reporter training procedures, and regular staff meetings. "But," he confesses, "nothing of a major nature." He adds: "I think the activities have been valuable."

Some of Spilman's reporters are less enthusiastic. Mottern has resigned from the paper, and the Journalists Committee, reiterating concern about "the quality, the values, the standards, the judgments, the honesty, and the integrity of these newspapers," in April began publication of an eight-page local review called *The Journalists Newsletter,* described as "the first of what we intend to be a continuing series of critical reports on the newspapers we work for." Copies were distributed free to selected individuals and organizations.

existed unopposed except by one or two editors. In the last year or two, however, many of the young women had been covering the black revolution and student unrest. As reporters they had listened to the rhetoric of "power to the people"; they had been "used" by militants who staged news conferences and other media events to get across their messages. When the *Newsweek* women decided to press their collective claims they arranged a media event: they timed the release of their complaint to the Equal Employment Opportunity Commission in Washington to coincide with the Monday morning newsstand appearance of the *Newsweek* cover story "Women in Revolt." They called a news conference and phoned contacts at other news organizations to insure full coverage. Then they appeared in force, well groomed and intelligent, flanking their lawyer, a young, attractive black woman named Eleanor Holmes Norton. Their widely covered action had the desired effect, galvanizing the top echelon of *Newsweek* into a long series of meetings with the women and winning from management pledges to open the entire editorial hierarchy to women.

The editor may justifiably grumble that the women should have come to his office first, but the women believe it was the public nature of their action that produced results. Their experience replicates that of a Minneapolis *Tribune* reporter who now believes the "only power that we staff members really have in these matters is the power to embarrass management." This power also was demonstrated in March 1970 when a group called Media Women flooded into the office of the *Ladies' Home Journal's* editor and publisher, John Mack Carter, to stage the first "liberation" of a mass magazine. The resulting publicity may not have immediately hurt the *Journal's* advertising revenues or circulation, but it certainly affected that evanescent quality known as aura—and it made many readers who heretofore had not paid much attention to the feminist cause conscious of the magazine's assumptions.

For the time being at least, the tactics of "liberation" have been the exception rather than the rule. If there is a pattern in developments around the country, it is the tactic of internally rather than publicly making the case for a larger staff role in policymaking. Thus, some sixty New York *Post* activists (over as well as under thirty) have been meeting with the *Post's* publisher, Mrs. Dorothy Schiff, to force a break from the penurious policies and lackluster journalism of the past. The reporters have asked for more specialist beats, a larger travel budget, more black and Puerto Rican staff, and more coverage of minority groups. At the New York *Times* a loose confederation of reporters and editors have also met to discuss a long list of grievances, some of them water-cooler complaints but others centering on the *Time's* coverage of politics, race, the Chicago Conspiracy trial, and the Black Panthers. Some of the *Times* reporters are chafing under what they consider the harsh yoke of Managing Editor A.M. Rosenthal and his bullpen editors, and one step being considered calls for the selection or election—in the *Le Monde* and Minneapolis models—of a top editor.

And in Philadelphia, the senior editors of the *Bulletin* have been conducting regular Monday afternoon "seminars" with some fifteen of the younger—and more activist-minded—staff reporters. The weekly seminars began in March 1970 after managing editor George Packard had heard complaints from staff members that story suggestions and opinions about news coverage were not "trickling upward." A typical meeting allows equal time for a senior editor to explain his particular operation (news desk, photo assignments, etc.) and for reporters to ask questions or otherwise respond. The trickle—some say, torrent—of underclass feelings loosed by the seminars has already resulted in some changes in the way the *Bulletin* handles racial identifications in stories. *Bulletin* editors are also opening up channels so that younger reporters can get story ideas into the paper's new "Enterprise" page, and no one seems more satisfied with these developments than Packard himself.

A number of issues could transform these informal internal discussions into overt action groups. Working reporters have been made visibly nervous by recent efforts to subpoena reporters' notes, raw files, and unused film [See CJR, Spring, 1970]. The Wall Street *Journal* "cell" and the Association of *Tribune* Journalists, among others, have formally protested to their managements about cooperating in such government fishing expeditions. More significantly, two groups of journalists, cutting across corporate and media lines, have banded together on the subpoena issue. One group consists of some seventy black men and women journalists who placed an ad to announce their intention to oppose the Government's efforts (the Government's first target in efforts to obtain reporters' notes was a black journalist for the New York *Times*, Earl Caldwell).

The second group, called the Reporter's Committee on Freedom of the Press, consists of both black and white newsmen, and J. Anthony Lukas of the New York *Times* has been one of its early organizers. The Reporter's Committee met early in March at the Georgetown University Law Center in Washington. The discussions—attended by men from the Washington *Star*, the Washington *Post*,

Time, Newsweek, the Los Angeles *Times,* NBC, and CBS—reflected some of the feelings of staff men that interests of management and employees may not always be congruent in the matter of subpoenas. Rather than rely on lawyers of their individual companies and corporations—who by and large have been uncertain trumpets in recent months—the Georgetown group wants to explore the legal thickets of the subpoena issue directly with law schools and scholars. Already, the group is cooperating with the Georgetown Law Center on an information center and clearing house, and with Stanford University on a legal study of the whole area of confidential material.

Two other issues could also serve to "radicalize" the working press. One issue is race. Black reporters in the San Francisco area and in New York City have organized their own associations, partly to get together to talk about matters of common interest and occasionally to speak out with a collective voice. The other radicalizing issue is the war in Indochina. Shortly after Mr. Nixon ordered American troops into Cambodia, more than 150 *Newsweek* employees met to debate whether they should bring pressure on their magazine to come out against the war; one form of action considered was an anti-war advertisement in *Newsweek.* At the New York *Daily News* more than 100 editorial employees attempted to place just such an ad in their paper, but were refused space by the paper even though they had collected $1,100 to pay for it. The *Daily News*men promptly took their ad to the New York *Times,* where it was accepted—double embarrassment for the *News'* management. [Editor's Note: The May, 1971 issue of *Chicago Journalism Review* reported that "nearly all" of the reporters and editors of the *Chicago Sun-Times* and *Chicago Daily News* supported Richard E. Friedman against Mayor Richard Daley. The papers of Marshall Field V endorsed Daley but complicated negotiations with management led to both the *Daily News* and *Sun-Times* carrying ads prepared by newsmen opposed to Daley. *Chicago Today* allowed thirty-one staffers to use a page opposite the editorial page for a rebuttal to its endorsement.]

Media activists have a great deal in their favor, including management's fear of a talent drain and its abhorrence of adverse publicity. Ultimately, too, they can count on the *amour propre* of the ownership: the proprietors have a selfish interest in listening. John Cowles, Jr., for example told his *Tribune* reporters that it wasn't at all pleasant to hear, in his words, that he was "the captain of the *Titanic.*" Perhaps a "dialogue" can achieve a new arrangement of authority that recognizes the best qualities of passion, spontaneity, and social concerns of the younger journalists while preserving the established professional virtues of fair play and balance.

Chapter III

INCREASING PROTECTION
FOR SOURCES OF NEWS

NEWSMEN AND THEIR CONFIDENTIAL SOURCES

Abraham S. Goldstein

The outrage with which the news media greeted recent efforts by federal prosecutors to subpoena reporters' notes and TV tapes, and the hasty retreat beaten by Attorney General Mitchell, has obscured from view just how unsatisfactory the ultimate resolution was. The public was left with the impression that Mitchell had violated a right of newsmen to keep their notes and tapes confidential and that indignation had brought him to heel. The fact, however, is that in the federal system and in three-fourths of the states, reporters have no more right than the rest of us to withhold information demanded by the subpoena of a court, grand jury or legislative committee. Nevertheless, Mitchell concluded that it would be impolite to press his power to the limit in the overheated atmosphere now surrounding Black Panthers and Weathermen. He proposed instead to negotiate in the future, rather than peremptorily to subpoena newsmen's files.

In short, the Attorney General reverted to what has long been the practice. Such "negotiation" inevitably involves a bargaining process in which the weak will feel pressed to divulge information while the strong will not. In 1945, for example, a congressional committee, which had voted a contempt citation for a well-known newsman who had refused to divulge his sources, reversed itself after it was subjected to a barrage of press criticism. And Mitchell himself is following the "prudent" course lest the major media beat him in the court of public opinion.

Abraham S. Goldstein, dean of the Yale University Law School, offers a different perspective to the problem of the subpoena which continues to plague the news media. The article is reprinted by permission of *The New Republic*, copyright 1970, Harrison-Blaine of New Jersey, Inc., where it appeared in the March 21, 1970 issue.

The uncertainty as to when and where the journalist and his records are to be protected is fed by the paucity of case law. The Supreme Court has never dealt with the issue, and there are relatively few state decisions, in part because "negotiation" keeps cases out of courts. If we lived in a time when government investigators were less demanding, or seemed more sensitive to the value of confidentiality, or when the need for a strong and critical press was less clear, the currently ambiguous situation might be tolerable. But this is not such a time. The paranoid tendencies latent in a mass society are running unusually strong these days and make all the more essential a clear standard which strikes the proper balance between the demands of confidentiality and those of the public interest, [see page 5].

The usual rule regarding subpoenas is that they compel disclosure of all information, written or oral, relevant to the concerns of the investigative or judicial body which issued them. The person who refuses to comply may be held in contempt and remitted to custody until he testifies. The underlying principle is that a rational society, and intelligent decision-making, depend upon a free exchange of information and that society is entitled to demand of its citizens that they make their knowledge available. Though it is currently fashionable to treat such demands as invasions of privacy, they can as easily be viewed as contributions to the common welfare. For every license to withhold information obviously carries with it the risk that a crime might not be discovered or successfully prosecuted, or that the innocence of a defendant might not be established, or that a legislative policy might not be intelligently formulated. It is after all an "establishment" press which will be withholding information from the official establishment. The sources and the information protected today may involve Black Panthers and the SDS. Tomorrow, they may involve disclosure of corruption or abuse of power among public officials or corporate executives.

The news media themselves have been the most vigorous champions of access to all sorts of records and proceedings. And when confronted by governmental agencies with claims of an executive or legislative privilege to withhold information, they have been justifiably suspicious that such claims might be made less to protect the public interest than to subvert it. In this spirit, they have sought legal endorsement for their position through "right to know" laws and the federal Freedom of Information Act. Newsmen, therefore, occupy the uneasy position of espousing a right of access to the government's files while denying governmental access to their files. In doing so, they are placing the need to protect their sources, and their news-gathering procedures and relationships, above the state's right to a full investigation or a fair trial.

Despite the inconsistency of this position, there is ample precedent for it. We find in constitutional law the principle that truth is not an end in itself. The most conspicuous illustration is the limit on official inquiry inhering in the privilege against self-incrimination. The testimonial privileges also restrict official inquiry: husband and wife may not be compelled to disclose their communications with one another; the priest may not disclose his penitent's confession; the attorney may not reveal the secrets of his client. In many states, comparable protection is given to communications between physician and patient, accountant and client, social worker and client, psychologist and patient.

The recent outcry of the news media is in effect a claim for parity of treatment with the other professional groups. They argue that there is a strong public interest in freedom of communication within the journalist-informant relationship, and that such interest transcends the particular legislative or judicial or investigative interest in learning the content of the communication. They argue, in addition, that the disclosures are usually made in reliance on a promise that they will be treated as confidential; that the failure to protect such disclosures will dry up essential sources of information; and that adherence to their professional code of ethics will expose them to charges of contempt.

These assertions are far more credible for newsmen than they are for the other professionals. Most disclosures are made to an attorney because the client wants the best possible advice and because he realizes that he will be the loser if he withholds the raw materials on which such advice should be predicated. The patient tells all to his physician because he wants to be diagnosed and treated properly. Information is given to social workers, teachers and guidance counselors because there is a problem which calls for help. The persons who make such communications probably know very little about the degree to which their confidences may be disclosed in the future; but if they did, the immediate interest in getting good advice would probably prevail, the communication would be made and the professional relationships would remain viable.

In the case of a journalist's privilege, the informant does not risk his health or liberty or fortune or soul by withholding information. He is likely to be moved by baser motives—spite or financial reward—or, on occasion, by a laudable desire to serve the public welfare if it can be done without too much jeopardy. His communication, more than the others, is probably the result of a calculation and more likely to be affected by the risk of exposure. In this instance, compelling the disclosure of a confidential source in one highly publicized case really is likely to restrict the flow of information to the news media. And by doing so, it may well interfere with the freedom of press guaranteed by the First Amendment.

In fourteen states, legislatures have been persuaded to enact statutes which protect the newsmen's sources. In eight of the states, the protection is absolute. In the remaining six, however, the privilege may be invoked only if the material derived from these sources has been published. Of the two solutions, the latter seems preferable because it strikes a balance in favor of the newsman only if he has indeed served the public by publishing the information and adding to society's store of knowledge. But it does not entirely meet either the need or the current problem. In some cases, the sources should be protected even if nothing has yet been presented to the public. And in others, the information should be protected as well as the source if vigorous reporting is to be encouraged. A newsman cannot be expected to learn what the Black Panthers or Weathermen or heroin users are doing unless he operates in an atmosphere of reciprocal confidentiality. He must be free to explore in detail, but at his own pace and in his own way. Interference with that exploration by official demands for information may make it immeasurably more difficult for the reporter to gain access in the future. For he will appear, after he has responded to a subpoena, to have been a police spy using deceptive practices in order to obtain information which would not otherwise have been disclosed to him.

The dilemma is a real one. It is relatively easy to justify protecting a confidential source when the public has been given the benefit of information obtained from that source. It is far more difficult when the newsman asks for immunity from subpoena for sources and information he may never expose to public view at all. For these problematic situations, a judge should be authorized, each time the privilege is asserted, to decide whether or not the investigative or adjudicative interest is great enough to override the public interest in confidentiality and a free press. As in the law of "government privilege" and self-incrimination, this could in most instances be determined by appraising the context in which the problem arises and the relative importance of the competing interests, without requiring the disclosure of the privileged material to the judge.* The bill recently

---

*There remains the question whether issues must be resolved by statute, or whether they might be dealt with as a matter of constitutional law under the First and Fourteenth Amendments.

introduced by Rep. Richard Ottinger (D, N.Y.) adopts such an approach for the federal government and, with some modifications, might serve as a model "Newsman's Privilege" statute for states as well.

Disclosures to journalists are only a special instance of a much larger problem which has not yet received the attention it deserves. Communications are regularly made to schools, employers, banks, stores and the military on the erroneous assumption either that they will remain confidential or that they will be used for a limited purpose. Inadequately protected by law, they make up a fund of information which is increasingly available to public and private investigators. As the pace of inquiry and computerization increases, so also will the temptation to use these "dossiers." The current controversy between the prosecutors and the news media serves to remind us once again that our confidences are protected far less than we realize, and that a more sensitive law of confidential communications is long overdue. [Editor's Note: See Introduction] .

THE SELLING OF THE PENTAGON: CBS VS. CONGRESS

Frank Stanton

I appear here today on a most serious matter. I have great respect for the Congress of the United States and for this important Subcommittee. I am mindful of my duty to comply with the requirements of a lawful Congressional subpoena. But I also have a duty to uphold the freedom of the broadcast press against Congressional abridgement. The conflict between these duties is the issue dividing us today. It raises a profound constitutional question going to the heart of the American democratic process.

Simultaneous to the Pentagon Papers dispute, CBS President Frank Stanton was defending the privacy of materials his network used in producing "The Selling of the Pentagon." Mr. Stanton told a special subcommittee that CBS was protected by the First Amendment and recent court rulings. The subcommittee was of the House Interstate and Foreign Commerce Committee, which has jurisdiction over the Federal Communications Commission. That committee found Mr. Stanton in contempt following this June 24, 1971 testimony, which is used with Mr. Stanton's permission. The House received the contempt citation in July, but after a bitter debate sent it back to the committee by a 226-181 vote. That maneuver killed the move against CBS.

My appearance is in response to the Subcommittee's subpoena dated May 26, 1971. That subpoena directs me to appear for the purpose of testifying and to bring with me "all film, workprints, outtakes, and sound-tape recordings, written scripts and/or transcripts utilized in whole or in part by CBS in connection with its documentary, 'The Selling of the Pentagon,' broadcast on February 23, 1971" except for "materials relating to segments not shown therein" and "official United States Government film that was utilized in the broadcast."

I would like to recapitulate the sequence of events that has led to my appearance here, and then to address the central and serious issues raised by your subpoena.

On February 23, the CBS Television Network broadcast a documentary, "CBS Reports: The Selling of the Pentagon," describing the public information activities of the Department of Defense. The broadcast was promptly acclaimed by many and sharply criticized by others. These criticisms were fully reported by CBS News.

On March 23, in response to the widespread public attention generated by the report, we rebroadcast it. At its conclusion, we broadcast a 22-minute postscript including earlier comments critical of the broadcast by Vice President Agnew, Secretary of Defense Laird, and Chairman Hebert of the House Armed Services Committee, as well as a response by Richard S. Salant, President of CBS News.

On April 18, in view of continued public interest in the substantive issues raised by the broadcast, we broadcast a CBS News Special Report, entitled "Perspective: The Selling of the Pentagon." This hour-long panel discussion presented contrasting points of view on the issues involved. Former Assistant Secretary of Defense for Public Affairs Arthur Sylvester, and General S.L.A. Marshall, a military commentator and historian, generally supported the Defense Department's public information program; Senator Fulbright and Adam Yarmolinsky, a Special Assistant to former Secretary of Defense McNamara, were critical of it.

Meanwhile, on April 7, this Subcommittee had issued a subpoena to CBS demanding the delivery of "all film, workprints, outtakes, sound-tape recordings, written scripts and/or transcripts" relating to the preparation of "The Selling of the Pentagon." On April 20, CBS furnished a film copy of the original broadcast and rebroadcast (with postscript) as well as transcripts of those broadcasts. But CBS respectfully challenged the Subcommittee's power to inquire by compulsory process into the editing of the broadcast and declined to produce materials not actually broadcast. The Subcommittee then allowed CBS 10 days to make a fuller response.

On April 30, without waiving its objections, CBS voluntarily supplied the Subcommittee with some general information unrelated to the editing process. And in support of its challenge to the Subcommittee's right of inquiry into this matter, CBS submitted an opinion of its counsel that the compulsory demand for production of materials not broadcast, for the purposes described in the Chairman's statement of April 20, was beyond the Subcommittee's power because of the First Amendment, and that CBS was under no legal duty to comply.

On May 26, the Chairman advised us that CBS had "satisfactorily met the requirements of Paragraphs 1, 3, 4 and 5 of the April 7 subpoena," but had failed to comply with Paragraph 2, which called for scripts, transcripts, workprints and other filmed materials *not* actually broadcast. The Subcommittee withdrew its April 7 subpoena and issued a new one. This May 26 subpoena requires me to appear for testimony and to produce the same materials called for in Paragraph 2, except that the letter accompanying the subpoena disclaimed any interest in transcripts and filmed materials of "interviews or events which did not appear, even in part, in the actual broadcast."

We have carefully reviewed with our counsel the May 26 letter and the accompanying subpoena. They have advised us that in their opinion* the subpoena still seeks to compel the production of materials compiled in preparing and editing the documentary but not actually broadcast; that the purpose of the Subcommittee investigation is still to make an official governmental inquiry into the editing process employed in producing the documentary; and that the Subcommittee may not constitutionally compel CBS to produce the subpoenaed materials or give oral testimony for such a purpose.

The First Amendment states that "Congress shall make no law. . . abridging the freedom of . . . the press." Clearly, the compulsory production of evidence for a Congressional investigation of this nature abridges the freedom of the press. The chilling effect of both the subpoena and the inquiry itself is plain beyond all question. If newsmen are told that their notes, films and tapes will be subject to compulsory process so that the government can determine whether the news has been satisfactorily edited, the scope, nature and vigor of

---

*Dated June 15, 1971, and submitted [to the subcommittee but not included here.]

Big Brother Is Monitoring You

their news gathering and reporting activities will inevitably be curtailed.

Our objection does not depend upon establishing that the government lacks power, under any and all circumstances, to subpoena a journalist or his unpublished materials. There are now pending before the Supreme Court several cases centering on the issue of whether the need of information for some important governmental purpose can under certain circumstances be so compelling as on balance to outweigh the repressive effect of such a subpoena. But this Subcommittee's legislative purpose—to prevent "distortions" or to control "editing practices" in broadcast news reports and thereby engage in official surveillance of journalistic judgments—has no constitutional warrant and therefore no benefit that can be balanced against the chilling effect of this subpoena, let alone outweigh it.

Based on the advice of our counsel and our own conviction that a fundamental principle of a free society is at stake, I must respectfully decline, as President of CBS, to produce the materials covered by the subpoena of May 26. For the same reasons, I must respectfully decline, as a witness summoned here by compulsory process, to answer any questions that may be addressed to me relating to the preparation of "The Selling of the Pentagon" or any other particular CBS news or documentary broadcast.

We take this position as a matter of conscience, because of our obligation to uphold the rights guaranteed by the First Amendment. That Amendment embodies our national commitment to freedom of the press. It protects the rights of journalists, not to make them into a privileged class, but to safeguard the liberties of us all by preserving one of the most indispensable elements of responsible democratic government—the right to report freely on the conduct of those in authority. In Judge Learned Hand's famous phrase: "To many this is, and always will be, folly; but we have staked upon it our all."

There can be no doubt in anyone's mind that the First Amendment would bar this subpoena if directed at the editing of a newspaper report, a book or a magazine article. Indeed, the Chairman has been quoted as having specifically conceded this point. However, it is urged that because broadcasters need governmental licenses while other media do not, the First Amendment permits such an intrusion into the freedom of broadcast journalism, although it admittedly forbids the identical intrusion into other press media. If broadcasters must comply with such subpoenas, broadcast journalism can never perform the independent and robust role in preserving those freedoms which the Constitution intended for American journalism.

Only two weeks ago, in a major case applying the First Amendment to protect a news broadcast, the Supreme Court placed broadcast and print journalists on precisely the same footing.

As broadcasters, it is our duty and responsibility in the public interest to resist any government action that threatens to transform a free and vigorous news medium into a controlled and timid one.

I shall, however, do my best to answer questions of the Subcommittee which do not seek to probe so deeply into the news process as to reach specific journalistic practices or the editing of particular broadcasts. The line is a difficult one to draw, and I hope the members of the Subcommittee will bear with me as I deal with your questions. I hope we can achieve a dialogue consistent with the stand we feel compelled to take as a matter of constitutional principle.

As we have previously indicated to the Subcommittee, comments on "The Selling of the Pentagon" have raised important issues as to the practices employed, or that ought to be employed, in the editing of documentary broadcasts. While responsible journalists may reasonably differ concerning particular practices in particular cases, we do not intend to ignore these differences or to shrink from continuing self-examination of our own practices. What we do object to is being subjected to compulsory questioning in a government inquiry, expressly intended to determine whether this or any other CBS news report meets government standards of truth.

The objection I am making has been urged not only by CBS and not only by those who believe that "The Selling of the Pentagon" was an excellent and valuable piece of journalism. The same objection has also been made by many groups and individuals, in and out of public office, who have criticized the broadcast in whole or in part. Scores of newspapers, representing the entire spectrum of political opinion and varying in their views of the merits of the broadcast, have expressed the deepest concern in editorials strongly supporting our position.

Leaders in the nation's educational, civic and religious life have protested the inescapable implications of the subpoenas addressed to us. Professional associations representing every segment of journalism have joined in the protest. These associations include the American Society of Newspaper Editors, the American Newspaper Publishers Association, the National Newspaper Publishers Association, the American Association of Schools and Departments of Journalism, the American Newspaper Guild, the Associated Press Broadcasters Association, the Association for Education in Journalism, the Association of American Publishers, the Authors League of America, the Radio Television News Directors Association, and Sigma Delta Chi. Government officials, including the Director of Communications for the Executive Branch, who criticized the broadcast, and the Chairman of the Federal Communications Commission, have stated their opposition to the subpoena. [Editor's Note: The FCC ruled that CBS had complied with the requirements of the "Fairness Doctrine."]

I can assure you that we at CBS have not taken lightly either your subpoena or the concern that prompted it. We recognize that journalists can make mistakes, that editing involves the exercise of judgment, and that we and other journalists can benefit by criticism. But I respectfully submit that where journalistic judgments are investigated in a Congressional hearing, especially by the Committee with jurisdiction to legislate about broadcast licenses, the official effort to compel evidence about our editing processes has an unconstitutionally chilling effect.

Let me close with the words of James Madison, written in 1799 and quoted by Mr. Justice Brennan in his opinion announcing the Court's decision two weeks ago applying the First Amendment to protect a news broadcast:

> "Among those principles deemed sacred in America, among those sacred rights considered as forming the bulwark of their liberty, which the Government contemplates with awful reverence and would approach only with the most cautious circumspection, there is no one of which the importance is more deeply impressed on the public mind than the liberty of the press. That this *liberty* is often carried to excess; that it has sometimes degenerated into *licentiousness*, is seen and lamented, *but the remedy has not yet been discovered. Perhaps it is an evil inseparable from the good with which it is allied; perhaps it is a shoot which cannot be stripped from the stalk without wounding vitally the plant from which it is torn. However desirable those measures might be which might correct without enslaving the press, they have never yet been devised in America.*"

Chapter IV

INCREASING RELEVANCE
OF REPORTING PRACTICES

IS MUCKRAKING COMING BACK?

Carey McWilliams

The existence of a continuing—but cyclical—tradition of reform journalism may be taken for granted; ongoing, it seems to disappear at certain times only to surface later. There is general agreement on the major factors which gave rise to muckraking journalism in the first decade of this century: technological changes which made it possible to reach out for a new mass audience at reduced unit costs; the emergence of a large audience of high-school-educated Americans who were interested in public affairs but unable to relate to such magazines as *Harper's, Atlantic, Scribner's,* and *Century*—for "the cultivated classes." More important, a mood of deep social concern and disaffection had emerged. The key to this mood and the political movement it brought into being was a feeling that "the system" itself might be somehow at fault. As Walter Lippmann pointed out, "The mere fact that muckraking was what the people wanted to hear is in many ways the most important revelation of the whole campaign. There is no other way of explaining the quick approval which the muckrakers won."

There is also general agreement on the factors which brought about the decline of muckraking. For one thing, the movement of which it was a part tended to merge with the Progressive Party. More important, the entire Progressive Movement—muckrakers and all— was eclipsed by World War I.

The turn-of-the-century muckrakers, however, had their precursors. The articles by Charles Francis Adams on the Tweed ring and

Carey McWilliams, editor of the *Nation* and for years an advocate of "reform journalism," prepared these ideas for the Fall, 1970 issue of *Columbia Journalism Review,* and along with the *CJR* gave his permission for republication.

"Chapters of Erie," which appeared in the *North American Review*, helped set the stage; John Jay Chapman's *Political Nursery*, which he edited in New York in 1897-1901, was as shrewd and realistic about the sources of corruption as anything Lincoln Steffens ever wrote; and as Harvey Swados points out, much of what the muckrakers had to say was to be found in H.D. Lloyd's *Wealth Against Commonwealth*, published in 1894.

A number of newspapers had conducted some aggressive muckraking campaigns before the turn of the century. In 1896, for example, Congress was set to consider the Funding Bill, an outrageous giveaway designed to add to the Southern Pacific's plunder. Hearst decided to fight it and to this end asked Ambrose Bierce, who was then writing a locally celebrated column for the San Francisco *Examiner*, to go to Washington and direct the campaign against the bill. Bierce accepted with alacrity, and for nearly a year directed an unremitting attack on the Southern Pacific and C.P. Huntington.

In one sense, as Swados notes, sensational or "yellow" newspaper journalism was a parallel development, but much more superficial and not so sharply focused on social issues. Then, too, the newspaper has been a basically local institution, largely dependent on local advertising and restricted to a local readership. The issues that began to concern the public at the turn of the century were largely national, and we then had no truly national newspapers.

The muckraking magazines were a distinct journalistic innovation. Taking advantage of the new technology, they cut costs, dropped the price, and reached out for the big new readership that McClure and others knew existed. They got the readership, which in turn produced the advertising. (At the turn of the century a new nationwide mass market for certain products was just emerging.) But by 1912 the pattern was clear. Once the new mass magazines had demonstrated the existence of the market, other publications moved in and, in effect, took over the invention of the pioneer muckraking journalists. The initial reform impulse abated.

Harvey Swados points out that our country recuperates from the greedy decades "almost like a repentant drunkard recovering from a debauch by trying to examine the causes of his drinking bout and by making earnest resolutions to sin no more." The difference between the nation and the drunkard, he suggests, may lie in the fact that in its moods of sober self-criticism the nation really does redress many of the wrongs, really does help those who cannot help themselves, and does thereby renew its world image as a state concerned not solely or even primarily with self-aggrandizement, but much more importantly with dignity, freedom, and decent self-respect.

Swados could get an argument on this proposition from some of today's rebels and dissenters; nevertheless I share his feeling. *Time*, on Sept. 19, 1969, took much the same position. "For reasons that seem to be rooted in the public mood," it stated, "muckraking is a cyclic form of journalism. If a society is troubled, it suspects that something is wrong with its system or its leadership; a free press responds by finding out what that is." Conversely in periods of apparent prosperity and well being, reform journalism loses its appeal, and the muckraking journalist is regarded as a spoilsport or an old-fashioned curmudgeon. The situation changes when the public—often a new public—becomes concerned over the course of events. The reform tradition never dies—there are always a few publications around to keep it alive—but it does seem to fade away at times.

The 1920s were such a period. As the great boom got under way, the *Saturday Evening Post* and *Collier's*, after the days of Norman Hapgood, celebrated the national virtues and pieties. As James Playsted Wood points out, the reform tradition was sustained during this decade by small-circulation magazines, in some respects more radical than the muckraking monthlies—namely, the *Nation, New Republic*, and one or two other publications. This was a familiar role for the *Nation;* again and again it has helped sustain the reform tradition when the cycle has turned against it.

We do not ordinarily think of Mencken or the *American Mercury* as part of the reform tradition, but as James Wood notes they were—at least during the 1920s. As the muckrakers had done before him, Mencken discovered a new audience, with new tastes, new interests, new attitudes. It is worth noting that like the *Nation* and the *New Republic*, the *Mercury* was not entirely dependent on advertising revenue. Like these magazines also, the *Mercury* cultivated a new group of writers and encouraged—across the country—a healthy skepticism. In some respects, *New Masses*, founded in 1926, also helped sustain the reform tradition.

After 1929 the scene changed. The first reactions to the stock market crash were shock, disbelief, and bewilderment. Then, rather slowly, a new current of concern and anger began to form. As the decade advanced, the world crisis began to mesh with the domestic, and pressures for change mounted. Old dogmas were questioned, and a thirst for new theories and a willingness to experiment emerged. The New Deal, of course, was a response to this mood. On the New Deal and the momentous happenings of the 1930s the press was divided—that is, owners and publishers were in general opposed to the New Deal and not inclined to rise to the challenge of the times, whereas the working press was sympathetic and did respond.

But it was not publishers alone who experienced a failure of nerve. In his *Autobiography*, published in 1931, Steffens not only said that the muckraking tradition was dead but that it had been a mistake. It had, he thought, stretched out the age of honest bunk and protracted the age of folly. He accused himself of having shared its illusions and of not realizing that muckraking was merely "a reflex of an old moral culture."

But Steffens spoke too soon. In the early 1930s, as he was saying farewell to the muckraking tradition, Matthew Josephson wrote a series of articles for the *New Yorker* about bulls and bears in the market. It occurred to Josephson that it might be worthwhile to turn back in time and examine their prototypes. *The Robber Barons*, directly in the muckraking tradition, was published in 1934 and has been selling steadily ever since. It was followed in 1938 by *The Politicos* and in 1940 by *The President Makers*, which extended the same analysis. Books, in fact, seem to have been the prime means by which the muckraking tradition was kept alive in the 1930s, as writers sought to muckrake American history or to give in-depth reports on the state of American life. *The Grapes of Wrath* (which grew out of a San Francisco newspaper series by Steinbeck) and *Factories in the Field* made the nation vividly aware of the social consequences of large-scale industrialized farming and brought the anti-labor activities of the Associated Farmers to public attention—without much help from the press.

In the *Nation* and *New Republic*, Carleton Beals, Heywood Broun, McAlister Coleman, Lewis Gannett, Louis Adamic, and others kept the muckraking tradition very much alive. Radio also played a key role in developing mass awareness of what was happening. Documentary films were important, as were photographs. The pamphlet, a neglected journalistic form, experienced a rebirth; the great labor organizing campaigns brought a flood of pamphlet material.

At the end of World War II we were, as William Barrett has written, "at the end of a long tunnel, there was light showing ahead, and beyond that all sorts of horizons opened." But this bright vision was never realized; the Cold War intervened. Instead of muckraking, red-baiting journalism became the order of the day. Full of high promise, *PM*, launched in 1940, struggled valiantly, and was succeeded by the *Star*, which continued the struggle for a time and then collapsed. George Seldes carried on the old muckraking tradition brilliantly and courageously with his newsletter *In Fact*, started in the 1930s because of his feeling that the press had not responded to the needs and challenges of the 1930s. But Mr. Wood, writing in

1956, smugly reports the demise of the muckraking tradition in these words:

> Magazine liberalism and iconoclasm have both declined in the years since World War II. The reasons in both instances are apparent. Most of the old idols have been smashed, and the clay feet of newer ones have not yet been identified. . . . Most of the immediate social gains have been gained, and newer causes either have not been invented or have not been formulated distinctly enough for journalistic clamor. . . .

We were confident we "had it made." We had become so infatuated with the great god GNP that we could not see the poor and underprivileged in our midst. It took independent investigators such as Michael Harrington, Dwight MacDonald, and Herman Miller to discover them. Even after the Montgomery bus boycott touched off the civil rights rebellion, the press still failed to zero in on the urban ghettos or to sense what was happening in them. For a decade or more it had, with notable exceptions, been "fighting communism" with an intensity that largely precluded concentration on domestic realities.

In these depressing years the small-media magazines once again kept the muckraking tradition alive. While the *Nation* devoted much space to a critical analysis of Cold-War policies, it also became increasingly concerned with domestic assaults on civil liberties which were the counterpart of these policies. We devoted major articles to the Ted Lamb case, the Oppenheimer case, the Remington tragedy, the Hiss case, and many similar situations.

At the same time the *Nation* pioneered in application of what might be called muckraking techniques to large-scale arms spending, first in Matthew Josephson's series on "The Big Guns" in 1956 and later with Fred J. Cook's "Juggernaut: The Warfare State" in 1961. We followed this with a special issue on "The CIA" in 1962—the first hard look at that institution. Previously, in 1958, we had devoted a special issue to another *verboten* subject, "The FBI." Aside from Max Lowenthal's fine book on the Federal Bureau of Investigation— which came out in 1950 and was in effect suppressed by FBI pressure—the press had failed to take an objective, critical view of the FBI. It had also failed to take a critical view of large arms spending or the CIA. After our special issues appeared the ice was broken, and many articles appeared on these subjects.

We demonstrated the acute need for old-style muckraking in a special 1956 issue—again by Fred Cook—on "The Shame of New York," the title of which reflects its parentage. This issue led directly to a very fine series in the New York *Herald Tribune*. We ran one of the first good articles on cigarette smoking and lung cancer, by Dr. Alton Ochsner, in 1953. We insisted, in 1957 and 1961, on giving attention to the wicked suggestion that perhaps a tax might be placed on advertising. We ran the first articles by Ralph Nader to appear in an American magazine, including his 1959 article "The Safe Car You Can't Buy."

The *Nation*, however, is not a news magazine. It is a journal of critical opinion. As a publication we are not well adapted to the needs of muckraking journalism. We have a small staff and meager resources. We have no full-time writers to assign to various subjects. We are unable to finance extensive research or investigation. It was presumptuous of us to undertake such an issue as "Juggernaut: The Warfare State," or the other Fred Cook special issues. Not a penny of foundation money was used to finance these projects, although it would have been welcome. What we did was to build up files of materials—all kinds of materials—and then turn them over to the enormously gifted, hard-working Fred Cook, who is the living embodiment of the muckraking tradition in journalism. We did something else I think is important and which other small-circulation magazines also do. We brought along many young writers: Dan Wakefield, Gene Marine, Stanley Meisler, Jennifer Cross, J.L. Pimsleur, Robert Sherrill, and many others.

Today journalism faces a new situation. The scene began to change in 1960; slowly at first, but then it began to accelerate. No journal now has a monopoly on dissent. The change has come about as a result of the two components which have, in the past, ushered in new chapters in the cyclical history of reform journalism: new technology and new interests and concerns.

The myth of affluence was beginning to dissipate by the time President Kennedy took office. Nor was it long before a war had been declared against poverty. The acceleration of the war in Vietnam discredited "establishment" opinion. And the rebellion of blacks and students shattered the prevailing complacency. These new concerns created an enormous new market, so to speak, for a modern version of reform journalism.

In September, 1969, we ran an article by our Washington correspondent, Robert Sherrill, on "The Pendleton Brig," which illustrates the point. That article was widely quoted by the press and the wire services and was twice used by Mike Wallace on CBS. It brought a House subcommittee to Pendleton almost before you could say "brig." If that report had been published in September, 1967, it would not have attracted the same attention. We have published tougher articles by Sherrill that received less notice. Once again, as Lippmann pointed out years ago, it is active public concern about a subject that compels the press to pay attention to it. Today new concerns, new apprehensions, new interests have ushered in a new chapter in reform journalism.

The new technology has pivoted on the emergence of television as a major news source. From rather modest beginnings, TV news has become a huge enterprise. At the same time, TV has gotten more and more advertising that formerly went to newspapers and magazines—particularly the large-circulation picture magazines. Newspaper owners have bought into TV when and where they could and, to the extent that they have succeeded, have taken a somewhat more relaxed view of the new competition. But magazines—notably those hardest hit—have begun to strike back. In general both newspapers and magazines have begun to feel that muckraking or investigative journalism is a useful means of countering network news.

Print media have certain inherent advantages in investigative reporting. Print constitutes a record that can be cited, quoted, filed, passed from hand to hand, and reprinted and distributed in large quantities. TV news is gone in a flash, and it is difficult to get transcripts of network programs. Also it is difficult to present complex situations, with facts and figures, on TV. For example, TV newsmen with whom I have spoken, including the producers of some excellent documentaries, concede that the medium has never done a truly effective expose of the military-industrial complex. All news is perhaps a form of entertainment, but the entertainment factor is much stronger on TV than in print.

There are other limitations on TV investigative reporting. No one in the industry needs to be reminded that TV is a licensed medium—Vice President Agnew's blast only underscores the point. The Fairness Doctrine does not present much of a problem, but the "personal attack" doctrine, as evolved by the FCC, is another matter. Under this doctrine if a TV documentary refers to someone in a derogatory manner the producer is obligated to seek out this person and offer him a chance—then and there—to respond to the statement. The mere fact that such an offer is made implies that the statement is, in some sense, derogatory. So if the person has something to hide, and is sophisticated, he will not accept the offer but will say, in effect, "run that sequence and I will sue you." This rule—which applies to documentaries, not to news—causes much distress to producers of documentaries that might be regarded as muckraking journalism. The inability of documentary producers to use concealed mikes or cameras is a further limitation.

Despite these inhibitions, some fine TV documentaries in the muckraking tradition have been made: *Biography of a Bookie, The Business of Heroin, Hunger in America, Health in America, Case History of a Rumor,* and NBC's hard look at Jim Garrison of New Orleans. But if there is a weakness in TV news it is in investigative journalism.

As it becomes increasingly difficult for the printed media to compete in "hard" news, it is not surprising to note a new interest by some newspapers in investigative reporting. Since February, 1967, *Newsday* has had an investigative team consisting of an editor (Robert Greene), three reporters, and a file clerk, who also functions as secretary and researcher. Greene had experience on the staff of the Senate Rackets Committee before he came to *Newsday;* he knows investigative techniques. The team works as a unit. It has its own files and records and a separate office. In addition to many minor stories the team has turned out about three major reports a year—each about 3,500 words—running for five days. Word of *Newsday's* enterprise has gotten around. When the American Press Institute at Columbia staged its second seminar on investigative journalism, attendance increased over the previous year.

The Associated Press also has set up a special assignment team, with ten reporters, under their own editor. One is a specialist in education, one in health and science; the others are all-purpose reporters. In 1969, AP reports, this team turned out 250 stories—that is, stories that were the product of investigative journalism.

One may hope that the new team of reporters at AP will remedy, to some extent, a weakness of wire service news. Again and again AP has failed to pick up excellent articles prepared by local reporters after much hard digging and investigation. Two examples are Sanford Watzman's fine series on defense procurement and renegotiation, which appeared in the Cleveland *Plain Dealer*, and Nick Kotz's excellent series for the Cowles papers on meat inspection. AP did distribute four or five key stories in the Kotz series but there were fifty or more in all. The *Nation* and *New Republic* were able to secure rewrites of some of the material, but it should have had, from the start, much wider national attention. I make it a business nowadays to scan the *Congressional Record* for series of this kind, which are often inserted by a senator or representative with a special interest in the subject. I learned of the Watzman and Kotz series in this way.

The "underground" press is, to some extent, trying to exploit what it regards as the general press' reluctance to engage in investigative journalism. Many offbeat journals, hard to categorize, belong in the muckraking tradition. They include I.F. Stone's indispensable newsletter; the *Chicago Journalism Review*, which has its counterpart in Montreal's *The Last Post; Hard Times;* Roldo Bartimole's *Point of View*, published in Cleveland; the *Bay Guardian* of San Francisco; and newsletters such as that of the North American Conference on Latin America. FM radio and documentary films have added something to the muckraking effort. And some investigative reporting in *Life* and *Look* has been first-rate—William Lambert's *Life* article about former Justice Abe Fortas, for example.

The book remains a major resource of reform journalism, as demonstrated by Rachel Carson's *Silent Spring*, Ralph Nader's *Unsafe at Any Speed*, and Joseph Goulden's remarkable study of the Gulf of Tonkin Resolution, *Truth Is the First Casualty*. (Indeed, it is instructive to read Frank Graham, Jr.'s *Since Silent Spring*, which documents massive and often personal attacks leveled against Miss Carson by a large part of the press. *Time*, for example, denounced her book as "an emotional and inaccurate outburst" and accused the author of "putting literary skill second to the task of frightening and arousing readers." But last fall, when the Government vindicated Miss Carson by banning DDT, *Time* reported complaints that the ban was inadequate.) Moreover, the paperback revolution has added a new dimension to the book's effectiveness. In Canada, after David and Nadine Nowlan prepared an eighty-page analysis of the Spadina Expressway, computerized typesetting and offset printing enabled reproduction of their book in three weeks, for a sale price of $1.25 a copy.

From all this, it should be apparent that the muckraking or reform tradition is very much alive in American journalism. But there is not nearly enough of it. The problem is not with personnel. We have some superb investigative reporters: Jack Nelson, Nick Kotz, Sanford Watzman, Robert Sherrill, Bernard Nossiter, Fred Cook, Morton Mintz, Richard Harris, Tom Whiteside, and many more. The problem is how the available personnel are used. Good investigative journalism takes time, money, and commitment on the part of a publisher. If there is a personnel problem it exists at this level. A few more publishers like the late William T. Evjue would be welcome.

Business Week in a cover article reported that the day of the mass magazine as we have known it has passed; the "hot" magazines are those with a special relationship to their readers—that is, the selective-audience magazines, be the audience surfers, skiers, or single girls. What this means, an executive of J. Walter Thompson told

Business Week, is "simply that print media, like everything else that is for sale, are gradually being moved into the traditional and modern marketing mold." In fact, some of the new selective-audience magazines are little more than means by which the publisher, who manufactures products related to the special interest of the magazine, can advertise these products. Newspapers, of course, could step into the breach. But will they? And how long will they be able to compete with TV for lucrative advertising accounts?

Another limitation is the libel laws, which, although they have been somewhat relaxed, still warn publications—particularly small-circulation publications—away from important subject matter. It has been my experience that individuals and corporations will threaten—and actually sue—small journals of opinion when they would hesitate to threaten or sue the New York *Times* for the same material. On occasion I have arranged for authors to testify before Congressional committees to get stories before the public simply because a publication such as the *Nation* cannot afford the luxury of winning a libel action. Recently we were sued for libel and the case was thrown out—but it cost us $7,500 to win.

Despite these difficulties, muckraking journalism seems to be staging a comeback. Today we have foundations that will occasionally underwrite the kind of research and travel that investigative journalism often requires. New technologies continue to push the press toward more and better investigative reporting. And on the horizon are a bewildering variety of greater technological possibilities of the kind Ralph Lee Smith discussed in the *Nation's* recent special issue, "The Wired Nation."

Leon Trotsky, like Lincoln Steffens, thought that criticism of existing institutions accomplished very little and that its chief function was to serve as "a safety valve for mass dissatisfaction." No doubt it does serve this function. But it is or should be a historical constant in any society that aspires to achieve a more rational social order.

Reform journalism can be effective. But its effectiveness has come to depend, now more than ever, on how searching it is and the extent to which it relates the part to the whole, the symptom to the cause. Reform journalists may not be "movers and shakers," but they do edge the world along a bit, they do get an innocent man out of jail occasionally, and they do win a round now and then—sometimes a significant round. A wealth of journalistic experience and much social wisdom is reflected in the title of George Seldes' book: *Never Tire of Protesting*. We never should.

THE REPORTER AS ACTIVIST: FOURTH REVOLUTION IN JOURNALISM

J.K. Hvistendahl

American journalism is embroiled in its fourth revolution, introduced to the country in the belligerent tones of Vice President Spiro T. Agnew in his Des Moines speech of November 1969. This revolution, like most social revolutions, has even those who are most directly involved in complete chaos and confusion. The revolution is real, those who are involved are in earnest, but the goal is not necessarily the demise of American journalism.

The first revolution was the freeing of the American Press from the threat of control by government. The first and fourteenth amendments to the constitution made it legal, and 18th Century rationalism made it philosophically desirable to criticize actions of the government. The editors of partisan newspapers after the revolution supplied somewhat more criticism than the government wanted.

The second revolution was the growth of the "objective press," brought about largely by the press associations which developed after the invention of the telegraph. Because they served many papers, with many and sometimes violently differing points of view, the press associations had to present the news as objectively as possible, without opinions or evaluations of the authors. The press association made a solid contribution to journalistic writing, and the objective style became the model for journalistic writing.

The third revolution was interpretive reporting, in which the reporter reported the facts objectively, but attempted to explain them or interpret them in a way that would make them meaningful to the reader and listener. Both World War I and World War II contributed to the growth of this type of reporting; readers and listeners wilted before a barrage of objective but totally confusing messages about the war. By interpreting the news to anxious audiences, H.V. Kaltenborn, Elmer Davis, Boake Carter and other "name" commentators commanded audiences of millions. Newspaper columnists like Raymond Clapper, Thomas L. Stokes, Marquis Childs, Walter Lippmann, and Ernest K. Lindley came on the scene for the same reasons.

J.K. Hvistendahl, member of the Iowa State journalism faculty and holder of the Ph.D. in mass communications from the University of Minnesota, has conducted extensive research in the newspaper field. This advocacy position is reprinted with the permission of *The Quill,* which published it for Sigma Delta Chi members in February, 1970.

Now the fourth revolution is upon us, and the revolutionists are activist reporters. The journalistic activist believes he has a right (indeed an obligation) to become personally and emotionally involved in the events of the day. He believes he should proclaim his beliefs if he wishes, and that it is not only permissible but desirable for him to cover the news from the viewpoint of his own intellectual commitment. He looks at traditional reporting as being sterile, and he considers reporters who refuse to commit themselves to a point of view as being cynical or hypocritical. The activist believes that attempting to describe the events of a complicated world objectively seldom results in the truth for anybody—the source, the reporter, or the reader or listener.

Some of the symptoms of the growing activism as reported in a recent *Wall Street Journal* article:

Some 500 Time, Inc. employees attended anti-war discussions in the company auditorium on Moratorium Day.

The *Chicago Journalism Review*, a publication by reporters dedicated to pointing out the lapses of the very papers for which they work, is now in its second year of publication.

Reporters on at least a half dozen major papers in the country have asked their publishers for a more active role in their paper's policy decisions, as have the employees of *Time*.

Two young women reporters on the New York *Post* were fired for refusing to have their bylines on stories which they thought demeaned women, but were rehired after other *Post* reporters eliminated their own bylines in sympathy.

Those of us who have been associated with University publications should have seen the fourth revolution coming. For surely the college and university press has provided the early warning system. College and university newspapers, some of the best in the country and some of the worst, have steadily de-emphasized "straight news." Opinion pieces abound, and not only on the editorial pages. The *Carletonian*, of Minnesota's prestigious Carleton College, has relegated all straight news to a daily bulletin, and has turned the entire college paper into a journal of "think" pieces, somewhere between a newspaper and a magazine in format.

"Truth-as-I-see it" reporting, rather than activist reporting, might be a more accurate description of the fourth revolution. The new reporters don't claim that they, or anybody else, have a corner on the truth. But they insist that the reporter, like the scientist, has an obligation to report the truth as he sees it. In the long run, they believe, the reporter who is seeking the truth will serve the reader and listener better than the traditional reporter who attempts to describe an event accurately, reduce it to symbols which fit the news conduits of the various media, and then pipe the product to the consumer who is to make of it what he will.

The activist believes the modern media "lie by sanitation" and sin by omission. The media omit important observations by the reporter because they are "editorial in nature." They clean up and homogenize the news to make it fit the orderly world of the establishment, of which the press is too much a part. Read this excerpt from a letter written by a young journalism graduate after his first job on a large Midwestern newspaper:

> In July I went on a walk through_____, the city's worst black ghetto, with the President of the American Public Health Association. We visited homes of five ghetto residents to talk with them about their health problems.
>
> My assignment was to pour out my heart in the story. I did. But by the time the copy desk got through with the material it was unrecognizable. Every reference to tenement was changed to "apartment" and all mention of rat tracks, month-old garbage, and abandoned buildings standing open to kids and arsonists (law requires all abandoned buildings in the city to be boarded up) was edited out.

The reporter thought that he'd been asked to "pour out his heart," but apparently not to the extent that he could describe a ghetto neighborhood in terms which showed his feelings and might in turn convey similar feelings to his readers.

The truth-as-I-see-it newsman rejects the conduit, or common carrier, theory of the press. The amount that can flow through the conduits is miniscule compared to the totality of available news. The consumer can't possibly be given all the facts about a situation as complicated as, for example, Vietnam. The process of news selection is and always has been subjective; there are no reliable external criteria (first-year journalism books to the contrary) by which anyone can decide with any precision what is news and what isn't news.

If it is indeed true that a news story starts out as a subjective decision on the part of the press service, city editor, or television program director, the question then arises as to whether the story shall be released without further responsibility on the part of the media. Vice President Agnew would probably say yes. But for the activists there are several reasons why the newsman's responsibility should continue. Because only a small part of the totality of relevant information can be presented to the reader or viewer, the situation (as far as truth-as-I-see-it goes) is one-sided and is likely to mislead the reader or listener. The content of a news event, within the reporter's own knowledge, may be patently false, exaggerated or misleading but is offered to the reader without comment and with the implication that it is true. "Objectivity" may be served but the truth isn't.

The classic example of "common carrier" reporting, of course, was that of the late Senator Joseph McCarthy. McCarthy made charges on the floor of the Senate which reporters knew were false, but they were obliged to report the stories without comment or warning because the newspapers they worked for were "common carriers." The reporter had no obligation to truth-as-they-knew-it other than to quote the senator correctly, but it was a frustrating experience for those who knew they were spreading false information.

A second example is Nixon's speech on Vietnam, which was evaluated immediately after delivery by television commentators, and which led to strong condemnation of the media by Vice President Agnew in his Des Moines speech. Agnew was perturbed in part because the commentators seemed to be in general agreement that there was nothing substantially new in Nixon's speech, a judgment that can be supported by even a casual reading of the President's speech. It is possible that President Nixon, being a skilled politician, hoped that the *impression* would be left that he had a new policy on Vietnam. Would the truth have better been served if the television commentators had acted as common carriers only, when their experience with politics and news had told them that the public needed some additional information which might bring them somewhat closer to the truth?

From the viewpoint of communication theory, the "objective" reporter or writer expends most of his responsibility with the source. He is obliged to quote the sources correctly, and accurately describe the news event. Further, he must not in any way permit his own views to provide a warning to the reader if he perceives the information to be false or defective. The reader or listener must be the judge; the writer has no responsibility to the audience other than to deliver the message. The activist reporter with his emphasis on truth-as-I-see-it feels responsibility to the audience. He asks, "If I deliver an 'objective' message to the reader, but that message is likely to take the reader farther from the truth rather than bring him closer to it, who has been served?"

Another area in which the truth-as-I-see-it journalist demands more of the share of the action is in the news selection process. The women reporters on the New York *Post* refused to have their bylines on an interview of Mrs. Gil Hodges. According to their value system, women are people and should appear in the news on their own merit, not on the merit of their husbands. (If this value were widespread in American journalism, Jackie Kennedy Onassis would soon have complete privacy.)

The point is not that one point-of-view is necessarily more valid than another, but there are *multiple points of view* in a diverse society and more of these should surface in the press. For the most part, the "gatekeepers" who make the news decisions in the media are in the bifocal set, and they inevitably make news judgments that reflect their own training and backgrounds. Like all of us, they are victims as well as beneficiaries of all they have experienced. They have "learned" that the public will lap up columns of type on murder cases, so they have given the public columns of type on the Sam Sheppard cases while Lake Erie gets little attention until it is biologically dead. As one young reporter expresses it, "The American press is always last to recognize the disease, but is first to report the funeral."

The activist believes that the base of news judgment should be broadened to include more newsmen with contemporary social conscience, who are actively interested in solutions to social problems, and who might make the press an active partner, rather than a passive chronicler of social change.

Truth-as-I-see-it reporting might not only help to eliminate some of the excesses of journalism but also the practice of making mountains out of trivial molehills. Astronaut "Buzz" Aldrin in a UPI story criticized news media for a practice that is so common that it is taught routinely in schools of journalism (it's called "getting the peg."). Aldrin says, "We were talking about the G (gravity) airplane, and simulations for one-sixth G and zero G and somebody happened to ask the question, did you ever get sick in the airplane?"

"I admitted it had happened—that I did once on one flight and this turned into 'Aldrin reveals lunar sickness' as a headline, and I think that's pretty misleading."

In another instance, Aldrin's uncle was talking to another passenger on an airplane, and happened to mention conversationally that some scientists had speculated that lunar rocks might burst into flame when exposed to oxygen. "Well, this turned into a headline, because the man was a reporter: 'Aldrin Fears Lunar Rocks.' " These stories may have had inconsequential effects, but the effect on George Romney's political future when newspapers chose to play up his famous remark that he'd been "brainwashed by American generals" in Vietnam probably ended his presidential hopes.

There are at least two other compelling reasons why it might be well to take a tolerant view of truth-as-I-see-it reporting. America faces tremendous environmental and political problems which can only be solved by concerted action. Outmoded forms of government must be changed. A new and saner view needs to be taken of the nation's defense. If the press is to act as a neutral bystander, waiting to report the symptoms of disaster as they appear, what social agency is to marshal the people and the institutions to the task at hand?

The second reason is that the institutions of our society are so vast that the truth about them may never emerge, or emerge so late as to be downright dangerous. It took 21 months for the "secret" to surface about the massacre of several hundred Vietnamese civilians by American troops. It took over a year to "discover" that the Air Force had spent an extra, unauthorized billion dollars on the development of a cargo plane. And whoever heard of Watts or Hough before the fire bombs started falling?

Like most revolutions, this one had its roots deep in the past. The libertarian tradition of the American press, as envisioned by Thomas Jefferson, assumed a free marketplace of ideas, from which the truth would emerge. The libertarian press did not encompass "objectivity," and it assumed that personal opinions would be expressed and the best of them would survive. (Jefferson couldn't possibly have contemplated the difficulty of the truth emerging into the marketplace from the Pentagon.) Being personally and emotionally involved in stories they are writing is nothing particularly new to American reporters. Almost every Pulitzer prize-winner has been an activist to the extent that he involved himself personally and emotionally in the story for which he won the prize. Clark Mollenhoff, reporter turned presidential assistant and press critic, was himself noted for his high personal involvement in the stories out of Washington which he wrote for the Des Moines *Register* and *Tribune*, and for which he won a Pulitzer prize. News magazines, *Time* especially, have bordered on this type of reporting for some time, although they have toned down the personal element by a cloak of anonymity. *Look* magazine owes at least a part of its post-war success to vigorous first-person reporting by concerned writers who were given their editorial head. The same week President Nixon delivered his policy speech on Vietnam, *Look* published a seven-page article by Foreign Editor J. Robert Moskin entitled "Vietnam: Get Out Now." The article was followed (not preceded by) a three-paragraph editorial supporting Moskin's stand.

Truth-as-I see-it reporting is not editorializing. It is an honest attempt on the part of the reporter to bring together all the material that he can on a subject on which he has strong feelings. The article may be onesided or it may be balanced. Perhaps his decision is to make no decision. But it is an honest attempt to seek the truth. If the reporter is honest, he will be accurate and he will be fair. But he'll follow the information he has to its logical conclusion, and make judgments, if judgment seems apparent to him.

Lest panic set in, it should be noted that not all reporting should or need be done by activists, and not all reporters may be dedicated to "truth-as-I-see-it." "Objective" news reporting did not entirely supplant the biased reporting of the partisan press. Partisan reporting is still present in labor publications, most of the underground press, and in the editorials of many a respected newspaper. Interpretive reporting did not replace objective reporting, and the need for interpretive reporting remains. And truth-as-I-see-it will no doubt supplement, rather than replace, other approaches to reporting.

For the most part, this type of reporting calls for specialists, highly trained in their specialty. Unlike editorials, it is by-line reporting representing the accumulated wisdom of one individual rather than of the newspaper or television station. Much of the necessary-but-routine reporting from obituaries to baseball scores could be done by high school or junior college graduates; the truth-as-I-see-it reporters should be university graduates, preferably with a Master's degree in a specialty field.

If the media are to function as catalysts for action in vital political and social institutions in America, as well as continue their functions as common carriers of information, the organization of the newsroom will have to change. Most newspapers are organized to process the news, not to originate it. A more realistic organization of daily papers would be along lines of special areas of knowledge—the economic editor, the environmental specialist, the political editor, the urban affairs editor, the transportation editor, the leisure time editor, the science editor. More responsibility would be thrust on editors and reporters to carve out their own stories.

The long-haired, mustachioed creatures from the colleges and universities beginning their apprenticeship on America's newspapers, magazines, radio and television stations represent what may be America's last chance for a vital and vigorous press. But if they are turned

off by an establishment press while the garbage mounts, law enforcement deteriorates, the ghettos grow as fast as the military budget, the
airports get ever more crowded while train service disappears, they
will turn to other pursuits. For on the whole the activist-type college
editors are the brightest, most talented of the current crop of young
journalists.

The established press can harness the vitality and concern of
this new breed of journalist to the nation's serious problems. Or the
press can retain its traditional status as a common carrier of news and
faithfully record the failures of America's social, political, religious,
and economic institutions as they occur. Then, says the young activist, they can comment at length on just what went wrong and who is
to blame. The comment would be on the editorial page, of course.

THE 'ORTHODOX' MEDIA UNDER FIRE:
CHICAGO AND THE PRESS

Nathan B. Blumberg

The news media of the United States were subjected to an
attack unprecedented in modern times for their coverage of events
during the Democratic National Convention in Chicago. The reason is
that the news media did their jobs in Chicago in a way unprecedented in modern times.

Mayor Richard Daley made several dreadful miscalculations in
his handling of the Democratic National Convention, but the decisive
mistake was a frontal attack on the men sent to cover the events in
the convention hall and on the streets. Two things happened that
didn't have to happen and that made all the difference. Unfortunately, it took some assaults on newsmen by police to push the print
media into telling a story that otherwise, we must assume from the
record, would have remained essentially untold, and it took some
ham-handed attempts at censorship by Chicago's political boss,
accustomed to having his way, to infuriate the television networks to
the point that they showed the way things were and are in Chicago.

Nathan B. Blumberg, former dean of the University of Montana School of Journalism, who has for years been calling for "relevance," originally published "A
Study of the 'Orthodox' Press: The Reporting of Dissent" in the *Montana Journalism Review*, No. 11, 1968. These excerpts from "The Orthodox Media Under
Fire: Chicago and the Press" in the *Montana Journalism Review*, No. 12, 1969,
are used with his permission.

Only 10 months earlier, when 100,000 persons assembled at the Lincoln Memorial to protest the war in Vietnam and more than 30,000 demonstrators later pressed against the Pentagon, the confrontation was reported by the news media in ways that only could have delighted the authorities—governmental, military, police and industrial. . . .

What happened in Chicago was that incidents of repression that in the past almost always had been kept hidden from the public were reported in detail. Naturally, those persons committed to perpetuating present policies and conditions were infuriated by this unexpected and unusual turn of events and they struck back with all the considerable power in their hands. They were joined by those millions of Americans who for varying reasons favor authoritarian repression of minority groups and minority opinions.

Conversely, events in Chicago were shocking to millions of other Americans because just as the orthodox press covered up what happened in the demonstration leading to the doors of the Pentagon, it has covered up illegal police behavior in countless cities where police officers daily harass and intimidate large numbers of our citizens. Chicago was a catalyst. It brought out in one agonizing ordeal all the frustrations that overwhelm our people—on one hand the young, the disenchanted, the revolutionary, the pacifistic and idealistic, the draft resisting, the McCarthy-supporting and those concerned with the desperate plight of the blacks and of a nation in a horrendous war; on the other hand the complacent and the content, the Nixonites and Humphreyites, the ones who have it made in government or in business or in the military, the people who don't want niggers next door or niggers taking their jobs. Agonizing, that is, to everyone except, in one of those poignant and delicious ironies of history, the blacks and the other aggrieved men and women of color who could stand back and watch in amusement Whitey's battle in which The Man took after The Kids.

(Chicago's brooding ghettos remained calm during the entire week of the convention because their black inhabitants knew very well why the troops were there. The reported 7,500 regular army troops—flown from Fort Hood, Fort Sill and Fort Carson and bivouacked in armories, at air stations, in Washington Park in the heart of Chicago's south side—were ready along with an announced 6,000 Illinois National Guardsmen, an estimated 1,000 Secret Service and FBI agents and about 12,000 Chicago police. In addition, three full regular army armored divisions, totaling more than 40,000 men, were earmarked for Chicago, if needed. The 26,000 men on hand were not there for the scruffy legions of pacifism and hipdom or the McCarthy kids or even the hard-eyed revolutionaries—in all the "weapons"

Law and Order

displayed by police as captured from demonstrators, not one gun had been picked off a protester. The soldiers were there for the blacks, who are armed. Mayor Daley had the sign up in blazing capitals: "YOU BETTER NOT MOVE." And if the blacks on the west and south sides did move, Daley and the police wanted troops ready for the battle in the streets, the sniping and the guerrilla warfare they fully expect, nervously await and patently escalate toward fulfillment. As a result, many black militant leaders moved out of Chicago before the delegates moved in and the others cooled it or watched in carnival spirit as the cops busted heads of the self-proclaimed new niggers in Lincoln and Grant parks, in front of the Hilton or the Palmer House, in Old Town or at 18th and Michigan.

Some publications of the orthodox press scantily reported that 43 black soldiers at Fort Hood were arrested after they refused to board planes to go from Texas to Chicago. But the orthodox press quickly dropped the matter and certainly did not try to explain why black soldiers preferred the stockade to duty in Chicago where they might be ordered to patrol ghetto streets. The black Chicago Daily Defender *named one of these soldiers from Chicago and quoted him: "I don't want to knife any one of my brothers or sisters. We fought for one whitey in Vietnam, and we don't want to go home and destroy the freedom that we fought in Vietnam for.")*

No doubt about it: The People of the United States split, if not down the middle somewhere close to it, over what happened in those four days that seemed like 40 to anyone who was there. Those thoroughly angry with American policies in Vietnam, with a fixed convention programmed to nominate a man who hadn't won a primary, with the lack of understanding of the plight of the minorities were arrayed against those other millions thoroughly fed up with noisy demonstrators, with bearded and often dirty youths, with uppity people, with those who mocked their desperate longing for a return to a time when, in retrospect, life was so ordered and pleasant.

An equally indisputable fact is that the closer reporters and cameramen were to the action in Chicago, the more they were infuriated by what they saw and experienced. The violence was far worse than what television showed; the savagery was too widespread to be picked up by a few cameras. No person of decent instincts could witness that hell on the streets and in the parks without revulsion, and that revulsion was communicated effectively. Whether the story would have been told so completely had not Mayor Daley's police clubbed and beaten and threatened scores of newsmen can of course be argued, but the overwhelming evidence is that it was the thumpings suffered by journalists that was decisive.... [Editor's Note: See "The Chicago Police and the Press" in Appendix.]

In the maelstrom that is Chicago politics, almost nothing can be regarded as unusual. The editorial unanimity of the Chicago daily press in support of a fourth term for Mayor Richard Daley in 1967 was not especially strange, although in the case of the *Tribune* and the mayor it meant the queerest sort of bedfellows: The bitchiest of Republicans sleeping with the kingmaker of Democrats. Nor was this curious consensus unexpected, since Chicago business executives, in the words of a pre-convention story in *U.S. News & World Report*, "keep organizing to help Mr. Daley win re-election," and the Chicago daily press throughout the 13 years of Daley's rule had treated him as some sort of sacred cow meriting no more than an occasional slap on the rump when some particularly scandalous caper among the herd was uncovered. This political-journalistic alliance was rudely severed when Chicago police began clubbing reporters and photographers. Suddenly—and it was so sudden that customary policies and procedures could not be put into effect—three of Chicago's four major dailies, in varying but nonetheless significant degrees, began reporting news about their police and their mayor as they never had before. It did not last long—from three to five days, depending on the newspaper involved—but they certainly were among the most glorious days in the history of Chicago journalism.

The first signs of the transition were only barely visible in the Monday morning *Sun-Times*, which buried the events of Sunday night in Lincoln Park and the Old Town area on page 5—behind at least six other convention stories—but nonetheless showed a deep concern for journalists who had been clubbed. The newspaper was especially disturbed about the beating administered to one of its photographers who "identified himself, but the police kept swinging." It had difficulty, however, adjusting to the demonstrators, whom it generally called "hippies" in headlines and "youths" in stories and photographs (where they often looked like young people anywhere), and on Monday it even described the protesters as "a mixed band of hippies, yippies, motorcyclists and flower children."

Chicago's American, once a Hearst newspaper and now a satellite launched daily from the Tribune Tower, appeals to an earthy group of readers, nearly 90 per cent of whom, according to an *American* poll reported on the eve of the convention, "indicated they would order police to 'shoot to kill' if they were attacked by militant civil rights agitators." On the Friday before the convention the paper had thought it hilarious to run on its front page a three-column photograph of a human being, a "fuzzy-haired delegate to the Pigasus 'nomination,'" under a line: "Yippies' Pig Goes to Pokey." Its coverage on Monday afternoon featured a banner over a page of photos, "Police Halt Hippie Invasion at the Bridge," which is, admittedly, one way of looking at the march that had developed after the demonstrators had been flushed from Lincoln Park.

The *Chicago Daily News* coverage of the Sunday night events included an evenhanded, enlightening front-page story concerning the views of some of the demonstrators. Another story served especially to tell how the situation was shaping up in Chicago. It began:

> Beneath the hoopla there was a grimness and—unlike other years—the cops had no time for jokes.
>
> And it wasn't only the hippies and the Yippies and the peace kids they were up tight about.
>
> It applied to ordinary, shirt-and-tie folks, too.

By Tuesday, however, following a night of indiscriminate beatings of newsmen, the three newspapers were almost equally incensed. The front page of the *Sun-Times* featured a photograph and caption: "Police knock down a fleeing demonstrator near Wells and Division early Tuesday morning after hundreds of young demonstrators were routed from Lincoln Park by police using clubs and tear gas."[. . .]

In the fantasy world of Chicago's incredible *Tribune*, every act of God or man is made to conform to an elaborately constructed journalistic masquerade. The warped, distorted view of the world that Robert R. McCormick pressed daily on his staff and readers until his death in 1955 is memorialized by his carefully selected successors.

The pre-convention Sunday *Tribune* announced in a headline on page 3 that "Tribune News Staff Is Tops" and proclaimed that "one of the largest and most experienced news teams of any newspaper in the country" would "bring to Chicago readers the vivid details of every exciting moment." By *Tribune* standards the qualification "one of" was an extraordinary concession to modesty on the part of the "World's Greatest Newspaper." It listed the 13 persons who would cover the convention but neglected to include the name of anyone assigned to cover possible disorders, although the front-page story that same day had suggested strongly that disorders by what it called "peaceniks" were likely. As it turned out, readers had no difficulty discovering that security and disorder stories clearly were the province of [a reporter] steeped in the *Tribune's* tradition of unremitting irrelevance and calculated viciousness.

On Monday the *Tribune* slightly stepped up its coverage. A front-page headline stated that "Police Repel Jeering Mob of Peaceniks," and in the story the protesters were called "peaceniks" (three times), "radicals" (twice), and "radical detachment," "anti-war demonstrators," "demonstrators," "hippies, yippies and other radical groups," and "hippie-clad people." No mention of police clubbing demonstrators was made in the story or in the cutlines accompanying four demure photographs. Mention was made of a *Tribune* automobile that was stoned and a *Tribune* reporter who was "pelted" but not seriously hurt, both by demonstrators. The one-column headline and story appeared next to a three-column color photograph of Mayor and Mrs. Richard J. Daley, "Host and Hostess," holding hands. On page 9 was the headline, "Mayor Finds Time to Be a Host, Father; His Honor Seems to Be Everywhere," which accurately reflected the tone, quality and content of the long story. The daily index of the news failed to include the events in Lincoln Park and environs as one of the eight important local stories of the preceding day, although they had been reported on the front page.

The Tuesday *Tribune* continued to play down the fact of convention week disorders, burying a short story under a one-column headline on the fifth page. Throughout the fanciful account, which differed extensively from what non-*Tribune* reporters saw, five separate references were made to injuries reportedly suffered by policemen while no mention was made of injuries to "hippies," which is what the demonstrators were called throughout. A second story, also under a one-column headline, briefly reported that "more newsmen were injured in the battles between hippies and police early today than either demonstrators or lawmen," and dismissed in one paragraph the "vigorous protests" filed by officials of the three television networks, the *Sun-Times* and the *Daily News*. (*Chicago's American* also had protested, according to itself, the *Sun-Times* and the *Daily News*, but it is owned by the *Tribune* and therefore could be omitted in the *Tribune's* fantasy-world reporting.)

While the three other major Chicago daily newspapers were furiously reporting what had happened Tuesday in Chicago, the Wednesday *Tribune* kept its cool. It ran a weird tale of the flushing of Lincoln Park which included the information that the protesters were "hippies, yippies, and other nondescripts." It referred to "50 Negroes wearing patches identifying them as Black Panthers, the California black nationalist group," a scoop of monumental proportions since no other reporter in Chicago mentioned their presence. Its readers also were treated to the following wildly simplified account of the Lyndon Johnson "un-birthday party."

> Before the largest group of hippies left the Coliseum, at 1513 Wabash ave., [Note the splendid example of significant detail] they were whipped up by provocative speeches made by Dick Gregory, comedian and civil

rights worker; Allen Ginsberg, hippie poet; William Burroughs, author; and Jean Genet, French writer.

The theme of the speeches was vigorously against the Chicago police [!], comparing them with Russian troops occupying Prague. At one point folk singer Phil Ochs sang an anti-war song called "We Won't Go Marching Anymore" [*sic*] and his performance was greeted with a 10-minute ovation and the burning of what were said to be draft cards by about a dozen persons in the audience. . . .

The primary journalistic—and ultimately, perhaps, historical—lesson of Chicago is that the news media of general circulation have been guilty of a massive failure, especially during the past decade, to describe and interpret what has been happening in the United States and in the world. The "orthodox" press, essentially satisfied with the prevailing conditions of life, has resisted or ignored the inequities of our society and has attempted to perpetuate governmental, economic and social abuses. It is not enough to open the columns and the electronic channels for a few hours or days to report what is really happening as they were opened during the battle of Chicago; the reports Americans saw and heard and read in much of the orthodox media should be their steady diet. Significantly, the "underground" newspapers had little to add to what happened in what it termed "Czechago" except for accounts of speeches delivered in Lincoln and Grant parks. In effect, by doing its job, the orthodox media briefly made the underground press irrelevant. . . .

And it is time, too, for recognition of the stark, naked but almost never spoken truth that hundreds—perhaps thousands—of reporters and copy editors and even editors who draw their pay from the owners of the orthodox press are disgusted with the policies of their employers, but the economic necessities of their situation force them to vent their frustrations in the bars, in letters to friends, in their homes or wherever they gather with fellow professionals. What, finally, can they do? Where, finally, can they go? With the orthodox press dominated by the Hearsts, the Scripps-Howards, the Pulliams, the Ridders, the Copleys, the McCormick heirs, they stick grimly and unhappily with their jobs. And even if they could go to the *New York Times*, the *Washington Post* the *St. Louis Post-Dispatch*, the Cowles or the Knight or the Field papers—to name a few of the newspapers that display at least some significant measure of decency, fairness and respectability—they have discovered they still are up against editors and publishers who order stories killed, or buried, or covered up when the pressures of the business community or the country club are applied. The men and women of the working press know better than anyone the truth of A.J. Liebling's essentially accurate aphorism that without a school for publishers no school of journalism can have meaning.

DISCUSSION QUESTIONS

1. Is Professor Barron's suggestion that newspapers be required to provide the less popular viewpoint in controversial issues consistent with the strong drive for news media freedom we find in the nation today? What dangers can you see with access requirements? What advantages?

2. Richard Jencks and Nicholas Johnson engage in a debate similar to the Barron-Daniel discussion. Who do you think is more reasonable in this instance? Regarding his responsibility to the public, should it make any difference if a man owns a broadcast station or a newspaper?

3. At what point would Nicholas Johnson and Fred Friendly agree regarding the development of community television stations?

4. Are the media capable of self-criticism and evaluation? What evidence is there to show efforts have been made to strengthen media performance, from both within and outside the profession?

5. What encouraging points can be found in the several national reports (see Appendix) which dealt in part with media performance during times of national stress? In your judgment, what was the greatest general failure of the media that you discovered in your reading of these documents?

6. Very simply, do you think the government, through Congress and the Federal Communications Commission, should have the right to examine the private working materials of broadcast newsmen—as the government requested during the CBS incident of 1971? If so, why? If not, why not?

7. Authors McWilliams, Hvistendahl and Blumberg tell in different ways that the press should become more relevant, should wake up to realities! Do you think Professor Hvistendahl's argument for "truth-as-I-see-it" reporting will help; or maybe is this something some staffs have used before; or would this be a dangerous attitude for a journalist?

PROJECT

Study a week's issues of two or more major metropolitan newspapers. Determine the emphasis on the news pages regarding the amount of international, national and local news. Secondly, determine to what degree the particular paper offered news stories which showed viewpoints divergent from that paper's usual editorial page stand. In general, which of these papers did the best job in conveying a week's news to its particular public? Take into account the audience because certainly the editors of the *New York Times* and *Los Angeles Times* think differently of their respective readerships and give them different diets of news.

FURTHER READINGS

The following articles which relate to the concepts described in Part I are a few of the many found in the leading journals and magazines.

Ackerman, Jerry L. "Editors Weigh Two Sides of Militancy in Newsroom." *Editor and Publisher* 103 (November, 1970):18.

"Any Way to Get Fairness Under Control?" *Broadcasting* 79 (September, 1970):21-6.

Barnett, Harold J. and Greenberg, Edward. "The Best Way to Get More Varied TV Programs." *TRANS-ACTION* 5 (May, 1968):39-45.

Barron, Jerome A. "Access—The Only Choice for the Media?" *Texas Law Review* 48 (March, 1970):694-733.

Bishop, Michael E. and Schorr, Andrew J. "Study Shows Foreign Correspondents System 'Works' But Coverage Often Thin." *RTNDA Bulletin* 24 (December, 1970):24-25.

Brucker, Herbert. "What's Wrong With Objectivity?" *Saturday Review* 52 (October, 1969):77-79.

Colburn, John. "Journalism Credibility in the Complex 1970's." *Nieman Reports* 24 (September, 1970):17-21.

Cranberg, Gilbert. "Is 'Right of Access' Coming?" *Saturday Review* 53 (August, 1970):48.

Dennis, Everett E., ed. *The Magic Writing Machine.* School of Journalism, University of Oregon, 1971.

Gilliam, Thomas B. "Newsmen's Sources and the Law." *Freedom of Information Report No. 259* (March, 1971).

Grotta, Gerald L. "Computers, Privacy and the Press." *Grassroots Editor* 11 (November-December, 1970):10-12.

Isaacs, Norman E. "Why We Lack a National Press Council." *Columbia Journalism Review* 9 (Fall, 1970):16-26.

Johnson, Nicholas. "The Media Barons and the Public Interest." *Atlantic* 221 (June, 1968):43-51.

"Ombudsman in Louisville." *Time* 96 (July, 1970):44.

Sevareid, Eric. "The Quest for Objectivity." *Nieman Reports* 24 (December, 1970):11-14.

Smith, Ralph L. "The Wired Nation." Nation 210 (May, 1970):582-606.

Tebbel, John. "The Stories the Newspapers Do Cover." *Saturday Review* 53 (April, 1970):66-67.

―――. "Who Owns Television?" *Saturday Review* 52 (July, 1970):75-76.

Part Two

Revolution in the
Mass Media

Changing technology, regulations and society have forced some startling, revolutionary changes in American mass media. In some ways, technology has the greatest role to play in change. An example is the newest revolution already upon us in the form of pre-recorded video cassettes and cartridges. Five major companies are in the field producing equipment and tapes, all incompatible with each other. Competition and cooperation are natural enemies.

Other technical improvements are just around the corner. AT&T plans to introduce a transcontinental cable capable of carrying 90,000 two-way telephone conversations—almost three times the capacity of the most advanced cable now in use. A Japanese company is preparing to market a two-way communication system between cable TV studios and subscriber homes. The Japanese also have experimented with electronic production of a newspaper page from a TV-like device.

Farther down the road is an entirely new radio spectrum—the millimeter-wave spectrum, so-called because its wave lengths are measured in millimeters, which are far shorter than those wave lengths currently being used. Theoretically, engineers tell us, one "channel" in the new spectrum has as much communications capacity as all channels now being used. Technical problems still must be overcome.

Regulation also plays an important role in change, particularly in the broadcasting industry. Two recent decisions, for instance, required the removal of all cigarette advertising from television and the reduction of network prime time broadcasting by three and one-half hours weekly. Our readings in television and newspapers concentrate on those changes brought by technology and regulation.

The traditional media also include books, film, music, and magazines. Here, however, we find economics and social change have had a profound impact. Books, the oldest print medium, have switched from literature to "nonliterary" publications, while film, always a mass medium, has lost most of its audience. Music has become a truly mass medium because of radio and long-play records, while magazines are finding a renaissance as specialized rather than mass media.

The influence of social factors on the communications field is seen most starkly in what is often called the "alternative media"; alternative, that is, to the traditional mass media. Alternative media are not new; they have existed in various forms in America from the colonial period, but the types discussed here have grown out of the social turmoil of the sixties and are radically different from those media they have either replaced or supplemented. The underground press is one expression of this social change, and with photo-offset printing anyone can be a publisher; the transitional ethnic and religious press are others. Our selection of readings is designed to expose these changes to a wider audience. Even here, however, change occurs so rapidly that it is hard to keep abreast of it. For instance, one manifestation of the underground press is a press for "Women's Lib." Perhaps this nascent creation will find its female Boswell.

New social concerns have combined with economic, technical and political considerations to revolutionize the "persuasive arts" of advertising and public relations. These "arts" are striving to affect society and the media and, in turn, are being affected by changes in society and the media. We include several articles and excerpts as means of assessing the influence of these different messages on the society and the mass media that they serve, use and, sometimes, abuse.

Finally, because of the role of the United States in world affairs, we record a brief glimpse of the accelerating influence our communication technology and expertise are having on international communications. These selections indicate that we may be exporting a different revolution from that which many Americans thought we were.

The articles in Part II vary greatly in content and style. They range from *Forbes'* statistic-laden prophecy on the decline of network television to Greil Marcus' personal essay on the mysticism of "rock 'n roll" to Herbert I. Schiller's concerned expression about Madison Avenue's international influence. All help, we hope, to illuminate some of the revolutionary changes occurring in the mass media.

Television "is unquestionably the wave of the future—as it is the wave of the present," according to *Forbes.* But in the special report that follows, *Forbes* argues persuasively that television of the future will not include network TV as we know it today. *Business Week,* looking at the same technical and marketing advancements, but from the perspective of one additional year, concludes that network "television, reported to be mortally wounded, has barely been scratched." Changes are taking place, the *Business Week* survey demonstrates, but much more slowly than had been predicted.

Metropolitan newspapers slashed job positions during 1970 as advertising revenues nose-dived. Ten of the fifteen advertising volume leaders showed losses in advertising revenue. This gloomy recession-caused picture is not characteristic of all American newspapers, according to a thorough survey of the industry by *Business Week.* Newspapers in general and John S. Knight's newspapers in particular are doing very well. Newspapers, the magazine claims, "are the next best thing to an indispensable medium," partly because there has been a "virtual elimination of competition among newspapers." Other reasons for a bull market in newspapers are contained in Richard L. Tobin's appraisal of "the era of electronic publishing," which he claims is already here. Tobin points out how the revolution in publishing will increasingly affect every facet of newspaper production, from reporter to printer.

Books, film, music, and magazines have been transformed. Despite gloomy forecasts in the sixties that books were obsolete, Curtis G. Benjamin documents the staggering growth of nonliterary books (of which this volume is an example). The most notable change in film—and music is the dramatic shift to a youth-oriented culture. *Newsweek's* cover article has been selected (and edited) because it surveys the new movies: new methods, new themes, and new personnel. A familiar conclusion is drawn, nevertheless: the film industry still is motivated by the desire to please the audience and to get a hefty return on the invested dollar. The same has been written of the new music business, which in one decade grew from $500 million annually in 1960 to $1.2 billion by 1970. Rock albums make up about 55 to 60 percent of all records purchased, which just emphasizes that rock 'n roll—a development of the fifties—still is with us. Though many writers tell of profits to be made in the name of counter-culture, Greil Marcus tries to explain rock's continuing impact on a generation of young people. Rock is metaphor, he asserts; it's "the defining idea for a situation or a time of one's life." The recent demise of *Look* has again pointed out the precarious nature of the mass magazine. The rise of the specialized magazine has been with us for sometime. Ben L. Moon documents the development of a little known part of that field; the city magazine.

Social change or, perhaps, the lack of social change, often creates the proper cultural conditions for a viable minority press. Jack A. Nelson surveys the causes for the creation of an underground press in America. Drugs and sex may have turned on many of these subculture newspapers, but it is political dissent, particularly with the Vietnam war, that keeps many of them going. Even the black press, which has a long history in America, is being transformed by black militancy, as L.F. Palmer, Jr. shows. Comparable change is occurring among Spanish-speaking Americans, or Chicanos as some groups call themselves. Frank del Olmo surveys the field and pinpoints basic changes in this segment of the press. Even the religious press is in ferment, as Terence Shea documents. The borders of restraint are being stretched and, in isolated cases, broken. They are not, however, being dismantled.

The "persuasive arts"—advertising and public relations—are changing our media and our politics. John Tebbel explores first the far-reaching influence of the TV and radio sales representatives, who sit between media and advertiser and, sometimes, advertising agencies. The "reps" exert major impact on programming, Tebbel argues, by determining when and what programs will be shown. They also substantially erode the position of advertising agencies by buying time for advertisers. Fairfax Cone looks at the changing media scene and suggests that advertising may *finally* serve the consumer's "own best interest," what with cable TV and the potential of "two-way communication established between receivers and cable stations." Richard M. Detwiler then checks the social scene, among others, and concludes that such movements as consumer protest over what certain products and companies are doing to the environment have created a situation where public relations must now enter the marketing process in a manner it has not entered before. "Segmentation" of the audience is the key, as Cone also explained. Finally our excerpt from *Survey of Broadcast Journalism* suggests that when advertiser and politician get together to use the powerful medium of television in campaigning, watch out. Following the primaries of 1970, one study reported that "The outstanding political upsets of 1970 have been made by men of great wealth, presenting their politics to the voters on television and spending their way from obscurity to success in a matter of weeks." As for the seventies, one bill which would have curtailed campaign spending is explained here, as is President Nixon's veto of that measure which would have completely changed the "system."

Telstar was the first satellite to relay a broadcast across the Atlantic. This took place in 1962. Today, Intelsat IVs are riding 22,300 miles high in the heavens linking countries and continents. Sig Mickelson discusses this revolutionary technology and its use by developing countries. Herbert I. Schiller also looks at foreign countries to see what effect American mass communications—particularly advertising, public relations, and public opinion research—are having on the mass media and culture of other nations. He is worried by what he sees.

Chapter V

<hr>

CHANGE IN THE TRADITIONAL MEDIA

<hr>

TELEVISION: NETWORKS VERSUS CABLE

TV: IS THE BLOOM OFF THE OLD ROSE?

Electronic communication, specifically television, is unquestionably the wave of the future—as it is the wave of the present. But not necessarily television as we know it today.

Right now network TV is riding the crest of the wave. Of some $3 billion a year in television broadcasting revenues, $1.5 billion of it will go to network operations, up from just $1.1 billion in 1965. Some $1 billion of the remaining rich TV take is in national spot advertising, and a sizable chunk, $280 million, flows to the 15 network-owned stations. Yet this particular crest seems to be receding.

It may well be that network TV stands where the mass magazines of this country stood two decades ago. In those days, the big communications market on a national scale was almost a monopoly of *The Saturday Evening Post, Reader's Digest*, the women's service magazines and a few brighter periodicals such as *Life* and *Look*. Combined, they had advertising revenues of $245 million, compared with $181 million for radio, $41 million for the then-infant TV.

Today the *Post* [and *Look* are] gone, and gone, too, are other long-established mass magazines. The survivors—*Life and McCall's*—are grievously hurting. Even the *Reader's Digest*, which had to start accepting advertising in 1955 to help meet soaring costs, relies on its books and records division for a majority of the magazine's net income, despite a worldwide gross of more than $400 million a year.

What's this got to do with TV? The same factors that squeezed the mass magazines are, a couple of decades later, threatening net-

Reprinted with the permission of *Forbes* magazine, which originally offered this analysis on the problems of television networks in the October 15, 1970 issue.

work TV. They are: (1) technology, (2) increasingly sophisticated tastes.

In the case of the mass magazines, the technology villain was TV itself, with its immediacy and live quality. Increased education and sophistication at the same time tended to fragment their mass markets.

The once-vast audiences tended to splinter into dozens of smaller special audiences, which the big magazines found it increasingly difficult to appeal to and, therefore, to deliver up to advertisers. The common denominator no longer sufficed; it had in fact become too common.

This did not, of course, mean the end of the magazine business. The special-interest magazines, as typified by FORBES and *Business Week, Sports Illustrated, Scientific American* and *Field & Stream,* and the news magazines, flourished as never before; for they could both satisfy the deeper interest of their selected group of readers as well as provide the advertiser with a smaller yet more affluent audience package.

The parallel in network television today threatens to be close. The technical changes that most affect the broadcasting networks now center around community antenna television. CATV already has been wired to 8% of the nation's TV sets and is breaking into the top 100 markets, the urbanized areas that provide 90% of broadcasting's income. Technologically, CATV offers impressive advantages in the number of channels that can be received and the clarity of their reception. And CATV is merely one example—pay TV is another—of the changes in and multiplication of communications channels that seem certain to shake network TV to its roots.

So far, the broadcasting industry has managed to stand off some of these threats by vigorous political action (like the "Save Free TV" campaigns, waged jointly with movie theater owners, that have thwarted several pay-television experiments). But it is a very hard job, in a technologically oriented society, to keep something that is technically feasible from at least being tried. Among the things soon to be tried: Beginning in April, 1971, CATV systems having more than 3,500 subscribers will be required by the Federal Communications Commission to originate some local programs, which also may carry advertising during natural program breaks. The same FCC ruling says that the networks, which had been buying up CATV systems until recently, will have to sell them.

CATV has its problems. There are subscriber charges, usually about $5 a month; and start-up costs for big-city cable systems can be overpowering. But since its inception in 1949 in the hills of Pennsylvania, CATV has developed into much more than a relay system for TV fringe areas. This year, systems are being installed in Michigan with up to 32 channels. "The relay is only 1% of CATV's value," says Sylvester (Pat) Weaver Jr., former president of the National Broadcasting Co. and now a broadcast consultant. "But the cable itself has a 99% value, for all kinds of other services—including the delivery of printed materials, shopping, burglar alarms and all the rest. And you can leave an inferior 525-line service and go to a superior 1,000-line picture using wall screens; a real home theater. . . . Such a home communication system can give the promise of revelation to every man."

Some industry observers minimize the threat of technical wonders and blame politics for current unsettling developments: "They're ganging up on television in Washington," says Les Brown, broadcasting columnist for the show-biz trade paper *Variety.* "There's been enough action down there to shake everyone to his boots," says Dan Del Rio, broadcasting analyst for the brokerage firm of Delafield & Delafield. President Frank Stanton of the Columbia Broadcasting System puts it in broader terms: "The networks shook people up by showing them vividly what's going on in the ghetto and in Vietnam. Naturally, some people don't like the messenger." In FCC Commissioner Nicholas Johnson's view, consumer thrusts such as the antismoking commercials have had a telling effect: "When people get a glimpse of what television really could be, they become dissatisfied and then outraged."

The reasons don't matter. The trend does. Like the magazine industry before it, the world of television is being transformed. The coming of CATV and other expansions of communications channels—including even the brisk growth in two-set and three-set families—have gone hand in hand with an increasing degree of audience fragmentation.

"The Big Three networks," says *Variety's* Les Brown, "have a real problem with demographies. Many of the audiences have grown older with the shows. Advertisers don't want to pay $4.50 per thousand [viewers] and get a bulk audience when they're after younger trade." He means that it might be more economical for advertisers to pay twice as much per head to get half as many people—but the right people for their products.

Television can deliver a mass audience, of course—30 million or more watching a single network show in prime time. But as David M. Blank, CBS's vice president for economics and research, showed in a recent analysis, it is really the older homebodies in this mass who watch TV. Adults 50 and over, says Blank, view 15% more than their numbers would indicate, and those 35 to 49 view in proportion to their numbers. But adults under 35 watch TV 15% less than their numbers. Package goods advertisers, however, often want to reach those under 35. John Scott Keck, programming director for the big advertising agency Needham, Harper & Steers, notes: "These days, if a show isn't hot in Nielsen ratings, it almost has to be skewing toward a younger audience to stay on the air."

Concern about audience age was behind the 1970 season's bumping of Jackie Gleason and the forced shift of Red Skelton to NBC. New shows were substituted like "Headmaster" and "The Storefront Lawyers." And the main rating company, A.C. Nielsen, agreed, for the first time, to break down audience figures regularly into five age groups so that advertisers can see exactly where their programs are penetrating.

If Washington did not start the fragmentation, it is certainly helping it along. The FCC finally adopted a rule that, as of Oct. 1, 1971, no local station may devote more than three of the 7 p.m.-11 p.m. prime time hours to network shows. Further, the networks will be required to sell off their program syndication units, and will be blocked from retaining subsidiary rights in programs.

These moves, together with the CATV changes, should force TV outlets into considerably greater amounts of independent local programming. It may be better programming. Or it may be worse. But it is certainly going to be different programming. Donald H. McGannon, president of Westinghouse Broadcasting Co., is itching to provide the local markets with shows. He's called in people like Dr. Margaret Mead, the anthropologist, and Harold Hayes, the editor of *Esquire*, to advise. And McGannon believes that opening up of prime time will draw a number of young, creative filmmakers into the television production business.

The advertising agencies, which have lost out to the networks and big movie studios as program packagers, would like to move stage center, too. And increasingly they are going in with their own shows to barter directly with local stations for air time. Young & Rubicam, for example, has found acceptance for its "Galloping Gourmet" show, and now has five other projects in the works. And the Corporation for Public Broadcasting kicked off its first real season of 19 shows in fall 1970 and plans to call on broadcast professionals for more program advice.

The change in the prime-time rule will in most cases cause the networks to cut back their program feed by only one-half hour. But the loss in revenue is estimated at $60 million to $70 million. And it will come on top of the $236-million annual loss of network cigarette advertising which will take effect Jan. 2, 1971.

It is true that the loss of cigarette advertising will soon be at least partly offset ("fortuitous timing," CBS' Stanton calls it) by the smaller number of prime-time hours up for sale; and partly as a result, RCA's NBC network claims to be nearly sold out, at $33,000-$65,000 per commercial minute, for the 1970-71 season. "We're replacing much of the cigarette advertising with products we've never handled before," says Julian Goodman, president of NBC. "We're going heavy into retail chain stores [Sears, Roebuck is expected to spend $30 million on TV ads in '70-'71], charge cards, insurance companies and bank advertising."

Overall, in spite of these setbacks, network TV revenues will rise about 3%. Network executives take comfort from this gain in what is, after all, a recession year. But it is also true that this gain is puny compared with 1969's 11% gain, or 1968's 10%. It is also true that the full impact of the increase in local programming will not be felt until 1971, and none of the cigarette loss will be felt until then. To search out the accounts Goodman was speaking about, the networks have organized new-business departments. But only one, ABC, has reported new business contracts, and these for $3 million. "I don't think there's much that's gone untapped," says Keck. "That leaves a lot of difference yet to make up for the cigarette advertising loss."

Bernard P. Gallagher, whose marketing newsletter has often sent tremors through Madison Avenue executive suites, believes the broadcasting leaders are shutting their eyes to reality. "They're in big trouble," he says. "If people knock off cigarettes, what's to keep them from knocking off the air proprietary drugs, cereals, hair dyes, autos and all kinds of other products on which TV depends?"

Gallagher is just as pessimistic about the effect on the networks of the new prime-time rule. "I think commercial television is in for a big tumble on the programming side," he goes on. "It may happen rather quickly, perhaps in the next two or three years. The networks may be left mostly with sports and news events."

All these pressures, along with another new FCC rule limiting new broadcast owners to one unit per market, have made themselves felt already in that most sensitive of indicators: the price of TV stations. For nearly two decades, station prices rose in a steady spiral. For example, L.B. Wilson, Inc., took over WLBW-TV in Miami in 1961 for $300,000. It was sold in 1969 to the Washington Post-Newsweek Stations for $18.4 million. KTAR-TV in Phoenix was purchased in 1954 by KTAR Broadcasting for $251,000, but Combined Communications Corp. paid $15 million for the station in 1968.

Now the market is topsy turvy. Capital Cities Broadcasting recently took $1 million less than originally promised for a Philadelphia radio station after local investors couldn't meet the $12.5-million sale price. And FM radio stations, once thrown in for virtually nothing with an AM, now go for a premium. United Artists Broadcasting recently purchased a Philadelphia FM for $950,000 even though it was off the air at the time. And two oil entrepreneurs recently picked up a Los Angeles FM, KCBH, for $1.6 million, a record, for an FM radio outlet.

Some of the big owners, who hoarded their stations for decades, are beginning to disgorge them. "Buyers are hard to find," says Howard E. Stark of New York, a leading station broker, "and we are selling off stations one by one rather than in packages." For example, Walter H. Annenberg's Triangle Publications recently shed three TV and six radio stations to Capital Cities for a total of $110 million. Then Stark stepped in to act as broker when Cap Cities, because of FCC ownership limitations, disposed of two TV and six radio stations.

"In most cases they went to individuals," says Stark. "A former station employee got the AM in New Haven, and the FM went to the station manager. The radio stations in Fresno went to different California residents. These are the types of owners that they [the sellers] thought the FCC would approve of."

Triangle is by no means the only group owner that has been selling off numbers of units. Storer Broadcasting is in the process of selling its five FM radio stations to three different buyers. Metromedia is giving away its costly UHF television station in San Francisco to an educational broadcasting group—but at a figure that will get it a substantial "profit" from tax savings. And the word is out in the industry that Time-Life Broadcasting wants to sell off its radio stations and use the money to expand in CATV.

For the big networks, all this is doubly ominous. Although they are limited by law to five VHF-TV stations each (plus two UHF-TV, seven AM radio and seven FM radio stations), they generally own their stations in the biggest and richest markets. These stations are known as O&Os (for owned and operated). The 15 television O&Os owned by the three major networks are immensely profitable; they netted $133 million in 1969 on revenues of $323 million. These profits, in fact, accounted for 60% of total network profits of $226 million. Whereas the networks netted only about 12 cents on the sales dollar from their network operations, they earned a rich 40 cents-plus from their O&O stations.

The problem is this: If network broadcasting declines in importance, the O&Os may become less important in their markets and more vulnerable to competition from non-network stations. Finally, there's the danger—distant at the moment but present all the same— that one day the FCC may move against chain broadcasters. On Chairman Dean Burch's docket is further rule-making that would split up present broadcast complexes and require that owners hold only one television, AM or FM station per market. The commission also has expanded its probe of broadcasting conglomerates. While now tuned in on the problems of reciprocal dealing, it could blossom out in much the same way that the Justice Department's attack on the manufacturing conglomerates did.

Whatever they say for public print about the future, the networks have been saying something different with their money. They are paying more attention these days to their activities outside of direct broadcasting. CBS recently formed and is spinning off a separate company to handle both its extensive CATV holdings and program syndication. "CBS is much more than broadcasting these days," emphasized Frank Stanton. Most recently the network has been buying up vocational and business schools to tie in with CBS' publishing firm, Holt, Rinehart & Winston. Some 60 schools may be purchased. William Paley, CBS chairman and Stanton hope for a 50-50 mix between regulated and non-regulated operations.

ABC continues to creep up on the audience advantages of CBS and NBC, and President Leonard Goldenson is looking again to ABC's 418 movie theaters. Once something of a millstone, the old downtown movie palaces are being replaced with smaller suburban houses. NBC, meanwhile, is pushing its records division and is vying with CBS to introduce practical cartridge TV and video recording units for home use. While NBC is the traditional heart of RCA, the parent seems to have its eyes focused elsewhere. RCA is still trying to make its computer operations into a winner, and in 1970 acquired firms as diverse as frozen food and real estate companies.

With broadcasting caught in many crosscurrents, it seems certain that the biggest targets, the networks, will suffer most. As the industry leader, CBS is probably the most vulnerable. Despite acquisitions and spin-offs, broadcasting still contributes more than 60% of its $1 billion-plus in revenues. And its O&O TV stations, notably the one in the Chicago area (WBBM-TV), have been losing market share. To shore up the broadcast division, D. Thomas Miller, an ex-station manager, was named president of the CBS-owned stations. ABC has a new TV broadcasting head in Elton Rule.

Also vulnerable, because so much of their profitable production is tied to network programming, are the big moviemakers such as Metro-Goldwyn-Mayer, Columbia Pictures Industries (Screen Gems), 20th Century-Fox, Walt Disney and MCA, through its Universal Television Division. As if to foreshadow some rough days to come, most of the moviemakers—excepting Fox—filed a Federal court suit to make CBS and ABC stop producing films. The networks, they claim, offer unfair competition. But the networks answer that it's the moviemakers themselves who want to control the program market. They already provide, for example, 30% of the prime-time entertainment programming on CBS.

While the explosive growth of group broadcasters appear finished, some of the more flexible ones, such as Westinghouse, Metromedia and Capital Cities, may discover fresh life—especially if they can create interesting new programs as more prime time opens up for the independents.

The important question is whether interesting shows can be brought in economically. Goldenson of ABC believes that "the public will be up in arms that they're being deprived of programming better done by the networks." And present-day programming costs are high. A one-hour situation comedy or spy drama can run $300,000. But the independents are confident that shows of quality and audience appeal can be turned out for a great deal less than that—possibly for half that much.

The electronics manufacturers and the cable companies, of course, are itching to take advantage of any new era in broadcasting. The recent merger of the largest cable firm, H&B American, into the fourth-biggest, TelePrompTer Corp., now gives TelePrompTer a foothold in 29 states. But while the CATV companies are spreading across state lines, the FCC is responding by trying to bring all cable activities, from programming to ownership, under its eye.

The influential Electronics Industries Association, representing 300 manufacturers, is restless about its idea for a wired nation, which would end over-the-air broadcasting as now practiced. Since October 1969, the FCC has been considering EIA's proposal to permit two wired telecommunications systems throughout the country. One, a switching network, would combine picturephone, facsimile and computer information gathering operations. The second, a Broadband Communications Network (BCN), would be aimed at providing broadcast TV, mail services, library material, educational offerings and a wide variety of printed material. EIA says it now has 20 firms, including Magnavox, the Los Angeles Times-Mirror and Encyclopaedia Britannica, interested in pushing the project along. They are considering launching, for $20 million, a pilot BCN that would combine both corporate and individual stockholders. "We see it as a kind of a private Comsat," says John P. Thompson of consultants Arthur D. Little, who led the wired nation study.

However disturbing all this is going to be to a good many businessmen, it is probably going to make U.S. TV something a good deal better than it is today. McGannon, Westinghouse Broadcasting's bright, iconoclastic president, says flatly: "People are just marinating in front of their TV sets today." McGannon means—and many people vehemently agree with him—that TV is behind in technology, in keeping up with people's tastes and with TV's educational and entertainment possibilities.

As we said in the beginning: TV is the wave of the future, but not the TV we know today.

These days, if a commercial broadcaster is having trouble selling his TV station, he may find bids coming from the oddest places—like from that weakling down the block, the educational TV operator.

BIG WINNER OF THE SEVENTIES?

"Why, we even had some people out in L.A. who raised $21 million to buy a commercial VHF station—and that's a tough market, you know. They couldn't get a sale, but I suspect we'll see more of that," says John W. Macy Jr., the career civil servant who became the first president of the Corporation for Public Broadcasting.

Macy has some reason to crow. He has just released data that shows educational TV—or "public broadcasting" as it has now been repackaged—actually increased its audience ratings in 25 large cities by 42% in a single season.

"We believe we have to promote our product as professionally as anyone else," Macy says in the slick corporate headquarters that CPB leases just one block from the White House. This suddenly healthy industry within an industry will have its advertising handled, by a hot Madison Avenue agency, Wells, Rich & Greene, Inc.

Noncommercial TV has always been hooked on appealing to

special audiences—a Manhattan executive recently found his wife plunked down in front of the set for five straight hours, not for soap operas but for live coverage of championship tennis. The fact is that today's educational product is making a conscious effort to entertain. Nowadays it merits serious attention in the largest mass-circulation magazine in the country, *TV Guide.* Writing in that magazine social critic Cleveland Amory made a telling point when he pointed out that "the 1969-70 season will go up in history for one thing—it was the year when educational TV came of age . . . elsewhere around the dial, the times, as the song tells us, were a-changing. On many an old show, the legs were going and age was showing. The 'Ed Sullivan Show' was still telecast live—but you had to take their word for it."

And in a September 1970 preview issue, the same weekly concluded simply that "public TV, the home of 'Sesame Street' and 'The Forsythe Saga,' is out to lure more viewers away from commercial channels this season. . . . For the first time the public stations will be part of a genuine network that will offer a full schedule of prime-time programs five evenings a week nationwide.

Everyone agrees, including Macy, whose government-supported corporation helped in the funding, that 1969 was "the Year of Sesame Street." "No question about it," says he, rubbing his gray crew cut as if for luck. "We were out there diversifying and trying to raise the quality of our programs, but 'Sesame Street'—that was the great leader. Now some congressmen are asking me: 'Okay, but where's the 'Son of Sesame Street?' "

The petite woman who put the name Sesame Street on everybody's road map, Joan Ganz Cooney says: "We in noncommercial broadcasting found that educational programming need not be grim." Grim it wasn't, with 6 million children tuning in every morning or catching repeats in the evening. Even commercial outlets in major markets such as New York signed up the educational product—despite the fact they can't interject cereal commercials every five minutes or so. In 1970 "Sesame Street" will air on possibly 200 stations, the most for any series, anytime.

With its own network now, public broadcasting is branching into regionally produced shows that could have national impact. In 1969, for instance, they were impressed when a tiny station in Orono, Me. put on a Down East storyteller to spin yarns every week in what was about the only true country humor on television. In 1970 Negroes will find they had their own western heroes, as "Black Frontier" starts. And Ralph Nader will report to the viewing public regularly for the first time.

"Based on ratings commonly used by the commercial networks," John Macy reports, "the evidence suggests that public television's audience for a certainty stands at least at 45 million persons."

The signs are, then, that the traditional tastemakers of TV are finding that the nation is in the beginning stages of the same sort of "mass *vs.* class" battle that has been rocking the popular magazines for over a decade now.

THE TV NETWORKS SHRUG OFF NEW COMPETITION

For television broadcasters, 1970 was the year of horrors. Growth slowed dramatically, and profits fell so sharply that even the ever-expanding television networks were forced to make drastic layoffs.

A hostile atmosphere seemed to develop at the Federal Communications Commission, which regulates the industry. It began to rule against the networks in cable television, in concentrated ownership of multiple outlets, and in the matter of prime-time programs, which it cut in number to make room for local shows.

New forms of competition—videocassettes, CATV, and pay-TV—threatened to reduce television to the status of the silent movie, or so rumor would have it. On top of everything, recession-wary advertisers kept their hands in their pockets, seemingly annoyed over commercial clutter and the ever-increasing costs of making commercials and buying TV time.

This year did not start out any better. Hurt by the ban on cigarette advertising, network ad revenues fell 15% in January and 9% in February. But, suddenly, in March, the industry sold more than $100-million worth of time—and at higher prices that promised good profits. So powerful is this upsurge that, when 9,000 members of the National Assn. of Broadcasters meet next week in Chicago at their annual convention, the chastened but optimistic executives will be carrying with them the thought that the worst is over.

Television, reported to be mortally wounded, has barely been scratched. True, the hard times of 1970 have made the networks leaner, but the industry thinks it now has answers to the serious doubts raised last year. Says James Duffy, president of ABC-TV; "We

Business Week writers researched the latest data and came up with a solid estimate of how television networks, racing tremendous financial and technological pressures, are reacting. The article is used with permission of *Business Week*, March 27, 1971.

got fat over the years or developed a defensive posture, but things are different now.''

Some of the differences, the network men admit, are negative factors. Growth rates, for one, will be smaller than in the past. The CBS and NBC networks now feed their programs to about 200 affiliated stations each, ABC supplies about 160, and the country has no room for more. Some 60.1-million U.S. homes, about 95% of the total, have one or more TV sets—85-million of them in all—and future audience size will depend on population growth. It will, that is, until "wristwatch" TV sets turn each individual into a regular viewer.

Network executives are aware, too, that they cannot forever pile on rate increases of 8% and 10% a year to cover their rising costs. Competition is nibbling at their audiences: Programs such as *Sesame Street* and *The Andersonville Trial* on public TV can attract some viewers away from network outlets. Affiliated stations infrequently "bump" network programs to carry a golf match or ski race fed to them by "occasional networks"—such as Howard Hughes' Sports Network or American Telesports Network—which buy the rights to such events, sell them to advertisers, and hook up as many stations as they can get to carry them.

But the competition and the all-pervading influence of television seem only to have made viewers like the medium more. At the start of the 1960s, the TV set in the average home was on for about five hours a day; in February, 1971 it was on for six hours and 53 minutes, according to A.C. Nielsen Co.'s research. The networks, which supply 70% of the affiliated station's programming on a typical weekday, believe that few advertisers can afford to ignore the huge audience viewing for so long a time—and building up advertising revenues is the basic problem of the television networks today.

But Michael H. Dann, the former program chief at CBS-TV who resigned last year to promote public television, thinks differently. So many forces are at work that "the network structure as we know it cannot survive," Dann warns. "There is no reason why we should be exempt from the vicissitudes of life, as we used to be," retorts David M. Blank, vice-president for economics and research for the CBS Broadcast Group. "But we must look at the threats that present a real challenge, and look at our strengths, and determine what can be done to insure the future."

Much of the talk at Chicago next week will concern the triple threat of videocassettes, cable-TV, and pay-TV. Anyone, it has been said, could destroy broadcasting as it exists; all three together might represent an overwhelming danger. But hard-thinking network men find little to fear in the new media, and some even see profit opportunities for their own operations.

VIDEOCASSETTES. For several years, there have been fanfares for devices that would permit viewers to play programs on their TV sets by merely inserting a cartridge of film or tape. Two of the most vocal proponents of the new medium have been CBS, Inc., and NBC's parent RCA corp., which led some observers to conclude that both companies must be preparing for a "peaking out" of regular TV operations. "Not so," says CBS President Frank Stanton. "It has always been my intention to diversify so that no more than 50% of the company is in a business that comes under regulatory agencies."

Few broadcasters doubt that the videocassette will eventually reach consumers. But they do not see them arriving in quantity within five years, and almost every top network official thinks it will be 10 years before as many as 1-million homes have players. The first news broke in mid-1967 of a "revolutionary electronic device" developed by CBS that would be "manufactured for about $280," marketed "in late 1969 or early 1970," and play film cartridges that would cost "from $7 to $14." But since then, the videocassette industry has been largely promotion, promise, and postponement.

CBS last month began delivering the first 500 of its Motorola-made EVR (Electronic Video Recording) players to a handful of industrial and educational users who pay $795 for the machine and $37.50 for a half-hour color-film cartridge. A dozen other companies—including Ampex, 3M, Sony, Avco, Magnavox, RCA, Matsushita, and A.E.G. Telfunken/British Decca—have shown prototypes of similar devices. But target dates keep getting pushed back, and suggested prices keep climbing. Avco's Cartrivision, initially announced for June, 1971, at a price of between $800 and $900, now will not be marketed "before early 1972," and the price will be $900 to $1,000. Sony, which talked last year of a $400 machine, next week will show an improved prototype that might reach the market in a year or two at $800.

Confusion in marketing plans centers on a manufacturers' debate over whether to sell their hardware in TV appliance stores and their program cartridges in record stores, or perhaps distribute cartridges by mail, or sell them in motion picture theater lobbies. The fact that most systems are totally incompatible with one another will not help sales.

Moreover, there is uncertainty over what programs a customer might want to buy or rent. At CBS, which will have invested $30-million in EVR by the end of 1971, Stanton says that no one has yet convinced him there is a market for any specific kind of consumer programs. This prompted the decision to sell EVR initially to industry, which can pay high costs and use the equipment as training aids. Undaunted, EVR President Robert Brockway predicts a $1-billion cartridge market by 1980 that will be made up of golf lessons, old movies, cartoons, and old Broadway shows. Theatrical producer Alexander Cohen, who listened to Brockway advise showmen to tape their shows for future cartridge sale, calls it "a terribly naive idea—we have to deal with 18 different unions to bring a snapshot Brownie into a theater."

There are plenty of cassette promoters around, and they can be easily recognized when they lace their pitches with phrases like "edutainment shows" and "interactive, self-paced programs with online manipulatives." A typical cassette man's claim came last year from Avco Cartrivision President Frank Stanton, who is not related to the CBS executive. Said he: "In 1971, we'll sell 100,000 playback decks. In 1972, we'll sell a half-million. We might even give them away free to some manufacturers—but don't quote me—just so we can start selling 2 1/2-million tapes a year. Once we get the razor— the player—into the home, we'll make our money off the blades—the cartridges." The Avco subsidiary thus far has spent nearly $5-million to develop a prototype player and is about to make a public offering that will help raise $15-million more it says it needs to get the first machines and cartridges to market.

Even if the fledgling industry solves its hardware and software problems, network men see little danger from it. David Blank doubts that the television industry will be harmed at all, even if millions of homes have cartridge players. He theorizes that the player would be used much as a phonograph is used today—selectively and infrequently. "The average adult uses a phonograph only about 60 hours a year, our research shows," says Blank. "He plays a radio about 800 hours, and uses the TV set about 1,300 hours."

CABLE TELEVISION. The threat of cable-TV grew slightly with recent FCC decisions to let cable operators sell advertising and originate their own programs for viewers. The decision on programming, which said that any system hooked to more than 3,500 homes must provide original programs, did not please all CATV owners, since it means added expense for them. Previously, most operators contented themselves with bringing clear pictures from distant stations (which they pick, free, out of the air) to subscribers in isolated areas, or where mountains, buildings, and other obstructions cause poor reception. Currently, about 4.5-million subscribers pay $5 to $6 a month to some 2,750 different cable-TV systems. (Some operators have only a few hundred homes wired to their service; the largest, TelePrompTer Corp., has about 540,000 in 100 different systems.)

The networks do not see this as a threat, either. "In the last five years," says NBC-TV President Donald Durgin, "cable-TV signed up less than 3.5-million homes. The number of regular TV homes increased by twice as many."

Cable's growth might seem stymied by the fact that most viewers who need CATV to get any kind of reception already subscribe to it. But the industry has its share of long-range forecasters who see bigger and better things.

One such prognosticator is Irving B. Kahn, the chunky, forceful dynamo who is president of TelePrompTer. Kahn says that the cable wire will someday provide 40 or 80 channels of programs, burglar and fire alarm systems, electronic reading of water and electric meters, instantaneous voting on political issues, and supermarket shopping from the living room. In the face of such entertainment and service opportunities, he says, the TV networks are bound to lose viewers.

Paul L. Klein, an audience research executive with NBC-TV who left last year to head a tiny company called Computer Television, Inc., is equally enthusiastic. He envisions a service that would enable an individual subscriber to dial a code number that will instantly bring to his screen a specific TV program selected from a catalogue and fed over the wires from a central library.

But these are long-range miracles. The more immediate reality for the cable industry is the problem of moving into big cities and "importing" TV programs from other cities. The FCC this month listened to a parade of 200 witnesses arguing for and against a proposal of this nature. The plan would allow a CATV system to give its subscribers programs from four non-network stations in distant markets in addition to the local stations it carries. Despite outcries from local stations, which say that this would cut into their audiences, the FCC will probably adopt the proposal.

The networks have analyzed the possible effects of such a plan on them, and they consider them minimal. Says CBS's Blank: "The most optimistic estimates are that 50% of the country might have cable in 10 years. I see 25%, and in a longer time. There is every evidence that subscribers pay first to get new, well-promoted network programs—*Gunsmoke, Lucy, Laugh-In.* Most people already get these without cable. They will pay less for the programming of a local independent station—old movies, old network series, local news.

They will pay still less to get the same kind of thing from stations that are far away."

Noting that the three network stations regularly divide 85% of all viewers in New York and Los Angeles, where they already compete with four independent stations, Blank estimates that the same thing might happen in 10 years in 25% or 50% of the homes that now get only network programs. "But it works out to a loss of 0.2% of the total audience a year," he says with a deprecatory wave.

PAY TELEVISION. The "menace" of pay-TV, which has come and gone several times in the last 15 years, came back to life briefly this month with the closed-circuit coverage of the Ali-Frazier fight. The promoters paid $5-million for the closed-circuit rights and some 1.5-million people paid an average of $10 each to see the bout in 350 theaters and arenas. Immediately, pundits conjectured that other events, notably the Superbowl and the World Series, might be bought away from the networks, depriving them of revenue.

Again, network executives do not think so. First, there is not enough good closed-circuit equipment around, making it difficult to attract and please audiences larger than the one that viewed the Ali-Frazier fight. For that event, theaters were jammed to overflowing, and much of the equipment was antique and faulty. Nor is it likely to be replaced or increased unless a continuing supply of programming is assured. Second, ticket prices for the fight were higher than could be charged for less ballyhooed events, which would mean a smaller box office.

CBS President Stanton cites two reasons why major sports events now on free TV will stay there. One is a strong feeling in Washington that the man-on-the-street has a right to view such programs even if he cannot scrape up the price of a ticket. The other is that the team owners have come to depend on the money they get from selling sports packages to the networks. And since the networks will not be eager buyers if the big draws such as the World Series or Superbowl are eliminated, Stanton feels it is unlikely that the teams will jeopardize the present relationship.

The TV industry's regulators at the FCC seem a less fearsome problem for the networks today than at almost any time in the last 18 months. When activist Chairman Dean Burch took over in 1969, the commission started off on a series of rulings that threatened the networks' power. It forced the networks to divest themselves of their cable-TV and program syndication businesses. It came out against single ownership of more than one broadcasting outlet in any one market and made the once "automatic" renewal of a station's license a thing of the past. It agreed to let cable-TV systems originate programs and sell advertising. And it demanded that each network give up one half-hour of prime time each night to local stations.

Since that flurry of action, the FCC has been easing up. Network executives speak cautiously, but they do detect a waning of the FCC's pressure. They cite in particular two recent moves by the commission:

■   Approval of the $110-million bid by Capital Cities Broadcasting Corp. to buy the TV and radio stations of Triangle Broadcasting Co. Before this decision, the commission made a year-long study of concentration of broadcasting ownership in large companies, and then came up with its surprising 7-0 vote for approval. Even FCC Commissioner Nicholas Johnson, who has usually been bitterly opposed to concentration of broadcasting ownership, went along.

■   The easing of an FCC rule that required an owner of an AM radio station, an FM radio station, and a TV station in the same market to sell two of the outlets. Now the commission is ready to allow AM-FM combinations, and it may permit broadcasters to own both a radio station and an ultra-high-frequency TV station. UHF stations, on channels 14 through 81, are often marginal or profitless operations.

The networks are not especially worried about having to get rid of radio stations in markets where they also own TV stations. For years, radio network operations and the owned NBC and CBS radio stations have been unprofitable though ABC's stations have made money by feeding listeners a diet of rock music. Nor are the networks crying about having to divest themselves of their cable-TV holdings and their program syndication service. "No one likes to lose any revenue," says NBC President Julian Goodman, "but syndication is not a significant part of our business. It's profitable, but not significant." The same applies at CBS, which is spinning off its cable and syndication interests into a separate company called Viacom; CBS gets less than $2-million of its net income of $64-million from syndication.

Far more threatening to the networks was the commission's tougher approach to renewal of TV station licenses. When the FCC refused to renew a Boston TV station's license and gave it to a challenging group late in 1969, the networks feared their stations would have to fight similar challenges. The loss of any of their owned TV stations would be a shattering blow to all three networks. The stations generate at least half the profits that NBC and CBS get from broadcasting. For ABC, the stations are even more vital. ABC's network operation has always been a money-loser, but its glossy programming helps its five stations attract ad dollars in neck-and-neck competition with those of the other networks. The stations' profits go a long way toward covering the network's losses.

The threat raised by challengers to the network stations' licenses seems far less serious now than it did a year ago. No challenge has succeeded in blocking renewal, and the FCC has explained that the Boston case was "exceptional."

The one FCC action that could prove costly is the cutback from three-and-a-half to three hours in the amount of prime time that the networks can fill. This could cut as much as $140-million year from network revenues. To a man, though, the network heads are convinced that the rule slicing 21 half-hours a week from their schedules (the 7:30 to 8 p.m. period) will be rescinded in a year or two. The commission's idea is to force local stations to put on their own shows and thereby increase program diversity.

Stations originally were told they could not use old network programs to fill the time. When informed, however, that recession-pinched budgets did not allow for a major increase in local production, the FCC agreed that for a year, beginning [September, 1971], stations may air whatever they choose. Most local outlets promptly began scrambling to buy up old and inexpensive five-night-a-week reruns or game shows such as *To Tell the Truth* and *This Is Your Life*. FCC chairman Dean Burch, casting one of two votes against the half-hour cutback, said its primary achievement would be "to bring Ralph Edwards back to television."

Westinghouse Broadcasting's President Donald H. McGannon, the philosophic broadcaster who first proposed the cutback to the FCC, now admits that it might not work initially. "Without the networks' support," McGannon says, "it's not likely that much diversity will be evident for a year or two. But I disagree with the contentions that a show is automatically junk if it didn't cost $150,000 a half-hour to produce, and that quality programs can't be done for less."

Even if the rule sticks, broadcasters remember that in 1958 the FCC moved to abolish something called "option time," which gave the networks first call on the air time of their affiliates in certain periods. Although they claimed that losing option time would destroy them, the networks prospered. They began airing longer programs, going from the standard half-hour format to one-hour shows, and affiliates had to give them more time. Also, as advertiser demand increased, the networks began programming earlier in the morning and later at night. Similar ideas might develop, but there are plans now to ask the commission to reconsider its rule next year, and the network chiefs are hopeful. For one thing, Ashbrook Bryant, who headed the FCC department that was instrumental in getting the rule accepted, left this month for a post on the Maritime Commission. And Chairman Burch is likely to get support from two new Nixon appointees to the FCC.

"Anything as big and powerful as TV has proven to be," says NBC's Goodman, "is always going to be under regulatory pressure." But he and other broadcasters feel that the commission has pretty well run through all the ideas that were kicking around for the past 10 or 15 years, and it might relax to see what effect its recent rulings have.

When network TV revenues began to slide in 1970, the reasons seemed obvious. The recession made many advertisers cautious about spending. The General Motors strike eliminated perhaps $20-million that the carmaker might have spent in network TV, and its competitors—Ford, Chrysler, American Motors—eased up on their own spending so as to have ammunition left when GM roared back.

But another factor was at work. Knowing that the networks would soon offer bargain rates to fill the time left open by the departing cigarette business, advertisers began holding off their commitments as long as they could. Prices tumbled. The falling rates—in January, they were down to $1.50 and $1.60 per 1,000 homes vs. the usual prime-nighttime price of $3.50—enabled advertisers to buy for less as much or more advertising as they had bought in the past, so they cut their budgets further.

To lure new money, CBS reduced the minimum amount of time that advertisers might buy, cutting down from a one-minute sale to a 30-second sale. ABC and NBC followed swiftly. "It actually was a built-in rate increase," says NBC's Durgin, "since we could get a little more for two 30-second announcements than for one minute." The networks pitched their bargain rates to new advertisers, and concentrated on companies in retailing, apparel, and furniture, which have always been major buyers of newspaper space.

Suddenly, in March the floodgates opened. "We knew it would happen," says Durgin. "We knew the money was there and that it would come in when major companies decided they had better not wait until the choice periods were gone." The networks responded to the crush by raising their rates 25%, getting them back near 1970 levels.

One basic reason that the broadcasters saw the money coming their way is put in a few simple words by ABC's Duffy: "Where else can a major advertiser go?" Specialized magazines? They reach small, select audiences at a high cost-per-thousand, he notes. And TV's critics tend to overlook the fact that the most successful specialized magazine is *TV guide*, bought by 16-million people each week.

"Besides," says Duffy, "television can zero in on select audiences, too. A golf match reaches an entirely different audience than a situation comedy." New research data that pinpoints viewers by age group, income, education, and the like, Duffy says, lets each advertiser choose programs that reach the type of audience he wants.

Advertisers seem to be going along with this thinking. Goodyear, which cuts its ad expenditures in half last year "because of budgetary pressure" and put its money into newspapers, came back with a $2-million buy of sports programs aimed at the male audience. Mutual of New York came into TV sports for the first time to reach the same audience. Even the U.S. Army, which has long relied on free public-service announcements for recruitment, is spending $3-million in a three-month effort to reach the 17-to-21-year-old viewer of such programs as *Mission Impossible.*

Advertiser irritation with "clutter"—the proliferation of commercials back-to-back-to-back-to-back—is a problem that could be eliminated tomorrow, says McGannon. All the networks need to do, he says, is to cut the number of commercials in a program break, and, if advertisers really are concerned, they will pay a little more to clean up the air. "It is not an insoluble problem."

Peter Bardach, a broadcast executive at the Foote, Cone & Belding, Inc., ad agency, thinks some advertisers soon will solve the clutter problem and get solid identification themselves by returning to full-year sponsorship of a single program—as in the days of the *Colgate Comedy Hour* or *Goodyear Playhouse.* If so, the business would lose some of the cyclical patterns that have developed over the past decade because advertisers made their commitments for 13-week periods or less. "I may sound like a speaker from the Television Bureau of Advertising," says Bardach, "but in five years the networks will be stronger than ever."

"The one thing that worries me," counters a Wall Street analyst, "is that the network boys have never been able to bring their costs down. Their solution to increased prices by their suppliers has always been to cut up the programs into smaller pieces, so more advertisers could share the pie. Now they are down from selling half-hour programs to selling 30-second announcements. They can't go much further."

Most TV executives agree, and admit they grew lazy and care-less as their revenues soared. "When we discovered years ago that film programs outperformed ones that were live or on tape," says Durgin, "we committed ourselves to an upward spiral of costs." Now there is a feeling that the recession has had a beneficial effect. "For the first time," Durgin says, "we have had to draw a line for our-selves and our suppliers. Instead of the usual 5% or 6% increase each season for programs, we have actually obtained a decrease this year."

There might even be an end to the spiraling cost of sports programs. True, sports has remained the one sold-out spot in net-work sales throughout the sluggish year, but costs have reduced profits. "I think the three networks together made about $3-million last season on the football packages," says one executive, "and that is on an investment of $58-million. It is just too risky, and I think there will be lower prices paid in the future."

The networks are also working to cut the cost of getting pro-grams to the audience. Topping the list is a satellite system that may save the networks as much as 50% of the $65-million they pay AT&T each year to distribute their programs. RCA and a dozen others have proposed such systems to the FCC. Meanwhile, a three-network task force is studying other ways to achieve the same objectives, perhaps

The End of a Long Climb

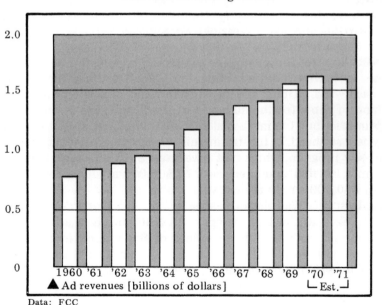

Data: FCC

by using ground lines set up independently at AT&T. "In the next five years," CBS's Blank predicts flatly, "there will be a significant reduction in our transmission costs."

NBC's Durgin speaks of cost-cutting developments in program production—"and I mean something more substantial than using 16mm film instead of 35mm, or tape instead of film." One such development was announced this month by CBS and Memorex Industries: a computerized editing system that greatly speeds the tedious process of manually splicing bits of film or tape to achieve the desired continuity of scenes. The device could cut $5,000 from the cost of each weekly program episode.

Perhaps most important, there are signs at the networks of a real awareness that today's urban-oriented and somewhat sophisticated TV viewer is not the same person who watched the tube in the past two decades. Last season's efforts to provide "relevant" programming—dealing with the drug scene, youthful rebellion, and the like—failed miserably. But programmers show signs of trying again. CBS's new *All in the Family*, which presents an outspoken bigot in a wildly humorous way, is a controversial show that in other days would have been promptly cancelled after a brief run. But it is scheduled to stay on next year. And the same network, which made much of the fact that it was modernizing its schedule last season by eliminating Red Skelton and a couple of hayseed comedies, now has gone all the way, dropping *Beverly Hillbillies, Hee-Haw, Green Acres, Andy Griffith*, and its 23-year-old *Ed Sullivan Show*, among other long-running hits.

NBC, too, cut loose on some top-rated programs for next season because they were not delivering the young, active audience that advertisers want. "Don't tell me *Laugh-In* and *Flip Wilson* are not a new kind of show for the audience of the 70's," says Durgin. "Call me optimistic, but I think a real acceleration of our ability to make money is just ahead." (Illustrating his confidence is the fact that the *Flip Wilson* program, which cost advertisers $45,000 a minute before its premier last fall and then went to $65,000 as audiences soared, will cost $80,000 a minute next year.)

At least one Wall Street analyst agrees with Durgin's optimism. A White, Weld & Co. bullish report on NBC guesses that its broadcasting operations had pretax earnings of $82-million in 1969 and $55-million last year. They may slip to $50-million this year—but will leap to $75-million in 1972 "when the slack generated by the cigarette advertising ban is expected to be taken up by increases in the promotion of other products."

Most network men are naturally keeping one eye on the immediate future to see how quickly they recover from the cigarette ad ban, but they also are looking further ahead—and are smiling. Behind them are two decades of uninterrupted growth, during which the networks came to count on $1.6-billion in annual ad revenues, primarily from the aggressive marketers of food, drugs, toiletries, and other non-durables.

Now the TV industry is working to add to this base a number of retail and financial service companies. New sales efforts—revolving around programs that should attract the right audiences and new numbers to prove the audience is there—are under way. With these, network TV will try to get back to its 8.6% annual compound growth rate of the 1960s. The rate was better than that for total advertising expenditures, which, at 5.7%, roughly paralleled the increase in gross national product.

Even during 1970, optimistic network salesmen point out, major clients such as Procter & Gamble and Lever Bros. increased their spending. As the economy gets moving again, they say, expenditures should shoot up, particularly when advertisers loose a flood of new products that were held back from the marketplace in the past 18 months.

"If things go the way the economists in and out of the Administration predict," says CBS's Blank, "we'll be right up there again. I say 'if,' because we wouldn't have been hit as hard as we were if we hadn't looked for an upturn in the last half of 1970, and had planned accordingly. But we went along with everybody else. And you know what happened."

PRINT: A GLOW OF HEALTH

WHY NEWSPAPERS ARE MAKING MONEY AGAIN

John S. Knight, Pulitzer Prize-winning columnist, editorial chairman of Knight Newspapers, Inc., and, at 75, one of the grand, old curmudgeons of American journalism, is a man of many opin-

A second look at the giants of the mass media is given the reader through the courtesy of *Business Week*, August 29, 1970. This time the Knight newspapers are described in an article which shows that for many reasons newspapers are not going broke.

ions. And these days his one overriding opinion, which may come as a surprise to anyone outside the newspaper business, is that daily newspapers are not only alive and well, but are becoming a full-fledged growth industry.

"Within the last eight or 10 years," Knight points out, "a lot of metropolitan papers disappeared, and everyone was saying that television would be the death of the daily paper." In New York City alone, four dailies suspended operations between 1962 and 1968. "What really happened," Knight says, "is that the industry underwent a long-overdue shakeout, then slowly consolidated. And now it is much, much stronger for it." [Editor's Note: An analysis of the Bureau of Advertising showed daily newspapers gained more new ad dollars than television and radio combined in 1970, $97 million, to $75 million for TV and $14 million for radio.]

Stewart Macdonald, executive director of the American Newspaper Publishers Assn. Foundation, trots out figures showing just how strong: Newspaper advertising revenues are up more than five times since 1946 (to a record $5.8-billion in 1969), daily circulation is up over 20% (to a record 62-million), and the industry now ranks as the country's fifth-largest employer. Every day, more than 98-million Americans—almost 80% of the adult population—read at least one newspaper. And while it is true that 11 dailies suspended publication in 1969, it is also true that 28 other dailies started up. "That," says Macdonald, "is growth."

Prime example. Perhaps the best proof is KNI itself. Though the company's editorial coverage falls short of a *New York Times* or *Washington Post* and tends toward what one former KNI editor describes as "safe, formula journalism," even rival publishers concede that the Knight papers comprise one of the best-managed, most profitable, and most aggressive chains in the country.

In one year alone, the company added five papers to its collection: the *Philadelphia Inquirer* and *Daily News*, the *Macon* (Ga.) *Telegraph* and *News*, and the *Boca Raton* (Fla.) *News*. Together with other papers in Miami, Detroit, Akron, (O.), Charlotte, (N.C.), and Tallahassee (Fla.), KNI's acquisitions raised its daily circulation to 2.2-million and its annual level of advertising to more than 340-million lines, while total revenues for the year spurted to a record $162.8-million and profits to a record $12.7-million. Along the way, KNI has also boosted its after-tax profits to nearly 8% of gross revenues, and talks confidently of the not-too-distant day when it will earn 10% to 11% on revenues. That compares with average newspaper profits of 6% to 7% and average magazine profits of 5% to 6%.

Today, as Knight likes to observe, there is not a single KNI paper that—over the long run—has not grown stronger in circulation, advertising, and profitability once KNI took control. Excluding those papers that have expanded through merger, the country's fastest-growing metropolitan daily is now KNI's *Detroit Free Press*, which picked up 42,000 new readers in the last year. And the company's *Miami Herald*, which ranks 12th in circulation among morning papers, is the nation's second-largest daily in total advertising—despite the fact that Miami is the 26th-largest market by population and 19th in retail sales.

There are still plenty of papers that have more troubles than a rusty press. In fact, a few years ago, many publishers in the industry were bearish about the future of all but the best newspapers—and, in some cases, felt it was a business that was becoming increasingly obsolete. But today the industry's broader trend is unquestionably up. And like KNI, many chains and individual papers are now riding higher than a banner headline:

■ *The New York Times*, despite a tight profit squeeze and costly union contracts, continues to pile up profits that run about 7% of gross revenues ($238.2-million in 1969). Francis Cox, the *Times* vice-president of finance, says the paper has had the idea of editorial expansion "under continuous study" and is "keeping the options open"—though it still carries the scars of its ill-fated West Coast edition, which folded in 1964.

■ *The Washington Post* is steadily expanding its advertising (72-million lines in 1969) and has built its daily circulation to 502,000—more than 60% higher than that of its main competitor, the evening *Washington Star*. At the same time, the *Post* is providing strong internal momentum for Katharine Graham's overall Washington Post Co. empire (*Newsweek*, a chunk of the *International Herald Tribune*, several radio and television stations)—described by one top newspaper broker as "the hottest property in the business."

■ Dow Jones & Co., which publishes the weekly *National Observer*, the *Wall Street Journal*, and a bevy of other financial services, branched out into general newspapers in July 1970, and paid $25.5-million in company stock for Ottoway, Inc., publisher of nine small Eastern dailies and three Sunday papers. "Newspapers are doing well generally," says Buren McCormack, Dow Jones executive vice-president. "And when an industry is doing well, you simply try for a bigger share." Ottoway also provides, says McCormack, "a good corporate vehicle for acquiring other papers."

The leading American newspaper is the *New York Times,* originally made famous in the early twentieth century by Adolph Ochs and Carr Van Anda, the publisher and managing editor who turned the *Times* into "the paper of record." The *Times* maintained the reputation with the publication of the Pentagon Papers, as shown here. Reporter Neil Sheehan gained access to the documents and a team of editors and reporters worked three months to prepare the series. As in the days of Ochs and Van Anda, the power of the *Times* was felt throughout the nation and pride in achievement was deep in the pressroom.

Rivaling the *New York Times* for attention is the West Coast giant, the *Los Angeles Times* of the young publisher Otis Chandler. A growing foreign staff and strong domestic coverage, plus the Chandler wealth, allows the *Times* to dominate California. The other paper in the "top three" is Katharine Graham's *Washington Post*. There are about 1,750 daily newspapers ranging in circulation from a few thousand to the *New York Daily News'* nearly two million readers.

■   Times Mirror Co., which owns the *Los Angeles Times* and several other ventures, closed a $24.5-million deal in May, 1969 for 51% ownership of Long Island's *Newsday*, the country's largest suburban daily. Then the Times Mirror dug deeper and for $49.5-million worth of stock bought the *Dallas Times Herald* and its broadcast interests. Times Mirror Chairman Franklin D. Murphy admits that while his company's acquisition appetite is satisfied for now, "that doesn't mean that if a very high-quality property were available, we wouldn't look at it." In fact, Times Mirror recently made an unsuccessful pitch for the *Houston Post*. Murphy has also privately admitted that he would "love to own" KNI's *Miami Herald*.

■   Newhouse Newspapers, Scripps-Howard, Gannett, and the country's other leading chains now account for more than 120 other papers. And nearly all the chains are trolling for more. "There are so many markets," says Gannett President Allen Neuharth, "that you can pick and choose. Some want metropolitan areas, some don't. Knight wants metropolitan. They have Philadelphia. We're in Camden (N.J.) with 120,000 circulation and rapid growth. There is no growth in Philadelphia, but you don't need continued growth to be profitable."

A big reason for the industry's prosperity, of course, is rising newspaper ad revenues. At $5.8-billion (vs. $3.6-billion for television), newspaper ad revenues in 1969 were up more than 11% above the year before. In today's television age, why are advertisers still flocking to newspapers? Simply because newspapers—unlike television, radio, or magazines—are the next best thing to an indispensable medium, if only because of the many service features they provide to their readership.

Besides important local and national happenings, newspapers dish up everything from hometown job, apartment, housing, movie, theater, stock market, and television listings to details on yesterday's garden club luncheon, last night's PTA meeting, and tonight's YMCA squash match, along with A&P's latest prices on sirloin and the department store's close-out bargains on minis. No one, in short, can afford to be without his local paper, especially at today's economy price of 10¢ or 15¢ a copy. As the *New York Times*' Francis Cox, pointing to the inflationary trend, puts it: "Most things—even a telephone call for a single item of information—cost a dime today."

Far more basically, there is one other big clincher for newspapers: the long-term shakeout of metropolitan dailies and the virtual elimination of competition among newspapers. While the total number of dailies published today (more than 1,700) is almost the same as in 1945, their distribution has shifted away from major metropolitan areas and toward the suburbs, along with the population and retailers. Right after World War II, there were 117 cities with two or more competing dailies. Today, there are only 45. And in 22 of those cities, a total of 44 papers have pooled their printing and business operations to cut costs. In July 1969, President Nixon even signed a bill into law, extending antitrust immunity to those joint operations where one of the papers might otherwise fail.

As they fatten up, more and more papers are also able to swing the purchase of big, fancy, labor-saving equipment—computerized typesetters and presses, photocomposition, and so on. Since 1965, Newhouse has sunk over $70-million into major capital improvements. In Philadelphia alone, Knight is spending $15-million on new equipment. At the *Ithaca* (N.Y.) *Journal*, which is Gannett's main proving ground for new equipment, production per man-hour has jumped 69% in five years.

As an added damper on costs, many publishers are investing in their own paper plants. "Until a few years ago," says Gannett's Neuharth, "there was none of this except in a few isolated examples such as the *Chicago Tribune*." For many years the *New York Times* depended on wholly owned Spruce Falls Paper Co. to pay its dividend. More papers are also able to afford regional or "zone" editions, thus refining their circulation and luring a few more advertisers. Newhouse's *Long Island Press*, for instance, boasts three geographic editions. "The whole mass numbers game in circulation is fading," says Thomas Vail, editor and publisher of the *Cleveland Plain Dealer*. "The magazine business overstepped itself in this circulation area," adds Brady Black, editor-in-chief of the *Cincinnati Enquirer*, "and some of them got so much circulation they couldn't find enough advertising to pay for it. We don't want to get into that position." As a publisher puts it: "Overall, top-management thinking is simply directed more toward how circulation relates to advertising."

At Knight Newspapers, the top-management thinking is done by four men: John Knight himself, company overlord and chief custodian of KNI's broader editorial philosophy; Knight's younger brother, James, 59, board chairman and chief executive officer who presides over the business side; Lee Hills, 64, president and a Pulitzer Prize winner in his own right, who operates just below John Knight on the editorial level; and Alvah Chapman, 49, executive vice-president and the No. 2 man on the financial side, just under James Knight. Oddly enough, the four maintain no central headquarters. John Knight summers in Akron and winters in Miami. Hills spends most of his time in Detroit. James Knight and Chapman operate out of Miami.

Despite management's far-flung nature, KNI's lines of authority and overall operating philosophy—as set down by John Knight—are as fixed and firm as a tray of type. Knight insists on full editorial independence and autonomy among his papers and complete separation of editorial and financial functions. "I'd have to confess," he says, "that every general manager is a frustrated editor. But I don't find too many editors who think they could do a better job of management."

Knight also insists that his editors and managers eschew any political or business alliances, including corporate directorships. "On the two occasions when I violated this rule," he admits, "the bank failed and my candidate faltered." A lifelong Republican himself, Knight proudly points out that many of his critics now call him a "Black Republican" for having supported more than 1,000 Democrats for public office. Other critics call him simply an opportunist who bends with every prevailing public wind. Either way, it keeps the reader guessing, and that is the way Knight likes it. Says he: "In this day of the credibility gap, we think this makes a newspaper believable."

Knight began hammering out his philosophy back in the 1920s when he was managing editor of the *Akron Beacon Journal*, one of three small Ohio dailies then owned by the family. At that time, his father, Charles L. Knight, was the editor and also a political aspirant. This, says Knight, "made every headline suspect in the eyes of our readers. What I learned from C.L's era was that newspapering and political involvements are incompatible." When his father died in 1933, Knight took charge of the *Beacon Journal* and four years later launched the company on its current trajectory. In 1937, the Knights bought the *Miami Herald;* in 1940, the *Detroit Free Press;* then in 1944, the *Chicago Daily News*, which was later sold.

As the chain grew larger, Knight saw an increasing need for tighter management and more financial coordination among his papers. So at the suggestion of Lee Hills, then executive editor in Detroit and Miami, Knight formed an executive committee in 1960 to make quarterly reviews of all KNI operations, including labor problems, personnel recruitment, operating costs, advertising, circulation, and acquisitions. "The net of all this," claims Jack Knight, "is that we don't have so many crises now. We're pretty orderly. But it isn't as much fun any longer."

That same year, Chapman joined KNI and brought what Knight

describes as "order and business discipline" to the chain. During six years as general manager of the *Miami Herald*, Chapman doubled the paper's revenues and tripled profits. As KNI executive vice-president, Chapman—working closely with Jim Knight—has now introduced budgeting on all KNI papers, a rarity among most small and medium-sized papers. "Some do their budgeting in bits and pieces," says Chapman. "But most of them just don't want to work that hard." Chapman also came up with "management by objective," the use of incentive bonuses for every noneditorial manager. Ad salesmen get bonuses for producing extra business, composing room foremen for rolling more pages on time, accounting managers for beating their deadlines.

Chapman and Jim Knight have wrought similar economies and savings in the composing room. Today, every KNI paper uses a computer not only for administration and typesetting, but to control presses and other equipment, as well. That even includes KNI's *Boca Raton News*, which has a circulation of only 6,169. KNI also uses optical scanners to produce type automatically from a typewritten page; computer-controlled display screens for redesigning ad layouts; and a facsimile system for transmitting ad layouts. KNI's *Miami Herald* even became the first major metropolitan daily to paint its presses white and equip the pressroom with "demisters," making the area as clean as any other part of the plant. "What we did," says the younger Knight, "was turn the composing room into a manufacturing center."

Out in the editorial offices, changes are slower in coming. "The Knight news level is good, though not superior," says one former KNI editor. But there have been improvements, adds one editor in the field, "and the Knight papers are starting to get more of a cutting edge." To hone its blade, Knight is going in for more investigative reporting, adding columnists of almost every political hue, and generally trying to upgrade the quality and quantity of its reporting. Here and there, the results have bordered on the spectacular. In 1968 alone, KNI won three Pulitzer Prizes and ran its total to 12—more than any other single chain. Among KNI's recent winners: the *Detroit Free Press* for its coverage of that city's 1967 race riots, the *Charlotte Observer* for its biting editorial cartoons, and the *Miami Herald* for gaining the freedom of a wrongly-convicted life-termer.

KNI is pouring money, as well, into that staple of every good daily: the service feature. On the *Philadelphia Inquirer*, for instance, KNI has spent more than $200,000 for its page-one "Action Line" column that now requires 12 reporters to handle the more than

1,500 calls and 500 letters that pour in every day. "Our whole approach is to make the *Inquirer* more personal, more down-to-earth," says *Inquirer* Executive Editor John McMullan, a deft, sharp-eyed KNI editor promoted from Miami. "We're trying to be more aggressive in our news coverage, to bring a fresh look to some of the dark corners around here."

Knight is becoming equally aggressive in its pursuit of acquisitions—once they satisfy a strict set of guidelines. KNI claims that it will not venture into a city where the competition has a commanding lead or the profit potential is marginal. The property must also be located in a city with a strong growth potential and a minimum population of 50,000. And needless to say, the price must be right. Jim Knight suggests a price of 15 times earnings, but chuckles at the thought of ever buying a metropolitan daily that cheaply, considering the hot and heavy bidding going on among the chains. KNI, for instance, paid 26 times earnings for the Macon papers.

Perhaps KNI's biggest all-around exception was 1969's purchase of its two Philadelphia papers. There, the company paid $55-million in cash and notes, or a price equal to 20 times earnings. On its $41-million worth of notes, KNI also agreed to pay a stiff 8% annual interest or whatever the prime rate happens to be.

Was it worth it? Over the previous five years, both papers had slid from a combined daily circulation of 811,000 to 719,000, and profit margins followed suit. Chapman points out, however, that the purchase involved no stock dilution, and expanded KNI's total revenues almost 50% without adding new shareholders. "When we get Philadelphia cleaned up and pay off the debt," Chapman claims, "our earnings will really be something." In fact, Chapman talks of doubling the profit margin within five years.

Others in the field have their doubts and question the company's whole system of guidelines. "When you buy a newspaper or broadcast station," says Norman Chandler, chairman of Times Mirror's executive committee, "you don't put a price-earnings ratio on it. You just buy it if it's available and if it's in a good market and making money, and as long as the acquisition doesn't dilute your earnings appreciably." John Purcell, Gannett's vice-president of finance and administration, insists that KNI picked the wrong city. "Look at our Camden paper," he says. "It serves Cherry Hill, and look at the statistics. The two Philadelphia papers have steadily declined and we have steadily increased."

Jack Knight himself admits that the Philadelphia purchase bothered him. "I raised 10 reasons why we should not buy, none why we should," he recalls. "But I'm a team player. Once the decision to go ahead is made, I join the rest." This does not mean that Knight discourages acquisitions. He is just choosy. "I believe we should make acquisitions gradually in sound growth areas. I don't want to own just to own. Nor do I want to buy simply to become a national chain. To me, we should look to areas where the brightest growth will be. And I can't disregard the fact that Philadelphia is the fourth-largest city in the country."

Question. How well KNI finally does in Philadelphia—and elsewhere around the country—will hinge largely, of course, on how well it does against industry's age-old bogey of rising costs. At the production and plant level, new modern equipment seems to be winning the day. At KNI's *Akron Beacon Journal,* general manager Sam McKeel says that computerized typesetting has trimmed the paper's annual increase in per-unit production costs from 5% to 6% in 1966 down to 1% to 2%. Over-all labor costs among all KNI papers have similarly declined from over 38% of total operating expenses five years ago to 37.3% in 1969.

One sticking point is the unions. Some go along, some do not. The *New York Times* management is now installing a high-speed, labor-saving press that is more than three times faster than the press it replaces. Yet in the *Times'* mailroom, there is a conveyor that has been idle more than a year because of a union dispute over how many men should "watch the papers go by."

To guard against such hassles, KNI has invested heavily in retraining programs for employees automated out of jobs. Chapman describes this as "the best money we ever spent."

Rather than production costs, the No. 1 problem of tomorrow, if not today, shapes up as distribution. It now accounts for some 8% to 10% of the industry's total operating expenses. Growing traffic congestion is slowing up deliveries. Medium-rise and high-rise apartments are swallowing up tenants and making them almost impossible to reach. Metropolitan papers are also losing a favorite, old outlet: the "Mom and Pop" store. In Pittsburgh alone, where circulation and distribution costs are rocketing 12% to 15% a year, 70 such stores closed in 1969. Then there is the problem of ghetto or core-city areas. "The papers can be delivered, but let the boys try to go back and collect," says Michael Tynan, director of circulation for the *Pittsburgh Press* and *Post Gazette.* "They're beaten and robbed. They can never get back with the money." In fact, the *Cincinnati Enquirer's* Brady Black questions whether "anyone is even breaking even in the core areas."

As one possible solution, the *Detroit News, Chicago Daily News*, and several other papers are experimenting with a "block-system" of deliveries and collections. Every one or two blocks, a bundle of papers is dropped off with some enterprising homeowner, and a sign is hung out, indicating that papers can be bought there.

As another answer, a West Coast paper even tried encouraging the use of charge cards. For its part KNI is now recruiting 25 bright, eager college graduates and training them in circulation and distribution. "We're trying to create specialists who can come up with answers," says Chapman, "because the traditional way of getting papers to people isn't working."

Further off in the future, the elder Knight and the rest of his management team have nothing but optimism for the prospects of their company and industry. Population increase alone, says Knight, assures a built-in growth factor. "In many industries," Hills adds, "rapid growth simply brings in more competition. Retail trade is one. But newspapers to a large extent have already gone through their era of excessive competition and the shakeout of weaker members. Besides, it's too costly for new newspapers to spring up."

If costs start getting out of hand, newspapers can simply hike their circulation rates. As it is, many publishers feel that rate increases have not kept pace, and that subscribers should be kicking in a bigger share of total revenues. Right now, circulation income accounts for an average 20% to 25% of total revenues compared with 75% to 80% for advertisers. A better balance, some say, would be a 65-35 ratio. Consider KNI's *Miami Herald*, which sells for 10¢ Monday through Saturday and 15¢ on Sunday—for a total of 75¢ a week. Of that 75¢, the carrier gets 23 1/2¢, leaving 51 1/2¢ for the *Herald*. "That 51 1/2¢," says Chapman, "doesn't even cover the cost of the newsprint, not to mention transportation or anything else. Just on raw newsprint alone, we lose $12 to $15 a year per subscriber." By raising the cost of the *Herald's* Sunday edition only 10¢—to 25¢—KNI would bring in another $2.5-million a year in revenues.

However, Chapman is quick to caution against any idea that newspapers could generally pay their way on circulation. "Circulation revenue is important," he says. "And it will vary slightly in ratio with advertising, depending on whether we raise our prices. But it's a blind alley. We could never make it on circulation alone."

As for his own personal prospects and future, the elder Knight gives no indication that he plans to step down from active participation in the company. Whether in Miami or Akron, he still shows up at 9 o'clock every morning and puts in a five-day week. "I'll retire when I no longer feel I can be effective," Knight vows, giving the impression that that will not be for some years to come.

PUBLISHING BY CATHODE RAY TUBE

Richard L. Tobin

By 1979, give or take a year, newspapers, and perhaps magazines, too, will be printed in your living room. This is the substance of a startling full-page ad that appeared in late 1970 in *Advertising Age*, the bible of Madison Avenue. The ad was inserted by McGraw-Hill in behalf of its electronics periodical, now published every two weeks. The ad went on: "All it will take is a compact printout unit attached to an ordinary TV set. When you are ready for the stock market closings, ball game scores, or movie listings, you'll simply push a button. Instant newspaper. And you'll be able to get any part of it, or all of it, any hour of the day or night."

Once upon a time the printing press had the world of news all to itself. Then came radio, later television, to rob the newspaper of its original reason for being, and by now almost all first reports of the world's news come through electronics rather than print. Soon, however, the cycle of news will have come full circle, for the printing press itself will have been replaced by something plugged into the electricity of your living room. In another generation most of the homes in America will have an electronic communication center connected to a national control for both entertainment and news. If you want live television you press one button; if you want a fresh daily newspaper printed right in your home, you will press another. The video cartridge, or cassette, will transform television by the mid-1970s, and for that matter phonographs and records, as we know them, may disappear because in this home electronic center anybody can bring to heel virtually anything he wants at any hour of the night or day in the line of amusement or information, by sight, sound, or both—and in color at that.

Almost one-third of the country's daily newspapers are already using computers to drive typesetting equipment. Harris-Intertype re-

Richard L. Tobin is vice president and associate editor of *Saturday Review*, which outlined "The Coming Age of News Monopoly" in its October 10, 1970 issue. The article is used with permission of *Saturday Review*, Inc., copyright 1970.

Electronic editing display terminals are being used by publishers in an effort to eliminate production bottlenecks by displaying newspaper and book copy for instantaneous editing, proofreading and correcting prior to photocomposition or linecasting. Both major wire services, Associated Press and United Press International (AP system shown here) use the cathode ray tube to send news to the newspapers, who receive the copy on similar looking screens. Input signals can be stored for future retrieval, also (used with permission of Wide World Photos, Inc.).

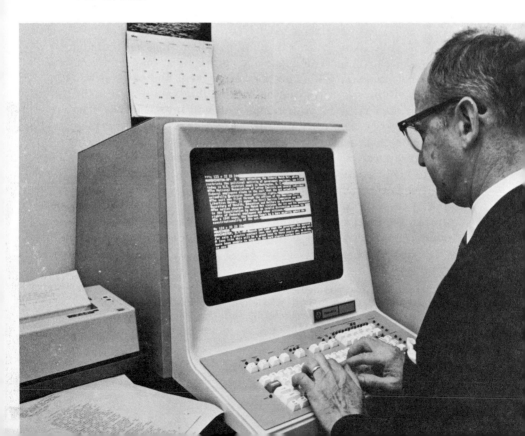

The miracles of electronic editing, computerized delivery systems and other innovations have eliminated much of the extra toil common to publishing. But there always will be reporters at the scene, like these Associated Press correspondents whose words can be moved around the world within minutes, indeed even seconds in the event of a "flash." Whether in the private company of a Secretary of State (Saul Pett), at the White House (Frank Cormier), or gaining the ideas of young people (Hugh Mulligan), this is where the action starts (used with permission of Wide World Photos, Inc.).

ports that many others are exploring or have already adopted a form of offset printing akin to electronic printing, photographic typesetting, high-speed data transmission, and mailroom computer automation. It isn't in the future, it is already here—the era of electronic publishing. In the end there may be no typesetters at all, no stereotypers, no pressmen or linotype operators as we now know them. An editor will simply speak into a microphone, punch some buttons, bring his artwork into focus electronically, then sit back and wait a few seconds for his inkless paper. To say that journalism is in the vortex of a technical revolution is to magnify the obvious.

Central to this revolution in publishing is a gadget called a video display terminal involving a technique probably more astonishing to most modern journalists than the surface of the moon itself. The principal element in the video display terminal is a cathode ray tube, abbreviated to CRT when discussing the publishing industry of the future. Scores of companies here and abroad make, or plan to make, CRTs, and there are quite a few of them already in operation. There are many ways that a great variety of CRTs can be put to use. Let's look at one system.

The editor sits before a CRT display terminal. By the use of a keyboard he can call onto the screen a story that has been stored earlier. He can edit the story just as though he had a pencil in his hand and the words had been typed on paper. He can delete words or paragraphs, write in his own changes, shift lines around, and so on. If he changes his mind about what he has done, he can call the whole thing back the way it was before he started. When he is finished, he can send the edited piece back on to a memory disc, or he can send it out for makeup.

Editing by this method is no faster than the time-honored way, but when combined with an automated system of printing it has unlimited applications. When the CRT is a part of a computer complex it becomes almost incredible. At a recent conference held by the American Newspaper Publishers Association's Research Institute, Stanton R. Cook, executive vice president of the Chicago *Tribune*, described a metropolitan newspaper of 1980 this way:

"Your production plant looks like a gigantic pinball machine, a bank of glowing dials and whirling tapes and multicolored buttons that occupies an entire wall. What's it all for? Composing, stereotype, warehouse, pressroom? Everything, everything. This is the central computer complex. Your entire plant is automated. . . . Our main inputs to the computer complex will be via cathode ray display terminals. There will be optical character recognition devices and graphics digitizing scanners that will convert photos and artwork into digital form for the computer. That guy over there is inputting marked-up copy to the computer with an Optical Character Reader (OCR) device. That lady is feeding a picture out of Washington through the digitizing scanner. The compositor working on makeup is sitting at a CRT display console. He's manipulating copy, photos, and artwork on the TV screen, instead of composing the ads from slugs of type, cuts, and engravings.

"Most classified ads will be inputted directly to the computer from CRT display terminals. Each ad flashes on a screen as it will appear in the paper. You also will see what the ad costs and receive a credit okay for the advertiser. If everything checks out, the ad-taker pushes a button and the ad goes to the computer storage bank. From instructions inputted by the ad-taker, the computer will automatically delete, skip, advance, or update any ads it has in storage. The classified storage bank fills until deadline time, when the computer shuts off for that day's insertions, then proceeds to completely make up the section.

"With the size determined, and with all ads allocated, the computer calls the makeup man for final page makeup and pagination. He and other editors will sit down at a CRT terminal and shorten or lengthen stories, change fonts or column measures, do what needs to be done to fit the news tightly but handsomely into the given space.

"When the editing is complete, the editors will pat the computer on the head, give it a squirt of oil as a reward, and go to work on the next edition. Though the editor's job is complete, the computer's job continues. It drives high-speed phototypesetters which produce the fully made-up pages."

Though Mr. Cook's prediction seems fantastic, it is a sober collection of facts from ANPA research and just around the corner from a technical standpoint. As of the moment there isn't an easy way to produce special offset for letterpress plates, but the remainder of Mr. Cook's procedures are already in use. Many small weeklies and dailies have already converted from letterpress to offset print; in a few years virtually all small-city dailies will operate in elegant offset. At that point the benefit of automated publishing is theirs, at the expense of pressing a button or two that will set a page of "type" in one second. CRT display terminals already are being tested in several places: the Huntington (W. Va.) *Herald-Dispatch*, the Chicago *Sun-Times*, the Los Angeles *Times*, the Lee papers in Davenport, Iowa, the Norwich (Conn.) *Bulletin*, *The New York Times*, and elsewhere. Everything is in a pioneer stage, so to speak, but technology is moving so fast that in a short time radical developments are anticipated. The wire services are racing to take advantage of the cathode ray tube. Both AP and UPI have been testing it. In fall 1970, AP put into service four display terminals in its New York headquarters, the start of a major installation. UPI, by 1972, will have from twenty-four to forty-eight CRTs operating, meaning that automation will take over just about completely.

The reporter will find the newsroom a different place. He will type his story on his own typewriter display connected directly to the computer. He can change and edit it as he goes along, calling back parts or all of it as he sees fit. For background information on the subject, he can go to a display screen and type a request to the library for stories appearing in the last ninety days pertaining to such and such. After reading the abstracts on the screen, he asks for a full print-out of the two or three stories that interest him, and a printer generates them in a matter of seconds. When he finishes writing his own story, he sends it into the computer, where the city editor can call for it when he is ready.

On a big daily paper, each department will probably have its own display terminals and perhaps will perform its own layout functions. The woman's page editor, the amusement editor, the sports editor, etc., will put together their own sections. Page 1, of course, will require the usual editorial conference. But at some point everything will come together where an editor, a makeup man, or some guiding power will put together that edition via CRT. As each page is okayed, he sends it off for photocomposition, a process that is accomplished in seconds. What this means is that editorial will have control of production. (All proofreading will have been done *before* text is released by editorial. Printing errors in a CRT system are so rare that they can be lived with.) The implications are great. But the role of the reporter is not endangered by the advent of CRT, and there is no reason to assume that the function of the pressman is endangered. He will be wearing clean clothes and pushing buttons. And the "pressman" will never get dirty.

It's a revolution all right. A century ago the linotype machine and photoengraving radically changed production methods in print media—ways of publishing that had progressed very little since Guttenberg. Now all of a sudden—and sudden is the precise word—technological lightning has hit the printed page. But however it comes to the reader, by press, ink, or computerized electronics, published language and those who edit it inevitably will be more involved and beset by what is to be transmitted than the devices that do the transmitting. If indeed we have come full circle and print and electronic news distribution have joined hands technically, the age of news monopoly is not only coming, it is already here, dragging with it vital questions of the centralization of power as fewer and fewer human beings tell more and more human beings the news of the day. These are storm-warning flags, and, regardless of the new techniques, and perhaps because of them, every journalist worth his salt has to be more vigilant than at any time since the founding of the Republic to be certain that 1984 is not what George Orwell gloomily foresaw.

OTHER MASS MEDIA: BOOKS, FILM, MUSIC, MAGAZINES

BOOK PUBLISHING'S HIDDEN BONANZA

Curtis G. Benjamin

The division of the book world most readily recognized by the general public is between textbook publishing and general (or "trade") book publishing. Indeed, the U.S. book industry has for many years divided itself in this way by maintaining two trade associations: the American Book Publishers Council for producers of general books, and the American Educational Publishers Institute for producers of textbooks and related teaching materials. But this dichotomy loses validity every year as educators continue to move sharply away from the traditional one-subject-one-book teaching practice. In fact, most publishers today, foreseeing a sure meeting of the twain, think their two trade associations should be merged; this move seems imminent.

Another division, and a more natural one, is between what are known within the industry as literary books and nonliterary books. The first category includes fiction, biography, poetry, drama, and general literature. The second encompasses several classifications of practical and professional works in such subject areas as agriculture,

Curtis G. Benjamin, director and consultant for McGraw-Hill, Inc., and former president and chairman of the McGraw-Hill Book Company, gives his expert opinion of trends in book publishing. The article (April 18, 1970) is used with his permission and that of *Saturday Review*, copyright 1970.

business, economics, education, law, medicine, science, and technology; and it includes a multitude of handbooks, manuals, directories, statistical reports, sets of numerical tables and data, and "how-to" guides. Most textbooks, by nature as well as subject matter, fall into this second category. The classifications of the respective categories have been used since the turn of the century by the *Publishers' Weekly* annual statistical reports.

This division represents two worlds of publishing, each quite different and separate, and sufficient unto itself. There is, in fact, a far greater distinction between literary and nonliterary houses than between textbook and nontextbook houses.

During the 1960s, there occurred an astonishing explosion of nonliterary books. This unexpected development was doubly astonishing in that it was within the hardcover realm, and it came at the end of a long and little noticed sea change that began some forty years earlier. Although the explosion was a big one, not many people heard it, or even heard about it. This was because it occurred in the hidden part of the book-industry iceberg, the much larger part that is all but invisible to the general public, and that is not much celebrated within the industry itself.

In the early years of the century, newly published literary works outnumbered nonliterary works by two to one. Then, starting with the 1930s, there came a change in this imbalance; the production of literary works declined, while that of nonliterary works increased in proportion. The decline of the former was caused presumably by restricted spending for nonessentials during the Depression.

In the following decade, the 1940s, literary works declined a little more, while nonliterary works climbed a little higher. Then both categories climbed sharply through the 1950s, and by the end of that decade the two were almost even. Happy days were here again for all kinds of literary books, and for fiction especially. Income from sales of reprint, book-club, and motion-picture rights gave novels a new lease on life, and restored their production to an interesting level of profitability.

Then came the 1960s and the spectacular leap ahead in the production of nonliterary works. In that decade alone, the number of such works produced annually increased by 164 per cent, while literary titles increased by only 29 per cent. The imbalance of the earlier years was completely reversed, and by 1969 new nonliterary works outnumbered new literary works by more than two to one.

The long-range change over this forty-year period was even

more striking: Annual nonliterary book production increased by some 380 per cent, while literary production increased by only 40 per cent. . . .

It is amusing to note the aloofness of certain lofty-minded literary publishers and commentators who like to describe many kinds of nonliterary works as "nonbooks." The publishers of these books laugh all the way to the bank over this disdainful characterization. They know that these "nonbooks" are in great demand, that they have high societal value, and that they are of large importance to the overall resources and economy of the book industry. They know, too, that in many a large, multi-interest publishing firm, the profit earned by nonliterary titles bankrolls the whole house; that more often than not this profit provides large sums for investments in glamorous but uncertain literary ventures of great worth and prestige—ventures of the very kind that always are warmly applauded by the literary buffs.

Another possible division of the book publishing world is the paperback/hardcover bisection. This division actually is not as sharp or as meaningful within the industry as it is in the public's mind. Strangely, one of the most persistent of current myths about book publishing is that the two kinds of books are locked in a battle for survival. Indeed, many people on the fringes of the publishing world now believe firmly that paperbacks are *in* and hardcovers are *out*. This belief has gone so far that many students today suspect the value of any book that has not been reprinted in somebody's paperback series. I, myself, often have to suffer the pity of certain of my young friends when I insist that hardcover books are here to stay. To them, paperbacks have a high public visibility—at bookstores, newsstands, drugstores, supermarkets, railroad stations, bus terminals, and airports everywhere. Besides, they have had the truth of the matter from their teachers and from numerous reporters, columnists, lecturers, TV commentators, and book reviewers.

As an example of how the public can be misinformed about the fortune of paperbacks and the fate of hardcovers, a statement in *The New York Times* of January 31, 1970 written as background to a review of a recently published history of the Houghton Mifflin Company, read:

> The economics of publishing today has reached such a stage that the hardcover book is almost a liability to the man who brings it out. Since all the money is in the subsidiary rights, in what can be spun off in the form of movie options, stage adaptations, paperback rights, digests and the like, the publisher wishes the hardcover would go away and leave him alone.

Imagine with what dismay this statement was read by those insiders who know for certain that in recent years hardcover books have provided almost 90 per cent of our industry's sales and about 95 per cent of its profits. Naturally, the question arises why the public fancy has been so far misled. Why has the paperback "explosion" been so overcelebrated? Why has its supposed impact on hardcover publishing been so overstated? The answer, of course, is that large segments of the general public, and some people in book publishing as well, want it that way. Indeed, they want it that way so badly that they refuse to believe hard facts and figures. They simply will not believe that mass-market paperback publishing is, economically speaking, only a small part of the total publishing world. Nor will they believe that the paperback explosion actually has been more helpful than hurtful to hardcover publishing.

The foregoing observation should not be taken in any way as a denial of the status of paperback publishing. Everyone knows that the paperback explosion of the 1950s had large importance of its own. Everyone recognizes that paperbacks, and especially mass-market paperbacks, also have high and special societal values. The insider knows, too, that paperbacks have made a large indirect contribution to the overall prosperity of the U.S. book industry. He sees that they serve to hook thousands of new readers every year who would never have started on the hardcover stuff. Thus, he knows that the importance of the many millions of paperbacks sold each year is far greater than the dollar income and profit derived from their sale.

In this light, it is especially regrettable that paperback publishing had several difficult years in the second half of the 1960s. Although between 300 million and 350 million copies of mass-market paperbacks were sold annually, some of their major producers had rather rough going. The trouble came not from a lack of buyers, but rather from excessive payments for reprint rights and from costly competition for market outlets. Some of this trouble was offset by newfound success with what have been dubbed "instant paperbacks"—meaning quick reprints in large quantities of certain public documents of wide popular appeal, such as the report of the Warren Commission. These quick reprints, in some instances, have put paperback books into fairly direct competition with the news media, and thus have given a "new dimension" to the book industry.

In fairness, the quotation from the *Times* is true of fiction; still, fiction represents less than 10 per cent of the present annual output of new books. In any case, it appears that the *Times* reviewer, like most other outside observers of the publishing scene, was totally unaware of the great hardcover explosion that had occurred on the nether side of his world.

The striking aspect of the book market as a total aggregate is that, while the annual production of new books of all kinds increased by only 40 per cent in the three decades that ended in 1959, the increase in the subsequent ten years was over 100 per cent. It was inevitable, of course, that there would come with this sharp increase an intensification of the perennial cry that too many books are being produced. Unfortunately, this cry has been repeated through even the years of the book industry's greatest and soundest growth. It comes from certain breast-beating publishers who loftily call for "fewer and better books." What they plainly want, of course, is to cut out the other fellow's trash. Often they want also to eliminate all those dull "nonbooks" that no one ever sees.

Nearly all these advocates of fewer and better books are literary buffs. Observing the publishing scene narrowly, they look no deeper than the rising total numbers of books produced annually, and then declare positively that the market cannot possibly absorb so many new titles. Often they wail, correlatively, that quality is being sacrificed for quantity, that bad books are driving out good books, and that the book industry is going to hell in a crassly overloaded handbasket. Such talk has always been popular with literary audiences and with reporters looking for stories about the charismatic world of publishing. Yet, it has never made sense, and it never made less sense than in the 1960s. For example, how could the great increase in scientific and technical books have anything whatever to do with the quality of the new fiction of the decade? And did the slowdown in published general literature really improve its quality? No, the postulate of fewer and better books patently has no general value as a working principle for the industry.

Far from being choked up in recent years, book markets have actually been expanding rapidly in size and receptivity. In fact, sales of almost all kinds of books climbed sharply through the 1960s. In that decade, total dollar volume of industry sales increased by almost 150 per cent, from $1.106-billion to $2.760-billion. Much of this gain came, to be sure, from higher prices and inflated dollars—about a fourth of it, roughly. With an adjustment for this inflation factor, the real ten-year gain was about 110 per cent. In the same period, the country's Gross National Product, after application of the same kind of implicit deflators, grew by only 50 per cent. It is clear, then, that the book industry's growth was far greater than that of the nation's economy as a whole.

In the longer view, looking back through the earlier years of sea change, the book industry as a whole in a way scored a truly remarkable long-term growth record, but in another way it seemed not to keep up with its true potential. Some interesting comparative figures on forty-year growth trends appear. According to these figures, the book industry in sales growth again far exceeded the long-term growth of the national economy. (The dollar figures for both book sales and GNP are adjusted to 1929 values—and who won't be shocked to see that the 2.760-billion of 1969 sales dollars converts to only 1.290-billion of 1929 sales dollars?)

On the other hand, looking at the long-term growth in the nation's population of college graduates, one can ask whether the book industry has not failed to make the most of its growing opportunity. Assuming that college graduates represent the country's hard core of book buyers, it appears that publishers have not kept up with the natural growth of their markets. (In the forty-year period, the college graduate population increased eightfold, while book sales increased only sixfold.) Indeed, it can be fairly said that the industry as a whole has been riding rather than making the long wave of its good fortune.

The publishers of educational and reference books rode high on the wave through the 1960s. The injection of massive federal funds into education and library budgets caused a soaring of sales that reached a truly dizzying height in 1966: In that year, an aberration in government disbursement practice caused most of the funds for two federal fiscal years to be spent in the one calendar year. In the following three years, there was a disappointing slackening in the sale of textbooks and related instructional materials, and of encyclopedias, dictionaries, atlases, etc. Still the publishers of such works, always more prosperous than general book publishers, never had it better. In the decade, their sales increased by 156 per cent. Their net profits failed to soar proportionately, largely because the costs of intensified competition exacted a heavy toll as more and more firms rushed to what was for them a newfound and unfamiliar mother lode.

Many inside observers were bemused by one particular behavioral response of educational publishers in the 1960s. This was the alacrity and enthusiasm with which many reputedly turgid textbook firms answered the call of educators for more and larger multi-unit instructional packages. When teachers began some years ago to move away from the conventional textbook as a monolithic instructional instrument, many textbook publishers pushed to the head of the parade. Sure, they could supply rather quickly the needed multi-unit packages containing core text materials, supplementary readers, laboratory manuals, workbooks, tests, and whatever else was wanted. Some could, and did, supply even larger and more costly multimedia packages (including films and tapes), which were scooped up by the more affluent school systems and certain government-financed special programs. All this explains in part the juiced-up growth in the educational publishers' sales volume. It also explains how many an old-line textbook firm quickly acquired a refreshing stimulant and a higher sense of professional responsibility. Thus again did progress and prosperity go hand in hand.

The curious phenomenon that helped to produce in the 1960s an inordinate increase of scientific and technical books had a powerful effect on publishing through many years; I have called this, by analogy, the "twigging phenomenon." It can best be described as the continual furcation and fractionation of scientific and technical knowledge, and, hence, of the subject matter of books in these fields. Naturally, this endless fractionation has resulted in the publication each year of hundreds of highly specialized books for groups of readers that are no larger today than they were ten or twenty years ago, despite the fact that our total population of scientists and engineers has almost quadrupled in the past two decades. The specialists need and write books on proliferated and refined subjects; the technical publisher who properly serves his clientele must, of course, publish them in proliferated numbers.

In my analogy, the subjects of such books represent the twigs on the tree of scientific and technical knowledge. Although the tree itself is perhaps five times as big as it was twenty years ago, the twigs are still the same size—and so are the markets for the specialized books. This phenomenon explains in large part why publishers of scientific and technical books have had to scramble to keep up with their markets, and why these particular markets have so readily absorbed the greatly escalated numbers of new titles published in the past decade.

Finally, another, but not so subtle, phenomenon that worked with force on the book industry in the 1960s was the wide impulse for corporate mergers and for related marriages, in some instances, between the electronics industry and book publishing. Many of the mergers were impelled by "cross-media" marriages, and all the latter were inspired by rationalized dreams of synergistically induced extra-dividend happiness. The industrial giants (hardware grooms) happily took to wife many carefully selected bedmates among the available book firms (software brides). "We have the hardware, they have the software," General Sarnoff is reported to have said when RCA acquired Random House in 1965.

Then what happened? It is, of course, too early to say for sure, but two things now seem quite obvious to insiders.

First, the hardware-software marriages, though widely celebrated in the press and greatly feared by many in the book industry, have been tried and found wanting. The synergistic effect has not come off as expected; to date, the unions have been disappointingly unproductive of profitable hybrids. Clearly, computers and books have not mixed so readily and effectively as many people believed they would. Consequently, some high-powered grooms already have been heard to grumble about their brides, many of which were bought at quite fancy prices. At the same time, many relatively low-powered book publishers have unexpectedly been enjoying life as millionaires. Thus, by the end of the decade, the miscegenetic marriages were rapidly going out of style. Maybe we shall see some annulments or spin-off divorces in the 1970s. Even so, many publishing houses will have been provided, meanwhile, with more adequate working capital and more progressive management.

Second, the many mergers and cross-media marriages have not resulted, as widely supposed, in a baneful concentration of book publishing in the hands of a few large and powerful corporate complexes and conglomerates. To be sure, many independent houses, both large and small, have become operating units in a wide variety of much larger corporate structures. But, at the same time, many new and growing firms have come along to take their places in the ranks of the independents. In fact, contrary to popular belief, these ranks have been more than filled every year. Actually, there were more independent book houses in the United States at the end than at the beginning of the 1960s, just as there were more at the end than at the beginning of the 1950s. Anyone who doubts this statement can be self-convinced by counting the number of independent firms listed in *Literary Market Place* (Bowker's annual guide to book publishing) for certain years. He will find that there were 508 in 1949; 638 in 1959; and 675 in 1969.

No, the book industry is not about to be gobbled up or monopolized by a few large and sinister industrial octopuses—not, at least, for some time to come.

THE NEW MOVIES

The great Hollywood empire that ruled American tastes for more than half a century lies in dust, its tyrannical moguls dead or deposed, its back lots empty, its sound stages still, its ranks diminished and in disarray. But out of the ruins of the city of dreams a new film industry is rising.

The studios have become, for the most part, financing and distribution arms for a proliferating army of independent filmmakers. And these new producers and directors, who account for three out of every four American movies today, no longer need the facilities of any big studio. Instead, backed by a new mobile technology, they are shooting in Vancouver, B.C., and Taos, N.M., in New York, New Jersey and New Orleans, in motor inns and on motor bikes.

Today's movies are being shaped by a nexus of forces that no one clearly understands. But certainly among the most powerful of these is the gradual emergence of a new audience, demonstrably younger (62 per cent of today's movie-goers are between 12 and 30), better educated, more selective and, most important of all, drastically smaller than the mass audience that supported the old Hollywood system. Over the past decade, it is the needs, tastes and temperament of this new audience that have given birth to a new kind of American movie.

Inevitably, there are those who see all new movies as signs of a golden age and those who see them, with their themes of dissent and alienation, their anything-goes sexuality, as more false idols of a decadent time. The truth is more complicated and more important. The new film focuses not on some backlot fantasy landscape, but on Times Square and Queens Boulevard, on the basements, bowling alleys and backyards of Middle America, on American subcultures like the motorcycle-racing circuit and the world of the oil rigger, the urban underworld, and the violence of the American streets.

These films feature men whose ordinary faces would have condemned them to the secondary status of character actors only a decade ago—like the frail, baldish Jack Nicholson and the unglamorous Dustin Hoffman—and have enlisted the considerable talents of new actresses whose unconventional good looks are as offbeat as the

Newsweek gave permission for its December 7, 1970 cover story on American films to be edited for this book. The original article contains many personality sketches of both new stars and producers. Condensed from *Newsweek*, copyright 1970.

roles they play. The life-styles and attitudes of these new heroes and heroines reflect the dissident outlook of the younger directors, who themselves question the prevailing values of American life. A personal cinema is being born, and in its films can be read the search for a better way of life.

The first flickerings of this new itinerant industry have already been seen in such successes as Dennis Hopper's "Easy Rider" and Robert Rafelson's "Five Easy Pieces," in "M*A*S*H" and "Joe" and "Diary of a Mad Housewife," in "Little Fauss and Big Halsy." But these are just the harbingers of a whole new wave of American films, conceived and developed by screenwriters and directors, not producers and studio chiefs, and focused in a personal way on American traditions and values. "There's only one place where American films are today," says David Picker, the bright, bearish, 39-year-old president of United Artists, "and that's in the heads of the people who are making them." Echoes Ned Tanen, who presides over independent productions at Universal, "The initiative has passed from the business people to the creative people."

This power shift still leaves the studios holding the trump card—money—but the situation is more open than it has been since the earliest informal days of American films. "A couple of years ago, if I wanted to direct a film, I couldn't have gotten to see anyone of any importance at the studios," says 31-year-old Richard Wechsler, co-producer of "Five Easy Pieces," who will soon be directing his first film, "A Way of Life." "Now I can go to the head of any studio and present my idea. That doesn't mean they'll finance it, but at least they're listening."

This sudden attentiveness is born not of charity but necessity. Profits are down, production schedules have been cut back, the old formulas about what films should make money no longer apply and no new formulas have been found. Panic haunts the executive offices, and confusion reigns at even the most profitable studios. "The rule book has been thrown away," concurs Richard Zanuck, the 35-year-old son of Darryl Zanuck and president of Twentieth Century-Fox, which has turned its sagging fortunes around with successes as varied as "M*A*S*H" and "Patton." "Today almost anything goes. Frankly, I go on what pleases me personally because I just can't tell what pleases the audience any more." [Editor's Note: Zanuck was removed as president of Twentieth Century Fox in a 1971 shakeup which also involved his famous father; "Patton" swept the Academy Awards with "old hero" George C. Scott in protest of the system, not attending the ceremony but instead sending the Oscar to a museum.]

Through this massive hole ripped in studio confidence have rushed all kinds of new talents. Suddenly, established actors are getting a shot at directing, like Alan Arkin, who has just finished filming Jules Feiffer's "Little Murders," and Jack Nicholson, who has completed Jeremy Larner's "Drive, He Said." Lawrence Turman, who produced "The Graduate," is now directing another Charles Webb novel, "The Marriage of a Young Stockbroker," and Monte Hellman, for years admired for his low-budget Westerns, is shooting a major production for Universal, "Two-Lane Blacktop," the story of a cross-country car race.

Screenwriter Charles Eastman refused for years to let the studios shoot his screenplays unless he directed. Finally, the author of "Little Fauss and Big Halsy" is directing "All-American Boy," his own story of an amateur boxer, starring Jon Voight. And Eastman's sister, Carol, who wrote "Five Easy Pieces" under the pen name of Adrien Joyce, will be directing her own screenplay, "The Second Interval."

The success of "Easy Rider" has opened Hollywood to young talents with no track record at all. Jeff Young, 27, showed a twenty-minute film to Paramount Pictures two years ago. Now he is putting the finishing touches on a $500,000 production of Richard Farina's "Been Down So Long It Looks Like Up to Me." Warner Bros. will release the futuristic "THX 1138," the collaboration of 25-year-old San Francisco-based director George Lucas and 26-year-old screenwriter John Milius, who has also written movies that will star Robert Redford and Frank Sinatra. "Today a guy can walk off the street and ask us to look at his $65,000 film," says John Calley, the 69-year-old production chief at Warner Bros. "The situation is wide open."

From the 1920s until after the second world war, Hollywood was a closed shop. Under the autocratic leadership of men like Harry Cohn at Columbia, Louis B. Mayer at M-G-M and Jack Warner at Warner Bros., Hollywood monopolized the movie industry, making virtually every American film on its own back lots. It held in thrall an American public that cheerfully spent 80 cents of every spectator-amusement dollar at the movies. And, to satisfy this massive consumption, the major companies devised an assembly-line studio system that could turn out a film a week on the premises.

Independent production was all but impossible. The banks abetted the Hollywood hegemony by lending money almost exclusively to the big studios. And, even if a producer could find the funds and facilities to make his own movie, where was he to show it since the studios owned or controlled most of the movie houses? But already, by the late 1940s, the autocracy was cracking. The star players rebelled, and the contract system collapsed. In 1950, the Supreme Court ruled that the studios restrained trade by owning chains of movie theaters. And then came television. The old audience and the sure-fire moneymaker vanished forever.

After a period of panic and sharply declining revenues through the 1950s, the studios met the challenge by turning out the kind of wide-screen, multimillion-dollar spectaculars that television couldn't rival. In the mid-'60s "The Sound of Music," which earned a record $72 million, salvaged Fox—and nearly ruined the industry by fathering a series of disasters aimed at imitating its success: "Dr. Dolittle," "Star!," "Goodbye, Mr. Chips." "We all spent too much money," concedes Richard Zanuck, "and we're just now coming out from under these enormous inventories."

At the same time, the success of Federico Fellini's "La Dolce Vita" attested to the presence of a large and educated audience eager for films with something to say. Frank and Eleanor Perry's low-budget success "David and Lisa" in 1962 demonstrated that America didn't have to rely on foreign films to bring in these people. "Some filmmakers realized that there was and still is a large audience whose interests had been left untapped," says screenwriter Buck Henry. "As the mass audience moved toward TV, an effort was made to accommodate these special tastes."

One such effort, "The Graduate," rewrote the moviemaking rules. "Every studio turned it down," recalls Henry, who wrote the screenplay. "They thought you had to have a movie star and they didn't think Anne Bancroft qualified. They thought you needed a young star to play Benjamin and no such animal existed. And they were suspicious of making a movie from a minor novel. But, of course, when the picture succeeded, all that thinking changed. 'The Graduate' made possible motion pictures in which the theme is the star and the star is the director."

Suddenly, a whole new set of faces appeared in leading roles: Dustin Hoffman, Jack Nicholson, Richard Benjamin, Alan Arkin, Donald Sutherland, Jon Voight, Elliott Gould, Dennis Hopper, Stacy Keach, Frank Langella and Gene Wilder. "Ten years ago, they wanted the kind of face that only a few hundred people in the world possess—the Hollywood face," says Wilder. "They didn't want people who looked like the people in the audience. Now they realize they can make money by letting the audience see actors with whom they can identify." Or, as Richard Zanuck puts it: "We're hiring the uglies." [. . .]

After the runaway success of "Easy Rider," the studios started operating on the slogan "Make it for under $1 million." But with the success of "Patton," which cost $12.5 million, and the $10.5 million "Airport," the industry returned to its present state of confusion. "There is definitely a place for big films today," asserts Stanley Schneider, president of Columbia Pictures, which is currently shooting "Nicholas and Alexandra" for a scheduled $8 million. "But when I say 'big,' I don't mean the $15 million to $20 million film. We can't afford to risk a company's life on a film that big."

Even if the major studios wanted to turn out one blockbuster after another, today's tight money market would preclude it. Fox, which spent $100 million on movies in 1969—including $25 million on "Tora! Tora! Tora!"—plans to spend only $25 million altogether for the coming year. Paramount, which used to be good for 30 films annually, will have turned out only fourteen in 1970. And the American film industry as a whole expects to distribute no more than 250 movies this year, or half of what Hollywood cranked out in its heyday. One result of this lowered production is a shortage of supply for the nation's movie theaters. Recently, Variety's list of the 50 top-grossing films of the week was led by "The Professionals," "In Cold Blood" and "It's a Mad, Mad, Mad, Mad World"—all reissues.

This cutdown in production has been dictated by a shift in audience attendance as well. "People used to go to the movies," says David Picker of United Artists. "Now they only go to see a particular movie. And that difference has changed the movie business altogether." Indeed, only 15 million Americans went to the movies weekly last year as against 87 million in 1947, before the advent of television. And this shrinkage has hurt everyone. M-G-M is in the deepest trouble. After auctioning off such sentimental keepsakes as the witch's hat from "The Wizard of Oz" and the Unsinkable Molly Brown's brass bed, M-G-M is still working off a $35.4 million loss last year. Some observers believe that if the new, $13.6 million David Lean film, "Ryan's Daughter," bombs at the box office, the Metro Lion may have roared his last.

Fox and Paramount are also digging out from under heavy debts. But even those companies that remain relatively prosperous, like Columbia, Warner Bros. and United Artists, have been forced by the selectivity of the new audience to become more selective themselves. "There's simply no point in financing a film unless it's got a chance of becoming important," says Universal's Ned Tanen. "If a film isn't successful today, it's a dead flop. There's no in-between."

This call for selectivity has accounted for the rise to power within the industry of a new and more discerning kind of executive whose artistic judgment is often as crucial as his business acumen. . . .

But the changes in the American film industry go beyond the transfer of class taste and the rise of new leadership. "What's being established right now is an entirely new business," declares UA's David Picker, "altogether unlike the movie business 30 years ago. The crisis that we're passing through right now—the frustrations and reorganizations—are basically healthy signs. Everybody is reevaluating what movies should be made for in the light of realistic economics."

No one has practiced the new movie economics more diligently than 27-year-old Dennis Friedland and Chris Dewey, age 26, who have run their company, Cannon Films, with the cool precision of insurance actuaries. Cannon began with a $30,000 sexploitation film called "Inga," went on to make sixteen more minibudget films and finally hit the jackpot with "Joe," a portrait of a Middle American that cost $300,000 and promises to return millions. "We believe that any movie can be made and made well for $500,000 or less," says Friedland, who went into the movie business straight out of law school and now has his father on the payroll. "Before we make a film we analyze the marketplace. If we make a motorcycle film, we want to know the most money one has ever made and the least and the average. Then we figure a budget that will pretty well guarantee a return on our investment."[. . .]

Advances in technology have permitted producers and directors to shoot their films without once venturing onto studio property. "Nobody uses sound stages any more," says Robert Rafelson, director of "Five Easy Pieces." "Instead, they use the Cinemobile Mark IV, a movie studio on wheels developed by 37-year-old Fouad Said, a diminutive Arab immigrant who has revolutionized filmmaking. The Cinemobile has replaced the cumbersome and costly caravan of trucks that used to accompany films on location. This 35-foot, bus-like behemoth contains dressing rooms and bathrooms, space for crew of 50 and an armada of lightweight equipment that, in itself, saves money. . . .

With these new movies, a new hero has emerged. He is often a surrogate for the director himself, outside society, alienated by mainstream American values, searching for his identity as he moves across the face of America. Like Jack Nicholson's Bobby Dupea in "Five Easy Pieces" or Robert Redford's Halsy Knox or the wandering cyclists of "Easy Rider," these new heroes are most often losers whose heroism is measured not in their ability to triumph but to survive. "In the old movies," says Richard Benjamin, who will play the lead in "The Marriage of a Young Stockbroker," "you were a hero if you cleaned up Dodge City. Today you're a hero if you somehow manage to keep your life your own."

Even Redford, whose charismatic good looks and romantic films suggest firm roots in an old-fashioned Hollywood tradition, is playing the superhero with a new, contemporary twist. "I want to make movies about a guy who is outside society, who is flawed and a loner," says Redford, "the kind of guy who appears to be a hero but isn't. The flawed hero is the movie I'm living myself."

In many ways, the new hero grows legitimately out of the films of the 1940s and '50s in which Mr. Smith went to Washington to stand alone against Congress, Shane rode in from nowhere and rode off at the end to nowhere, in which Humphrey Bogart followed his own independent, Hemingwayish ethic. But the old heroes, played by men like Fonda and Stewart and Cooper and Gable, may have been alienated but they couldn't talk about it. "It wasn't part of the male myth to intellectualize," says director Alan J. Pakula. "The old heroes didn't articulate their predicament." Adds Buck Henry: "Now they're beginning to talk about things that have to do with their own behavior. Heroes can now be intellectuals, which they never were in American films. Perhaps it's because, until recently, the audience was so profoundly anti-intellectual itself. But the younger audience identifies with a melodrama of ideas."

The new hero often stands squarely in opposition to society's accepted values, whether that challenge takes the form of the irreverence expressed by Elliott Gould and Donald Sutherland as the medics in "M*A*S*H" or the direct political action embraced by Jon Voight as "The Revolutionary." "The movie heroes I grew up with were the guys who killed Japs," says Gould, who is starring in Ingmar Bergman's first English-language film, "The Touch." "The hero today is someone who questions, who goes to jail instead of joining the Army, who demonstrates and winds up saying, 'Screw God Bless America'." "The old heroes used to protect society from its enemies," says Paul Newman, who is starring in the film of Ken Kesey's novel "Sometimes a Great Nation." "Now it's society itself that's the enemy." [. . .]

THE BOMP: WAY OF LIFE, NOT A SIDESHOW

Greil Marcus

The Beatles revolutionized rock 'n' roll by bringing it back to its sources and traditions. The new era, in America, began with a song, a joyous song, which had what one friend of mine calls the "takeover sound"—music that breaks from the radio and is impossible to resist. The first notes of *I Want To Hold Your Hand* were there, day after day. Everyone knew something different had happened. For months, every new Beatles song had part of that first record in it—that was just the way you had to hear it; that's what a new beginning, a sense of a new beginning means. All the rules were changing, as they'd changed in the fifties. Like the Beatles, groups had to write their own lyrics and music, and play their own instruments—they had to be as involved as possible. With the coming of the Rolling Stones, a new pattern was set: for the first time in the entertainment world, singers and musicians would appear, in photographs and on stage, in the clothes they wore every day. The music and the mystique were coming closer and closer to life as we lived it. For the new groups and for those of us who listened, rock 'n' roll became more a way of life than a sideshow. There was a hint that those stars up on stage might even be the same kind of people as the ones in the audience. Rock became more comfortable and more exciting at the same time.

Rock 'n' roll seeks to do something that earlier popular music had always denied—to establish and confirm, to heighten and deepen, to create and re-create the present moment. Rock, as a medium, knows that it is only up to a certain point that this can be done. To keep a moment of time alive it's necessary to make a song new every time it's performed, every time it's played, every time it's heard. When a song gets stale it only fills time, marks time, expends itself over two or three or ten minutes, but it doesn't *obliterate* time and allow you to move freely in the space that the music can give you. When a song is alive, the mind and the body respond—they race, merge with the music, find an idea or an emotion, and return. When a song is dead, the mind only waits for it to be over, hoping that something living will follow.

Excerpted from "Who Put the Bomp" from *Rock and Roll Will Stand*, Beacon Press, 1969, copyright Greil Marcus, this is one of many pieces about music and community authored by Mr. Marcus. A student in American political thought at Berkeley, he has been an editor on the *Rolling Stone* staff, coauthored *Woodstock*, edited *Rock and Roll Will Stand* and has most recently contributed to *Creem*.

Judy Garland has sung *Over the Rainbow* some thousands of times; there's a man who keeps count. The tally is published in the newspapers occasionally, like the Gross National Product, which is really what it is: Judy Garland's GNP. You measure her progress that way. The same kind of mentality that demands this tune from Judy Garland, the same kind of mentality that makes her want to sing it, made a Santa Monica grandmother watch *The Sound of Music* over seven hundred times, once a day, at five o'clock. Listening to a rock song over and over, seeing *A Hard Day's Night* a dozen times, isn't the same—with that you participate when you must, stay away when you desire. The mind is free to remake the experience, but it isn't a prisoner. You don't demand the same songs from Bob Dylan every time he gives a concert—you understand that he's a human being, a changing person, and you try to translate his newness into your own.

This movement of the re-creation of the moment, with the constant changing of the dynamic, is mostly the result of the radio, the way it gives one music. When a song is new, and you like it, when it possesses that intangible grace that makes it part of you, you wait and hope all day that it will come out of the radio and into your ears. You listen, stop what you're doing, and participate. Finally, you'll get tired of it, ignoring the song when it comes on. Months or years later, when it returns as an oldie, the initial experience will be repeated, but with understanding, with a sense of how it all happened. You can't pretend that grace is there when it's not. When *Like A Rolling Stone* was released, I liked it, but I got tired of it pretty quickly. A few months later I put it on the phonograph and it jumped out and claimed me. I think it's the greatest rock 'n' roll record ever made—but I didn't decide that, I accepted it.

An incredible number of songs provide this sort of experience. Because of this, because of the way songs are heard, with an intensity that one provides for himself, they become part of one's mind, one's thought and subconscious, and they shape one's mental patterns. People sense this: there is a conscious effort by the members of the generation I'm talking about to preserve and heighten the experiences of rock 'n' roll, to intensify the connection between the individual and his music, between one's group of friends and the music they share. That effort takes the form of games and contests. These games reinforce the knowledge that this music is ours, that it doesn't and can't belong to anyone else. The kids who'll follow us will have a lot of it, but they can never really know the absolute beginnings of rock 'n' roll—that's our treasure. The generations that came before us are simply somewhere else. In a strange, protective way, people who are now in middle age aren't *allowed* to possess the music we have. When the Beatles were becoming acceptable, listenable for adults, with *Michelle* and *Yesterday*, the foursome responded with hard rock and experimental music, with sitars and tape machines and driving guitars. *Day Tripper* and *Strawberry Fields Forever* blasted the Beatles back home to students, kids, intellectuals, dropouts. The exclusiveness of rock 'n' roll is well-guarded. If the adults can take it, we'll probably reject it. In a way we want to share it, but in the end, it's better that we can't. If we're to be different, we'd best protect the sources of our differences, whenever they are re-created. That is what the Beatles did when they sang *I'm Down*, the toughest rock 'n' roll since Little Richard—they returned to the beginnings, even as they stayed far ahead of everyone else.

And we preserve our possession with games. As small boys quiz each other on baseball statistics, young people today are constantly renewing each other's memories of rock 'n' roll. If you can't identify an old song by the first few bars, something's wrong. "Who did *Come Go With Me?*" "The Del-Vikings, 1957." That's a conversation between Yale and Harvard football players, caught on the field. Once, in an elevator on the Berkeley campus, a friend and I were singing "Who put the bomp in the bomp de-bomp de-bomp, who put the dang in the rama lamma ding dang, who was . . ." ". . . that man, I'd like to shake his hand . . ." joined in another passenger. "He made my baby fall in love with me!" sang a girl entering the elevator, completing the verse. Another friend of mine once made a list of all the Beatle songs released up to the time, about eighty then, identifying the songs only by the first letter of each word in the title. He quizzed everyone on it. Two years later I asked him about the list— he remembered, and started the game all over again. Then there was the guy who, when about twelve, set up an incredible routine for responding to the current hits. He'd budget enough money to buy five records a week, and he'd buy the ones he dug the most. Then, when he got them home, having also picked up a copy of the most recent Top Forty survey, the ritual would begin: he'd draw elaborate tables, as he correlated his taste with that of the record-buying public, re-drawing the graphs each week as a song moved up or down the charts; and he had elaborate sets of figures establishing and revising the position of his all-time favorites on the same sort of scale. The next week would bring more new songs, adding to his mathematical history of his love for rock 'n' roll. And then there was the disk jockey on an FM rock show who played some records, and then announced: "You've just heard *Since I Don't Have You* by the Skyliners, and *Ain't That Just Like Me* by the Searchers, both of which formerly tied for the all-time record in repetitions of a final rock 'n' roll chorus, and *A Quick One While He's Away*, by the Who, a song that *destroyed* that record by going over *thirty!*" In live performance, the Who have taken *A Quick One* past one hundred. Anyone who's seen them do it knows why that's important.

Rock 'n' roll has always had an awareness of its music as a special thing, reserved for a certain audience. There are dozens of songs *about* rock 'n' roll, a game within a game. There's *Roll Over Beethoven* and *Rock and Roll Music* by Chuck Berry, Little Richard's *All Around the World (Rock 'n' Roll Is All They Play)*, the magnificent *Do You Believe in Magic* by the Lovin' Spoonful, and the classic *It Will Stand* by the Showmen, released at a time when it looked like rock and roll might not:

> They're always trying to ruin
> Forgive them, for they know not what they're doin'
> Cause rock and roll forever will stand. . .

The vitality and determination of these songs, that consciousness of rock as a special thing, something to be cherished, has reached the listener, who might have come to it on his own anyway, and helped him into the greatest game of all, the use of lyrics and phrases, verbal, "nonsense," and musical, as metaphors to describe and enclose situations, events, and ideas. "Da do ron ron' to you too," wrote a reader in the letters column of a rock newspaper, responding to an offensive article on Phil Spector's Ronettes, and revealing at the same time the wealth of undefined and undefinable meaning possessed by that phrase David Susskind just couldn't understand.

This is a great game that never stops; and it's more than a game, it's a way of responding to life. Situations are "set"; one puts himself down; reveals an irony; takes comfort in the knowledge that someone has been there before him. There is a feeling that if we could only hear enough, and remember all we hear, that the answers would be there on the thousands of rock 'n' roll records that have brought us to the present. It is the intensity of this game of metaphors that allows one to feel this way, to have this kind of innocent confidence. It's not that people haven't used metaphors before; "metaphors," as opposed to "explanations," have been drawn from all of literature and art for the same kinds of reasons. What is different is that rock 'n' roll is a medium that is ever-present, thanks to the radio, and repetitive, thanks to Top Forty and oldies and record players, so that the habit of using metaphors in this way comes so naturally it is a characteristic of how the more articulate part of this generation thinks at any time and responds to any situation. The fact that rock 'n' roll is a body of myths private to this generation only heightens the fact.

People quote lines and phrases from songs to their elders, who can't possibly have any idea of what they're talking about; they quote them to friends, who do know. A line from Dylan can stop whatever action is in progress and return the group to the warmth of a mental community. Since the renaissance of rock 'n' roll, people are finding out that what they thought was their private fetish is the style of a generation. There is a shared body of myths, a common style of feeling and responding, a love of a music that allows one to feel the totality of an experience without missing the nuances and secrets—and as we become aware of our myths we deepen them and practice our own mythmaking. The metaphors drawn from these myths aren't just a matter of fitting the proper words to the proper situation, but of knowing the music is there, somehow, in the same place that the idea is, that somewhere the two have met, and that you have been allowed to see the connection. It is a way of thinking that allows one to give mood and emotion the force of fact, to believe one's instinctual reaction more than someone else's statistical analysis or logical argument.

The music is all around. There's a radio in every car, at least one in every apartment. They are on much of the time—maybe all day. There's a record player, more and more, as people become aware of their music, finding "Oldies But Goodies" and "Greatest Hits" albums on it, as it also plays today's music. A hit song, one you like, is heard at least a hundred times. For the month or so it's popular, it becomes part of the day's experience. If it's on a record you buy, you have control over that part of your experience, instead of receiving it as a surprise from the radio. But playing a favorite song on your own record player lacks the grateful thrill of hearing it cascade from the radio as a gift of smoky airwaves. Rock exists—something makes one want not to control it, but to accept and experience it as it comes. After a record has passed from the charts, it will come back, as an oldie, every once in a while. You only need the rarity of renewal. It's like the surprise of hearing the Beatles' *All You Need Is Love* for the first time, with all those old songs, some virtually legends, jumping and twisting in and out of the chorus: *Greensleeves, In the Mood*, and a line from *She Loves You* with just a hint of *Yesterday*.

The incessant, happy repetition of words and music that is provided when a song is a hit on the radio or a favorite on the record player makes the song part of one's mind. The musical patterns and lyrics become second nature, as they merge and separate. The fact and experience of repetition, a song half-heard, half-enjoyed, a quick turning up the sound when a favorite chord comes, then withdrawal—this makes a difference as to how one thinks or subconsciously reacts to a situation. Once a song becomes part of you it is accepted. Then you are more naturally inclined to take that song, or any song, as a metaphor, to "name" the place you're in, and leave it at that. A person who feels this wouldn't employ *For What It's Worth* by the Buffalo Springfield to help explain the Sunset Strip riots, as did two writers in the *New York Review of Books;* he'd just say, "Listen to *For What It's Worth—*it's all there." The habit and facility of taking metaphors from music, taking music *as* metaphor, and even more important, using these metaphors in a simple and absolute way, is, I think, the result of the musical experiences I've tried to describe. The metaphor isn't even principally the "meaning" of the words to a song; more often it is that the music, or a phrase, or two words heard, jumping out as the rest are lost, seem to fit one's emotional perception of a situation, event, or idea. A pattern of notes or the way in which a few words happen to fit together hit a chord of memory and a perception takes place, a perception which structures and "rationalizes" itself into a metaphor, not on the basis of a "logical" relationship, but because of the power of music and song to reach into the patterns of memory and response. "If you could just listen to it, you'd know what I mean, completely. It's all there."

"It's all there" is an expression used so often in the making of a song or a musical experience into a metaphor it's as if some members of this generation had a secret language, with this phrase as the signal that an exclusive kind of discourse is about to begin. But no two people ever hear the same song in the same way, or connect the song with the same things. An organ movement in the "live" recording of Dylan's *Just Like Tom Thumb's Blues* is to me the terrifying presence of an evil serpent, swallowing the singer; to someone else, that part of the music slips by unheard, and the notes of the guitar become tears.

What this means is that a strange kind of communication must take place. In one sense, the communication is perfect—one person has complete trust in the other when he is told that a song holds all the truth of a moment or an experience. They both know it; they both accept the validity of the metaphor. Thus, on a non-verbal, non-visual level, they understand each other and the way in which they both think, and they share the knowledge that only certain people can understand them. They realize the privacy and the publicness of their communication. The repetition, over and over, of a two or three minute musical experience has given them an effortless metaphorical consciousness. One knows what the other is talking about. There is an identification, and a sharing. It is the language of people who comprehend instinctually and immediately. To know "where it's at" isn't rational, it's automatic. "You can't talk about it, you have to groove with it." Of course that can be valid. Two people may try to talk about it, perhaps; but they'll get closer to the truth by placing the experience in front of them, starting with a shared understanding of a common purpose and an unspoken language of intuition and emotion, ending with a respect for the experience as well as for each other. Thus the communication is perfect, among those lucky enough to be a part of it.

But on another level, communication is impossibly difficult and confused. One person will not hear what another has heard in a song. It is hard, and wrong, to force another to put specific meanings on music he can hear for himself. It will bring forth associations for him as well. They both know the truth is there; that is not in doubt. What's there? Who can tell? I know, you know—what else matters? What is vital is that the situation has been captured, robbed, made livable by understanding with a depth that is private and public, perfectly and impossibly communicable. Perfectly communicable in that there is mutual trust that the situation is *ours*, that we have each and together made it our own; it can't destroy us; it can only be relived and reexperienced with each hearing of our metaphor. Impossibly communicable in that we never know exactly what our friend *is* experiencing. But that can be accepted, when one can create or be given metaphors—imperfect knowledge that is perfect understanding, our kind of roots to joy and tragedy. In John Barth's *Giles Goat-Boy*, the various characters of the novel all go to the theatre, where the Barthian paraphrase of *Oedipus Rex* ("Taliped Decanus") is presented. All know that the drama has affected them profoundly, but none knows just how, for himself or for the others. Yet all trust the play to give them the metaphors by which they will shape and interpret their lives, their actions, and the actions of the others. Each knows, by grace of the gift of art, that they will accept, instinctually and non-rationally, the validity of the others' pictures. All trust the play, as we trust our music. The Greeks perhaps lived with this kind of depth, within this pattern of myth. The same treasure the Greeks of the tragic era possessed is, in some prosaic way, ours again.

Out of the experience of growing up with rock 'n' roll, we have found out that rock has more to give us than we ever knew. With a joyful immediacy, it has taught us to participate with ourselves, and with each other. A repetitive history of songs and secrets has given us a memory patterned by games, within a consciousness of a shared experience exclusive to our generation. Fifteen years of a beat, and thousands of songs that had just enough humor in those words that are so hard to hear, have brought us a style of thought that allows ideas to create themselves out of feeling and emotion, a style of thought that accepts metaphors as myths. Those myths, when we find them, are strong enough to sustain belief and action, strong enough to allow us to fashion a sense of reality out of those things that are important to us. This is not an attempt to "justify" rock 'n' roll by linking it to something "bigger" than itself—we have nothing bigger than rock 'n' roll, and nothing more is needed to "justify" it than a good song.

The kind of thinking I've tried to describe, the manner of response, the consciousness and unconsciousness of metaphor, the subtle confidence of mystique that leads to the permanence of myth—such an intellectual mood, I think, will have a deep and lasting effect on the vision and the style of the "students" of this generation. They will, and already do, embrace an instinctual kind of knowledge. This is partly a reaction against a programmed, technological culture—but so is rock 'n' roll, a dynamic kaleidoscope of sound that constantly invents new contexts within which to celebrate its own exhilarating power to create a language of emotional communication, sending messages to the body as well as to the mind, reaching the soul in the end.

What rock 'n' roll has done to us won't leave us. Faced with the bleakness of social and political life in America, we will return again and again to rock 'n' roll, as a place of creativity and renewal, to return from it with a strange, media-enforced consciousness increasingly a part of our thinking and our emotions, two elements of life that we will less and less trouble to separate.

This is a kind of freedom we are learning about. Affecting our own perspectives—artistic, social, and political—it makes the tangible and the factual that much more reprehensible, that much more deadening. The intellectual leap, the habit of free association, the facility of making a single rock 'n' roll metaphor the defining idea for a situation or a time of one's life—that is the kind of thinking that makes sense. It is the factual made mystical, with a mythic consciousness given the force of fact, that is our translation of society's messages. It's the elusive situation or idea that fascinates, not the weight of proof or conclusion, and that fascination, captured by metaphor, will be, I think, our kind of knowledge, leading to our kind of vision.

The isolation that is already ours will be increased, of course; but that isolation, as politics and as art, is here now. If it isn't comfortable, there is at least a kind of fraternity to be discovered within its limits.

CITY MAGAZINES, PAST AND PRESENT

Ben L. Moon

"The expectation of failure is connected with the very name magazine," observed Noah Webster in 1788, and the history of city magazines has supported his statement until recently. City magazines have existed since before the turn of the century, but during the early and mid-sixties the medium began a rapid growth and metamorphosis. Today they number more than 60 across the nation.

The first American publication of magazine format that concentrated its editorial content primarily on a city was perhaps *Town Topics*, founded by Colonel William Mann in New York City before 1900. The magazine was aimed at New York society, containing gossip and general light news of interest to its readers. It collapsed in 1932, its publishers charged with having blackmailed wealthy persons into buying stock.

On February 19, 1925, the first issue of the *New Yorker* magazine appeared—in the words of Harold Ross, its first editor, "a magazine avowedly published for a metropolitan audience" and one which "expects a considerable national circulation. . . ." Eventually the circulation of *New Yorker* outside the city of New York far outnumbered its circulation in the city, and a number of other publishers in other large cities tried to start imitations in their own cities.

Competitors and Emulators. A number of these imitators were themselves in New York. *Panorama*, which attempted to emulate the

Ben L. Moon, director of publications at the Georgia Institute of Technology, completed a M.A. thesis in 1969 on city magazines. Part of this study was reprinted in the Winter, 1970 issue of *Journalism Quarterly*, Vol. 47, No. 4, and is used with the permission of that scholarly publication.

Illustrated London News, served its readers a diverse mixture of content; "neither pictures nor articles were apropos anything in particular." Some, such as the *American Sketch*, were unsuccessful and were merged with competitors. Others, such as *New York Woman*, were aimed at business and professional women in the city; *New Broadway Brevities* was "a potpourri of Broadway gossip, interspersed by smoking car humor." Slick-paper hotel magazines and modest local community publications abounded, and there were guides to local arts and entertainment such as *Cue*, which appeared in 1934.

The magazine *Senator* attempted to emulate the *New Yorker* and to provide a "light and cheerful review of events in Washington"; like *New Yorker*, while concentrating on the "political, social, sports, dramatics and music affairs within 150 miles of Washington," *Senator* hoped for national circulation. Earlier, in 1931, the five-year-old *Washingtonian* magazine had begun "publishing less and less news of society, more and more pungent comment on politics," conceivably in response to the success of the *New Yorker*.

Chicago also gave birth to imitators; *The Chicagoan* was "created in the image of the *New Yorker*" in 1926. Years later, in 1955, *Chicago* magazine was started as an attempt "to create a magazine to serve Chicago as the *New Yorker* serves New York," but lasted only one year.

Other cities rushed to share in the success of the *New Yorker*. Cleveland had its *Parade*, which "exhibited well *New Yorker* technique but missed the master's polished dough and a sigh." Pittsburgh boasted its *Bulletin-Index*, which later failed. "Philadelphians laid out 25¢ and purchased *The Philadelphian* . . . a Philadelphianization of the weekly *New Yorker*," but were disappointed by a poor product. Delaware County, a suburban county near Philadelphia, had its own magazine formed from the local weekly newspaper, the *Advocate*. The *New Orleanian* candidly followed the *New Yorker* pattern, as did *The Bostonian*, *Town Tidings* of Buffalo, *The Chicagoan*, *The Bystander* of Cleveland and *The San Franciscan*. In 1946 the old *Boston Transcript* was resurrected as a magazine intended for Bostonians and had an editorial policy "to keep articles on a national scale." *Script* magazine tried to be *New Yorker* to the Hollywood community, but later died. *Tally* magazine was founded for Wethersfield, a suburb of Hartford, Connecticut.

Some of the emulators were avowed muckrakers, such as *Los Angeles* magazine, which announced its aim "to rid the city of such persons as Mayor Porter and Rev. Robert ('Fighting Bob') Shuler, and show up other long hairs who try for fame or money by limiting the personal liberty of Americans." The editor and one of his writers were shot by a man who allegedly refused to "frame" the local police chief for the magazine.

The emulators had small circulations, even considering that they aimed at high-income audiences. None was extremely successful, and their rate of failure was high. Many obviously lacked in quality and in clearly-defined editorial format. Peterson feels that "perhaps the magazines failed to hold readers because they tried too hard to transplant the *New Yorker* to their own localities instead of developing as indigenous products."

> The audiences they did attract were not large enough to be worth the attention of the big national advertisers whose accounts were necessary if a publication were to become financially successful. The *New Yorker*, as its national circulation grew, may well have eliminated any economic justification for its local imitators, for through the *New Yorker*, a national advertiser could perhaps reach as large a discriminating audience in, say, Chicago as he could through a local Chicago magazine.

A New Life for City Magazines. In 1967, [Theodore] Peterson identified a trend in communications that would seem to favor the development of city magazines, however dim their history had been.

> To me one of the fascinating developments among the mass media since World War II has been their tendency to address themselves to ever more clearly defined targets. The media may define their audiences on the basis of cultural interests, educational level, *geography* [italics mine], income level or some leisure-time activity. Whatever the basis, they are addressing themselves to increasingly homogeneous audiences, and I am willing to bet that the trend will continue. . . . Magazines, too, have been narrowing their audiences geographically, largely for the benefit of the advertiser. Today more than 230 consumer and farm magazines, by offering split-run and regional editions, allow advertisers to buy space in only a part of their total circulations.

In 1968, the city magazine was described as "a 50-year-old medium which has just come into its own."

> The business press was first to notice last year that a kind of publishing which had long been dismissed as self-serving Chamber of Commerce propaganda had changed significantly and was now not only a growing medium, offering a new market to advertisers, but one whose magazines had begun to act more like civic gadflies than tame publicity purveyors. It is difficult to determine exactly how many of these magazines exist, but there are at least 60 of them; their number has doubled in the past five years. In circulation, *New York* may prove that the last shall be first, since its magazine projects an initial printing of 100,000, while the Los Angeles periodical (a monthly) has been the leader until now with 60,000. The others range from that figure down to 10,000, in Dayton, Ohio.

There are a number of other feisty city magazines, in fact, with circulations as low as 6,000.

In February of 1967 a group of 23 city magazines formed the Metropolitan Publishers Association and signed with Select Media, Inc. to develop national advertising on a collective basis. Select Media is a subsidiary of Maloney, Regan & Schmitt, Inc., a New York national newspaper advertising representative firm. Motions have been made to merge the membership of the Metropolitan Publishers Association with that of the Magazine Publishers Association.

The publishers and advertising representatives of the city magazines have been accumulating solid and impressive research data on their products—eight out of ten readers live in homes they own with an average market value of $47,760; nearly nine out of ten subscribing households use or serve alcoholic beverages; over a third of the heads of subscribing households have done post-graduate work, two-thirds have college degrees, and over 85% have attended college; seven out of ten households own two or more cars; three out of four are stockholders; nearly nine out of ten households have a member who has flown in a commercial air liner within the preceding year; almost eight of ten heads of households are in the professional, managerial, official or proprietor level of occupation; and almost half of the households earn $25,000 or more per year. National advertisers are being urged by the advertising trade press to wake up to the flexibility, efficiency, and effectiveness offered by city magazines. Select Media claims for the medium local impact, selective audience, editorial vitality, efficiency and economy, good markets, attraction of both sexes and permanence.

These new magazines not only offer attractive packages to advertisers—they also seem to have a sense of purpose and seem to be a thoroughly professional effort in every sense.

> Handsomely put together, they keep talking about local concerns. In this day of vastly increased regionalism and great world concerns . . . , this may prove tremendously important. It adds . . . a new balance to journalism. One that . . . is needed.
> The motto of the new type of local magazine journalism is know thyself, and forget other people's cities. As the editor of one . . . succinctly puts it: "Our job is to plug the city—and to attack the city and its problems. . . ." *My* city, right *and* wrong.

Thus, perhaps this generation of city magazines will avoid the bland, over-general format and diffuse national orientation that Peterson sees as being the downfall of their predecessors of the 1920s and 1930s.

The city magazine is extremely well suited for this role of in-depth criticism and praise.

> By their nature, magazines are well equipped to dig into city affairs where exhumation is needed. They have the time to do the digging which, among newspapers, only the largest city dailies can afford, and magazine layout provides an opportunity for sharp, incisive display of a story, with color as an added attraction—a feature which most newspapers cannot match. The professional skill with which city magazines are put together is one of their outstanding characteristics; in design and editing some of them equal the better consumer magazines.

The field of city magazines is divided into chamber-sponsored magazines and independent commercial ventures. Many of the chamber magazines were founded early in the century, and quite a few have revamped their format and purpose to join the throng of new city magazines.

Even with such encouraging signs, however, problems are still present. Perhaps financing is the gravest problem facing magazines that are independent commercial ventures. *New York* magazine started on $1.1 million, and more was soon needed; advertisers were slow responding. Many others operate in the red, continually needing infusions from wealthy publishers or investors.

Chamber-sponsored city magazines, while backed financially by an organization, face still other problems of maintaining editorial independence and winning reader credibility. Studies conducted by some chamber magazines have indicated that while over half of their readers favored the magazine going into in-depth reporting of social issues, many had "some reservations about the Chamber's being able to maintain 'objectivity.' " A number of the chamber-owned books claim to achieve such objectivity; however, they fight a negative image so strong that it affects even the independent city magazines.

But whatever their problems, both independent and chamber-owned city magazines are saying things that need to be said. The bellwethers of the new breed are generally agreed to be *Atlanta* magazine in the chamber ranks and *Philadelphia* among the independent magazines. *Atlanta* has treated the high suicide rate and organized crime in its city, the question of whether to bring horse racing to Atlanta, and, critically, the John Birch Society. *Philadelphia* has attacked the Annenburg newspaper empire, the Pearl Buck Foundation and the military-industrial complex. No thunder-countenanced reformers are these; the job is accomplished with wit, polish and no small portion of humor.

An indirect means of gaining insight to the effectiveness of city magazines is to study the lot of the editors—their position in the organization structure, their freedom to run the magazine in accordance with their best judgment and the pressures operating on them. Such a study was conducted by the author in the summer of 1969. The editors of 60 city magazines throughout the United States were surveyed by mail questionnaire; in addition, 11 of the editors in cities throughout the country were selected for personal interviews.

Independent magazines were found to have the usual publisher-editor form of organization for the most part, while most chamber magazines were found to have the editor reporting directly to the executive vice-president of the chamber. The personality of the executive vice-president was found to be critical to the nature and success of the magazine under such an organization, for he could strangle it in fear of an unfavorable reflection upon him. One chamber avoids this problem by having the editor report directly to its board of directors. Some independent magazines are only one facet of a multi-enterprise corporation, and some chamber-*endorsed* magazines are run by independent local interests.

The pressures acting upon chamber editors and upon independent editors were found to form a distinct pattern in each case. Even though there is a striking similarity between chamber magazines and independent magazines in the process of editorial policy formulation, the chamber editor always has more people looking over his shoulder and more points of view to consider than does the independent editor. More chamber editors than independent editors reported submitting to pre-publication review of editorial content. The chamber editor is often called upon to handle public relations for the chamber in addition to his editorial duties. On the other hand, independent editors tend to suffer slightly more pressure from advertisers than do chamber editors; "with a somewhat shaky economic foundation, it is not politic to offend potential advertisers," admitted the editor of a struggling independent magazine. Chamber editors, however, seem to be more susceptible to pressure from governmental officials than are independent editors, perhaps because of frequent cooperation between the chamber of commerce and the local government. "I wouldn't want the magazine to embarrass city hall if I can help it," said one chamber editor.

A significant number of chamber editors reported pressure from chamber members who feel justified in "calling the shots" by virtue of their membership. Again on the opposite side of the balance, independent magazines seem to be more sensitive to pressure from public opinion than are chamber magazines. One of the most subtle pressures operating on an independent magazine is the need to be exciting, sometimes to the extent of emphasizing sensation for its own sake primarily. "We have to be shriller to get attention," admitted one independent editor. The chamber editor can afford to plan his format and content from a more lofty position in relation to public opinion, covering unexciting issues simply because they deserve coverage.

Perhaps the most notable finding was that city magazines sponsored by chambers of commerce seem to be gradually evolving toward broad, farsighted community service, toward being a voice directed at the concerned citizens of the community, and toward being a critic of the city's ills as well as a champion of its virtues. Only half of the chamber editors prefer chamber ownership to independent ownership, however. With all its advantages of stability, chamber ownership was generally agreed to be more restricting than independent ownership in the attainment of professional standards of journalism. As one chamber editor put it, "I would like to see this magazine independent, but I'm being terribly practical in saying how could it be?" All of the independent editors preferred independent ownership.

A reason for the attitudes of the editors is suggested by their responses to questions about editorial freedom. Almost all of the independent editors said that their magazines are free to "impartially wade into controversial issues with complete freedom," whereas only 40% of the chamber magazines enjoy the same degree of freedom. Many chamber editors envy the degree of freedom that they think independent editors enjoy, admitting "there is an unavoidable degree of restraint whenever a publication is designed to foster and promote the interests of a certain group." Thus, even though the long-range, enlightened self-interest of a chamber of commerce is well served by a hard-hitting, critical city magazine, complicating factors such as vested interest often interfere with a chamber's ability to sponsor a city magazine truly cast in the new mold. However, as the new mold is a highly idealistic concept, the realities of the commercial world also often curtail the realization of the ideal through an entrepreneurial venture. Unique circumstances in a given city will dictate which of the two forms of ownership is best there, and at a given time.

The future of the city magazine field as a whole seems strong. The city magazine of today, whether independent or owned by a chamber of commerce, has a more serious intent than did its predecessor of the 1920s and 1930s, a primary orientation toward service instead of profit or special pleading. It is an indigenous product, aimed primarily at its own city and using its own city as its foremost subject, rather than being a magazine of national or regional emphasis only incidentally located in a given city. City magazines have thus carved out a unique market.

Chapter VI

CREATING ALTERNATIVE MEDIA FOR MINORITIES

THE UNDERGROUND PRESS

Jack A. Nelson

The emergence in recent years of large numbers of so-called "underground newspapers" has caused speculation that traditional American newspapers face a serious credibility gap with their readers.

For the past several years, public opinion polls have shown that the public trusts newspapers less than formerly. In a recently published ten-year study, the Roper Research Associates found among those queried a drop from 32 per cent in 1959 to 21 per cent in 1968 of those who viewed newspapers as the most believable mass communication medium.

Now, say some critics, the apparent popularity of the newspapers of protest is an indication that the traditional press is not filling the needs of society. The speculation is that the underground papers are generally successful because they do fill that need.

Since 1963 some 200 newspapers have begun operations in this country with an approach to journalism that has made conventional society wince. These newspapers speak for a sub-culture that usually centers around the disenchanted, the anarchist, the hippie—the youthful drop-outs who reject society's traditional values. Loud, blatant, colorful, often obscene and amateurish, the underground newspapers nevertheless strike a note that merits examination.

Jack A. Nelson, member of journalism faculty at Humboldt State College, California, holds the Ph.D. from the University of Missouri. His research on the underground press was published in the August, 1969 *Freedom of Information Reports* and is used with permission of the FOI Center.

Many critics have damned the papers as pornographic, and dismissed the whole movement as fleeting and silly. At the same time others have said that it offers hope for shaking traditional journalism from the doldrums they see it foundering in. This paper will present the development, the characteristics, the directions, and some of the sidelights of the underground press.

In a sense, a dissenting press is not new to this country. After all, the first American newspaper, Benjamin Harris's *Publick Occurrences*, lasted only one issue back in 1690 because Boston authorities found it overly critical. And 30 years later Benjamin Franklin's brother James went to jail for satirizing local government in his *New England Courant*. During the Revolutionary War there was a "fugitive press" and, prior to the Civil War, an "abolitionist press" that published in spite of official sentiment.

There is a major difference, however, between the dissenting press of the past and the current underground press. The former protesters essentially were rejecting the political structure. The new press of dissent claims to be rejecting the whole fabric of society, and many of these newspapers state plainly that their goal is to bring down the walls of the present establishment structure.

Perhaps the closest thing to a modern predecessor to the underground papers is the *Village Voice*, a saucy tabloid begun in 1955 and still published in New York's Greenwich Village. It has stood to the left of regular newspapers politically and beyond them in imagination and artistry, according to many of its readers. The *Voice* does not run news as such, but is full of reviews, features, and filler items that are too racy for the regular press. An observer writing in the *Nation* says that the successful formula of the *Voice*—"always feed the reader something that outdoes the regular press"—has been copied by the underground press.

The average underground paper presents a startling departure from the tenets of regular journalism. Often the front page is wrapped in a bewildering combination of photomontages, eye-bending artwork, chaotic splashes of color, laced with headlines running all over the page—and set off by language until now deemed more or less unprintable. In content the paper reflects views that are not popular. Some regularly call for impeachment of the President and an unconditional withdrawal from South Vietnam. Such features as advice on avoiding the draft, the efficacy of a particular contraceptive, or ways of detecting inferior quality drugs occur regularly. The papers represent the voice of the underground culture, and they have found that there is a demand for what they have to say.

Frequently the editorial staffs have had little previous experience putting out a newspaper, and the writing shows marked contrast to traditional standards. They make no claim to objectivity, and in fact see subjectivity as a virtue.

"The theory is that truth is rooted in deep personal experience," said a report in the New York *Times*, "and that the standard news media, by insisting on impartial and detached coverage, omit and distort the underlying reality of crucial news events."

In answer to the charge that their product is amateurish and not worthy to be called journalism, Allan Katzman, co-founder of the popular *East Village Other* of New York, wrote in an article in *Look:*

> We're not based on perfection. We're based on our own reliable responses to what's going on. If at times we're extremely obscene, it's because we're feeling obscene. We're not afraid of expressing our feelings. . . . it's journalism through your fingertips.

Obviously much of the intent of the papers is to shock. At Boston University the campus newspaper—ostensibly free from administration control and thus counting itself among the underground—once ran a front page picture of a couple engaged in sexual intercourse.

In another instance, the *East Village Other*, following the death of Cardinal Spellman, devoted its front page to a photograph of the late cardinal, smiling broadly. A gigantic headline read, "Congratulations, Cardinal, On Your Promotion And Merry Xmas Wherever You Are."

But beyond the attempts to startle society, these papers offer news that is not likely to be found in the standard press. For instance, the New York *Times* told of an issue of the New York *Rat* that carried, among other things, these stories: an account of a Mexican guerilla band, first-person stories and exclusive pictures of the spring turmoil at Columbia University, accounts of the violence of the June demonstrations in Berkeley, and a "guide to survival" for demonstrators at the then upcoming Democratic convention in Chicago.

In one of the most popular underground papers, the Berkeley *Barb*, the best-read feature is a medical column written by a young physician at the student health center at the University of California. Called "Dr. HIPpocrates," the column gives medical advice slanted to the hippie culture—advice not likely to be forthcoming from the family doctor. *Time* magazine recounted this sample of the letters written to and answered by Dr. Hip: "Question: 'Will any harm come to our nursing baby if my wife smokes marijuana?' Answer: 'Your baby is on a good trip anyway at its mother's breast. Why take a chance?'" Among other things, Dr. Hip is permissive about marijuana, concluding that medical evidence of harm to normal people is lacking.

The purpose of much of this admittedly is to create disturbance and unrest. Jeff Shero, editor of the *Rat*, is quoted in *Editor & Publisher* as telling a group of Sigma Delta Chi Headliners, "At every level the social structure is breaking down. What is happening is the ungluing of the institutions that hold the country together. We want to make more of it come unglued."

On the other hand, others are somewhat more constructive. In a statement in *Avant Garde*, Walter Bowart of the *East Village Other* demonstrates the sense of mission that some of the staffs feel:

> Our purposes are altruistic. We're part of a revolution that is occurring. In 1776 was the revolution of the body . . . . a clique of writers led by Emerson began the revolution of the intellect. And now, 1968, we're engaged in the revolution toward the liberation of the spirit.

This sense of dedication is one of the marks of the staffs of the papers, whatever their goals. There is an abundant supply of volunteer labor. Many staff members make up for their lack of formal journalism training by their willingness to work for little or nothing to help spread their views. Often the same people who write and edit the papers later sell them on the streets. Usually the underground papers are sold on the streets by unkempt youths who make enough from the sales to continue their unorthodox existence. With such sales methods, circulation booms in the warm summer months when there are more salesmen and then drops during the cold winter months. Others of the more established papers depend heavily on newsstand sales.

Just how many of the underground newspapers are publishing at any one time is difficult to estimate. In March, 1968, the *Wall Street Journal* estimated "more than 50." In a similar survey at the same time *Newsweek* guessed "more than 150." Readership estimates vary even more, with the *Wall Street Journal* placing the underground audience at a conservative third of a million. Other surveys place the readership at more than four million. However, Marshall Bloom of the Liberation News Service, a news network founded for the underground papers, said in the *Nation* that his organization serviced 280 publications, of which 125 were underground, 80 were peace-oriented papers, and the rest college papers not controlled by their administrations.

There is little doubt that some underground papers have had

substantial success. The following experience of magazine editor Tom Hyman as recounted in *Avant Garde* illustrates the rise of the new press. Hyman was walking with another editor in November of 1965 when they came across a street salesman with the *East Village Other*, which was just getting started then. It was a four-page issue folded so that it ripped when it was opened. They decided it was the "most incomprehensible piece of trash we had ever seen." Hyman described the articles as "insane," the layouts as "bizarre," the type as "sloppy" and ridden with errors. "We could only suppose that the thing had been produced by a drunken gang of hebephrenics who had somehow gained access to a printing plant." The two editors were positive the paper could not survive to publish another issue.

Yet three years later the fragile four-page paper had grown into a giant 40-page psychedelic success with circulation of 40,000. Employees who had formerly worked for $15 a week were by 1968 receiving $100 weekly.

Perhaps even more startling is the case of the Los Angeles *Free Press*, generally recognized as the most financially successful of the underground papers. According to the *Wall Street Journal*, editor-publisher Art Kunkin started the paper in 1964 with a total outlay of $15, which was the cost of printing the paper and mailing letters to advertisers. Kunkin, a former printer, said he began his publication to fill a "political vacuum" left by the establishment papers' support of the two major parties. By 1967 he had a circulation of 17,000, which had jumped to 60,000 by 1968 and to 85,000 by 1969. At the latter time the *Free Press* had 40 full-time editorial and clerical employees and revenues from advertising were $5,000 weekly.

Such success stories natually have raised questions about the reasons behind the popularity of the new publications. What is the attraction?

Originally, the papers were aimed at hippies and other drop-outs of society. But in addition they found a ready audience among such other diverse groups as college students, young radicals, housewives and professors. The papers were exciting, different, ribald, and with a taste of the forbidden about them. One of their major attractions was the advertising. The Berkeley *Barb*, the *East Village Other* and the L.A. *Free Press* led the way by opening their classified columns to advertisers soliciting sex partners, nude models and drugs. Other papers quickly followed. Now the classified sections are generally the best-read portions of the papers.

Another important factor in the success of the underground papers is the low start-up costs. This is a crucial point considering the fact that for years journalists have bewailed that it is no longer possible to start a newspaper on a shoestring. The costs of owning a printing plant had made newspaper ownership out of reach of all but a few. But with the recent emergence of photo-offset printing, this all changed. In Los Angeles, according to the *Wall Street Journal*, anyone can have 5,000 copies of an eight-page paper run off at an offset print shop for about $80. Now, as in the days of Benjamin Franklin, anyone can be a publisher again.

Other factors contributing to the success of the underground papers were noted by Thomas Pepper, former newsman on the Winston-Salem (N.C.) *Journal*, in the *Nation*. He said that besides low operating costs, a new permissiveness regarding obscenity has created a climate that tolerates the excesses of the protest papers. In addition, Pepper noted, a large percentage of today's young rebels are from relatively-wealthy parents and have money to spend, making it profitable for such advertisers as record companies to patronize the newspapers.

As to the reasons for the appeal of such anti-establishment papers, some writers see it as an indication of a weakness in current society. John Kronenberger, writing in *Look*, sees some underlying deficiencies.

> In the last few years, an awakened awareness of American racism and the special menace of war they alone are asked to fight have undercut young Americans' faith in the status quo. The chemical wonders of the Pill and psychedelic drugs have badly bruised traditional morality. And the advocacy of protest and pot has brought down upon the heads of the young a police toughness previously reserved for less educated and less articulate minorities. Unsurprisingly, it's become "us against them" for many restive adolescents and young adults—not just hippies. ... The straight press belongs to the institutional America; they don't trust it.

A recurrent theme among the disenchanted is that the new press is necessary because the establishment press has failed them. They see it as speaking only from the viewpoint of its big-business owners, out of touch with the people. In general, the charges of the underground press against its big brothers, as summarized in *Editor & Publisher* are these:

1. The established press does not give an editorial voice to deviant minorities.
2. The press does not report the whole truth, but instead filters the news to reinforce established society.
3. The press treats deviant groups in news columns with sensationalism which either inflates their significance or causes their demise.
4. The press does not believe in total freedom of expression.
5. It is not contemporary, a kind of anachronism in the electric age.

In the underground press itself there has come a change of focus in the last two or three years. Originally the papers were a reflection of the withdrawn style of life of hippies and other drop-outs. Their formula for success then was sex, drugs, rock music, oriental religion and psychedelic art. But about two years ago a change took place, according to an article in the New York *Times*, and the orientation was to coverage of student uprisings, the peace movement, draft resistance and attacks on the political and social system.

The *Times* saw the change as a disenchantment with the withdrawn way of life of the flower people, those who turned their backs on society to find solace in illusion and contemplation. "It's now impossible to believe in any kind of salvation from drugs," the *Times* quoted Jeff Shero, editor of the *Rat*, as saying "Kids get drafted or hit by the cops. . . . The outside world keeps barging through your door and you've got to confront it."

Thus the move was toward speaking up on issues that seemed important, and political coverage increased. When that happened, the "New Left" in American politics gained new voices.

In order to service a burgeoning market of newspapers often inadequately staffed, several press services have sprung up in the underground. The two most important bear a rough similarity to the Associated Press and the United Press International. The Underground Press Service (UPS) is a kind of cooperative that allows its some 60 papers to reprint one another's articles without charge. On the other hand, the Liberation News Service (LNS) sells its articles, art, reviews, poems and essays to subscribers for about $180 a year. While LNS formerly used the mails to service its clients, teletype machines were introduced in 1968.

Reporters from these news services are well received in the underground where establishment journalists are not tolerated. During the demonstrations of Spring, 1968, at Columbia University, LNS reporters were permitted access to the buildings under student occupation. Their member papers received scoops, but they refused to sell any of their hundreds of photos to overground publications.

There are now about 100 organizations—including such diverse groups as TASS, New China News Agency, CBS, *Life*, and the Library of Congress—that subscribe to the LNS service. More than 200 underground publications make up the majority of its clients—including such colorful titles as the *Great Speckled Bird* of Atlanta and the *Ungarbled Word* of New Orleans. Some 100 individuals, including Pulitzer Prize-winning writer Norman Mailer and the controversial Dr. Benjamin Spock, are subscribers to the service.

The voices of dissent have found expression even in the military. On a growing number of military reservations, underground newspapers are produced in varying degrees of secrecy by enlisted men.

There are published on these military bases an estimated 20 tabloids which claim circulations ranging from 500 to 23,000. Their content ranges from protests against the Vietnam War, the draft, and alleged racial discrimination in the armed services to advice on how to harass superior officers.

Although obviously nettled, the Army points out that in what is essentially a civilian army that draws heavily on college-age youths, this has to be expected.

Some commanders, however, are taking a dim view of the publications. The army's first formal disciplinary action involved Pfc. Dennis Davis, editor of the *Last Harass*. Davis was given an undesirable discharge only three weeks before his service time would have been up.

Davis' record as a soldier had been unblemished, and the legal question has been raised of whether the army has the right to discharge a soldier for activities not related to his military duties. His attorneys said that the case is being appealed.

In another case, an anti-war group at Fort Hood, Tex., has charged the fort command with court-martialing the editor of an underground paper there because of his private views. The group ran a full-page ad in the New York *Times* claiming that Pfc. Bruce Peterson, editor of the *Fatigue Press*, was convicted falsely of possession of marijuana. According to the ad, the Army said marijuana was found in the lint of his trousers pockets, but was destroyed in the process of analysis. The ad called for a full investigation of the case and similar incidents involving underground editors.

The Army denied having any knowledge of Peterson's anti-war activities at the time of the court martial.

The first edition of another military newspaper, *Shakedown*, published at Fort Dix, N.J., produced threats of confiscation and arrest by military and local police. Soldiers reported being warned by their company officers not to read the newspaper and other anti-war literature.

Some observers see the military underground press as having far-reaching effects. New York *Times* writer Benjamin A. Franklin summed up the implications of this dissent among the ranks this way: "In the rigid structure of the military . . . a very little dissent goes a long way . . . the G.I. anti-war movement already is keeping the brass awake at night. . . . For the fact is, if it lasts, that G.I. dissent could be the most effective form of anti-war protest thought up yet."

Another trend has been the proliferation of publications on college and high school campuses. Until recently, the long-established campus newspapers enjoyed a monopoly. But now many schools are seeing the birth of new publications which regard the other campus papers as little more than controlled bulletin boards for coming events and sports scoreboards.

At Harvard, a group which considers the traditional Harvard *Crimson* as "stuffy, very establishment," started a 16-page tabloid last summer called the *Old Mole*. The name was taken from Marx's reference to the underground activity of the model revolution. According to the *Nation*, however, the *Old Mole* shifted its activities away from Harvard later and is now considered a spokesman for the Students for a Democratic Society in the New England region.

Financing for the college publications has been difficult, however. An article in the *Nation* predicted that this phase of the underground press probably will not last.

Perhaps more meaningful is the tremendous growth of papers that has taken place in the high schools. An article in the *Saturday Review* claimed that by the beginning of 1969 there was a network of nearly 500 underground newspapers produced by high school students, with even another press service to feed them.

Of widely varying quality, the papers are usually a mixture of serious radicalism and youthful gags. With such names as *The Pearl Before Swine*, *The Roach*, *The Finger*, *Big Momma*, *The South Dakota Seditionist Monthly*, and even *The New York Herald-Tribune*, often they are audacious in scope, attacking boldly the great issues facing mankind. For instance, the first mimeographed issue of the Eugene (Ore.) *Strobe* was devoted almost entirely to opposition to the Vietnam war.

One of the high school papers rated best by Diane Divok, writing for the *Saturday Review*, is the *New York High School Free Press*, which reportedly distributes 10,000 copies every three weeks. The price is 5 cents for students, 15 cents for faculty members.

The national focus of the high school underground is HIPS, High School Independent Press Service of New York. It offers weekly mailed packets of news and illustrative features—often involving high school uprisings and advice on flaunting dress codes and discipline.

A staffer of HIPS explained the function of his news service to Miss Divok, an education writer, like this:

HIPS is very much in the revolutionary bag. I suppose we're just as bad as the *Times* at being biased. But the underground papers are more interesting to read than the *Times.* They don't start with usual "who, where, when, what, and why." HIPS gets people to think. Gets them radicalized before they get into college. If that happens, chances are a fourth of them will never get to college.

Before it became apparent what direction the underground press would take, reaction from school administrators and the communities was mild. When an underground opposition newspaper called *Alternative* appeared on the campus of Harbor College near Los Angeles in 1967, the Los Angeles *Times* commented editorially:

It strikes us that what is happening is a healthy thing, worth emulation elsewhere. Young people nowadays are vigorous, questing and questioning. Unless this expression of protest degenerates into pointless obscenity, the best course is to let them enjoy this measure of off-campus freedom.

Such reaction was not to last, especially among high school administrations. After the first issue of Ann Arbor (Mich.) High School's *Us,* the editor commented:

The suppression we encountered was frightening. The Savage in Huxley's *Brave New World* comments on our situation, saying to the controller, "You got rid of them. Yes, that's just like you. Getting rid of everything unpleasant instead of learning to put up with it. . . . "

The existence of anti-distribution laws for student literature is the major objection. This is a violation of our constitutional rights. If this journalistic venture is a failure, it can easily be forgotten. But if you or they force us to stop, we are all failures. Then this school, city, and country and the principles they supposedly represent are lies.

Miss Divok sees such suppression as posing a far greater danger for our system of society than the publications could ever threaten. She says that such over-reaction defeats its own purpose.

For instance, at a high school near Seattle, Wash., John Freeburg, an honor roll senior who spent summers working with diabetic children, began to edit and publish a mimeographed newspaper. Noted as a "clean-cut youth," Freeburg was one of three chosen by the faculty as "outstanding students," and he was a student council representative and winner of the Veterans of Foreign Wars "What Democracy Means To Me" contest. His newspaper was critical of the Vietnam war. But before publication he submitted the articles to the school administration for approval.

Yet three months before graduation he was suspended. His parents' efforts to have him reinstated proved fruitless. Then the American Civil Liberties Union stepped in and obtained a court order for his reinstatement in the face of the school district's claim that his activities were disruptive to school operation.

Miss Divok sees in his case an expression of the whole problem of an establishment that is unable to cope with idealism:

> John Freeburg has gone from idealism to skepticism about the "system" that found his exercise of freedom of the press an embarrassment to be eliminated in the face of pressures from right wing groups in the small community. His school said he was old enough to praise democracy publicly, but not to speak about its seamier aspects. Rather than practicing the ideals of freedom and tolerance it preached, the school used its power to suppress ideas.

On the other hand, along with the success of the left wing newspapers, some right wing groups have started their own newspapers with a view to balancing the available opinions. On the campus of Stanford University, for example, the *Stanford Daily* has undergone nominal competition since 1967 from the *Stanford Arena*, a weekly started by conservative elements which considered the *Daily* as too far left.

And in St. Louis, 17-year-old Jim Merkel started a monthly mimeographed paper, *Alternatives*, to counteract the effect of a left wing underground paper published there. Merkel said he hoped to distribute 25,000 free copies to the 40 high schools in the region. The paper is financed by contributions from adults who, according to Merkel, "are sick and tired of getting just one viewpoint in the high schools."

In spite of their success, some of the underground papers are subject to certain hazards because of the nature of their content. Not the least of these is interference from law officials who view the publications as obscene or dangerous.

Typical cases include:

—Boston's *Avatar* found its use of certain four, eight, and ten-letter words so enraged the Cambridge City Council that the paper's street salesmen were consistently arrested in Harvard Square. Their solution was to make the salesmen and the offending words even more prominent, printing one verb in letters four inches high. After 58 arrests had been made, a local court found the content not obscene. A truce was then reached when *Avatar* agreed to quit selling its paper to anyone under 18. But because of the frequent brushes with the law, many newsstands had already agreed to stop handling the newspaper, causing a drastic drop in circulation.

—In Los Angeles in November of 1968, the editor of the underground newspaper *Open City* was fined $1,000 for printing an "obscene advertisement" depicting a nude woman.

—Damages are being sought from the Los Angeles *Free Press* for $25 million in connection with the newspaper's publication of state narcotics officers' names.

The paper published the names, addresses and telephone numbers of 80 state narcotics agents.

A senior narcotics agent filed a $15 million suit against the *Free Press* for that article; and State Attorney General Thomas C. Lynch brought a $10 million suit against the newspaper charging it with the "wrongful disclosure of confidential information which jeopardized the lives, health and safety of law enforcement officers and their families."

Lynch also obtained from a judge an order preventing the *Free Press* from publishing confidential information from [California state agencies.] [Editor's Note: The Free Press continued its fight for Los Angeles Police Department press passes in 1971, even though the U.S. Supreme Court refused to hear that case; out of court settlements totaling about $50,000 ended the other cases, with editor Art Kunkin admitting in a page one statement that he was in error in running the names of agents in his fight against secret police tactics.]

—A Montgomery County, Md., judge sentenced the editor of the Washington *Free Press* to six months in jail for publishing an "obscene editorial cartoon." The cartoon depicted a nude judge masturbating as he presided over a courtroom.

—The Chicago *Seed* ran in its Christmas 1967 issue a collage depicting portions of nude bodies, unnatural sex acts, a floating skull, and a picture of a policeman swinging a club. When arrested the young editor protested: "I don't see where the state becomes involved in a matter of taste. The definition of obscenity is personal."

—In Florida when the first issue of the Miami *Free Press* hit the streets in April of 1969, police promptly arrested the three teen-aged street vendors. They were charged with possession of obscene material. Along with provocative articles both from the underground news services and locally written, the issue carried artwork depicting President Nixon and Mao Tse-tung superimposed on a nude woman.

The editors involved see these frequent arrests as harassment to be expected from the establishment. Jerry Leggerri, one of the staff of the *East Village Other*, calls them "a political device to gain attention for lazy politicians."

It is still early perhaps to make an assessment of the significance of the apparent success of the underground press. A correspondent for the *IPI Report* pointed out that the audience for these papers is young, and that the decreasing average age of the American population may be a factor in determining the direction of future publications. In that report the correspondent, Gaye Sandler Smith, asked if these young people—growing up with the iconoclastic content, the liveliness and forthright style of the underground press—will be content with the traditional established press when they become consumers.

Smith pointed out that already some observers see the changes in recent years in display advertising as influenced by the liveliness of the underground press. "Within the past year," he said, "advertisements for ladies' fashions and for soft drinks have appeared in the total-impact style of overall design and dazzling color so familiar to readers of underground papers."

As to what the future holds for this press of dissent there is little agreement. Although generalities are difficult when there is such a variety of voices, the trend is toward militancy. The drug-and-introspection-oriented San Francisco *Oracle* is an exception, and it is looked upon with disdain by the big papers like the Los Angeles *Free Press* and *Avatar* because it dares to be so concerned with psychedelia when the country is in such bad shape.

Most commonly, the underground papers are irreverent, independent, anti-war, anti-establishment and pro-marijuana. Beyond that, generalizations fall apart, except that what is probably most important of all is that they are being read.

As an indication, the first issue of the *Underground Digest* in January, 1968 defined the underground press as:

> The youthful voice of rebellion. The exciting new style of journalism. The literature that *Time* assigns editors to follow coast to coast. The movement that *Esquire* wraps an entire issue around. It's what you've been reading about—and seeing just a smattering of.

That final statement is less and less true. The underground newspapers have spread down from the big cities into the smaller towns and schools.

For all its success, some critics predict that these voices from the underground will pass like any other fad. Nevertheless, there is generally an uneasiness about what the success of these strident voices with all their excesses means for traditional journalism.

Thomas Pepper in the *Nation* commented on both the inadequacies and the promise of the underground papers:

> The underground papers are not a quality press, because they pander to their readers with a dexterity befitting the establishment papers they criticize so bitterly. They offer little more than a stylized theory of protest.

[But] one should give credit where credit is due; by making a financial and a cultural hit with their appeal to a rich and identifiable market, the underground papers have awakened virtually all concerned to a real deficiency in American newspaper journalism. . . . the fact that regular metropolitan dailies do not communicate with sub-cultures.

Who will remedy this deficiency—whether the expanding newspapers of the underground will stabilize and spread their influence permanently or whether the establishment press will waken and fill the gap themselves—is a question to be answered perhaps after another five or ten years. Undoubtedly one of the major factors contributing to the existence and success of the underground press is the social condition under which it exists. This may change radically.

Indeed, it is apparent that unique conditions must exist to account for the whirlwind rise and continued presence of any widespread underground press. Summarized, these would include:

1. Climate of dissent and protest.

2. Dedicated souls who are willing to work for little or nothing, who believe passionately in what they are doing, and who will hawk the papers on the streets themselves if necessary. In the decade of the 1950's, college students were known as "the uncommitted generation" and would probably not have bothered to espouse their cause so fervently—even had they felt it—as today's youth.

3. A means of production to provide for an effective, cheap and easy way of publishing. The emergence of photo-offset printing in recent years provided this.

Thus while the journalistic fraternity waits slightly aghast to see what the eventual outcome of the movement will be, the underground papers go their amateurish but successful way, publishing in their strident voices. There were two anthologies of their writings published in 1968: *The Hippie Papers*, edited by Jerry Hopkins and published by New American Library; and *Notes from the New Underground*, published by Viking and edited by Jerry Kornbluth.

Kornbluth perhaps echoes the voice of the underground best when he offers in his volume this analysis of the future of the new press:

The underground has surfaced—it is everywhere. . . . the underground newspapers are the flimsiest manifestation of such sentiments; they are perhaps only the first tangible beginning of a disaffection so radical that it will frighten America as much as the black revolt.

Whether Kornbluth is correct or not will have to be seen later. In the meantime, the *Great Speckled Bird* of Atlanta, the *Avatar* of

Boston, the *Ungarbled Word* of New Orleans and the *Berkeley Barb* go on publishing and being read.

THE BLACK PRESS IN TRANSITION

L.F. Palmer, Jr.

In 1945, when Gunnar Myrdal's classic study *An American Dilemma* was published, this country had 150 Negro newspapers with a total circulation estimated at 1.6 million, and Myrdal could write: "The Negro press . . . is rightly characterized as the greatest single power in the Negro race." There were three circulation "giants" in the field: the Pittsburgh *Courier* (approximately 257,000); the Chicago *Defender* (202,000); and the Baltimore *Afro-American* (137,000). Twenty-five years later there are about 175 Negro newspapers with a circulation of more than 3 1/2 million; they are referred to as the black press; and there is considerable question about the power they wield in black communities.

The circulation "giants," using 1971 *Editor and Publisher* figures: *Muhammad Speaks*, Chicago, 700,000; *The Voice*, Jamaica, N.Y., 90,000; *Amsterdam News*, N.Y. 83,000; *Sentinel-Bulletin*, Tampa, 75,000; *Black Panther*, San Francisco, figure unavailable, 1969 estimate 110,000. [Editor's Note: E&P says 108 papers had a 1970 circulation of 10,000 or more, seven with better than 50,000; five have founding dates before 1900. Philadelphia *Tribune* (1885), Houston *Informer* (1892), Baltimore *Afro-American* (1892), Des Moines *Iowa Bystander* (1894) and Indianapolis *Recorder* (1895).]

Like the readership it serves, the black press is in transition. Characteristically, the field is changing so fast that it virtually defies measurement. Some editions aren't sold, but are given away; large numbers of publications know only a miraculously marginal existence; and small publications come and go in erratic spurts. But it is apparent that the press of, by, and for black people has entered a new evolutionary stage.

L.F. Palmer, Jr., reporter-columnist for the *Chicago Daily News*, formerly worked on the *Chicago Defender* and the *Chicago Courier*. His research is used with his permission and that of *Columbia Journalism Review*, where it appeared in the Spring, 1970 issue.

The changes in the "big three" of 1945 alone illustrate this. At the close of World War II, the *Courier, Defender,* and *Afro-American* all were national weeklies and could be purchased as easily in Biloxi, Montgomery, or Fort Lauderdale as in Pittsburgh, Chicago, and Baltimore. Today the *Defender* is one of two local black "dailies" in the country (the other is the Atlanta *Daily World* which publishes four times a week.) The *Defender's* 1970 circulation was 33,000 Monday through Thursday, and 37,000 for its weekend edition. But the Pittsburgh *Courier* also has dropped in circulation as has the *Afro-American.*

Among other great names to have withdrawn from the national field is the Norfolk *Journal and Guide,* consistently credited with being the nation's best-edited and best-dressed black newspaper. Now more of a regional sheet, it has dipped from 64,368 in 1946 to 30,000. Meanwhile, both the Michigan *Chronicle* and Los Angeles *Sentinel* have made dramatic local gains—the *Chronicle* (published in Detroit) from 25,868 circulation in 1946 to 63,000; and the *Sentinel* from 15,892 in 1946 to 39,227. The *Chronicle,* whose editor and general manager, Longworth Quinn, is considered to be one of the best administrators in the field, achieved sizeable increases by winning and holding many readers during Detroit's daily newspaper strikes of 1964 and 1967-68. In Los Angeles, the *Sentinel's* steady gains along with those of the *Central News* and *Herald-Dispatch,* parallel the city's growth and the migration of blacks westward.

Though copies of the largest black papers can still be found outside their home territories, the end of the national black newspaper is clearly in sight. "Most black papers have to limit their circulation base because it is too costly to maintain far-flung distribution," says John "Rover" Jordan, acting publisher of the *Journal and Guide.* "We can't afford field men any longer, and transportation is too complicated and expensive. It is virtually impossible to provide adequate coverage of the national scene anyway."

Television has made inroads on black newspapers' readership—as it has on that of whites—and, because inner-city blacks are audio-oriented, black-focused radio has hurt, too. As one black editor in Chicago said: "The four black-oriented radio stations here reach more listeners in an hour than the black newspaper has readers in a month."

The limited expansion of black newspapers' advertising bases also is a problem. Although the *Afro-American* is among the fortunate few with no financial crisis, publisher John Murphy says, "We are really not able to get into the mainstream of the American economy. We just haven't been able to break through the institutionalized discrimination by advertisers." There has been "some success" in obtaining food copy, he says, but little in such fields as department store advertising. In fact, when Macy's started advertising in the New York *Amsterdam News* in 1965 the newspaper turned the milestone into a front-page headline. Similarly, officials of the Chicago *Daily Defender* did not try to hide their elation when Marshall Field & Company signed with them. "We are delighted, of course," says John H. Sengstacke, *Defender* publisher. "This is the first time Marshall Field has advertised in black media, and we've been after them for a long, long time."

Sengstacke, the nephew of the *Defender's* founder, Robert S. Abbott, has become the black newspaper baron of the nation with ten papers. He became president of the *Defender's* parent company after Abbott's death in 1940, turned the *Defender* into a daily in 1956, and in 1967 purchased the *Courier* chain. His main plant at 2400 South Michigan Avenue in Chicago is the best equipped of any black newspaper facility, and his papers circulate in every region but the West. In addition to the *Daily Defender* and Michigan *Chronicle*, they include: the Chicago *National Defender*, *Tri-State Defender* (Tennessee, Mississippi, Arkansas), Georgia *Courier*, Pittsburgh *Courier*, Florida *Courier*, Ohio *Courier*, Philadelphia *Courier*, *National Courier*.

Then there is the problem of recruitment. "It's hard getting people who are qualified," says C.B. Powell, seventy-four-year-old publisher of the *Amsterdam News*, "and that goes not only for reporters but in advertising and circulation and management as well. I tried three white advertising managers but it just didn't work out." The *Amsterdam News*, the only black paper with a Newspaper Guild contract, pays the highest average salaries, but even these are below the scale of metropolitan dailies. Echoing Powell, John Murphy of the *Afro-American* says the black press has "become the training ground for the white metropolitan newspapers and radio and television stations ever since they recognized that it is advantageous to have a black reporter or two on their staffs."

The dearth of qualified editorial personnel is reflected in the black press' basic staple—news. Black newspapers, recognizing that they are in no position to compete with the metropolitan press in coverage of black communities, are greedy for handouts. In many instances, the black newspaper seems to have thrown in the towel. The metropolitan press, however, concerns itself largely with the most dramatic and sensational aspects of black life—conflict situations, militancy, unusual achievements of "celebrity blacks," and, of course, crime. Because they have the resources available, white dailies—often with reporters hired from black newspapers—give lengthy coverage to such stories. Thus black readers look increasingly to metropolitan dailies for articles about blacks, even though their treatment may be suspect.

However, when it comes to routine coverage of black communities—social life, church activities, births, marriages, deaths, club and fraternal news, etc.—the black press has an open field and takes full advantage of its monopoly. As one black editor put it: "People like to see their names and their pictures in the paper. Just as sure as day follows night, the average black man or woman will never make the daily newspaper unless he commits a crime, and a serious one at that."

This is why, for example, the Chicago *Courier*, which is rare in that it prints no crime news, in a recent twenty-page issue carried two full pages of business news, a page of entertainment notes, a generous amount of church and social news, and sixty-seven pictures. A sixteen-page edition of the Cincinnati *Herald* included two church pages, two sports pages, and one entertainment page, as well as a full page of pictures, all of different weddings. The *Afro-American* and Pittsburgh *Courier* routinely carry two or three pages of women's and society news. It is not unusual for black weeklies to devote two pages to school notes, crammed with names. Once the reader gets off the front page of a black newspaper, he is rarely confronted with hard news.

The front page of most black newspapers, however, are fairly predictable. Banner heads are likely to herald a crime or a racial issue. Typical banners in a recent week: in the Chicago *Daily Defender* weekend edition, E. CHICAGO HTS. RANGER TO DIE IN CHAIR; RAP SCHOOL OFFICIAL FOR STUDENT UNREST; in the *Journal and Guide*, FIRE KILLS 8; FATHER SAVES 3 BEFORE DYING; TROOPS PATROL AT VORHEES; in the *Louisiana Weekly*, COURT HITS RACISM IN ASBESTOS TRADES; INTRUDER SLAIN IN APPLIANCE STORE.

The black press dates to 1827, when John B. Russwurm and the Rev. Samuel Cornish went to the editor of the old New York *Sun* and asked him to run a story about a black organization to which they belonged. The editor is reported to have told them: "The *Sun* shines bright for all white men but never for the black man." Rev. Cornish and Russwurm walked out and founded the nation's first black newspaper, *Freedom's Journal*. It did not survive long, but the crusading spirit of its founders did. [Editor's Note: The famous New York *Sun* appeared in 1833, six years after the *Freedom Journal* was started in 1827; the *Sun* of Benjamin Day did have a motto, "It Shines for All" but the rest of the saying is probably just a tale.]

Early black newspapers cried out against the injustices of slavery and, after emancipation, against the plight of the freedmen. Through the lynching years the black press protested loud and long. Robert S. Abbott and his Chicago *Defender* concentrated on the tortured life in the South with such zeal that he contributed greatly to the northward migration of blacks beginning in World War I. During World War II the black press attacked and exposed discrimination against blacks in the armed forces. This relentless crusade led President Harry Truman to issue an executive order ending Jim Crow in the service. The first historic March on Washington in 1941 was dramatized almost exclusively by the black press. The direct result was President Franklin D. Roosevelt's executive order creating the first declaration for federal fair employment practices.

Today, with the black revolution at its zenith, the question is raised throughout the ghettos: where is the black press? The answer is that the established black press is squarely in the middle of a dilemma. It finds itself trying not to be too conservative for the black revolutionaries, and not too revolutionary for white conservatives upon whom it depends for advertising. Murphy of the *Afro-American* speaks candidly about the tightrope the black press walks: "Newspapers are small businesses and publishers are businessmen. Surely you'd have to describe black publishers as conservatives, I suppose. In earlier years, black newspapers were spearheads of protest. Today we're much more informational."

Powell of the *Amsterdam News* concedes that "we have not kept up with the black revolution as we should have. But you've got to realize that we don't see our role as leaders. We are not out to revolutionize. When the *Amsterdam News* sees issues that are too revolutionary, we speak out against them." Louis Martin, vice president and editor of the Sengstacke Newspapers and the former deputy chairman of the National Democratic Committee, says the black press is "reflecting the rise in black awareness" but admits that "some of the older publishers were a little too slow responding." Now, he says, "even some of our most conservative black newspapers are bowing to the winds of change."

Many black readers wonder if "bowing to the winds of change" is enough. An editor in the Midwest says no. "Playing catch-up is not the name of the game," he declares. "The black revolution has left the black press behind. And one of the reasons is that in the good old days of the black press income came almost exclusively from circulation because there just wasn't any real advertising available. Today, the papers are picking up some pretty good accounts and, aside from wrestling with the increasingly complex economics of keeping a newspaper alive, black publishers have to make sure they don't become too revolutionary in tone for fear of losing those new white accounts."

William Robertson, assistant to publisher Leon Washington of the Los Angeles *Sentinel*, suggests another reason why the black press has relinquished its title of crusader: "I think we have lost much of our penchant for protest because we just don't have the staff to dig out the stories like we used to."

Some reporters on black newspapers, moreover, do not appear to have the dedication to the black cause which characterized black newsmen a couple of decades ago. A former reporter for the *Amsterdam News* was quoted in a New York *Times* Magazine article recently: "You don't feel that you have to stay working there like you do on some jobs because you're doing good works or really helping to change the community around you. It's just a job. . . . You know the publisher's in it to make money, not to reform the black world and that kind of spirit pervades the place. When I was there, my attitude was what the hell, if he's in it for the money, I am, too."

This attitude parallels that of a reporter for a Chicago black newspaper who told this writer: "Look, man, you get tired of brothers and sisters bugging you on the street because your paper just isn't with The Movement. You know, one day our paper looks like it might be getting with it and the next day it sounds like the *Trib* [Chicago *Tribune*]."

Probably the classic example of the black press' ambivalence on militancy is the way it has reacted to the Black Panther Party. At first black papers tried to ignore the Panthers. As the Panthers' brand of activism stepped up to where it could not be overlooked, black newspapers, for the most part, reported their conflicts with police but consciously sought to hew a line that would not identify with the Panther ideology. About a year ago, after the Illinois Black Panther Party served notice that the Chicago *Daily Defender* "will have to become relevant or we will have to deal with it," the *Defender* began carrying more news about the Panthers—their breakfast-for-children program and other activities not tied to police confrontation. When Panther leader Fred Hampton was killed in December, 1969 in a police raid in his Chicago apartment, black newspapers—

like many white newspapers—took a new look at the Panthers and
began questioning the role of the Establishment in dealing with this
ultra-militant group.

How are less explosive issues handled in the black press today?
An excellent insight is offered by Harold Barger, who has studied
nine black newspapers in the Chicago area for a Northwestern University Ph.D. dissertation. Though there may be isolated differences
in black newspapers' handling of news across the nation, Barger's
findings apply generally to the established black press. He found two
news areas in which there was what he called "an almost total negative image": the Nixon Administration and police activity in black
communities.

"Virtually all of the references to Nixon are negative," Barger
says. "This is not entirely surprising. Yet it is significant that references to the federal government tend to be favorable. It is when the
references are made in more specific terms—the Nixon Administration, the Justice Department, etc.—that the bitterness shows through.
Blacks tend to respect the basic traditions of this government—the
rhetoric of American democracy, so to speak—and yet they clearly
see their own identification as that of second-class citizenship."

Barger sees this apparent ambivalence toward the federal government as a paradox, yet it is easily explained since blacks have
always looked to the federal government as their "hope." When the
arms of the federal government are viewed individually, they show
blatant failures to implement the American promise. Put another
way, what Barger affirms is that black newspapers reflect blacks'
general support of the American system, but record their readers'
beliefs that the system is not working. (References to the Supreme
Court were usually positive, but stories on housing, real estate men,
jobs, labor unions, and the education, health, and welfare systems
had negative images.) The most consistent positive theme Barger
found was black unity, allied with the call for community control,
particularly of schools. At the same time, he found black newspapers
encouraging integration as a means of shaping a kind of society in
which both blacks and whites can live in harmony.

These are, indeed, the general images which reflect from the
established black press—that segment of the black newspaper institution which publishes as much for commercial motives as others. But
there is a bold new dimension in the black press in the form of the
organizational newspaper that in some instances is a profit-making
venture but in all instances is a propaganda instrument. These papers
are appearing all over the nation, especially in major urban areas, and

they are having an impact on their readers and on the established black press. One thing sets them apart—militancy.

Two such papers, national in scope with circulations that outstrip virtually all other black newspapers, are *Muhammad Speaks*, published in Chicago by the Black Muslims, and the *Black Panther*, printed in San Francisco by the Black Panther Party. *Muhammad Speaks*—by far the largest of any black newspaper—is published in the Black Muslims' modern $1.5-million-dollar offset plant. The Panthers' tabloid, according to Black Panther Chief of Staff David Hilliard, sells 110,000 weekly. Significantly, neither paper depends on advertising for revenue and both are sold enthusiastically by members on street corners. Both are remarkably alike in approach, though not in ideology: each issue of the *Black Panther* carries the party platform and its 10-point program; each edition of *Muhammad Speaks* runs the Muslims' program, also a 10-point platform.

Muhammad Speaks, which sells for 15 cents in Illinois and 20 cents elsewhere, runs stories under such headlines as THE SLAVE TRADE, WHITE EXPLOITERS BUILD NUCLEAR ARSENAL IN AFRICA, LINK STRUGGLE OF U.S. BLACKS, VIETNAMESE, as well as numerous messages from Elijah Muhammad, "Messenger of Allah." There also are reports from various Black Muslim Mosques. Only about half of the editorial staff is Muslim, and most top editors are trained in journalism. The acting editor in Chicago—the base for thirty-two staff members—is a Harvard graduate; the New York editor is an alumnus of the Columbia Graduate School of Journalism. Although the newspaper subscribes to United Press International, it does not use much UPI material, depending more on news contacts in key cities and lifting and rewriting of material from other black newspapers. The paper has an office in Cairo and is opening another one soon in London.

The staff of the *Black Panther*—which sells for 25 cents a copy—is mostly volunteer, depending heavily on reports from Ministers of Information in Panther chapters. The paper's pages are saturated with Panther-police confrontations, progress reports on trials involving Panthers, and activities such as free breakfast and health programs. Typical *Black Panther* headlines scream: BLACK YOUTH MURDERED IN COLD BLOOD BY RACIST S.F. PIG; "RAP" BROWN LAW PUT TO USE BY POWER STRUCTURE; MOZAMBIQUE GUERRILLAS DETERMINED TO CARRY ARMED STRUGGLE THROUGH TO THE END; THE ANATOMY OF EXTERMINATION, A POLITICAL ASSASSINATION.

The fact that these two papers consistently circulate in figures far larger than their memberships affirms that there is a market for the more militant, anti-establishment black newspaper. Indeed, sizeable but unknown numbers of small organizational newspapers are now in existence, with an undetermined but obviously significant aggregate circulation: in Chicago, for example, the bi-weekly *Black Truth* circulates 30,000; the bi-weekly *Torch* 15,000; the weekly *Observer* 25,000; the monthly *Black Liberator* 10,000; and the monthly *Black Women's Committee News* 5,000.

The established black publishers look warily on these militant organs. Sengstacke Newspapers' Martin comments: "It's the same story in every city I've been in. The big weeklies apparently are not able to give these organizations and their points of view the kind of attention they demand." Because they are subsidized by organizations they are less dependent on advertising; and the editors—generally untrained in journalism but committed to the militant black cause—exercise wide freedom in their "news" presentation, which has great appeal to blacks who want action along with words.

Whether the established black press will move more in this direction remains to be seen. But its survival does not appear to be threatened. Publishers, though expressing mixed feelings about their individual futures, agree on that. "As long as there is white racism, we'll have black newspapers," Martin says. "But there is no question about it, we have to change our points of view and presentation of the news as the demands of black people are recognized. We'll have to if we are to be relevant."

CHICANO JOURNALISM:
NEW MEDIUM FOR NEW CONSCIOUSNESS

Frank del Olmo

> Bueno, pues que hubo, como les va?
>
> Que lindo dia para cantar
>
> Noticias que han llegado
>
> De Nuevo Mexico . . .
>
> > from "Que hubo Raza,"
> > a modern Mexican-American corrido

This modern day Mexican-American, or Chicano, corrido (folk song) sings about "news that has arrived from New Mexico"—more specifically, it tells of the *Alianza* movement led in that state by the Chicano leader Reies Lopes Tijerina.

The Chicano movement, like all movements that have ever involved Mexicans, has been immortalized in songs—the earthy *corridos* and *rancheras*, as well as the more romantic *boleros*. Unfortunately, in these days of instant mass-communication, there is a need for more efficient and consistent (albeit less romantic) means of carrying news.

Perhaps as many as fifty Chicano newspapers have sprung up since the early 1960's to publicize and help push the "Mexican-American civil rights movement" (to use for once the mass-media label for the complex social ferment now going on in our community).

Chicano papers can be found in almost every major city of the Southwest, and even as far away as Kansas City (*Adelante* or Forward) Chicago (*Lado*), Florida (*Nuestra Lucha*, or Our Struggle) and Wisconsin (*La Voz Mexicana* in Wautoma and *La Guardia* in Milwaukee). Most of these publications are members of the semi-formal Chicano Press Association (CPA).

Frank del Olmo, *Los Angeles Times* reporter and member of the Mexican-American Studies Department at San Fernando Valley State College, California, contributes one of the first published looks at the Chicano Press and the Chicano Press Association. He traveled throughout the Southwest for the *Times*, analyzing conditions in Mexican-American communities.

The CPA was formed as a semi-official "confederation" among the earliest Chicano community newspapers. They agreed to share articles and features with each other. They also opened membership to "all other publications committed to improve the news media in the Spanish speaking community," as their statement of goals and philosophy says.

"Chicano" newspapers and newsletters are distinct from the many Spanish-language news media found in the Southwest, where the radio and television stations, and newspapers, are not as politically and socially activist as are the CPA members. In most cases, these more established media present the usual diet of daily world, national and local news—only in Spanish. (The word "Chicano" is a Spanish slang term used by many Mexican-Americans to refer to themselves. It has no literal translation into English, and its origin is obscure.)

As other Chicano papers were established, they also became members of the CPA. From the first few, they have multiplied to over 25 CPA members, with possibly another 25 non-affiliated Chicano papers, according to one CPA editor. The first of these papers emerged with the event that many social observers say was the start of the current Chicano (or Mexican-American) movement—the California grapeworkers strike.

In 1964, grapeworkers under the leadership of Cesar Chavez walked out of the Delano, Calif., fields to begin their strike and form the United Farm Workers Organizing Committee, their new union. They also founded a union newspaper, *El Malcriado* (which means a precocious, ill-bred child in Spanish).

Today *El Malcriado* still publishes bi-monthly in Delano, as the "voice of the farmworker." It operates out of a small and unbelievably cluttered shack livened by multicolored posters, on a bare strip of land called Forty Acres (which the UFWOC hopes to someday develop into a national farmworkers center).

The tiny, almost claustrophobic office is quite in contrast with the clear, flat California croplands that stretch away from Forty Acres. Far from the quiet and broad croplands of the San Joaquin Valley and Forty Acres, one can find the offices of a second major Chicano paper, which recently adopted a magazine format.

The offices of *La Raza* are located just off the noisy traffic lanes of the busy San Bernardino Freeway which speeds commuters through the sprawling urban barrio (ghetto) of East Los Angeles, where nearly one-half million Mexican-Americans are concentrated. Small, aging homes recline on the steep hills that loom above the old concrete building that is used as both office and layout shop for what is generally acknowledged as the leader of Los Angeles' Chicano press.

Since it was founded in 1967, *La Raza* has spawned many imitators in the Los Angeles area. Among them are *regeneracion* (Regeneration), *Inside Eastside, Chicano Student Movement* (which merged with *La Raza* is a not-so-new newspaper deal), *Machete, La Causa* (The Cause), and *El Popo* (named after the Mexican volcano Popocatepetl). In turn, these papers have seen colleagues begin publication in California cities from San Diego to San Jose, in New Mexico, Arizona, Texas, Colorado and a few other scattered areas.

Whether they publish in rural areas like Delano, or a metropolitan center like Los Angeles, these Chicano newspapers share common traits. Only a few of them are organs for specific organizations. *El Malcriado* represents Cesar Chavez' UFWOC. *La Voz* (The Voice) in Los Angeles is published by the Community Service Organization, and San Jose's *Forumeer* is the newsletter for the local G.I. Forum, a Mexican-American civic organization. The rest attempt to publicize all organizations in their community.

Like most underground papers, they are photo-offset and quite free in their use of artwork. They tend to be quite inventive in layout of both type and photos. CPA papers make no pretense toward being objective. They are deeply involved in the communities around them and, while they often do give information, they also serve as an organ for the political and social causes of the Chicano *movimiento*. As one CPA editor said, "sometimes every story we run is an editorial."

Generally regarded as the more well-known of these political papers are the aforementioned *La Raza,* and *El Grito del Norte* in New Mexico, which is a supporter of the fiery and controversial Reies Lopez Tijerina. Others are *La Verdad* (The Truth) in San Diego and *El Gallo* (The Rooster) in Denver, which is the publication of the Crusade for Justice, a major Chicano organization in that city.

In 1970 a group called Los Siete de La Raza began publishing a paper in San Jose and Oakland called *Basta Ya!* (Enough).

All of the CPA papers are bilingual. *El Malcriado* publishes one edition in Spanish and another in English. The other papers carry articles in both languages in each issue. Finally, few CPA papers carry any advertising. They tend to be fiercely independent and are usually determined to stay that way.

"This paper is not a business venture," Joe Razo, a member of *La Raza's* editorial board, explained. "It is an organizational tool. Our aim is not to make money, but to organize our people. We want to make them aware and sensitive to what goes on both within the community and in the establishment outside."

Another thing CPA papers have in common, according to Razo, is that "they always lose money." Razo, and other Chicano newspapermen, see this as a virtue, although gathering funds to back their papers is often a struggle.

Another editorial board member of *La Raza* is the former editor of *Chicano Student Movement*, (the papers merged in September of 1969 and in Spring of 1970, *La Raza* appeared with a magazine format). Raul Ruiz said he does not worry about ads. "We worry about relevant things that have to be said, and hustle up the money."

Most of these papers do have to "hustle." Although they are sometimes supported by an organization, as UFWOC supports *El Malcriado*, and Crusade for Justice helps *El Gallo*. More often, like *La Raza*, they get donations from sympathetic supporters of the organizations it publicizes. (Donations from a liberal, social-action oriented Los Angeles church group were helpful in getting *La Raza* started in 1967, and an editor of *La Verdad* said his paper received some aid from a small foundation grant).

The major exceptions to the no-advertising rule are *El Malcriado*, San Bernardino's *El Chicano*, and the *Chicano Times* in San Antonio.

CPA writers and editors tend to dismiss traditional journalistic objectivity as irrelevant to their situation, and sincerely feel they are aiding their community by emphasizing political controversy over straight news reporting.

As Ruiz bluntly put it, as he leaned back from one of the battered old desks in the *La Raza* offices, "the purpose of *La Raza* is not just to report all the news that is fit. We participate in what we print, we cannot separate ourselves from the community. If we did we would be committing the same sins the establishment media does, we would become noninvolved and irrelevant."

La Raza's reputation spread after the 1970 East Los Angeles riot when photos by Razo and Ruiz of law enforcement officers in firing position were republished in a huge Los Angeles *Times* display. They also were shown on television at an emotional coroner's inquest. At that time KMEX, serving the Mexican-American community, telecast the inquest live, unifying the people who mourned the loss of Mexican newsman Ruben Salazar, killed by a tear gas shell allegedly fired by an officer.

Why have so many Chicano newspapers sprouted up recently? The reasons are varied. A staff member of *El Malcriado* offered a pragmatic explanation. "The huelga (strike) here in Delano turned on the younger generation," he said. "And offset-printing enables a small group to put out a paper with little capital or equipment."

Another CPA member answered more philosophically. Tomas Trimble, former writer-photographer for *La Raza*, said the CPA was "trying to fill a vacuum." "Our people have had few chances to read about themselves," he said, "because the regular press carries little about them." "There has always been some mistrust of the Anglo press in our communities," he added. "In the past the media have not represented us properly. This includes works of history and social interpretation as well as newspapers."

"I think a whole new kind of Chicano expression is coming out for the first time. There is a renaissance going on in the *barrios* that these papers are the start of. Later we will get novels and plays written by Chicano authors. The CPA is just filling a gap right now."

At least one observer of the Chicano community in the Southwest echoed these sentiments. Dr. Rudy Acuna, former chairman of the Chicano Studies department at San Fernando Valley State College, also described the CPA papers as training grounds for the future literary spokesmen for the Chicano. "You cannot have a movement without ideas," he said. "Before any real Chicano leaders can emerge, we will need ideas, and this is a function the Chicano papers are serving now."

Dr. Acuna said that the Chicano papers were "probably the main mode of expression we have, the only way we can express ourselves. Even the blacks have their point of view told more readily, because they have greater access to the media."

"Our ways of expressing ourselves in Chicano papers may not be in the patterns of traditional Anglo journalism," he admitted, "but it is good to me. I read the Chicano papers and they articulate many of the things I feel."

Dr. Acuna brought up an example of the *Los Angeles Times* on a typical morning. "I think I found one article on Chicanos in there this morning, and it has over one million Chicanos in its service area. Compare that with the society page. How many persons are really involved in that? But look at the coverage they get." "I think it's natural for us to have our own papers," he said, "since we've been written out of most other literature."

When queried, most CPA editors and writers are frankly unsure about whether they have real influence in their communities. The safest assumption is that they are most widely read among the younger Chicanos of high school and college age, and among community activists of all ages.

The contributors to CPA newspapers also tend to be young and/or activist. Dr. Acuna said there might be a disadvantage to this youth orientation. "A lot of the writers are inexperienced, and haven't learned to mix their materials," he said. "They tend to be too political, and don't mix in enough social news or human interest stories."

They also tend to use rough, militant language which Dr. Acuna said alienates many potential readers. Nevertheless, he said that there has been an improvement in most Chicano papers since they began, and he expects it to continue.

"You can see a marked evolution in *La Raza*, for example," he said, "It started out as a political rap sheet that made generalizations without backing them up. Now its articles present good points to back up logical arguments." "The longer these papers operate," he concluded, "the more good young writers will be attracted to them. I think the quality of these papers will continue to improve and may even become better than the conventional press."

However, at least some CPA members see newspapers—even quality ones—as only one part in an overall plan to build up *barrio* communications media. Raul Ruiz explained his hope that the *La Raza* offices might someday become a full scale publishing house. "Instead of having other people approve our writers before they can be published, we want to be able to print our own Chicano materials," he said.

While, with their arty layout and lack of objectivity ("We may be slanted as the establishment press defines it, but we tell the truth as the Chicano sees it," one writer said) the Chicano newspapers may not represent journalism at its best, they do represent the respect many young Chicanos have for the printed word as a tool to be used for the betterment of what they proudly call "la Raza," "el Movimiento," and "la Causa."

The names these Chicano newspapermen give their papers reflect both their militant cultural pride and their restless determination to better their people: *Bronze* in San Jose, Calif.; *Inferno* and *La Raza Nueva* (The New Race) in San Antonio, Texas; *La Revolucion* in Uvalde, Texas; *Coraje* (Anger) in Tucson, Ariz.; *El Grito del Norte* (The Truth) in San Diego; and *El Yaqui* in Houston (named for an Indian Tribe in Mexico, known for its fierceness).

Finally, another notable San Antonio paper is *El Rebozo* (named after a traditional wrap-around garment worn by Mexican women). Written and published by women, it is primarily aimed at the increasingly militant "women of la Raza."

As Ruiz put it, "The seriousness of the movement demands a dependable and consistent press, and we feel that we cannot rely on the establishment press to provide this."

The Chicano newspapermen of the CPA are not alone in this view. An increasing number of other young writers and potential newsmen in minority communities are going in the same direction (another example, one native American organization publishes *The Warpath* in San Francisco).

All of these minority representatives are in essence telling the outside world of the white majority that, if there is interpretation and uplifting of their communities and people to be done, they are going to try and do most of it themselves.

ARE RELIGIOUS MAGAZINES OBSCENE?

Terence Shea

The 32,000 subscribers to *motive*, an ambitious Methodist religious magazine, got a thin surprise when they opened the May 1969 issue. The postman had delivered only the empty covers.

A mistake there may have been, but it wasn't made in the print shop. The empty covers arrived with a letter from the editors, explaining why. In the previous month's issue, one devoted entirely to the role of women, the authors had studded their copy with four-letter words and reference to sex and homosexuality.

"This issue appears with the four-letter words intact because the authors used them intentionally," the editors had said. But the explanation wasn't good enough for the publishers—the church authorities. They ordered the next issue canceled; hence, the empty covers.

B.J. Stiles, 36, a Methodist minister whose term as editor ended with the issue, suggests that the dispute over the earthy Anglo-Saxon words was only the symptom of the troubles at *motive*; editors of other religious publications cite similar symptoms.

Terence Shea's examination of various church publications is used with permission of the *National Observer*, where he is the religion writer. The original piece was reprinted in the December, 1969 *Seminar Quarterly*. Mr. Shea is a nationally known writer whose ideas are often as thought provoking as the ones presented here.

Almost all publications, religious or otherwise, are accountable to someone, whether to a publisher, a church, or a group of stockholders. But there's a rising demand by editors of religious publications for more independence.

motive is a striking, graphic, and thoroughly liberal examiner of philosophy, politics, religion, poetry, the arts, and social issues. Among many religion-publication editors it has set a pace—usually more envied than imitated—in design and editorial concepts. Few publications resemble *motive* but several watch it as a barometer of religion publishing. A few defend it.

Christian Century said: "We do not favor the conversion of never-never words into common public vocabulary. But the discrediting of outstanding editors and the denial of a whole issue of a magazine to its readers because the editors have chosen to let the discontented speak in their own vernacular is a greater obscenity than any four-letter word."

Among America's 1,700 religion-based publications, *Christian Century, Commonweal,* and *America* are a few of the more liberal commentaries. The broad middle range of general-readership publications includes such magazines as *Presbyterian Life,* the *Episcopalian, U.S. Catholic,* and *Christian Herald,* plus scores of locally oriented newspapers. The range of smaller, special-interest magazines includes those such as the topical *Christian Advocate* for Methodist pastors, the innovative monthly *Catechist* for religion teachers, a widening number of attractive youth publications, and a proliferation of journals concerned with particular church activities.

Many publications have changed substantially in response to changes in churches through the past decade, but some editors now sense a stiffening of opposition to the directions of their editorial policies. The former editor of a major Protestant periodical says, "There's a great reaction setting in."

He adds, "If you work for the church as a journalist you are working, theoretically, for the most idealistic institution in the world." But, he argues, publishing decisions are sometimes made for reasons that are petty rather than idealistic, and it seems to him that the momentum of change in the church is lost.

In August 1969, the Very Rev. Msgr. Vincent Yzermans, an outspoken proponent of increased editorial freedom in the Catholic press, resigned as editor of America's largest national Catholic newspaper, *Our Sunday Visitor.* He said he was weary of waging the "old liberal-conservative battles."

When B.J. Stiles resigned from *motive* he complained that the magazine lacked support from its publishers, the Division of Higher Education of the United Methodist Board of Education. He doubts that the church body wants to sponsor any magazine that deals in criticism, controversy, and occasional radicalism.

Within a year, *motive* may have a new publisher, he says, perhaps an *ad hoc* board of the United Methodist Church. The Rev. Myron Wicke, general secretary of the Division of Higher Education, says "a new ecumenical home" might be found for the magazine.

Whatever happens, says Mr. Stiles, *motive* will probably never again produce an issue like the last March-April number, wholly dedicated to the "liberation" of women and introduced with an editorial entitled, "Here's to You, Mrs. Robinson." The editorial was written by a pretty, miniskirted Randolph-Macon Woman's College graduate who calls herself the "token woman" on the *motive* staff.

Joanne Cooke, 23, planned and directed the issue. "The woman thing" demands radical rethinking, she wrote, and anticipating some raised eyebrows about what would follow in the art, articles, and poems, including the four-letter words, she continued: "Our society has permitted certain words to become weapons, often used against women and taboo to them. We have to learn to be shocked, not at 'bad' words but at the 'bad' concepts behind their use."

She listed and defined several familiar expletives, and she commented on two denoting sexual intercourse: "(They) mean not intercourse but its depersonalized version, involving the physical use of a woman one cares nothing about. These last two words are being used increasingly by women to refer to the male concept of impersonal sex. These words should have been demythologized and disarmed long ago."

One article characterized the low esteem of women scholars, another dealt with the women's-liberation movement, and in an essay promoting witchery an anonymous author said: "A witch lives and laughs in every woman. She is the free part of each of us. . . ." An article entitled "The Subversion of Betty Crocker" portrayed the image of woman in the "commodity culture," and another dissection of the female essence was titled "Woman as Secretary, Sexpot, Spender, Sow, Civic Actor, Sickie."

The authors of the article "The Realities of Lesbianism," which discussed the social and psychological frameworks of female homosexuality, complained that there are too few coffee houses and other acceptable gathering places for homosexuals. Attempts to form such places, they contended, "have lacked the influential backing of, say, the church, to provide protection against police harassment while creating a wholesome social fabric for the teen-age homosexual."

The reaction was predictably heavy and it cost *motive* some of its dwindling circulation, currently at 32,000. Some of the anger was aimed at Mr. Stiles, who had already resigned, with the implication that the issue was the vindictive stroke of a lame-duck editor against the church officials he disputed. In fact, Mr. Stiles had argued for a less-flamboyant women's-liberation issue, and half of the magazine's staff agreed with him.

Miss Cooke successfully argued for a lopsided issue. "I felt that any statement we could have made to temper it would have destroyed its impact," she says. "I didn't want to qualify it. I didn't want any Uncle Toms." The following issue, which was canceled, would have been the last for B.J. Stiles.

He had resigned almost a year before, after returning from a leave of absence for work in Robert Kennedy's Presidential campaign. He stayed with *motive* through the publishing year, which ended this spring, and now he is an executive with the Robert F. Kennedy Memorial Foundation, in Washington, D.C.

The biggest change he made at *motive* he says, was to abolish the "Christianity and . . ." approach to matters such as race, poverty, war, politics, and contemporary issues. He moved against the tradition that a Methodist magazine ought to be written by Methodists if possible, and he opened *motive* to such topics as secularism and "death of God" theology. He bought articles from literary and theological figures such as Thomas Merton, Harvey Cox, Michael Novak, Nat Hentoff, and other well-known writers.

The magazine's annual income doubled to $110,000, it's circulation rose to 45,000, it opened up to elaborate and expensive art and graphics. As Mr. Stiles says, *motive* came to be included in the publishing circles of *Harper's*, the *Atlantic*, and *Saturday Review*. That was one of his aims, and that was one of the problems.

"*motive* had more or less lost its way," says Dr. Wicke, its publisher. "We don't need to publish a magazine that tries to beat *Atlantic* and *Harper's* and *Ramparts*. *motive* was founded to speak to the campuses about campus issues in a Christian theological framework."

His hope for the restoration of *motive* has come to rest now on Robert Maurer.

Mr. Maurer is 27, a year younger than *motive*, and he stands only two inches short of seven feet. Unlike the magazines' previous editors, he is neither a Methodist nor a minister. He is a graduate of Wesleyan University and of Union Theological Seminary. He is a member of the United Church of Christ, and he was an active com-

munity organizer when *motive* hired him. The special board that
interviewed him gave him what he describes as a friendly "inquisi-
tion."

"They asked me questions like whether I smoke or drink," he
says. He takes a little soda in his Bourbon and he likes a good Medoc.
They never asked him what he would do with four-letter words, he
says—"but if they had . . . ." he would have said that he would allow
such language "in the context of the obscenities and violence that
they express for certain people."

He will aim *motive* at the 25-to-32 age group. "I want to get to
the roommates of those people who went to Selma," he says, "the
ones who heard it was pretty exciting down there but didn't go, the
ones who are making all that money now and maybe feeling a little
uneasy about it."

motive is put together in Nashville by a staff of 10 in a little,
old, brown, two-story house across the street from the United Methodist Board of Publication, the church's huge publishing complex
and a place under fire of its own from some church activists for its
operational policies.

Half of the *motive* staff has resigned, and Mr. Maurer says his
first task is to rebuild morale. Those who remained, including Miss
Cooke, may have to adjust from the ways of Mr. Stiles, a tailored and
urbane man conscious of trends and of sophistication in publishing,
to the manners of the tousled Mr. Maurer, whose boyish visage and
easy-going manner belie a certain activism, a recognized brilliance,
and firm intent.

He talks of de-emphasizing the striking typography and makeup of *motive*. They appeal to New York tastes, he says, but most of
his readers are in the Midwest. Such authors as Harvey Cox, the
theologian, and Daniel Berrigan, the activist anti-war Catholic priest,
will be rarer in the magazine's pages from now on, he says, to make
room for unknown new writers and, perhaps, for younger radicals.

Mr. Maurer will try to win back some of the subscribers who
recently quit, both those who left in disgust because the March-April
issue was printed, and those who left in dismay after the May issue
was canceled. It will be a hard but perhaps not impossible task.

One man who rebuilt a magazine's readership is the editor of
the United Church of Christ's religious-education monthly, *Colloquy*.
John Westerhoff III lost half of his 40,000 subscribers when he made
a new, modern publication out of two older, smaller periodicals.
"Every magazine has its own problems of getting its own market," he
says, "and in church publishing it's a real problem." He has solved it,

though, building his circulation to 70,000 in two years with consistently good editorial content that is broad enough to appeal to religion teachers of several denominations.

Another magazine that has shuffled its readership is *Home Missions*, published by the Southern Baptist Convention's Home Mission Board. Its circulation is 97,000, down from the 135,000 figure of several years ago when, says associate editor Dallas Lee, "Everybody (in mission work) just took it as a badge of membership."

In recent years, editor Walker Knight has used new design techniques, color, the photography of Don Rutledge, and his own editorials to stir the social consciousness of his readers. "The magazine is being talked about," says Mr. Lee, "and the decline of hate mail shows how far we've come. We're getting a better, more mature type of reaction."

The magazine with a defined audience and a single concern can be more direct in its editorial approach than can a more general religious publication such as *Presbyterian Life* or the *Episcopalian.*

"As an instrument created by the General Convention," the *Episcopalian's* editors recently wrote, "we exist primarily as an information exchange for lay people within the whole Episcopal Church. We serve largely the same purpose on the national level as a parish bulletin within a single congregation, and a diocesan paper within a single jurisdiction. . . . The editorial content of the *Episcopalian*, then, is a mixture of many messages."

Occasionally, a church magazine of general readership will risk its popularity by changing its editorial mind. The *Christian Herald*, an interdenominational monthly magazine with a 400,000 circulation and directed by the Rev. David Poling, recently announced it was publishing a story it had shelved in 1967—a criticism of the Vietnam War by Hoch Reid, a New York lawyer.

"It was and is a serious thing to question an action of our Government on legal and moral grounds," the introductory note said. "But things have changed in two years. The Administration in Washington has changed. We have changed. The nation has changed. What has not changed is the war in Vietnam."

The arguable topics and the strongest opinions are usually left to the smaller, less generally circulated religion magazines. A few are totally independent of church control, some are historically but not currently linked to certain churches, and some are closely affiliated with churches or religion-based groups.

The more specialized publications concerned to any degree with issues in religion range from the little weekly *Mennonite* with its crystalline essays for social change or the solidly intellectual *Commentary* published by the American Jewish Committee, to the moderate monthly *Lutheran Forum*, and *Christianity Today*, "a fortnightly magazine of evangelical conviction" that covers almost every event and trend in religion.

The weekly magazine *America*, owned and edited by the Roman Catholic Church's Society of Jesus, takes stands on matters of politics, war, economics, defense, international affairs, education, poverty, and the concerns of blacks. The magazine also examines more strictly religious matters such as the church's birth-control and authority positions, ideas about worship, the actions of the Vatican and of cardinals and bishops, and such issues as atheism, abortion, and priestly celibacy.

"I'd be wrong to say we don't have the Pope, the general (the international head of the Jesuits), and the bishops in mind when we write," says the Rev. Donald Campion, S.J. editor of *America*. "But we try to talk to them, not kick them."

Yet, for all their efforts to be professionally competent, vigorous, and fair-minded, can publications owned by church groups ever be fully free?

"I'm afraid I'd have to say no," answers B.J. Stiles. Other editors agree. Idealism eventually acknowledges reality in religious journalism too.

Chapter VII

FERMENT IN THE PERSUASIVE ARTS

BROADCASTING'S HIDDEN POWER: THE TV-RADIO REPS

John Tebbel

While no one was looking, a business within a business has grown up in television and radio during the past two decades that, in the words of one trade journal, has become "the most far-reaching business influence in broadcasting today." This little known, and even less understood, power is national spot sales representation, embodied in the companies that represent television and radio spot advertising to national sales and marketing organizations.

It is not surprising that the viewing and listening public is almost wholly unaware of the "TV and radio sales reps," as they are known in the trade. The public reacts either with boredom or with varying degrees of interest to the ubiquitous "spots" that surround its entertainment, but has no idea how they got there, and in most cases, doesn't care. What *is* astonishing, however, is the degree of ignorance in the business community itself about the sales reps. Many businessmen would be unable to define what these companies are, and only a few have any real knowledge of what they do.

The general shortage of savvy stems from a lack of knowledge about the economics of broadcasting. It is widely assumed that local stations exist because of the bounty derived from their network affiliation, but this is far from the case. For example, in 1968, television's total advertising revenue was $1,504,484,000. Of this figure, network revenue accounted for $247,618,000, but national and re-

John Tebbel, professor of journalism at New York University and distinguished author, frequently has contributed articles such as this one on the invisible power of the broadcasting representative. The article (December 13, 1969) is published with his permission and that of *Saturday Review*, copyright 1969.

gional spot advertising totaled $998,036,000. Even more significantly, network sales were up only 0.7 per cent from the year before, while the figure was 14.5 per cent for the national regional spots.

In radio advertising, there is virtually no network business. In 1967, it represented only $47-million out of a total revenue of $946-million, or 5 per cent of all radio advertising, and the figure is declining. By contrast, national spot advertising accounted for $289-million, or 31 per cent of all radio dollars in the same year, while local spots brought in $609-million, or 64 per cent of the total.

Dealing in figures like these, it is all the more startling that a major industry should be operating in such virtual anonymity, so much so that even many advertising agency staff members, (outside the media department, of course) have only vague ideas about what the reps are and what they do. Not that the reps need the publicity. Quietly, they chalk up about $882-million a year in time sales, and about 90 per cent of this business is divided among only fifteen firms. There are few, if any, industries where so few companies, employing such a small number of people, account for so many dollars of revenue.

What the increasing power and multiplying activities of the reps mean to the viewer lies in the major impact they have on programing. For a long time after the business began in 1937, the reps did little more than send out their rate cards, but now they profoundly influence a station's programs, since their job is to relate them to the station's market in terms of advertising. Thus, they decide such questions as when children's programs are best presented, whether the local news program should precede or follow network news, and what kind of shows are best adapted to the station's area.

In doing so, the reps have to take into account the nature of a broadcaster's audience, and it is fair to say that in an economy that has been market researched to the point of exhaustion, no audience for any product has been so thoroughly dissected and analyzed as the television and radio consumer. Nothing illustrates the antiquity of the Willie Loman image of salesmanship better than the massive jungle of statistics available to the TV sales rep as he goes about his work. Selling time in West Palm Beach, for example, is far different from doing the same job in Hawaii. In the Florida city, not surprisingly, the most popular television show has been *Meet the Doctor*, a locally produced program appealing to the predominantly elderly population. In Hawaii, on the other hand, the approach is heavily concentrated toward young people. Moreover, since everything has to come on tape from the mainland, it is possible to juggle the programs into time slots calculated to catch the attention of the young audience. The reps play a major part in the juggling.

In other areas of broad popular interest, the reps have also become determining factors. That staple of broadcasting, motion pictures, was once largely in the hands of the networks, but the reps have shown the local stations that they can buy their own movies for less and the reps will sell the advertising time. This also makes it possible for the local stations to buy movies that will please the audience in their own area. Obviously, the tastes of predominantly rural or smalltown viewers will not always be the same as for a more sophisticated urban audience.

Such buying is part of the trend toward local programing, according to James F. O'Grady, vice president and general manager of RKO-Radio Representatives, Inc. This movement is currently being stimulated, O'Grady points out, by the challenge to station owners offered by local groups seeking to obtain the licenses from the FCC for themselves. The challenge is nearly always based on the contention that the station is not properly serving local interests with its programing (meaning, among other things, that too many programs are network originated). Consequently, owners and managers have been moving rapidly toward more home origination, a move in which the reps are taking an important part. As more and more stations pre-empt network programs for local shows, the reps will have an even larger role in the development of programing.

Here again the facts contradict popular belief that the networks own the stations. In fact, by law no one is permitted to own more than seven television stations, of which no more than five may be on the VHF band. The major networks have increasingly come to act as distributing agents for programs that they buy from producing organizations; they originate comparatively few of their own. But the reps can also be distributing agents, and more and more they are assuming this function. Network-produced shows—and these would include those done by RKO-General, Westinghouse Group W, Metromedia, Triangle Broadcasting, and Storer, as well as the major networks—are now made available to other stations in addition to their own affiliates.

Reps believe that major network football is doomed and that it is coming into their province, along with the motion picture business. The new sports network set up by Howard Hughes, they say, may well supersede the others in distributing the games, and the reps will sell the time on a local basis. Similarly, where the major nets once had the advantage in news programs and dominated the field, the moonshot demonstrated that the smaller organizations are coming into their own here, too. Westinghouse, Metromedia, and RKO all had their own broadcasting teams operating for this event. It is significant that RKO-General has one of the fifty desks in the White House newsroom, and one of the five precious darkrooms available to develop news film on the spot.

The influence of the reps, invisible to the public and to much of the broadcasting business as well, is felt everywhere. They are aggressive in their encouragement of advertisers both large and small to use spot TV; some of the largest rep companies have formal departments and full-time personnel who concentrate on companies that advertise very little or not at all in spot television. The stations themselves, it must be noted, are not geared to do this kind of selling to national and regional advertisers; if it were not for the reps, it would never be done.

Today there is scarcely a facet of station operation that does not involve the reps; the legal and engineering departments are the only exceptions. The reps are particularly active in rate setting, research, and audience and sales promotion. They furnish their stations with promotional and research data, sales brochures, and full-scale presentations. They go to the Census Bureau to try to add (or subtract) counties from Standard Metropolitan Areas, as this category is called, and they work constantly with the rating services to improve audience measurement techniques. Reps even work on billing and collection problems.

Unofficially, representatives are the bumblebees of the advertising world, disseminating information in the industry like pollen. Sometimes they are the first to know when advertising accounts are shaky, and they act as an effective if informal personnel bureau for media and account people.

There are about sixty "independent" reps, as they are known, and about six or seven "limited list" reps, usually associated with such group-owned operations as Westinghouse and RKO. There are also more than fifty regional reps. All told, the national reps maintain approximately 350 offices and employ about 2,000 people, of whom roughly 850 are salesmen. Total annual payroll for these firms exceeds $15-million, and they sell spot advertising for more than 2,000 radio stations as well as nearly 500 television stations.

Among the group owners in television, Westinghouse Broadcasting was the first to establish a bona fide rep organization, TvAR, a subsidiary of Westinghouse Electric, to represent its television properties. According to its president, Howard H. Marsh, TvAR also became the first such firm to represent outside stations, and it pioneered the concept of limited list representation. Since TvAR was founded in July 1959, five major station groups and one network have established their own national rep firms.

Spot television is the only broadcast medium competing with the networks, and reps are the only force that advocates and sells spots. Both national representation and spot are mutually dependent; neither could exist in their present form without the other.

Advertising agencies have traditionally regarded spots with mixed feelings. Undeniably, they admit, the medium is an effective seller of goods and services, but it is much more expensive to handle and administrate than most other media, including network TV and radio. Consequently, many agencies either do not purchase spots—particularly spot radio—in the volume warranted by the medium's efficiency, or when they do, it is in a manner without sufficient controls and checks. This situation has had two significant effects on the advertising community:

1. Television, and especially radio, reps have in some cases short-circuited the traditional procedures of selling exclusively in advertising agencies' media departments, and have made their selling approaches directly to the advertisers. In fact, some reps have instituted units designed for the purpose, and have concentrated directly on selling to advertisers on a concerted basis. Recently, large purchases of radio spots have been made by advertisers who have not even consulted their agencies, but the agencies get commissions on the buys (after the fact).

2. Time-buying organizations have been springing up recently, devoted only to that function. Already there are two major companies in the field, Timebuying Services, Inc., and U.S. Media, along with several smaller organizations. Their business is expanding so rapidly that the entrepreneurs can scarcely keep up in terms of space and personnel.

The significance of these changes can hardly be underestimated; they constitute a major trend in communications advertising. Until now the industry has witnessed the odd spectacle of advertisers who demand a careful accounting of every aspect of their businesses—except for the $10- to $20-million a year they invest in spot television. Before, they had to pray they would get their money's worth. Sometimes they did; more often they did not. Today, say the reps, they are getting true value for the first time.

Some agency media people deny this contention, but those in

the business informed enough to be concerned about it, understand that the position of the advertising agency in this particular area is being substantially eroded by the reps.

WHEN ADVERTISING TALKS TO EVERYONE

Fairfax Cone

When publicly contemplating the future of almost anything, there is nothing safer than to see in it all manner of drastic change, even to the point of disaster. Then, if trouble comes, the viewer with alarm can smugly regard the situation that he has predicted and be called a wise soothsayer. If, on the other hand, the prophet of crack-up and break-down turns out to be wrong, no one is hurt, and he need only say that his timing was off or that vastly changed circumstances made the difference. I am going to take the long chance.

If we are indeed entering an era of news monopoly in terms of both national and world news, it seems more than likely that regional and local news services actually will be increased. The development of small-town and suburban community newspapers at a time when many big-city newspapers have ceased publication has been a phenomenon of the last two or three decades. Now, with local cable television coming to communities of all sizes, it can be predicted that this new emphasis on local news and interests will be intensified.

A recent broadcasting event in Newport Beach, California, illustrates this. The cable television station there invited thirty candidates for public offices ranging from the U.S. Senate to the local village council to tell their stories in terms of their own interests. All accepted with the result that hundreds of citizens of this small southern California seaside community for the first time saw candidates in the light of their own problems.

In much the same way, I believe we are entering a time when much advertising also will become more local and more meaningful.

Fairfax M. Cone told the story of his forty years in advertising in 1969 when he published *With All Its Faults* (Boston: Little, Brown). The final chapter is recommended for its estimate of how advertising can better serve the society in which it exists. This article on the future electronic age (October 10, 1970) is reprinted with permission of *Saturday Review*, copyright 1970.

Advertising aimed precisely at what might be termed need-groups promises a new and welcome relevancy.

When advertising tries to talk to everyone, the result is no different than it is when any other form of communication is aimed at the largest possible audience. The days of yellow journalism at the turn of the century are an example. The heyday of the great mass magazines in the 1950s is another. Neither could last, for audiences tire of unchanging fare, and either break up into separate interest groups or find new sources for their enlightenment and their entertainment. Both of these developments are occurring in broadcasting at this moment, and their effect on advertising will be profound.

One of the unhappy concomitants of today's television, with its enormous time and production costs for advertising, has been the unwillingness of many major advertisers to depart from commercial routines that have proved to be successful economically, no matter how wearisome they may be to millions of viewers. It is a demonstrable fact that one's reaction to almost any advertising message breaks down into two parts: the form in which the message is presented and the promise itself. The result is that the form may be, and often is, a subject of ridicule (e.g., the white tornado that blows through the kitchen or the eye-winking plumber who clears a clogged drain with nothing more than a sprinkling of powder that is available from your nearest friendly grocer), while the proposition that is made for the product involved is totally accepted.

If this sounds impossible, or even improbable, I can only explain it in terms of noises to which one becomes accustomed to the point of not hearing them at all, while a special sound of much lesser intensity comes through loud and clear. However, this is hardly an excuse for the foolishness that makes so many commercial minutes seem ugly and interminable.

The trouble lies in the lack of creative ability in the people in advertising agencies and production studios, and among the advertisers, who are caught between two deadly dilemmas. One is to follow the leader with the implausible dramas of fun and games at the sink or in the bathroom or laundry; the other is to try anything at all that is different—for that reason alone. Of the two, it is questionable which is harder to take if one pays attention.

Both, however, may well be headed for the discard, for paying attention to the commercials is no longer a requirement of the television experience. In the beginning it was said, and it was probably true, that viewers gladly accepted the advertising as a reasonable price of admission to the shows they watched. But the audience has become more sophisticated. There has developed a little mechanism in the brain of almost everyone of us that can automatically shut off our attention to a point where only certain sounds come through: mostly product names and promises and pertinent details of unusual services.

To be sure, there are exceptions to the general low interest in commercial messages. Some are full of fun and the fun is to the point. Others, such as commercials for many food and household products, present demonstrations that help the homemaker with her relentless job. Still others substitute dramatic facts for throaty claims for automobile tires and batteries and insurance, etc.

The changes that one can foresee in advertising in the next few years, and that should make much of it more attractive and useful for everyone concerned, are becoming apparent in an about-face in advertising philosophy that will bring it into line with growing interest in the consumer as an object of concern and respect and not a faceless, nearly mindless purchasing unit. To say this another way, I believe the impersonality is going out of advertising much as I believe that it is going to be replaced in business for the very good reason that this works both ways: Customer loyalty simply cannot be maintained by an impersonal supplier, and business and advertising must, in the long run, depend on that loyalty. That they must also earn it is the reason for the inevitable changes.

The alternative is the complete breakdown of an imperfect system. The imperfection may be the result of growth and standardization, and the temporary subjugation of the individual during a period of great economic change and concentration of power. Whatever the reason, no one can doubt that as a nation we have arrived at a time when skepticism may be our most outstanding characteristic. Vietnam is only one reason for this. Rightly or wrongly, the maturing generation believes that we have been lied to and manipulated by business and government, and even in our educational and legal systems, and the young men and women who supply this generation with its conviction and strength see advertising as one of the worst sins of a venal establishment. Nor is this a question particularly of dishonesty or sharp practice. Unhappily, these evils are largely taken for granted. The overriding objection is to the mass appeal of advertising at a time when all the emphasis our young people can muster is on individuality. There is a thing called life-style that simply cannot be dictated by anyone—advertisers least of all.

This will unquestionably mean more special-interest publications, both magazines and community news organs (either printed or electronically reproduced), with special-interest advertising. Still, the biggest change will probably be in television and television advertising, where the messages for many products and services will be delivered almost as professional buyers' guides by a nationwide corps of competent local authorities who will evaluate and recommend products and services according to their own standards and experience. Products of only general interest (or those lacking interest at any given moment, such as analgesics) will continue to be advertised over the networks in national news and sports programs and the more popular comedy and variety and dramatic hours.

Despite considerable speculation to the contrary, it seems unlikely that either pay television or the cassette will mean the end of the big variety or dramatic programs or the ace news commentators as we have come to expect these from the networks. For one thing, entertainment that one must pay for must be a good deal better than entertainment that is free, and this may be hard to come by for more than a few hours in any week, for the costs will be considerable. Also, news cannot be canned; it must be contemporaneous. On the other hand, hundreds of independent cable television stations are going to compete, and successfully, I believe, with the run-of-mine programs by offering a conglomerate of special interest features for limited but extremely receptive audiences.

Cable television was introduced as a means of establishing or improving physical reception in remote areas, and this it has done very successfully. While no one knows precisely what its effect will be in metropolitan centers, where reception is satisfactory for the most part and where there is already a choice of channels and programs, the likelihood is that it will become not so much an extension of television as we now know it, but an essentially new medium.

It is not difficult to imagine the attraction of a station that performs service to the community by broadcasting purely local news and commentary and an almost unlimited number of programs of unique interest. The key factor, of course, is the freedom of the cable station operator from the demands for a large audience by any advertiser, for his audience is made up of paid subscribers. Such advertisers as there may be, and I expect there will be many, will be satisfied with any reasonable, and reasonably priced, audience whose special interest they share.

This, then, is where the greatest change in advertising is likely to take place. In recent years, most large advertisers increasingly have aimed their messages at the largest available audiences at the lowest possible cost per thousand. This led to the disastrous circulation races among the mass magazines, the strain of which caused the demise of half a dozen of them, and a gradual diminution in the number of daily newspapers. Neither could compete successfully with a medium that was wholly advertiser-supported and adored by advertiser and public alike. This was in television's long honeymoon stage. Today many an advertiser is beginning to wonder whether the large audiences are really worth the total expenditures involved, no matter how low the cost per thousand. The questions arise partly out of a desire to save money and so increase profits and partly out of a determination to talk only to one's most logical prospects. Clearly, such a change in advertising strategy should dictate a much more thoughtful and much less blatant use of all advertising media.

It is safe to say that television is today the principal source of news as well as entertainment for the majority of American families. If this presaged a monopoly of either one by a monolithic television system, I would be fearful of the result. But I think the imminence of community cable television negates the possibility, in the very same way that it promises advertising that is less dictated and confined by formula.

It is necessary here to remember that all advertising is not alike either in its making or intention. Manufacturers' advertising, for the most part, announces innovations and product changes and improvements, and this advertising appears mostly in magazines and on television and radio. The advertising of retailers, which is concerned primarily with the values in those products in terms of style, size, price, etc., makes up the bulk of newspaper advertising, except for want ads.

The changes that I foresee will have little or no effect upon the division of advertising between the various media. It should stay much as it is, with only some diversion of special-interest advertising from the general magazines to the growing list of special-interest publications.

On the other hand, I believe that advertising may be greatly changed by still another factor. With two-way communication established between receivers and cable stations, whereby subscribers may dial requests for any information under the sun, which will be available by computer, it is unlikely that consumer reports will not be included. No service could be more natural or have greater effect upon advertising. For the reply to the subscriber's query and the advertising that floats freely through the air on the same subject must allow no disparity. Both must serve the recipient in his own best interest.

This is something that advertising has always promised to do. But the promise has not always been kept. In large measure, it may now be.

PR IN THE MARKETING MIX

Richard M. Detwiler

Since the day it was born public relations has achieved many wonderful things but it never amounted to much as an ingredient in the marketing mix.

Up until 1970, at least. Now all that may be changing. It could be that public relations ends up as the superingredient in the marketing mix, the *sine qua non*.

Prior to 1970 public relations as a component of marketing mostly got overlooked. It simply did not figure in the thinking or comprehension of most marketing management. It's a fair surmise even today that most marketing plans don't include a public relations section, and that it isn't even on a checklist when a marketing strategy is being put together.

Advertising Age, the largest and most influential of the marketing publications, does not recognize public relations as a factor in marketing. The Harvard Business School does not include it in its marketing courses.

When public relations does show up in marketing it is generally as an afterthought called product publicity—after the marketing plan is all locked up. There is nothing wrong with product publicity, except that it doesn't even hint at the potential of public relations fully integrated into the marketing process.

The reason for this neglect need not detain us long. It may be as simple as—of all things—a lack of communication between public relations people and marketing management, and probably a lack of a common nomenclature. The thinness of the literature on the subject may be the tip-off. Public relations people generally do not seem to be terribly interested or concerned in this unaltruistic phase of the business.

Richard M. Detwiler, vice president of Batten, Barton Durstine and Osborn, Inc., New York, sees an increased need for public relations techniques. Reprinted from the *Public Relations Journal*, by permission, copyright October, 1970.

In this *annus mirabilis* of 1970 some interesting things have been taking shape which may give public relations a stronger cachet with the marketing people, and present the public relations people with a lot more challenge in marketing. And not least, the prospect of new responsibilities and new business for them IF they can relate their capabilities and services to the needs and goals of marketing management.

The big breakthrough in 1970 was this: Probably for the first time marketing management fully recognized that public relations might not only be a factor in marketing, but possibly the decisive factor. This shock of recognition was the result of the cresting of consumer protest.

Under the pressure of consumer protest and government harassment, marketing has been going through some kind of Great Reformation. The day may not be far off when public relations sits in judgement on whether or not a certain product comes on the market, or stays on the market, or gets withdrawn from the market. And what kind of advertising gets created for the product, and what that advertising says and can't say.

Hairy though this prospect may be for ad men and marketing managers, the signs are clear.

In 1970 Olin Corporation voluntarily discontinued its DDT business before the end of the product life cycle. Dow Chemical got out of napalm a year earlier.

And so its goes. When General Motors gets demonstrated against and pressured on grounds of public accountability not to produce cars that develop noxious emissions, that is at least as much a public relations problem as it is a marketing problem.

The same goes for detergent manufacturers who come under pressure from the public and government agencies because of phosphates and eutrophication.

When Arthur Godfrey put the rap on the very product that he was getting paid to tout, it had to be at least partly a public relations consideration which permitted this hallowed huckster to keep his job pitching Axion for so long in spite of his apostasy.

Public relations may soon determine the marketing destiny of a great many products. In fact, 1970 may have seen the ultimate triumph of public relations virtue over marketing expediency—when in paid advertising Consolidated Edison confessed its power deficiencies and warned the public of impending brownouts within its marketing area.

It would be sheer madness to presume that public relations

professionals will automatically be doing all this sitting in judgement. But at least the public relations *function* will. For a while at least we will be exercising this territorial imperative in company with the lawyers.

Yet the problem today has gone beyond legality. Mere legal compliance—of an advertising message, for example—will not necessarily absolve an advertiser of his public vulnerability. The product or the message may be perfectly legal, and yet the public or an organized consumer protection group within it could react with outrage.

So in 1970 we got the attention of marketing management. They now have to recognize that products and marketing processes, for better or for worse, operate in a public relations environment.

How, specifically, can we relate public relations to marketing and the components of the marketing plan?

It would be shortsighted to hope for a big future for public relations in the distress of the marketing function. We are all fishing in the same pond. Nevertheless, marketing all along the line is under pressure, and these problems and stresses represent opportunities for public relations to help. It has unique capabilities to help solve the problems or outflank them.

Let's review some of the problems which are debated and deplored constantly by authorities inside and outside of marketing, and which get aired regularly in the advertising and marketing trade press.

The mortality rate for new products introduced to the market is close to 80 per cent—eight out of ten new products bomb out. The cost of introducing a new product—exclusive of research and development costs—can run to $30 million for a national introduction of, say, a soap or detergent.

The cost of new product failure each year has been estimated at about $2 billion.

There are a lot of reasons why these products fail. One cogent reason is that marketing management is just not observing that grand old principle of military tactics—the cooperation of all arms.

Public relations as an arm of marketing is "undercooperated," but it seems reasonable to expect—the way things are going—that beleaguered marketing management may have to take a look at every weapon in sight, and maybe discover that public relations packs quite a bit of firepower.

The rising *cost* of marketing and advertising is another nagging problem. The cost of media alone is going up at the rate of about 5 per cent a year. In other words, the advertiser today has to spend half again as much as he did in 1960 to bring the same advertising weight against his target audience. Or if he's not spending that much more, he is sacrificing weight and frequency—which maybe he can't afford to do in light of the increasing competition, plus a 2 per cent annual population growth.

Public relations offers some interesting alternatives and reinforcements for reaching the target audiences—with considerable cost efficiency.

The solution to the cost problem is not as easy as just being able to afford the higher price tag for the same advertising weight and frequency. The message itself—the impact and penetration of the selling message—is worrying marketing management.

The consumer is being bombarded with more and more advertisng messages, and he is tuning out more and more. In the past five years, for example, with the trend toward more 20- and 30-second commercials as opposed to the standard 60's of a few years back, the noise level, the sheer number of TV commercials, has increased by nearly 60 per cent. Ad people talk about "cluttervision" and "message pollution."

There has been escalation of the commercial content of TV all along the line. The situation with overstuffed print media is equally grim.

In the face of all this overcommercialization, the opportunity for public relations has been well articulated by the well-known marketing authority, Theodore Levitt, in his book, "The Marketing Mode."

"The very fact of advertising's enormous ubiquity, and the consequent difficult and costly struggle for the consumer's attention, makes it especially surprising that public relations is so marginally employed in the communications mix of heavy advertisers.

"If advertising's very abundance creates a high coefficient of agnosticism, then public relations has a special claim to merit. Its distinction is the greater credibility of its message."

The problem of the effectiveness and credibility of advertising is by no means the most serious problem. The right to advertise, the very existence of advertising, is being challenged as never before. The pattern of challenge has emerged clearly in the course of actions by the Federal Trade Commission and other government agencies, the U.S. Supreme Court and a number of militant consumers groups.

For example, there looms the prospect of limitations on the amount of advertising a large advertiser, with a dominant position in the market (e.g., cereals) can do, on the grounds that superior advertising leverage fosters monopoly.

If, indeed, there is going to be a ceiling imposed on advertising, this should certainly open up enormous opportunities for public relations.

Restrictions on the message, on what advertising can say, are tightening. It appears that an advertiser now is obliged to prove the claims in his advertising, and that indeed an advertising message is an implied warranty. The net of this is that there may be less and less competitive brand advertising. Less persuasion, more information.

If advertising is forced to become more bland and less persuasive, it seems entirely logical that public relations could help to take up the slack in articulating the selling message, by way of third party endorsement, editorial sanction or whatever else the useful flanking maneuvers of public relations might be called.

What are some of the pressure points to push with marketing management to demonstrate how public relations can fill the widening gaps in the marketing plan resulting mainly from an interesting phenomenon known as market concentration?

Market concentration works like this.

A batch of new products get introduced to the market—in 1968, about 10,000 in the package goods field alone.

This results in more market segmentation—the more a particular product category gets crowded with more products, each with some relatively minute differentiation or specialized appeal, the more that product category breaks up into sub markets with each product settling for a progressively smaller and smaller share of the market. The need to compromise on a smaller share of market enforces on marketing management the discipline known as market concentration, which assumes that for every product there is a prime prospect or key buying influence—the heavy user who accounts for the lion's share of consumption of that particular product.

For example, in the beer market it is that 20 per cent of the consumers who account for 80 per cent of the beer consumption. In instant coffee, the 17 per cent who drink 79 per cent of the product. The 25 per cent who buy 75 per cent of the aspirin. That 12 per cent of cough drop users who eat 67 per cent of the crop. That happy 14 per cent who drink 90 per cent of the bourbon.

So we see the trend—to concentrate more and more weight and frequency against a smaller and smaller group of the people, who must get the lion's share of the advertising pressure or the product is in trouble. Those marginal types, the people who *might* use the product, well, they are expendable because the marketer can't afford to reach them. He must concentrate to keep competitive. If he gets greedy and dilutes his appeal by trying to talk to everybody, he risks losing everybody.

What is developing here—in all this market segmentation and concentration—is a case of *gaposis*. Marketing has come a bit unzippered. The more the advertising coverage shrinks to concentrate increasing weight and frequency against the heavy user the more other potentials are left uncovered.

To the practiced eye of any good public relations man a marketing plan appears as full of holes as Swiss cheese. A lot of the marketing terrain is in defilade to the weapons of advertising. The most prodigal advertising budget simply can't afford to cover all the markets and all the audiences and media.

Consider cigarettes. It would be surprising if the cigarette manufacturers did not unlimber a lot of public relations to support their brands after cigarette advertising goes off TV at the end of 1970.

This kind of complementary support has worked successfully in the case of distillers. Although by industry agreement advertising of distilled spirits in the broadcast media has been prohibited, imaginative public relations has managed to get exposure and liquor brand identification on TV with good effect. One major distiller worked such a program several years ago. Not only were the results in terms of consumer response gratifying, but the trade impact stirred up interest far beyond expectations—in an industry where trade excitement is important mainly because there is no high-impact advertising such as TV offers.

Efficient marketing assumes that it is better to talk to the right 20 per cent of the market over and over, than to talk to everybody just a few times.

Public relations might reasonably be assigned to talk to the other 80 per cent of the people who are off the center of the target for advertising—plus adding some extra frequency by non-advertising means against the prime 20 per cent. In other words, it might increase both reach and frequency.

A novel example of this principle in action is the promotion of the coffee industry. Faced with a declining market the coffee industry has unlimbered an impressive public relations program to support its advertising.

One important target audience is teenagers. Traditionalists might gag at this idea, but coffee for kids makes good marketing sense. These are the consumers of the future, the ones to be wooed away from soft drinks and other competitive beverages.

However, this market would not be a lucrative target for advertising. The pre-teens are not heavy users or key buying influences in it. But it is a market essential to cover—and here public relations get the job.

This felicitous dovetailing of public relations with advertising can be demonstrated at just about every stage of the process—in the marketing strategy, the media strategy, the creative strategy, etc.

Demographies, for example. If the focus is on the 18-25 urban WASP female with 1.6 children, public relations can aim at singles, the geriatrics group, teeny boppers, males, Moslems, and anybody else who may be off the center of the target for advertising. And it can add extra weight against the prime prospect.

Seasonality. Public relations can maintain coverage in the off-season for advertising, plus backup in the in-season.

Trade coverage, which often gets skimped. Imaginative public relations can provide a dimension of excitement for the trade, which can be tremendously effective because it takes some pretty impressive consumer advertising to get the generally blasé trade folks stirred up.

The opportunities for public relations to lock into the media strategy and increase both reach and frequency are getting better and better. The selection of advertising media to reach a specific audience is getting more and more complex as the fragmentation of the media grows apace. For example, in 1950 the Milton Berle show delivered 70 per cent of the homes. Today the top-rated show is around 26 per cent, and the average prime time show is about 19 per cent.

The big mass circulation general magazines are no longer as efficient as they used to be in concentrating on the kind of specific audience that today's pinpoint marketing demands.

Obviously this fragmentation of the media will continue with the introduction of more UHF TV, public TV, pay TV, cable TV and EVR, all in addition to commercial TV. The trend in magazines is to more and more publications, each with a specific editorial focus for a specific readership.

In effect public relations can increase the frequency and reach of the selling message by working in the same media as the advertising—and thus beefing up the weight against the prime prospect—plus covering a wide range of media which would be unaffordable for advertising but which still reach worthwhile target audiences.

For example, take a beauty care product. This would be an unlikely choice for advertising in an outdoor or hunting and fishing magazine. But for public relations, what's wrong with a story on how a woman can keep dainty on safari? In other words, waste circulation, which makes advertising people so nervous, is not really a factor in public relations.

An extension of this argument is that public relations works in contexts outside the traditional measured media. There is some evidence that youth is not tuning into the traditional media as of old. Advertising and marketing people are uncomfortable when they have to work in non-measureable situations—this is probably the greatest single obstacle to the effective use of public relations marketing—but the day may come when folk rocks in the boondocks are the most efficient media buy for certain situations. And this type of "media" responsibility may come within the purview of public relations.

The logic for public relations in marketing applies equally well to the creative strategy, which is aimed at delivering more impact per prospect. It is entirely reasonable that public relations can increase this impact by supporting advertising messages via the editorial departments of media, with all the advantages of third party endorsement and "the greater credibility of the message," as Theodore Levitt has stated.

The value of the editorial message will grow if the advertising message has to be toned down as a result of government restrictions on competitive brand advertising. Furthermore, exposure by editorial means is likely to enhance the acceptance and credibility of the advertising message.

Public relations also offers a greater variety and flexibility of appeals and selling points than the advertising. In the interests of concentration and focus on the prime prospect, advertising is limited to a basic theme and a limited number of selling propositions which are directed to the high consumption areas. On the other hand, public relations can work with a great variety of news points (has to, in fact, to fulfill the media's demand for new news) and offbeat consumption situations. Soup on the rocks (beef broth over ice) and soup for breakfast have been perennially successful newsmaking themes that would not warrant advertising support.

In brief summary, the potential for public relations in marketing would seem to shape up thus:

1. Marketing is under pressure all along the line; its problems represent opportunities for public relations.
2. Public relations has unique capabilities to help solve or outflank these problems and marketing management is increasingly receptive to solutions.
3. The effective application of public relations capabilities to marketing depends on the ability of public relations people

to sell marketing management in terms of the latter's needs and goals and nomenclature.

4. Public relations can best relate to the needs and goals in terms of the marketing plan, which is full of conspicuous gaps which public relations can help to cover (in marketing strategy, media, creativity, etc.)

5. The basic selling point with marketing management is that public relations support can make marketing more efficient, get "more bang for the buck."

TELEVISION AND POLITICAL CAMPAIGNING

How politicians use television in their campaigns ought to be of no less concern to broadcast journalists, who report their activities, than to broadcast management, which must furnish them time. It has been the privilege and duty of the journalist in the United States to inquire into the qualifications and observe the behavior of the nation's officials, particularly at election time. This privilege and duty showed serious signs of erosion in the elections of 1968, and the erosion deepened in the primaries and general elections of 1970.

The blame was not all on one side.

Long before the days of television, it took a certain amount of money (yours and your "friends' ") to run for high political office in the United States. And more money (the taxpayers') to keep it. It was left to television, however, to demonstrate just how intolerable to a democracy such a simple formula could become.

In September 1969 Representative Torbert MacDonald of Massachusetts introduced legislation designed to control the use of television by his fellow politicians. In his accompanying remarks he said that if the country permitted the "television blitz" to continue unrestrained, it would be "tantamount to saying, at worst, that we condone the purchase of political office." MacDonald got three dozen other Congressmen to join him in sponsoring the measure.

This selection is reprinted with permission of the *Alfred I. duPont-Columbia University Survey of Broadcast Journalism*, which each fall gives an evaluation of the previous season's news and public affairs broadcasting. A network of seventy correspondents contributes to the book, edited by Marvin Barrett and published in both hardcover and paperback by Grosset and Dunlap. Jurors headed by Dean Elie Abel of the Columbia University Graduate School of Journalism oversee the yearly project. Copyright 1970.

Legislation was later introduced in the Senate by Senator John Pastore of Rhode Island.

Data about the magnitude and manner of broadcast campaigning in 1968 had been accumulating ever since the polls closed.

In its March 1970 issue, *Fortune* magazine reported that "spending in campaigns for all offices at stake in 1968, from county commissioner to the presidency, totaled at least $300 million. That was a 50 percent increase over the $200 million spent in 1964, which was itself a record breaker."*

The payments to broadcasters out of this total were $58.9 million, about 70 percent more than it had cost politicians to put their messages on radio and television in 1964.

In the post-convention presidential campaign, Nixon spent over $12 million on broadcasting. The Humphrey forces spent a little more than half that amount.

Prices being what they are in modern America, it might still have been possible to overlook these staggering numbers—had Nixon not won the election and done it with all expenses paid. Eighteen months later the Democratic National Committee was still $9.3 million in debt. After the deluge of 1968, important studies on the rising cost of electronic politics were begun in an effort to find some equalizing solution.† Before their recommendations could be made, *The Selling of the President* by Joe McGinnis, a short, sour story of the behind-the-scenes action in the Republican presidential campaign of 1968, gave more reasons for concern.

"It is not surprising," wrote McGinnis, "that politicians and advertising men should have discovered one another. And, once they recognized that the citizen did not so much vote for a candidate as make a psychological purchase of him, it is not surprising that they began to work together." None of the activity described in McGinnis's book was illegal. In terms of current mores nothing could be described as out of the ordinary, and yet an uneasy sense of manipulation and misrepresentation grew out of the account. Nixon had refused any of the free exposure offered him on television news interview shows. He gave no press conferences and stuck with his

---

*"A Financial Landslide for the G.O.P.," by Herbert E. Alexander and Harold B. Meyers. The figures used came from the non-partisan, non-profit Citizen's Research Foundation of Princeton, New Jersey.
†Notably those of the National Committee for an Effective Congress and the Twentieth Century Fund's Commission on Campaign Costs in the Electronic Era, which played an important role in the hearings held later on Congressman MacDonald's proposed legislation.

own time, controllable and paid for in cash, until the last Sunday before the election. Such behavior had to be disturbing to television journalists. Equally distracting was the success of his advisors in controlling the day-to-day coverage of his campaign and in making sponsored programs appear as though they were legitimate news events. McGinnis labeled the use of broadcasting in 1968 as electronic exaggeration and exploitation and obviously found it deplorable.

The book was on the best-seller lists for thirty-one weeks and some 200,000 copies were sold in the first twelve months. Its author was one of the first witnesses called to testify in Senate hearings on the proposed legislation.

Meanwhile, evidence was accumulating across the country that the Nixon approach to electronic politics had not stopped with the 1968 campaigns, nor was it limited to one party.*

One of the first instances in point of time was the campaign of John Lindsay, who lost the New York mayoralty primary to a conservative Republican, John Marchi, in June 1969. He re-entered the race as an independent, and in November was re-elected. In the interim he had spent roughly $1,800,000—more than four times what any of his opponents had spent—almost half of it for radio and television spots produced by David Garth, the liberal counterpart of the new breed of electronic image-makers portrayed in McGinnis's book.

After Lindsay there were many even more dramatic examples of just what could be done to win votes with television and money.

In the Democratic primary for U.S. Senator in Ohio, Howard Metzenbaum, a millionaire Cleveland labor lawyer and parking-lot owner, won out over John Glenn, former astronaut and more recently a businessman. Metzenbaum had been in Ohio Democratic politics for many years. However, he started his campaign with a recognition factor among Ohio voters of less than 15 per cent. Glenn—the first American to orbit the earth—was recognized by 97 per cent of all Ohioans. As to issues, there was little to choose between the two men, both liberal Democrats. The differences were Glenn's overwhelming reputation, Metzenbaum's comparative obscurity, and the amount of money apparently available to each of them.

---

*The *Congressional Quarterly* followed a political survey made in the summer of 1970 with the comment, "The outstanding political upsets of 1970 have been made by men of great wealth, presenting their politics to the voters on television and spending their way from obscurity to success in a matter of weeks."

Metzenbaum hired the Washington political consulting firm of Joseph Napolitan Associates, and also Charles Guggenheim, a political filmmaker who had to his credit two Academy Awards for documentary films and thirty campaigns (twenty successful, including George McGovern, Abraham Ribicoff, Robert Kennedy). Fourteen television spots ranging up to five minutes in length were produced, and for four months heavily covered the state at a reported total cost of $385,000.*

Glenn spent most of his original television funds—$26,000—in a brief two-market electronic splurge (Cleveland and Youngstown) in March 1970. At first Glenn refused offers of free air time for debates and other appearances on the logical assumption that it was Metzenbaum, not he, who needed exposure. Given such circumstances, a shut-down on legitimate journalistic exploration of political issues and personalities had worked before. But this time the balance was disrupted. With clever packaging and wide distribution of Metzenbaum's spots, and without the corrective of real-life confrontation, the campaign moved into the realm of pure merchandising.

When Glenn's forces saw an almost incredible possibility that Metzenbaum might win, they began scrambling after the free time they had earlier rejected and went into debt at the last minute to buy a thirty-minute television film. Lack of money still kept them from showing it anywhere but in Cleveland, where Metzenbaum had already bought sixty-three television spots for the final week. Glenn lost by 14,000 votes. Metzenbaum justified his blitz with the comment, "You know, Glenn had a three-and-a-half billion dollar television spectacular when he orbited the earth." Glenn's personal judgment was that Metzenbaum's victory proved that "you can buy an election" in America. Whoever was right, neither man had advanced the cause of political journalism.

An ironic footnote lay in the fact that Metzenbaum, facing Republican candidate Robert Taft, who had at least as much money at his disposal, immediately negotiated a ceiling on television spending. [Editor's Note: Taft won.]

A much more flagrant effort to stampede the electorate by an electronic onslaught was undertaken in California by Norton Simon, the multimillionaire collector of corporations (Hunt Foods, McCall's

---

*Example: Film of grocer talking to Metzenbaum:
Grocer says: "He should stick to astronauting. I'm a salesman. You're a Senator."
Metzenbaum: "Well, I'm not yet. I hope to be."
Grocer: "You will be. Believe me—you will be."

Canada Dry) and art (Rembrandt, Goya, Picasso). Simon, with a recognition factor close to zero, entered the senatorial race on the last possible day against incumbent Senator, and former movie star, George Murphy. Simon poured $1,900,000 into his two-month campaign, only $100,000 of it from sources other than himself and his family. ("It's my money. I earned it and I can spend it any way I choose.") At the same time, he avoided the sort of political activity—speeches, rallies, panels, walking tours, debates—that a journalist might legitimately cover. By buying time on twenty-five television stations and thirty-five radio stations and space in fifteen key newspapers—"Norton Simon, a capitalist for the United States Senate"—he brought his recognition factor, an essential statistic in all electronic campaigning, up to 55 per cent a week before the election. It wasn't enough for him to defeat Murphy, but it was one more awesome display of what money could buy. Of the Republican vote in the country's most populous state, 33 per cent had gone to a man who, two months earlier, was a virtual political unknown.

The same advantage helped Representative John V. Tunney win over George Brown in the California Democratic senatorial primary.* Television would be an important factor in the gubernatorial race, where Governor Reagan bought time to announce his candidacy and was rumored to have $1 million earmarked for television, the medium which was his former employer and natural element. His opponent, Democrat Jesse Unruh, notably untelegenic and short of funds, chose to dramatize his handicap by saying he was boycotting television advertising entirely. Columnist Marquis Childs commented after viewing the California primaries: "Here in the Golden West you don't run for office, you pose for office. Image is all important and television is supreme."

In Texas, a conservative Democrat and millionaire insurance man, Lloyd M. Bentsen, Jr., eliminated the incumbent liberal Senator Ralph Yarborough in the primary with an intensive campaign of television spots. Here, unlike the other cases cited, there was some question of misrepresentation of his opponent's real position via the television commercials, which flooded the airwaves at the last minute. Even if Yarborough had had the funds, he could not have commandeered the time to answer.

In Michigan, Lenore Romney, whose husband is a millionaire as well as Secretary of Housing and Urban Development, called in some

---

*Tunney, defeating Murphy in the fall, earmarked $1,300,000 to blitz the top ten California television markets and retained David Garth as his television adviser.

of the President's 1968 image-makers to help her in her race against incumbent Democratic Senator Philip Hart. The result was a $50,000 twenty-eight-minute film called "Lenore." According to the *Wall Street Journal*, although a charming portrait of a personable grandmother, it had "no more substance than a blob of cotton candy." [Editor's Note: Mrs. Romney lost.]

In Tennessee, liberal Senator Albert Gore, fighting for his political life, survived the primaries thanks to one of the most artful television advertisements of the season. Again the work of Charles Guggenheim, it cost $70,000 to produce and showed the sixty-seven-year-old Senator, healthy and pink, riding across the family acreage on a white horse in the company of his son. Off-camera a narrator said:

> The pace and direction a man sets for his life can tell you a lot about his inner spirit. . . . The people of Tennessee have learned to take the measure of Albert Gore by the battles he's fought for them along the way—for TVA, tax reform, Medicare, interstate highways, Social Security and education. . . I may have run ahead of the pack sometimes, he says, but I'm usually headed in the right direction.

"It's going to backfire," said Gore's opponent Hudley Crockett, who had spent ten years as a television newscaster in Tennessee* and had one-third Gore's television budget. "Mark my words. The people of Tennessee know it's packaged by an out-of-state man and paid for by out-of-state funds." It didn't backfire. Gore won with a 32,000-vote margin, and the widespread use of the "white horse" commercial undoubtedly helped. [Editor's Note: Gore lost in the fall elections.]

In Florida where a television blitz by Senator Edward Gurney was given credit for defeating Governor LeRoy Collins in the senatorial race two years ago, the legislature had passed a law setting the total campaign spending ceiling at $350,000 per candidate for primaries, $350,000 for the general election. Expected to benefit Gov-

---

*The radio-television journalist and personality-turned-politician (and the equal-time problems he presented) were growing more common across the country. The employer of Barry Farber, radio interviewer on WOR in New York City, had to offer Mrs. Bella Abzug, his opponent for Congress, her own talk show. Mrs. Abzug, claiming she knew nothing about talk shows, held out for spots and was turned down by the FCC. Farber stayed on the air.

WMT in Cedar Rapids, Iowa, had two newsmen who left to run for office. Their employer said he would not employ them again even if they lost, since he felt their "credibility" had been damaged by their political activities. Ten more instances of television newsmen turned politicians were cited in a New York *Times* article of September 6, 1970.

ernor Kirk as the incumbent, it did little to inhibit a millionaire druggist John Eckerd, who managed to dispose of $801,000 before the law took effect on July 1, 1970. He also continued to advertise his 166 drugstores on television with the slogan, "Eckerd . . . a name you can trust," a bit of subliminal campaigning that did not have to be counted. In charge of Eckerd's television schedule was Roger Ailes, President Nixon's television producer in 1968 and current television consultant. Although he did not win, Eckerd collected enough votes to force Governor Kirk into a run-off.

In adjoining Alabama, incumbent Governor Albert Brewer lost to George Wallace in what Brewer called "the dirtiest campaign I've ever observed in Alabama." Wallace employed radio and television to outflank unfriendly newspapers and put across some fairly unpleasant messages. One radio spot, aimed at a black action group's demand for integrated state troopers, said, "Suppose your wife is driving home at eleven o'clock at night. She is stopped by a highway patrolman. He turns out to be black. Think about it . . . elect George C. Wallace."

Network television was useful to Wallace in an unexpected way. Because of the national political implications of his comeback, network newsmen were out in force to cover his appearances, a fact he never neglected to point out to his audiences, thus arousing both their dander and their sympathy.

Virginia, usually considered a low-cost state for political campaigning, in 1970 suddenly became very expensive thanks to television. Costs for primary and general election for Republicans and Democrats totaled $2.5 million.

In New York, the state with the most money, the distorting pressures of available cash were evident in every major race, and television was the principal ogre. The situation was deplored, but nothing was done about it. Westchester Representative Richard Ottinger, who had three terms in the House of Representatives but was known to less than one third of New York Democrats four months before the Democratic senatorial primary, won against an equally little-known Congressman, Buffalo's Representative Richard McCarthy, and lawyers Paul O'Dwyer and Theodore Sorensen—both high on political credentials and low on cash.

Ottinger, the heir to a plywood fortune, was criticized throughout the campaign for his heavy expenditure of personal funds on television time. "Ideally," said Ottinger, "we ought to have free television, free radio and free newspaper space. But in this campaign I've got to reach sixteen million people and even though I start at six

A.M. and campaign until midnight, I can only see a fraction of them personally. I have to use television." Ottinger reported expenses of $1,841,750, while those of his three opponents together totaled $233,000. Political impresario David Garth, who prepared the Ottinger television and radio commercials, admitted that he had had at least a million to play around with.

But Ottinger's expenditures were, if not peanuts, at least modest in comparison to what Nelson Rockefeller was planning to lay out to stay in the Governor's mansion in Albany. Rockefeller faced a prestigious, if hard up, Arthur Goldberg (who had broken through the advantage of a very expensive television primary campaign— $60,000 per week on television commercials—served up by plastics millionaire Howard Samuels). The Governor refused to send a representative to a conference held by Goldberg and candidates for governor and senator in hopes of scaling down expenses to a reasonable level. Estimates of Rockefeller's total campaign budget went as high as $12.6 million, with as much as $2 million for the big television and radio push. His television attack began several weeks before the traditional Labor Day starting point. Polls were to be taken and the most effective advertisement—mainly sixty-second spots—would be increased until Election Day.* Arthur Goldberg, hard-pressed for campaign money, had established a broadcast budget of under one-half million dollars for his big effort.

Unedifying as was this emphasis on money and packaging over issues and qualifications, the most disturbing fact was that at least two of the more credible Democratic candidates for New York Governor, Robert Morgenthau, the former U.S. Attorney, and Eugene Nickerson, the top official in New York's populous Nassau County, dropped out before anyone had a chance to vote for them—both for the announced reason that they could not afford the tab. Another disturbing fact was that for all the hulabaloo on television, three out of four of the registered Democrats in New York State failed to vote in the June primary.

In a last-minute plea Goldberg had suggested that he and Rockefeller voluntarily impose the same limitation (in New York approximately $460,000) on themselves as that required by the legislation which during the summer had moved slowly through the Congress. Rockefeller replied by comparing radio and television to "the town

---

*Polls had become a standard expense in television electioneering. In the well-run campaign, the polls (the political equivalent of ratings and market research) would be run on an average of once a week and the use of television ads adjusted on the basis of the results.

meeting" and "the village green" as a means of communication between candidate and voter. He added that, of course, if the legislation passed, he would abide by it. Goldberg answered wryly, "Television may be 'the modern village green,' but the green stuff involved in getting on television is not grass."*

A few days later in Washington, the House was so depleted by premature departures for the late-summer politicking recess, that the bill was not presented for a vote and thus missed the chance of being applied in the fall general elections.

The measure, a compromise between the proposals of Representative MacDonald's bill and those of Senator Pastore, would:

• Limit the amount each candidate for President and Vice President, the Congress, Governor, and Lieutenant Governor could spend on broadcast time to seven cents for each vote cast for the same office in the previous general election. The limit included spending in behalf of the candidate by others. This would mean less than $6 million for each major party in the 1972 presidential race, $460,000 for each candidate in the New York State gubernatorial election, $496,000 in California. For sparsely populated states there was a $20,000 minimum.

• Permanently repeal the equal-time requirement for presidential and vice presidential campaign broadcasts, thus allowing stations to give time to the major candidates without having to give equal time to fringe candidates.

• Require broadcasters to charge all candidates—federal and state—the lowest unit cost for the time they purchase, thus assuring them the low rates usually obtained by commercial advertisers who buy large blocks of time over long periods. This could reduce charges by 25 per cent to 50 per cent, with 35 per cent expected to be the average reduction. No candidate could buy time unless he first stated in writing to the station that his purchase would not boost his spending over the prescribed limit. Violation could mean two years in jail or the loss of his seat if he won.

---

*At the opposite extreme, in the Union's most sparsely settled state, Alaska, with its seven television stations and vast distances, G.O.P. Senator Mike Gravel said a single half-hour television movie about himself got him elected in 1968. (Gravel had the help of Mike Rowan, a Napolitan associate.) "My opponent thought it was immoral, but I'm in the United States Senate today and he's not. If it hadn't been for the film, he'd still be in the Senate and I'd be relegated to oblivion, still selling real estate in Alaska."

- Allow states to extend the bill's provisions to other elections.
- Limit spending on primaries (except for President and Vice President) to half that for general election campaigns starting in 1971.

The bill was finally passed on September 23 by large majorities in both the House and the Senate. Two weeks later it was vetoed by President Nixon who said that although its motives were laudable, it was partial and imperfect.

There were other possible reasons for the veto. If it had passed, the Republicans would not be able to take advantage of the money which they unquestionably had in much greater abundance than the Democrats. Nixon's distaste for debates might prejudice him against the equal-time repeal. Politicians from both sides grumbled about the unfair advantage the bill would give to incumbents, thus making it almost impossible for unknowns to break through. This argument ignored the fact that economic considerations had heretofore prevented highly qualified men from even considering running for office.

The station owners and the National Association of Broadcasters made the identical complaint they had made about the prohibition of cigarette advertising, due to go off the air January 2, 1971. The legislation, they said, singled them out for special punitive treatment while permitting the other media to go on the same as before. There were also murmurs about "the government's going into the business of setting television rates" and "forcing broadcasters to subsidize politicians."

Many of the advertising men and "political consultants" were sympathetic to the legislation, although they might lose large fees and commissions (their share was usually 15 per cent of the total broadcast charges). In April, veteran ad man Carl Ally remarked that the proposed legislation had not gone far enough, that all private funds should be eliminated and the government should subsidize all campaigning. "Money should be removed as a factor and so should the theatrics, but television should be used because it is the closest thing to the stump."

Of all the provisions of the bill, perhaps the one greeted with most enthusiasm by proponents of full television coverage of politics was the elimination of the equal-time requirement of the Communications Act for presidential and vice presidential campaigns. This section has long given an excuse to unwilling politicians who thought it to their advantage to remain silent and to networks and

individual stations which objected to giving lesser or minor candidates too much free time.*

Whether the House and the Senate overrode President Nixon's
veto or not, the problem would not be finally solved probably short
of the complete elimination of political advertising. Then the television journalists' role in the political campaigns might take on some
of the importance it has in Great Britain. There, campaigns are severely limited in length and procedure, no political advertising is
permitted on television and radio, and parties are allotted equal time
for their leaders to present their positions. There the politician's real
impact depends not so much on money or clever packaging, but
rather on his exploration of the issues and his eloquence in presenting them in press conference, speeches, and television interviews.
There the professional skill and news judgment of the broadcaster
can be crucial.

Because of geographical expanse, the hundreds of thousands of
U.S. office-seekers, and the generally impacted character of U.S. television, such a free flow of political fact and comment might have to
await the advent of CATV and its multiple channels and capacity for
selecting and dividing audiences.

---

*There was no guarantee that the stations or the politicos would take advantage
of it. In a special study made in 1968 devoted to races where only two candidates ran for office, there was no evidence of increase in free time offered by the
broadcasters.

On the other hand, WSB Atlanta, abiding by the equal time rule and
offering regular prime-time exposure to all political candidates in the mayoralty
race, found itself with twelve legitimate contenders. All of them got on the air.

WTOP-TV Washington, doing the same for gubernatorial and congressional
candidates in its area of Maryland and Virginia during a four-week period before
both the primaries and general elections, scheduling prime-time debates and
permitting qualified political candidates to buy fixed position announcements at
one-half the current base rate, estimated the cost to the station at a minimum of
$56,000 for free time alone.

Chapter VIII

ACCELERATING CHANGE
IN INTERNATIONAL COMMUNICATIONS

THE FIRST EIGHT YEARS

Sig Mickelson

When communications satellites are mentioned, the average American probably thinks of some dramatic television event associated with them: man's first moon walk, the Olympic Games from Tokyo or Mexico City, Pope Paul's Christmas message, the investiture of the Prince of Wales. To watch international news events "live" on home TV screens is now so commonplace it is almost taken for granted.

But the communications revolution has not been limited to long-distance delivery of television signals. Miracles of international telephonic communications are being performed daily and hourly that would have been unthinkable prior to the late 1960s. The average individual can now pick up his home phone, ask for an overseas operator, place a call to Chile, Iran, or Indonesia, and have reasonable expectations of quick service and high quality. Anyone who tried as recently as [1968] would instantly recognize the difference; the noisy, unpredictable, rising and fading radio frequencies on which he had to depend have been replaced by satellite circuits equal in signal quality to that on intercity calls within the United States.

One of the most significant developments in satellite communications is the linkage being provided between the developed and the developing world and among the developing countries. Communications in the period of the cable and radio generally bypassed the less

Sig Mickelson, for many years a CBS executive and now with the Encyclopaedia Britannica Corp., possesses intimate knowledge of the satellite revolution and what the future holds. These ideas originally appeared in *Saturday Review*, October 24, 1970 and are used with permission of *Saturday Review*, Inc., Copyright 1970.

developed countries and followed high-density traffic routes. Just as quick, high-quality communication with South America previously was almost nonexistent, Africa, South Asia, and Southeast Asia were left in the backwaters of communications development.

The startling change in this pattern was dramatically signaled when the Shah of Iran, after dedicating a ground station near Tehran, went to Washington, D.C. His meeting with President Johnson was captured on TV and relayed, live, back to televiewers in Iran, in a sort of up-to-date Arabian Nights performance. About the same time, the Sheik of Bahrein was dedicating a satellite ground station in his country, with service going into Morocco, Lebanon, Brazil, and Indonesia.

Airlines and international hotel chains are using satellite communications for worldwide instant reservation service. Surgeons in Geneva have observed open-heart surgery taking place in Houston—asking questions about the operation as it proceeded. Weather data and maps are moving via satellite communications coupled with facsimile machines. The U.S. Army transmits battle-front information directly from Vietnam to the White House by specialized military satellite, and now is transmitting surveillance photographs from the Middle East for examination in Washington only minutes after high-flying planes return from the Suez Canal.

The first satellite to relay a broadcast across the Atlantic was Telstar, in 1962. An Earth station at Andover, Maine, was linked to another at Pleumeur Bodou, France. The broadcast, involving greetings from American Telephone and Telegraph officials in the United States to PTT (Poste-Telephone-Telegraphe) officials in France, ran for twenty-two minutes before fading because the streaking satellite had run out of range of both ground stations.

The initial commercial satellite service started in June 1965 with Early Bird—the first vehicle launched by the new Communications Satellite Corporation (Comsat) for the International Telecommunications Satellite consortium (Intelsat). But Early Bird had only enough capacity for 240 simultaneous voice circuits or one TV signal. Furthermore, it could link only two points. At that stage it didn't make much difference—during its early lifetime there was only one sending-and-receiving station in North America (Andover), and only two in Europe: one in England and one in France.

The tiny Early Bird had the burden of the full load of transatlantic traffic for more than eighteen months, until the Intelsat II series made its appearance in January 1967. The first Intelsat II was lost in space, but the second went into service over the Pacific Ocean and the third over the Atlantic. This second generation had no greater circuit capacity, but could broadcast simultaneously to several Earth stations. And now there was a Pacific service linking Asia with North America and in turn with Europe.

The satellites themselves, of course, were only one main element in the service chain; the other was the Earth station. By the end of 1966, both Germany and Italy had stations to add to the operating facilities in France and the United Kingdom. In 1966, Canada was added; in 1967, Spain; in 1968, Chile and Panama; and in 1969, Argentina, Brazil, Iran, Lebanon, Mexico, Morocco, and Peru. At the same time, second or even third and fourth stations were being added in England, France, Germany, Italy, Australia, Japan, Canada, and the United States, giving more flexibility to the whole system.

As 1970 nears an end, some twenty-five countries are tied into the Intelsat system. At least another ten—including Kenya, India, Korea, Nigeria, Senegal, Cameroon, and Ethiopia—are expected to be ready with Earth stations in 1971, and a minimum of seven more in 1972. The current cost of a standard Earth station is approximately $2.25 million, but portable stations have been built for less than $500,000, and some experts are predicting that one can shortly be built for between $100,000 and $250,000. As Earth-station costs decline, more countries undoubtedly will participate in the world-wide system.

Meanwhile, there also has been growth in the air. Early Bird has been retired. So have some of the second-generation satellites. The workhorse now is the Intelsat III, which carries 1,200 voice circuits or four TV signals, in contrast to the 240 voice circuits or one TV signal of the earlier generations. It has "multiple-drop" capacity, rather than point-to-point service. Even Intelsat III, however, is only an interim step. The consortium is preparing to launch in early 1971 a fourth-generation Intelsat IV series with an average capacity of approximately 6,000 voice circuits and twelve TV signals. There have been informal predictions that Intelsat V, when and if it should be launched, may be able to carry in the vicinity of 20,000 voice circuits.

Not only is the impact of this vast increase in circuit capacity reflected in the greater ease in obtaining satellite service; even more startling is the lowered cost of furnishing the service. Comsat estimates that its investment per circuit per year in the Early Bird satellite was approximately $25,000. In the Intelsat II generation, the investment had dropped to $13,500; in the Intelsat III's now in service, it is put at $4,500; and when the Intelsat IV's go into service in 1971, the figure will be $1,000—a 25-to-1 reduction in roughly five years.

In turn, the charge for a three-minute, station-to-station, off-hours telephone call to London from New York has been reduced from $9 to $5.40; charges for one hour of color TV service across the North Atlantic have been reduced by 81 per cent in two years; and charges to communications companies for transatlantic voice-grade circuits have been cut almost in half, with the further prospect that by 1975 they will be about 25 per cent of the 1968 figure.

The miracle worker that has made all this possible is not a very large or impressive-appearing device. The largest communications satellite now in use is only 56 inches in diameter and 41 inches in length—about the size of a large patio planter—and weighs 334 pounds as it enters space. It is, however, a versatile bird that sits 22,300 miles in the sky over the equator, catches signals sent up to it from Earth, amplifies them, and relays them back to a receiving station on the Earth's surface. In their 44,600-mile trip up and down again, the signals leap with ease over oceans and thick jungles, and penetrate into areas barely out of the tom-tom stage of communication.

The signal projected toward Earth from the satellite takes the shape of a flashlight beam. By adjusting the focus—accomplished in the satellite by regulating the configuration of the antenna—it is possible to widen or narrow the beam. As with a flashlight ray, the wider the beam, the less the signal strength. Specially designed Earth stations are required for sending signals to the satellites and receiving from them. Their size and cost vary according to the strength of the beam from the satellites they work with.

The satellite signal has another characteristic of the flashlight beam; it will not bend around the Earth's curvature. But this is not unduly restrictive. From 22,300 miles in space just three beams will cover most of the Earth's surface. The signal weakens a little as it nears the two poles, but this effect is important only to Canada and the Soviet Union which need service in the Arctic areas; the great bulk of the populated areas of the world lie in the Temperate and Tropical zones.

One of the most satisfactory features of satellite operations is a very high degree of reliability. The only major crisis occurred just before the *Apollo II* moon flight, in late June 1969, when the most advanced high-capacity satellite in operation over the Atlantic suddenly went dark. Fortunately, there were spare vehicles in orbit—including the ever willing Early Bird—that were quickly pressed into service, and the world was able to watch the moon walk with no further complications. Just one month later, the misbehaving satellite had been repaired and put back into service—all of this at 22,300 miles from the repairmen, who had no opportunity to fly to the scene with wrenches, pliers, and screwdrivers.

So far the satellites in use have had only one objective: to deliver a signal, whether it be telephone, teletype, facsimile, data, or TV, over long distances. Succeeding this type of satellite probably will be a "distributional" satellite aimed at delivering service in much smaller geographical areas. The Federal Communications Commission recently invited applications for operation of a distribution satellite system for the United States. Canada has plans for an all-Canadian service. Japan also is planning a facility of its own, and a number of plans are under consideration in Europe. These distribution satellites would be largely supplemental, adding to the facilities now available through land lines and microwave relays.

The third developmental stage would be a direct-to-home broadcast delivered through what is commonly called a broadcast satellite. This step may be technically feasible by the late 1970s, but necessary economic, political, and legal preparations probably cannot be made for its common usage before 1985. Many skeptics think that direct-to-home satellite broadcasting will never take place. Most likely, a cross between a distribution satellite and a broadcast satellite will serve underdeveloped regions by delivering service into schools, community buildings, or community antenna systems where programs can be watched by groups.

To date, however, it has been the long-range communications satellite that has commanded the most attention, including that of diplomats. And formulation of a mechanism to plan, launch, and manage a worldwide system of such satellites has necessitated a breakthrough in international relations.

The American entity, Comsat, was formed by a 1962 act of Congress. Originally, 50 per cent of its stock was held by U.S. communications companies and 50 per cent by the public, but some of the carriers' shares have since been sold to private individuals. Twenty per cent of its directors are appointed by the President, the other 80 per cent are elected by shareholders. Comsat, in turn, is the official U.S. representative in the International Telecommunications Satellite consortium formed in 1964, and owns 53 per cent of its stock. Other Intelsat members, however, have taken steps to reduce Comsat's sway in both stock ownership and management, and while no decision has yet been reached, it is evident that Comsat's ownership share will be reduced substantially and its management decisions will have to be cleared through some type of board of directors or secretariat.

Intelsat, which has approximately seventy members, is the actual owner of the satellites now in commercial operation. Through Comsat it contracts for construction of the satellites, pays NASA for launchings from Cape Kennedy, sets tariffs, and operates the system. Profits, if any, are divided among Intelsat members according to their percentage of ownership of the consortium.

The Soviet Union, though represented at recent conferences in Washington at which the future of Intelsat was discussed, has established its own satellite system, which it calls Orbita. (Orbita uses a nonsynchronous ovalorbit satellite to furnish service across Eastern Europe and Siberia.) The Soviets several times have suggested that other countries join an Intelsat-like system, which the Russians call Inter-Sputnik, but there has been little response.

As would be expected, the United States and the United Kingdom use the majority of Intelsat circuit capacity—approximately 59 per cent. But there is surprisingly high usage by the Philippines, Argentina, Brazil, Chile, Thailand, Iran, Kuwait, Indonesia, and Lebanon.

The story of Chile and Argentina is particularly interesting. Chile now leases forty-four full-time circuits, twenty-three for communications with other Latin American countries and Spain, and twenty-one for the remainder of the world; Argentina leases twelve circuits. The surprising fact about the Chilean-Argentine circuits is that previously there was virtually no communication between the two countries—even though they have a thousand-mile common boundary and their capital cities of Santiago and Buenos Aires are less than an hour apart by jet. The Andes were simply an insuperable barrier to communications.

This suggests that the most dramatic developments of the future well may come in large, sprawling countries in which construction of earth-bound facilities would be too costly and time-consuming to consider. Indonesia, for example, has roughly the same land area as Alaska and consists of three thousand islands spread over hundreds of thousands of square miles of the Southwest Pacific. Only a satellite could efficiently link these isolated segments. Brazil is stymied by thousands of square miles of virtually impenetrable interior, and India by the twin problems of size and poverty. Within a relatively short time, regional or distribution satellites should be able to deliver strong enough signals so that inexpensive Earth stations in these countries could provide a communications system comparable to Intelsat's worldwide service.

India was scheduled to have such an experimental service in 1972, but the United States—which had agreed to provide use of a satellite for the experiment—recently announced a postponement of at least two years due to federal budget cuts. India's only TV transmitter now is in New Delhi, serving fewer than 10,000 sets. Under the experimental plan, the Indian government will provide 5,000 villages with $500 receiving sets for community viewing, then produce programs in family planning, improved agricultural practices, and national culture.

The eight years since Telstar's brief moment in the international spotlight in 1962 indeed has produced startling, even incredible progress. And the pace of the revolution is accelerating. What the next eight years will bring is almost beyond comprehension.

MADISON AVENUE IMPERIALISM

Herbert I. Schiller

Many currents feed the international flow of communications. Tourists, governmental agents and officials, student travelers, trade (exports and imports), international games and sports, religious organizations and cultural exchanges are only some of the better recognized contributors to international communications. While each element does not necessarily match the next in volume, force or impact, in theory, at least, there is supposed to be no dominant thrusting single component that overshadows the rest. There is, it is claimed, a diffusion of influence, with culture, entertainment, travel and commerce nicely balancing each other in an international equilibrium that offers advantage to all participants. We hear, therefore, that "Trade is good," "Cultural exchanges create understanding," and "Travel is broadening." All this folk wisdom contributes ultimately to the most mystical and revered concept of the "free flow of information." The free flow of information, until recently at any rate, has been regarded as the ultimate good for which all sensible nations should strive.

Herbert I. Schiller, professor of communication at the University of California, San Diego, originally published this article in the March/April 1971 issue of *TRANS-ACTION*. A full analysis of the "system" is found in his book, *Mass Communication and American Empire*, Beacon paperback, 1971.

Actually, this view of beneficial and pluralistic international communications is about as realistic as the economists' model of free competition and the self-adjusting market economy. Not surprisingly, both systems are disrupted by the same force. Domestically, the giant corporation, as Galbraith and others have effectively demonstrated, makes a shambles of the notion of a free market of countless uninfluential producers and consumers. Internationally, the multinational corporation, the intercontinental extension of the domestic behemoth, now dominates similarly the global economy and has become the chief organizer and manufacturer of the international flow of communications.

The internationally active corporation is not an altogether new phenomenon but its extensive involvement in overseas communications is relatively recent. Since the end of World War II, both the volume and the character of international economic activity have changed considerably. Perhaps $70 billion of direct overseas investment is owned and controlled by a few hundred U.S.-based companies, the so-called multinational corporations. The massive build-up of private U.S. investment abroad requires no elaboration here. Though American-controlled raw materials and extractive industries have maintained and even extended their holdings around the world, the largest part of the postwar American investment flow abroad has been into manufacturing and service industries in already developed regions and countries (Western Europe, Canada, Australia). The changing nature of this investment has affected directly and consequentially both the apparatus and content of international communications. A trade publication has commented on this shift of activity of private U.S. investment overseas:

> For the international advertiser and marketeer, (for instance), this means expanded horizons. The shift in investment means a greater concentration by international business in the production of goods and services and a more rapid development of consumer markets. *Hence, a growing emphasis on the advertising and marketing of those goods and services is to be expected.*

U.S. raw materials and heavy goods producer interests overseas in the pre-World War II days availed themselves of some communications talent to provide their local activities with favorable imagery, but such expenditures were marginal at best. Today the situation is entirely reversed. Now the mass media, wherever U.S. manufacturing companies operate, have been summoned to promote the global expansion of American consumer goods sales and services.

The international community is being inundated by a stream of commercial messages that derive from the marketing requirements of (mostly) American multinational companies. The structure of national communications systems and the programming they offer are being transformed according to the specifications of international marketeers.

Advertising requires total access to the mass media. It is through the multimillion circulation magazines, the car and kitchen radio and the home screen that the marketing message comes across incessantly and effectively. Advertising cannot tolerate, if it wishes to be successful, mass communications channels that exclude its commercials and its commercially oriented "recreational" programming. It strives untiringly, therefore, to penetrate each available communications outlet that has a sizable audience. Advertising's appetite is insatiable and nothing less than the total domination of every medium is always its objective. Once subordinated, the medium, whatever its original attributes, becomes an instrument of the commercial culture.

Accordingly, one measure of a nation's loss of control of its own mass media, (apart from the obvious loss through foreign ownership), is the degree of penetration of foreign advertising agencies in the mechanics of national marketing. Such a penetration signals also fundamental changes in the country's cultural ecology, as a changed communications structure increasingly transmits and reinforces attitudes that fit nicely with the requirements of the multinational corporate goods producers that are financing the new system.

The emerging pattern reveals a mixture of economics and electronics that is enormously powerful.

Sophisticated communications methodologies—those which have proved themselves the most effective in regimenting and securing the attachment of the domestic population—are being applied internationally at an accelerating tempo. The culture of commerce, or more precisely, of corporate power, is radiating from its American base in a dazzling display of vitality. To sell its goods and products and itself, U.S. business overseas employs the familiar services of advertising, public relations, opinion surveys and market research. And to carry the carefully synthesized messages of these bought services, it enlists or subverts the mass media of the many national states in which it operates.

Take television, for example. A couple of years ago I described the process by which Western European broadcasting was being commercialized. "In Western Europe, the most stable noncommercial broadcasting structures of sovereign states are unable to resist the forces that are arrayed against them." Here is one description (from

Television Age) of how commercials defy national boundaries, especially in the compact North Atlantic region:

> Of course, the continued expansion of commercial television, despite powerful opposition, is playing a major role in making unity of diversity. Although many important countries, particularly in Europe, still forbid TV advertising, there is a certain "spillover" effect that tends to spread commercials even to those countries that originally were adamant. Only in 1971 did the 11-year-old government-controlled Swiss TV service permit commercials on its three regional networks. The move was in large part prompted by the concern of Swiss manufacturers who knew their customers were viewing Italian and German TV across the border. The same process is expected to unfold in the Netherlands, a large part of which is open to German programming and advertising messages. If Netherland TV goes commercial, then Belgium is expected to follow shortly thereafter. Then France and Scandinavia will be the last big holdouts... If French television goes commercial, an executive at J. Walter Thompson remarks, then there truly will be a common market for the TV advertiser.

All of this has come true with a vengeance. In Western Europe today, the only countries that have not "gone commercial" are Sweden and Denmark. Beginning in Britain in 1954 and continuing on through the last 16 years, country after country has accepted some form or another of commercial influence. Around the world, except in the Chinese and Soviet blocs, commercialism in broadcasting is now the dominant mode of organization. In the less developed nations, the dependence on outside capital assistance makes it inevitable that commercial broadcasting be established, and such has been the case.

Advertising has become the indispensible adjutant of the business system. Not surprisingly, perhaps, its own organizational structure is not different in many ways from the corporations whose interests it promotes and represents. Ad agencies, like the rest of American enterprise, show the same pattern of consolidation and concentration. In 1968, less than 10 per cent of the firms in the industry received almost three-quarters of the domestic business (billings). International billings are much more heavily concentrated.

The major U.S. ad agencies, much like the manufacturing companies they service, possess resources and obtain revenues that put them far ahead of most of their international competitors. Of the world's ten largest agencies in 1969, only one was not an American firm, and in the top 25 international agencies, 23 were American companies.

The rich domestic consumer market in the United States was the original stimulus for the growth of these word and image factories. It hastened their initial development. Now they are grazing in pastures far from home. The stupendous growth of directly owned American business overseas, has brought with it, of necessity, the marketeers. American factories worth more than $10 billion are manufacturing their products in Western Europe. Another $10 billion worth of U.S. plant is in Canada. Latin America, Africa and the Middle East, though mainly still serving as raw material depots of Western enterprise, have some U.S. manufacturing capacity too. The ad men follow their manufacturing clients wherever the potential markets lead, generally where the capital investment is set down. In 1968 American ad agencies operating outside the United States had billings exceeding $1.5 billion, a large part of which, though by no means all, was accounted for by the advertising programs of U.S. companies overseas. In 1971 U.S. companies advertising expenditures abroad are expected to reach $5 billion.

And the big U.S. agencies got most of the business. J. Walter Thompson; McCann-Erickson; Ted Bates; Young & Rubicam; Ogilvy and Mather; Norman, Craig & Kummel; Leo Burnett Co.; Foote, Cone and Belding; Compton; and Kenyon and Eckhardt are the elite ten American agencies in the world marketing swim.

No part of the globe (except, and perhaps only temporarily, the socialist-organized sector) avoids the penetration of the internationally active American ad agency. In a special international issue of *Printers' Ink* in 1967 titled "Who's Where Around the World," 45 U.S. agencies were listed with hundreds of overseas affiliates. Consider, for example, the far-flung activities of the largest agency in the world, J. Walter Thompson. In 1969, JWT had $740 million in billings of which $292 million, a sizable 39 per cent, originated in 28 countries outside the United States. JWT world-wide has 700 accounts and employs 8,000 people in 42 offices, in some instances several in one country. It operates in Argentina, Uruguay, Austria, Australia, Belgium, Brazil, Canada, Ceylon, Chile, France, Denmark, Britain, India, Italy, Switzerland, Spain, Japan, Mexico, Holland, Pakistan, Peru, the Philippines, Puerto Rico, South Africa (with five offices throughout the country and billings of $10,000,000) and Venezuela. JWT is the largest ad agency in seven countries outside the United States.

As of 1970, only two of the top 25 U.S. ad agencies still did not have overseas offices. If anything, the expansion of U.S. ad agencies is accelerating and foreign competition is being brought increasingly under the American umbrella. For instance, Leo Burnett Company, fifth-ranked U.S. agency in 1969, announced the acquisition of the

two largest ad agency subsidiaries of the London Press Exchange—
LPE Ltd., one of England's largest agencies, and LPE International,
Ltd., a combination of 19 agencies in Europe, Latin America, Africa
and Asia. "It is a natural alliance," said Philip H. Schaff, Jr., chairman of Burnett. "Leo Burnett is strong in the United States and
Canada and very weak outside. London Press Exchange is strong
outside but very weak here."

The internationalization of the American advertising business is
an integral part of the expansion of U.S. industry abroad. It is the
latter's voracious marketing requirements that elicit and support the
agencies' world-wide activities. The client list of American ad agencies operating internationally is a roster of *Fortune's* Directory of the
largest 500 U.S. nonfinancial corporations, supplemented by a heavy
representation of major European companies.

In Canada, for instance, the main revenues of commercial
radio-television broadcasting come mostly from the giant U.S. companies operating across the border. In 1969, the top ten broadcasting
advertisers were: General Motors of Canada Ltd., Procter and Gamble of Canada Ltd., Canadian Breweries, General Foods Ltd., Im-
perial Tobacco of Canada, Colgate-Palmolive Ltd., Ford Motor Company of Canada, Lever Bros. Ltd., Government of Canada and
Bristol-Myers of Canada.

Ninth-ranked U.S. ad agency Ogilvy and Mather, with one-third
of its income earned outside the United States and with 30 offices in
14 countries, notes in its 1969 annual report that it serves 17 clients
in three or more countries: Air Canada, American Express, Bristol
Myers, General Foods, Gillette, Hertz, ICI, Lever, Mars, Mercedes
Benz, Rountree, Schweppes, Shell Chemical, Shell, U.S. Travel Service.

In their 1968 Annual Report, the eighth-ranked U.S. agency,
Foote, Cone and Belding includes among its clients abroad Mon-
santo, BOAC, Gillette, B.F. Goodrich, Clairol, Kimberly-Clark Cor-
poration, International Harvester, GM, Hughes Aircraft, Smith-Kline
& French, Mead Johnson, Singer Company, Armour-Dial, Kraft
Foods and Zenith Radio Corporation.

The omnipresent advertising message, jarring or insinuatingly
effective, now constitutes a major voice in international communications. The mass media are the ideal instruments of transmission,
especially television which captures the viewer in his own, allegedly
secure, living room. The media, if they were not commercial to begin
with as they were in the United States, end up eventually as business
auxiliaries. The lure of advertising revenues is too tempting. Further-

more, the business system cannot permit as influential a "sales tool" as radio-television to function noncommercially, free to reject the transmission of its consumer messages.

It is no surprise, therefore, to discover that American advertising agencies have made deep inroads in most of the already-industrialized states. In Great Britain, for example, according to the *Financial Times*, "The situation now is that of the top twenty London advertising agencies, only seven are totally British. All the rest are American owned, or, in a few cases, have strong American links. In the top ten, the U.S. dominance is even greater, with only two of the ten retaining total independence." In West Germany, France, Italy and even Japan, U.S. ad agencies now account for the bulk of nationally-placed advertising, says *Advertising Age*. On the other side of the world there is the same loss of national control of the image-making apparatus. A report from *Advertising and Newspaper News* notes that "Overseas agencies gain whole or partial control of 15 of 24 largest Australian ad agencies and Australians berate themselves for lack of self-faith."

In many of the less developed states, the control of internal communications by foreign (generally U.S.) business interests, is often overwhelming. *Le Monde* reports, for example, that in Peru "more than 80 percent of the advertising carried by Peruvian newspapers, radio and television is channeled through big American advertising firms, such as J. Walter Thomson *(sic)*, McKann Erickson *(sic)*, Grant Advertising and Katts Acciones, Inc." Venezuela is even more monopolized by U.S. agencies and a similar pattern, varying in degree, applies in Rhodesia, Kenya, Nigeria, India, Malaysia, Pakistan, Thailand and many other low-income nations.

Advertising, and the mass media which it eventually traduces are, therefore, the leading agents in the business of culture, and the culture of business. Other services such as public relations, marketing research and opinion surveying, all of which are utilized to make the marketing effort more effective, feed further the stream of international commercial communications.

Public relations, a practice of American business since the early years of the twentieth century, also has become an international phenomenon, following the migration of American capital overseas. Compared with the growth of international advertising, PR is still a rather modest but steadily expanding activity. Whereas advertising commonly aims to sell the corporation's output, PR's goal more specifically is to sell the company itself—as a useful, productive and beneficial entity to the society in which it is located. As American capital floods into a country and wrests control of key industries, this is no mean task. Here is the problem as seen by the executive vice-president of Hill & Knowlton, Inc., the most important American company engaged in international public relations.

> Let us review the situation confronting the American corporation today in Western Europe, [Mr. William A. Durbin suggests:] For a time following World War II, American companies found European countries eager for dollar investment—and the markets seemed almost limitless. In the past decade or so, American business responded with a tremendous increase in direct U.S. investments in Western Europe. In 1965 the total approached $14 billion, compared with $1.7 billion in 1950 [closer to $20 billion in 1969—HS].

> In recent years the climate has changed: the 'welcome' sign has been replaced with one reading 'Yankee Go Home.' A recent survey of Opinion Research Corporation disclosed considerable pressures to restrict the growth of U.S. firms in four Common Market countries. Fifty-six percent of the *businessmen* (my italics) in Germany believe their government should discourage U.S. investment. For Italy the figure was 44 percent, France 40 percent, and the Netherlands, 31 percent.

> . . . Under these circumstances, American corporations face difficult problems. They cannot merely withdraw—they must work harder than ever—and much of their attention must be given to the public relations aspects of their international operations.

Or put otherwise, it is the task of U.S. corporate-supported public relations to overcome widespread resistance to American penetrations of the national economy wherever they may be occurring.

The manipulation of symbols to achieve this objective is applied skillfully, generally unobtrusively and intensively by the professional image-makers. As noted in one business bulletin, "Worldwide PR is, quite simply, the art of using ideas and information through all available means of communications, to create a favorable climate of opinion for products, services and the corporation itself."

When PR has its way, the flow of communications becomes a stream of unidentifiable (by source) promotional messages for the sponsoring company or complex or even the entire business system itself. Years ago, a U.S. business periodical observed: "As expert communicator, PR plays a unique and quite startling role in the whole flow of communications between the business community and the public. This role is often glossed over, but the simple fact is that much of the current news coverage of business by the American press, radio and television is subsidized by company PR effort . . . one hundred thousand public relations practitioners serve as a tremendous source of communications manpower. Without them, only a handful of newspapers and radio or television stations would have the staff or resources to cover business activities . . ."

Emphasizing the fanciful means that are required to promote modern business, a later study concluded: "The relative significance of public relations cannot be gauged by estimating total expenditures for this work. We have no such estimates, and the figure would probably be small in comparison with advertising proper. The most telling test of the significance would be to determine the portion of the contents of our newspapers [and television and radio programming—HS] that has originated from public-relations offices. This portion is probably quite remarkable."

In this curiously inverted state of affairs, the public is supposed to benefit from the privately-prepared press releases which are fed into the mass media, because the latter would be unable, if left to its own resources, to produce enough of such material. Now the international community is receiving these communications benefits as well. *Business Week*, a decade ago, estimated that "among the top three hundred companies in the country, three out of four have full-fledged PR departments, a broad jump from the one out of fifty reported in 1936. New corporation PR departments are starting at the rate of one hundred a year." The top 300 companies, it may be recalled, are the major exporters of capital and are the main owners of overseas plants and facilities. In a survey undertaken by Opinion Research Corporation in January 1968, the 500 largest industrial corporations listed in the *Fortune* directory were asked to fill out questionnaires about their foreign public relations programs. Only 153 replies were received and of these, 43 reported no overseas PR activities. The Survey therefore represents a self-selected response of 110 major U.S. companies engaged in foreign public relations. The basic findings with respect to these firms were:

The number of companies engaging in international public relations activities has increased markedly in recent years.

These companies are carrying out public relations programs on every continent and in every major country.

The programs are usually handled by staff members based in the overseas countries.

Only one-third of the respondents use either a public relations firm or advertising agency to implement their overseas public relations programs.

The principal activities are "press releases, product publicity, and exhibits and special events." Other activities include community relations, employee relations and government regulations. *Public*

Relations Quarterly sums up the study in these words: "Not only are more companies entering the overseas public relations field, they also seem to be more active."

National and local mass media systems are infiltrated by business messages not necessarily identified by their sources of origin. Hill and Knowlton have prepared a guidebook to familiarize less knowledgeable PR-men with the techniques of overseas promotion and concern with the local media has the highest priority.

With the advent of space communications, the opportunity to achieve a world-wide audience for promotional ends has not been ignored. In June, 1969, for example, the space satellite system was used to herald the opening of an iron ore complex in Australia, owned and operated by an American multinational corporation in association with other business companies. "Co-ordinated planning, American techniques and Intelsat make Australian mine openings a world event," reported the *Public Relations Journal.*

Two other media-related services supplement the information-generation business which engages so much of the attention and resources of American companies active in international markets. These are the opinion survey organizations and the market research companies which are also involved in opinion-taking as well as in more detailed market analysis.

Opinion polls are considered generally as part of the contemporary political infrastructure of parliamentary-electoral societies. In fact, by volume and character of the work, market-economic undertakings account for a substantial part of the poll-takers' overall business. The distinction between survey and market research is often extremely thin, and the techniques of uncovering political attitudes and desires may serve to give orientation to economic activities and politics. For example, the Opinion Research Corporation recently announced the establishment of a new company, Market and Opinion Research International, Ltd., (MORI) with headquarters in London. This is a joint venture with NOP Market Research Ltd., London. MORI, the new outfit, is expected to provide facilities for research in North America, the United Kingdom and Europe.

The Gallup Organization, Inc., the most well known United States opinion-surveying company, identifies itself as providing "marketing and attitude research." Gallup-International, which includes its autonomous overseas associates in a loose network of affiliate relationships, "covers 36 countries or regions throughout the world. It undertakes surveys on a world-wide or European scale in the fields of marketing research and of public opinion and behavioral sciences, to be conducted on a contract and client basis."

A.C. Neilsen Co., the major market research company in the United States, engages in surveys as a matter of course and operates in 20 different countries on four continents. It supplies some of its research services to 86 international organizations with parent companies located in eight different countries. Its television audience research services have been established directly in Canada and Japan and through joint ventures in Ireland and West Germany. This rating service which creates frenzy amongst commercial TV broadcasters scrambling to achieve high viewing ratios, is described by Arthur C. Nielsen, founder of the company, in this way:

> ... (Since) this type of research exerts a significant and favorable effect on the efficiency of one of the most important methods of moving goods from producer to consumer (television)—it is lowering the cost of distribution and creating increased profits for manufacturers and greater values for consumers.

The view of television as essentially a "method of moving goods from producer to consumer" explains, of course, the pathetic condition of television in the United States. The "increased efficiency" that the medium provides for the marketing function can be balanced against the human dysfunction imposed on its audience.

Another firm, International Research Associates, Inc., (INRA) conducts market and opinion research in the United States, Latin America, Europe, Africa and the Middle East, Southeast Asia and the Far East. The company has a network of associated research organizations operating in more than 40 countries and principalities around the world.

The opinion survey—whether conducted under national or foreign auspices, which is, incidentally, no easy matter to ascertain—is ostensibly designed to acquire information, not to create it. In fact, however, it often creates not only information but attitudes that it is supposed only to poll. The problem lies not with faulty sampling or poor interviewing; even the questions can be phrased with complete objectivity. Deficiencies in these matters can and do appear, but with increasingly sophisticated polling techniques available, amongst well-established organizations, technical errors are likely to be minimal.

A less acknowledged consequence of opinion surveying, however, is what might be termed its legitimization effect. This means that once political, social or economic questions are put in a fixed perspective and called to the attention of the respondent, a validation of certain ideas or even of a frame of reference may occur. Consumer preference studies, for instance, inquire about choices between one product or another, not whether either or both of the products should have been produced in the first place. Political inquiries ask individuals to choose between candidates thereby validating the electoral process rather than questioning its mechanics.

In short, in most instances, and not necessarily with a deliberate intent to influence, the question-answer format creates for the respondent (and the viewer, listener or reader of the poll's published results) a pattern with which to view reality. This is set according to the structure of the inquiry. The conditions of the response are set by the poll-taker in the way he already views the relationships he wishes to uncover. The respondent is forced into that mold once he accepts the role of participant in the survey.

A case in point as an illustration. A Roper poll, conducted and paid for by the National Association of Broadcasters (the commercial broadcasters), asked its respondents, "Do you agree or disagree that having commercials is a fair price to pay for being able to watch [television]?" Roper reports, no doubt to the great satisfaction of the NAB, that "people agreed, eight to one, with the concept that having commercials is a 'fair price to pay.'" Yet what has been learned from this question and the overwhelming affirmative response it obtained? Alternatives of having television without commercials were not offered to the respondents. A commercial structure of relationships was assumed by the question formulated by Roper, and those answering, by the very fact of responding, had to accept the underlying set of assumptions. In effect, the prevailing institutional pattern of commercial television was sanctioned in the very process of poll-taking.

In this way surveys of opinion too often either create opinion or inhibit opinion-creating by restricting the framework in which genuine alternatives can be expressed or considered.

Gallup-International, financed by whomever will foot the bill, conducts periodic omnibus surveys in:

> Argentina (every other month); Australia (every other month); Austria (four times a year); Belgium (each week); Chile (every other month); Great Britain (every week); Greece (every two weeks); India (four times a year); The Netherlands (every week); Norway (every month); Philippines (once a year); Sweden (every month); Switzerland (four times a year); Union of South Africa (alternate months, when the "European" adult population is sampled); Uruguay, (every other month); Vietnam (four times a year); West Germany (every month).

Published findings may be expected to have the effect of solidifying status quo sentiments in a generalized though fundamental sense. Moreover, polls conducted under obscure sponsorship may provide information to those with limited social responsibility, which increases their potential for further manipulation of local populations.

In any event, opinion surveys conducted for American corporations or governmental information agencies, present a twofold threat to the societies in which they are undertaken. The polls are structured commercially and when published as national sentiment cannot fail to aggravate the marketeering influence in the country, by legitimizing still further, existing inclinations to consumerism. Of more moment, perhaps, they probe surreptitiously for national opinions that may determine or increase the scope of U.S. official or private information makers' future policy in that country. Certainly, the information that is derived from American-financed overseas surveys hardly promotes the two-way flow of communication which is the objective of so much UNESCO rhetoric.

It should also be clear that in many advanced, industrial market societies, local market research and polling occur alongside of and sometimes without competition from American supported operations in the same territory. To the extent that they do exist independently, they provide for their domestic sponsors the same methodology of control and manipulation that these activities offer their American counterparts. Though this discussion is concerned primarily with the promotion of American business ideology overseas through advertising, PR, polls and market research, the imposition of a value structure riddled with commercialism is made easier to the extent that it finds societies already prepared and enmeshed in these practices.

The economic power of American corporate capitalism has long been manifest. Its postwar global expansion has made it an international system which affects, and is affected by, national decision-making in scores of countries on all continents. Its economic impact, if not thoroughly documented, at least is generally recognized and includes raw material flows and explorations, balance of payments conflicts, dividend and profit repatriation pressures, migrations of human talent ("the brain drain"), currency and gold speculation, and shifting shares of world markets. Political consequences of the international operations of American companies are also beginning to be appreciated. Instabilities or at least tensions in local political structures are sometimes analysed with respect to inflows of American capital.

Only the cultural-informational sphere has gone almost unacknowledged in the appraisal of America's global influence. Yet today the control of men and of societies requires, before anything else, the manipulation of words and images. Whatever the degree of raw power that can be brought to bear on a people, it is unavailing in the long run (which may not be so very long in arriving) if it cannot make its objectives seem, if not attractive, at least benign to those it seeks to control. The methods and the messages of communications therefore are the most significant and indispensible instruments of modern power wielders. Neglect of communications in any analysis of contemporary international relations overlooks one of the sources of ultimate power in our time. For the attitudinal state of a population helps to determine its political behavior. And beliefs and opinions are remarkably vulnerable to the sort of modern mass communications which the American system of power uses with fantastic dexterity.

Commercially-produced entertainment and recreation are the chief channels that convey internationally the values and life styles of U.S. corporate capitalism, but the information generated directly by the sizable American business community overseas also is imposing and far reaching in its effects. It is difficult to overstate the impact of the promotional and "research" activities of the large corporations on peoples subjected to them. Moreover, since the agent of influence is often unrecognized as such, the more powerful though less measurable it is likely to be.

The great American stream of business-financed and commercially-saturated communications, pouring through the mass media, is aimed at protecting the physical operations of U.S. enterprises abroad as well as in fostering values and attitudes of privatism and consumerism, which are the ultimate supports of the business system. Few are the regions removed from this wave of commercialism. The culture of American business is enveloping everything in its path as it appeals to individualistic instincts while it reinforces its messages with the imagery of technological gadgetry and consumer delights.

It derives strength also from its utilization of two of the currently strongest human desires—the yearning of people everywhere for an end to bloody conflict and warfare and in their place some condition of universality, and the equally powerful popular impulse to freedom. Accordingly, the rhetoric of corporate communications, disseminated one way or another through the mass media, makes much of internationalism and freedom, of the special sort that maximizes private benefits. The identification of human freedom with property ownership and classifying the world-wide activities of business corporations as an inspiring model of internationalism, provide the chief ideological underpinnings of today's business-oriented messages. For instance, the advice of Tom Sutton, executive vice-president-International of J. Walter Thompson Company, the world's largest advertising agency, on this subject is forthright: "I believe it is the job of international organizations such as [the] International Advertising Association and the International Chamber of Commerce to preach the gospel of freedom and to see that the best systems of control and restraint—in areas where there may have to be some—are exported for adoption everywhere, and not the worst."

On the internationalist theme, Robert Sarnoff, chairman of the board and president of RCA Co., the electronics supercorporation, invokes the image of a boundary-free world, accessible to everyone but especially to the undertakings of the few hundred multinational corporations. In a call for a "global common market of communications," Sarnoff enthusiastically recommends reducing national responsibility in communications so that it can be considered a "global resource." Such a development he claims "would foster an increasing worldwide flow of information that would bring benefits as tangible as the increasing trade among the countries of Western Europe. The distribution of knowledge by such a system would provide greater stimulus to growth than any conceivable program of economic aid."

"For the public of all countries, it would provide entertainment, cultural and informational programming from abroad as a routine rather than a rarity." And, furthermore, Sarnoff adds: "As data transmission becomes less and less expensive, we will see greater use of computerized controls and even long-distance time-sharing to strengthen the multinational firm as a vehicle for the transfer of technology. The increases in production and productivity, resulting from the global surge of business information, could parallel the economic advances made in the common market over the past 20 years."

All this would apparently occur in the absence of genuine international structures of control and alongside diminished national authority. Beneficiaries in this context could only be the giant, transnational corporations.

Economic output, technological mastery and military power have been the traditional strengths of the American corporate economy. Now, increasing reliance is being placed on communications control. The heavy informational flow produced and supported by American companies overseas makes a powerful contribution to the domestic maintenance and global extension of the business system and its value.

DISCUSSION QUESTIONS

1. If you were redesigning America's television system, how would you do it? Which problems would still exist when you were finished?

2. Marshall McLuhan claims in some of his writings that print is on the way out. Do you believe this is a valid statement?

3. New movies and the rock music are topics which are discussed every day. Which medium (publications like *Rolling Stone* or *Village Voice*, underground films, television clips) does the best job explaining these new ideas and feelings? What chance do parents have of learning about their childrens' world?

4. What danger do you see in these "multiplying media voices" such as the underground, minority or religious press systems? Or is this a completely healthy situation for community communication? What can the establishment media learn from these publications and broadcast outlets?

5. What can the average person do to protect himself against the "selling" of a political candidate as described in the *Survey of Broadcast Journalism* piece? What can professional media people do to help protect the public?

6. Herbert Schiller has some strong ideas regarding American involvement in foreign affairs. How does he link the media to his argument?

7. On the other hand, the Sig Mickelson article on satellites shows benefits being derived from strong international involvement. What advances can you predict—or imagine—regarding satellite transmission?

PROJECT

Being as realistic as possible and using the facts and predictions of the articles in Part II as a base, describe the media world of 1980. Include your ideas about the changing roles of different media persons, such as the large city newspaper editor, the public relations expert, the community journalist. How will Americans receive their information and entertainment? Will there be diversity and freedom in this media revolution or will there be stereotyped presentations and economic barriers?

FURTHER READINGS

The following articles relate to the revolution in the mass media as discussed in Part II and are but some of the many published during the past few years:

"20th Fund Delivers 2nd Satellite Report." *Broadcasting* 79 (October, 1970):52.

"Helen Gurley Brown Only Wants to Help." *Esquire* 74 (February, 1970): 74-75, 117-118.

"Troubles of Television and A Coming Revolution." *U.S. News and World Report.* 69 (December, 1970):58-60.

"A Video Cartridge Bows—to Muffled Applause." *Business Week* 2150 (November, 1970):100-102. Also see *Life* 69 (October, 1970):46-53.

"What's Ahead for TV." *Newsweek* 77 (May, 1971):72-78.

Asimov, Isaac, *et al.* "Toward the Global Village." *Saturday Review* (October, 1970):17-25.

Bernstein, Henry R. "Naderites in TV Debate with Advertisers on Truthfulness." *Advertising Age* 41 (December, 1970):16.

Burgheim, Richard. "Performing Arts: Television Reviewing." *Harper's* 239 (August, 1969):98-101.

Chazen, Leonard. "The Price of Free TV." *Atlantic* 223 (March, 1969):59-61.

Cowlan, Bert. "Ethnic Radio." *Centre Magazine* 2 (January, 1969):94-96.

Engberg, Edward. "A Free and Responsible Press," "Where Are They Now?" *Centre Magazine* 1 (October-November, 1967):23-25.

Fischer, John. "The Perils of Publishing." *Harper's* 236 (May, 1968):13-14, 18-20.

Fulbright, J. William. "The Governance of the Pentagon." *Saturday Review* 53 (November, 1970):22-25.

Garland, Phyl. "Blacks Challenge the Airwaves." *Ebony* 26 (November, 1970):35-44.

Hoffman, Hallock. "A Centre Report/Failure to Communicate." *Centre Magazine* 1 (September, 1968):24-32.

Lewis, David L. "The Outstanding PR Professionals." *Public Relations Journal* 26 (October, 1970):78-80.

McGinnis, Joe. "The Selling of the President 1968." *Harper's* 239 (August, 1969):46-60.

Trayes, Edward J. "Still Few Blacks on Dailies, but 50% More in J-Schools, Recent Surveys Indicate." *Journalism Quarterly* 47 (Summer, 1970):356-60.

Part Three

Multiplying Media Debates

Basic conflicts glare in Part III. A rising level of consciousness regarding investigative reporting (the secret Pentagon papers, My Lai, Tonkin Gulf), the treatment of minorities (even in comic strips), style of expression (books and movie ads) and media mistakes (there could be too much violence) is quite apparent. But just as clear is the attitude of the Vice-President, the difficulty of arriving at the truth in dealing with public issues, and the frustration of changing established patterns.

Spiro Agnew launched his general attack on the news media in Des Moines, November 13, 1969. Ripping into the television news industry, he attempted to show that millions of Americans were nightly victims of the liberal views and many mistakes of a "little group of men who not only enjoy a right of instant rebuttal to every Presidential address [the rebuttal to President Nixon's Vietnam speech is the first topic in Agnew's speech] but, more importantly, wield a free hand in selecting, presenting and interpreting the great issues in our nation." Using statistics and quotations to make his point, Agnew even borrowed an old quote from Fred Friendly, who along with the late Edward R. Murrow believed that television had a fault because it was missing the ingredients of "conviction, controversy and a point of view." Agnew claimed the networks had compensated for their earlier lapses in public affairs reporting with "a vengeance."

The next day in San Diego, at the national convention of Sigma Delta Chi, the professional journalistic society, CBS News Correspondent Daniel Schorr delivered a long rebuttal to Agnew's statements, during which the highly respected veteran reporter included his fear for the safety of open reporting and comment. But outside the conference room the late Merriman Smith, United Press International White House reporter since the days of Franklin Roosevelt, was telling delegates that Agnew should be compared to a pitcher "throwing a high, hard fastball at the batter's head, trying just to brush him off, not trying to hit him." Whatever the true case, in this instance the fastball came close enough to cause an uproar in the world of journalism.

By giving extra space to the Agnew story we do not mean to study just the particular statements of the Vice-President. Instead we intend to reflect upon the phenomena of heavy government criticism of the news media by officials on all levels—something which will continue as long as we have our adversary system of government.

Agnew's sniping at the press did not cease; it only diminished at times. While claiming all along that he did not mean to "intimidate" the news media, Agnew managed to raise strong suspicions from even his media supporters, like Howard K. Smith, that "a tone of intimidation" was there. This is why Agnew's statements and his influence warrant considerable attention, now and in the future.

Smith of ABC did not flinch when interviewed in saying that Agnew was basically correct. Although he considered himself to be left-of-center on most public issues, Smith claimed too many of his colleagues had been swayed by the excitement caused by the New Left and now automatically condemn conservatives like President Nixon and California Governor Ronald Reagan, no matter what they say. Eric Sevareid, attempting to destroy Agnew's claim that Eastern media leaders "talk constantly to one another," snorted that he had not seen "Huntley or Brinkley for about two or three years." Sevareid offered his usual graceful and balanced opinion in describing the Agnew phenomena. He admitted it is not difficult to get into a rut where one type of story is overemphasized for a while, but stoutly defended the men who put the news shows together, saying whether liberal or conservative their views are not evident as they work.

Often overlooked in the discussion of the role of television news is that putting together a television news program is very complex; it can be a nightmare before it becomes a reality. Wondering out loud about Agnew's generalizations, Daniel St. Albin Greene told *National Observer* readers how it is done at NBC in New York. The views of Chet Huntley enter into the conversation, as do the complaints of newsmen that both liberal and conservative citizens do not like what they see on the screen.

Part of the reason behind political attacks against the media is that there is a natural fear of the power of the press. The Vice-President hammered at the *New York Times* and the *Washington Post* while being toasted in Montgomery, Alabama, on November 20—a week after his Iowa speech. Agnew declared that the day is past when the *New York Times* can enjoy "a form of diplomatic immunity from comment and criticism of what they said."

Ironically, it was the *New York Times* and *Washington Post* which figured in one of journalism history's most important and perplexing court cases in June, 1971. The Nixon administration was thwarted by the Supreme Court in its attempt to stop publication of the secret Pentagon Papers, originally given to the *Times* by a disillusioned former Pentagon and Rand Corporation analyst. Does the President have an "inherent right" in the name of national security to stop the media from publishing news? Will the future see more government attempts to use the courts against the media?

But while some in high office worried excessively about the power of the media to move public opinion in a liberal direction, others were concerned that the media itself was guilty of being establishment or too conservative. One longtime mass media critic, Bryce W. Rucker, charged monopolistic newspaper and television owners threatened to cut out the diversity which makes for a truly open mass media system. Urging his fellow journalism educators to join in local and national fights against self-interest on the part of the media barons, Rucker engaged in a type of professional criticism similar to that referred to in Part I.

Another establishment under attack from several directions is the journalism school. While many professionals scoff at journalism education through ignorance of what is actually being taught, others criticize J-schools in hopes that their pleas for more professionalism will be heard. It was with this spirit that John Tebbel suggested college classrooms were the last best hope for media improvement. A scarcity of solid writers and editors bothered Tebbel, who managed to throw a few barbs at Ph.D.'s before urging concentration on the more traditional journalism subjects.

Joseph Lyford praises "highly literate press critics" and FCC Commissioners Nicholas Johnson and Kenneth Cox, but finds little else of happy note as he examines the media scene. The riddles are there: Why doesn't television respond with quality, why do editors "gut" interesting offerings of syndicated reporters, why don't the media as a whole try to be more than a "mirror to the world?" He does find encouragement in the fact there is an underground press and that people like Joan Baez can make it onto the "Today" show, but the hopeful signs are scarce.

One area where there is some real hope is in minority recruitment. The Association for Education in Journalism (AEJ) and Sigma Delta Chi have been working for several years, admittedly belatedly, in this area. Nevertheless, the harsh observations of those interviewed by Melvin Mencher remain valid. The media have a long way to go before these critical ideas can be dropped.

As evidence that there is room for hope, Jack E. White discovered the existence of "color in the comics." It has often been said that the future is in the hands of those who reach today's preschoolers. And that does include the cartoonist as well as the producer of the Saturday morning horror show.

The Preface implied one reason there has been an increasing number of debates about the media is that basic concepts about the role and function of the media have changed. The content of articles that reflect these changes creates both anger and delight. Terry Ann Knopf leads off the final segment with detailed examples of media reaction to violence—the type which she says only confuses the public and sometimes even "panders to the public prejudice."

Student and racial demonstrations—Cornell, Detroit, Cleveland, elsewhere—are the objects of study. While the crisis situation calls for an increase in news, she says, the news media have failed to explain that events like racial violence are part of the natural social process. She points to the proliferation of underground newspapers and radio stations as evidence that the media are seen to lack the necessary "sensitivity, sophistication and skepticism" necessary to present reasonable accounts of violent events.

Much of the overall debate about media performance centers around whether the media are open to new ideas. Lee H. Smith found that there is not much that cannot be printed if a writer or editor has the desire. The so-called sexual revolution has caused book, magazine and even newspaper editors to loosen up when it comes to describing sexual experiences, when they are part of a legitimate story. David Susskind and Hugh Hefner had their say as did a reserved *Chicago Tribune* editor. As in the following article by John Thompson on "Pornography and Propaganda," the reader has to move along with an open mind, being ready to appreciate reasons for the obvious changes but also arguments why Times Square should be considered a disgrace.

Clear-mindedness is also required while reading the Seymour Hersh and Don Stillman articles. Hersh won a Pulitzer Prize for his efforts in uncovering the My Lai massacre and Mike Wallace of CBS was nominated for a 1971 news-documentary Emmy for a "60 Minutes" magazine-type program on the Tonkin Gulf discrepancies. Finally, in early 1971, public opinion polls revealed that a majority of Americans felt they had been denied the truth about major events in Asia.

Truth has been the "first casualty" of the Vietnam War in many ways. Hersh tells of the reaction of the nation's major newspapers to his My Lai investigation—the initial negative response stands out—but he ends on a more positive note because the media finally did respond (and even overcovered the story at times, causing more wonderment).

Stillman traced the statements of those who questioned the Tonkin Gulf incident from the beginning, notably Senator Wayne Morse of Oregon, and discovered that the media used Pentagon information for the bulk of its coverage. Most citizens believed the military and trusted the Congress which gave President Johnson broad power to conduct war, and yet the actual facts were not known until later. Like CBS' Mike Wallace, Stillman came to the conclusion that the Tonkin incident was a disaster for the nation. He praises Washington writer I.F. Stone for being the "only one to cover in detail the charges raised by Morse." And he, like many of the contributors to this book, finds a ray of hope despite the darkness of the particular problem. In this case Stillman said more independent coverage of the *Pueblo* affair might be attributed to the lessons of Tonkin.

Whatever their differences about specific matters, or even large ones like the Vietnam War, the professional journalists interviewed and studied in this section seem to agree with the April, 1971, statement of ABC's Harry Reasoner. Reasoner, teaming with Howard K. Smith, told his audience that professional journalists should all move an arm's length away from government, "and then a few inches more," to insure skeptical, independent reporting.

The writers, whose work dealt with racial problems, violence and matters of taste, seemed to agree generally with Lee H. Smith's comment, "The story of the candid society is too big to be ignored and from all indications it will run for a long time." While American society continues to be explored in different degrees by different types of media, the critics—professional and political—will continue to be as candid in their words as the newsmakers are in their bold actions. The seventies will continue to be exciting but hopefully will not end as the sixties did, with the media holding post-mortems on one side and being blamed for causing the "terrible sixties" on the other. Perhaps all of this discussion will develop more aware and honest citizens who will have learned to appreciate both the power and the limitations of the media.

Chapter IX

TELEVISION NEWS
AND OBJECTIVITY

THE DES MOINES SPEECH

Spiro T. Agnew

Tonight I want to discuss the importance of the television news medium to the American people. No nation depends more on the intelligent judgment of its citizens. No medium has a more profound influence over public opinion. Nowhere in our system are there fewer checks on vast power. So, nowhere should there be more conscientious responsibility exercised than by the news media. The question is, Are we demanding enough of our television news presentations? And are the men of this medium demanding enough of themselves?

Monday night a week ago, President Nixon delivered the most important address of his Administration, one of the most important of our decade. His subject was Vietnam. His hope was to rally the American people to see the conflict through to a lasting and just peace in the Pacific. For thirty-two minutes, he reasoned with a nation that has suffered almost a third of a million casualties in the longest war in its history.

When the President completed his address—an address, incidentally, that he spent weeks in the preparation of—his words and policies were subjected to instant analysis and querulous criticism. The audience of seventy million Americans gathered to hear the President of the United States was inherited by a small band of network commentators and self-appointed analysts, the majority of whom

The most discussed activities of Spiro T. Agnew, vice-president of the United States, have been in relation to the performance of the mass media, particularly the work of television news reporters, commentators and documentary writers and producers. This speech of November 13, 1969 was made to a group of Iowa Republicans.

expressed, in one way or another, their hostility to what he had to say.

It was obvious that their minds were made up in advance. Those who recall the fumbling and groping that followed President Johnson's dramatic disclosure of his intention not to seek another term have seen these men in a genuine state of non-preparedness. This was not it.

One commentator twice contradicted the President's statement about the exchange of correspondence with Ho Chi Minh. Another challenged the President's abilities as a politician. A third asserted that the President was "following a Pentagon line." Others, by the expression on their faces, the tone of their questions and the sarcasm of their responses, made clear their sharp disapproval.

To guarantee in advance that the President's plea for national unity would be challenged, one network trotted out Averell Harriman for the occasion. Throughout the President's message, he waited in the wings. When the President concluded, Mr. Harriman recited perfectly. He attacked the Thieu Government as unrepresentative; he criticized the President's speech for various deficiencies; he twice issued a call to the Senate Foreign Relations Committee to debate Vietnam once again; he stated his belief that the Vietcong or North Vietnamese did not really want a military takeover of South Vietnam; and he told a little anecdote about a "very, very responsible" fellow he had met in the North Vietnamese delegation.

All in all, Mr. Harriman offered a broad range of gratuitous advice, challenging and contradicting the policies outlined by the President of the United States. Where the President had issued a call for unity, Mr. Harriman was encouraging the country not to listen to him.

A word about Mr. Harriman. For ten months he was America's chief negotiator at the Paris peace talks—a period in which the United States swapped some of the greatest military concessions in the history of warfare for an enemy agreement on the shape of the bargaining table. Like Coleridge's Ancient Mariner, Mr. Harriman seems to be under some heavy compulsion to justify his failure to anyone who will listen. And the networks have shown themselves willing to give him all the air time he desires.

Now every American has a right to disagree with the President of the United States, and to express publicly that disagreement. But the President of the United States has a right to communicate directly with the people who elected him, and the people of this country have the right to make up their own minds and form their own opinions about a Presidential address without having a President's words and thoughts characterized through the prejudices of hostile critics before they can even be digested.

When Winston Churchill rallied public opinion to stay the course against Hitler's Germany, he didn't have to contend with a gaggle of commentators raising doubts about whether he was reading public opinion right, or whether Britain had the stamina to see the war through.

When President Kennedy rallied the nation in the Cuban missile crisis, his address to the people was not chewed over by a roundtable of critics who disparaged the course of action he'd asked Americans to follow.

The purpose of my remarks tonight is to focus your attention on this little group of men who not only enjoy a right of instant rebuttal to every Presidential address, but, more importantly, wield a free hand in selecting, presenting and interpreting the great issues in our nation.

First, let's define that power. At least forty million Americans every night, it's estimated, watch the network news. Seven million of them view ABC, the remainder being divided between NBC and CBS. [Editor's Note: Many of these millions plus about 25-million other Americans also have the benefit of receiving world and national news from their local stations, which are not bound to give the same emphasis as the networks; indeed, some local newscasters give their own very conservative twists to "big" news through film and commentary.]

According to Harris polls and other studies, for millions of Americans the networks are the sole source of national and world news. In Will Roger's observation, what you knew was what you read in the newspaper. Today for growing millions of Americans, it's what they see and hear on their television sets.

Now how is this network news determined? A small group of men, numbering perhaps no more than a dozen anchormen, commentators and executive producers, settle upon the 20 minutes or so of film and commentary that's to reach the public. This selection is made from the 90 to 180 minutes that may be available. Their powers of choice are broad.

They decide what 40 to 50 million Americans will learn of the day's events in the nation and the world.

We cannot measure this power and influence by the traditional democratic standards, for these men can create national issues overnight.

'A small elite group of men decided what you
would or would not see on television. . .'

They can make or break by their coverage and commentary, a Moratorium on the war.

They can elevate men from obscurity to national prominence within a week. They can reward some politicians with national exposure and ignore others.

For millions of Americans the network reporter who covers a continuing issue—like the ABM or civil rights—becomes, in effect, the presiding judge in a national trial by jury.

It must be recognized that the networks have made important contributions to the national knowledge—through news, documentaries and specials they have often used their power constructively and creatively to awaken the public conscience to critical problems. The networks made "hunger" and "black lung disease" national issues overnight. The TV networks have done what no other medium could have done in terms of dramatizing the horrors of war. The networks have tackled our most difficult social problems with a directness and an immediacy that's the gift of their medium. They focus the nation's attention on its environment abuses—on pollution in the Great Lakes and the threatened ecology of the Everglades.

But it was also the networks that elevated Stokely Carmichael and George Lincoln Rockwell from obscurity to national prominence.

Nor is their power confined to the substantive. A raised eyebrow, an inflection of the voice, a caustic remark dropped in the middle of a broadcast can raise doubts in a million minds about the veracity of a public official or the wisdom of a government policy.

One Federal Communications Commissioner considers the powers of the networks equal to that of local, state, and federal governments all combined. Certainly it represents a concentration of power over American public opinion unknown in history.

Now what do Americans know of the men who wield this power? Of the men who produce and direct the network news, the nation knows practically nothing. Of the commentators, most Americans know little other than that they reflect an urbane and assured presence, seemingly well-informed on every important matter.

We do know that to a man these commentators and producers live and work in the geographical and intellectual confines of Washington, D.C., or New York City, the latter of which James Reston terms the "most unrepresentative community in the entire United States."

Both communities bask in their own provincialism, their own parochialism.

We can deduce that these men read the same newspapers. They draw their political and social views from the same sources. Worse, they talk constantly to one another, thereby providing artificial reinforcement to their shared viewpoints.

Do they allow their biases to influence the selection and presentation of the news? David Brinkley states "objectively is impossible to normal human behavior." Rather, he says, we should strive for "fairness."

Another anchorman on a network news show contends, and I quote: "You can't expunge all your private convictions just because you sit in a seat like this and a camera starts to stare at you. I think your program has to reflect what your basic feelings are. I'll plead guilty to that."

Less than a week before the 1968 election, this same commentator charged that President Nixon's campaign commitments were no more durable than campaign balloons. He claimed that, were it not for the fear of hostile reactions, Richard Nixon would be giving into, and I quote him exactly, "his natural instinct to smash the enemy with a club or go after him with a meat axe."

Had this slander been made by one political candidate about another, it would have been dismissed by most commentators as a partisan attack. But this attack emanated from the privileged sanctuary of a network studio and therefore had the apparent dignity of an objective statement.

The American people would rightly not tolerate this concentration of power in government.

Is it not fair and relevant to question its concentration in the hands of a tiny, enclosed fraternity of privileged men elected by no one and enjoying a monopoly sanctioned and licensed by government?

The views of the majority of this fraternity do not—and I repeat, not—represent the views of America.

That is why such a great gulf existed between how the nation received the President's address and how the networks reviewed it.

Not only did the country receive the President's address more warmly than the networks, but so also did the Congress of the United States.

Yesterday, the President was notified that 300 individual Congressmen and 50 Senators of both parties had endorsed his efforts for peace.

As with other American institutions, perhaps it is time that the networks were made more responsive to the views of the nation and more responsible to the people they serve.

Now I want to make myself perfectly clear. I'm not asking for government censorship or any other kind of censorship. I'm asking whether a form of censorship already exists when the news that 40 million Americans receive each night is determined by a handful of men responsible only to their corporate employers and is filtered through a handful of commentators who admit to their own set of biases.

The questions I'm raising here tonight should have been raised by others long ago. They should have been raised by those Americans who have traditionally considered the preservation of freedom of speech and freedom of the press their special provinces of responsibility.

They should have been raised by those Americans who share the view of the late Justice Learned Hand that "right conclusions are more likely to be gathered out of a multitude of tongues than through any kind of authoritative selection."

Advocates for the networks have claimed a First Amendment right to the same unlimited freedoms held by the great newspapers of America.

But the situations are not identical. Where the New York *Times* reaches 800,000 people, NBC reaches 20 times that number on its evening news. Nor can the tremendous impact of seeing television film and hearing commentary be compared with reading the printed page.

A decade ago, before the network news acquired such dominance over public opinion, Walter Lippmann spoke to the issue. He said: "there's an essential and radical difference between television and printing. The three or four competing television stations control virtually all that can be received over the air by ordinary television sets. But besides the mass circulation dailies, there are weeklies, monthlies, out-of-town newspapers and books. If a man doesn't like his newspaper, he can read another from out of town, or wait for a weekly news magazine. It is not ideal, but it is infinitely better than the situation in television. There, if a man does not like what the networks offer him, all he can do is turn them off, and listen to a phonograph." "Networks," he stated, "which are few in number, have a virtual monopoly of a whole medium of communication." The newspapers of mass circulation have no monopoly on the medium of print.

Now a "virtual monopoly of a whole medium of communication" is not something that a democratic people should blindly ignore. And we are not going to cut off our television sets and listen to the phonograph just because the airwaves belong to the networks. They don't. They belong to the people.

As Justice Byron White wrote in his landmark opinion six months ago, "it's the right of the viewers and listeners, not the right of the broadcasters, which is paramount."

Now it's argued that this power presents no danger in the hands of those who have used it responsibly. But, as to whether or not the networks have abused the power they enjoy, let us call as our first witness former Vice President Humphrey and the city of Chicago. According to Theodore White, television's intercutting of the film from the streets of Chicago with the "current proceedings on the floor of the convention created the most striking and false political picture of 1968—the nomination of a man for the American Presidency by the brutality and violence of merciless police." [Editor's Note: It must be noted that the only reason Americans did not see the street demonstrations when they occurred, but instead saw film which had to be quickly edited at the convention site, was that a telephone strike had made it impossible to telecast live from downtown Chicago. Johnson-Humphrey Democrats agreed with these decisions. White's book also tells of the continual harassment of TV men by Mayor Daley and police, including threats to men delivering film to the main convention hall, see p. 307.]

If we are to believe a recent report of the House of Representatives Commerce Committee, then television's presentation of the violence in the streets worked an injustice on the reputation of the Chicago police. According to the committee findings, one network in particular presented, and I quote, "a one-sided picture which in large measure exonerates the demonstrators and protesters." Film of provocations of police that was available never saw the light of day, while the film of a police response which the protesters provoked was shown to millions.

Another network showed virtually the same scene of violence from three separate angles without making clear it was the same scene. And, while the full report is reticent in drawing conclusions, it is not a document to inspire confidence in the fairness of the network news.

Our knowledge of the impact of network news on the national mind is far from complete, but some early returns are available. Again, we have enough information to raise serious questions about its effect on a democratic society. Several years ago Fred Friendly, one of the pioneers of network news, wrote that its missing ingredients were "conviction, controversy and a point of view." The networks have compensated with a vengeance.

And in the networks' endless pursuit of controversy, we should ask: What is the end value—to enlighten or to profit? What is the end result—to inform or to confuse? How does the ongoing exploration for more action, more excitement, more drama serve our national search for internal peace and stability?

Gresham's Law seems to be operating in the network news. Bad news drives out good news. The irrational is more controversial than the rational. Concurrence can no longer compete with dissent.

One minute of Eldridge Cleaver is worth ten minutes of Roy Wilkins. The labor crisis settled at the negotiating table is nothing compared to the confrontation that results in a strike—or better yet, violence along the picket lines. Normality has become the nemesis of the network news.

Now the upshot of all this controversy is that a narrow and distorted picture of America often emerges from the televised news. A single, dramatic piece of the mosaic becomes, in the minds of millions, the entire picture. And the American who relies upon television for his news might conclude that the majority of American students are embittered radicals. That the majority of black Americans feel no regard for their country. That violence and lawlessness are the rule rather than the exception on the American campus. We know that none of these conclusions is true.

Perhaps the place to start looking for a credibility gap is not in the offices of the government in Washington but in the studios of the networks in New York.

Television may have destroyed the old sterotypes, but has it not created new ones in their places?

What has this passionate pursuit of "controversy" done to the politics of progress through local compromise essential to the functioning of a democratic society?

The members of Congress or the Senate who follow their principles and philosophy quietly in a spirit of compromise are unknown to many Americans, while the loudest and most extreme dissenters on every issue are known to every man in the street.

How many marches and demonstrations would we have if the marchers did not know that the ever-faithful TV cameras would be there to record their antics for the next news show?

We've heard demands that Senators and Congressmen and judges make known all their financial connections so that the public will know who and what influences their decisions and their votes. Strong arguments can be made for that view.

But when a single commentator or producer, night after night, determines for millions of people how much of each side of a great issue they are going to see and hear, should he not first disclose his personal views on the issues as well?

In this search for excitement and controversy, has more than equal time gone to the minority of Americans who specialize in attacking the United States—its institutions and its citizens?

Tonight I've raised questions. I've made no attempt to suggest the answers. The answers must come from the media men. They are challenged to turn their critical powers on themselves, to direct their energy, their talent and their conviction toward improving the quality and objectivity of news presentation.

They are challenged to structure their own civic ethics to relate their great freedom to the great responsibilities they hold.

And the people of America are challenged, too, challenged to press for responsible news presentations. The people can let the networks know that they want their news straight and objective. The people can register their complaints on bias through mail to the networks and phone calls to local stations. This is one case where the people must defend themselves; where the citizen, not the government, must be the reformer; where the consumer can be the most effective crusader.

By way of conclusion, let me say that every elected leader in the United States depends on these men of the media. Whether what I've said to you tonight will be heard and seen at all by the nation is not my decision, it's not your decision, it's their decision.

In tomorrow's edition of the Des Moines *Register*, you'll be able to read a news story detailing what I've said tonight. Editorial comment will be reserved for the editorial page, where it belongs.

Should not the same wall of separation exist between news and comment on the nation's networks?

Now, my friends, we'd never trust such power, as I've described, over public opinion in the hands of an elected government. It's time we questioned it in the hands of a small and unelected elite.

The great networks have dominated America's airways for decades. The people are entitled to a full accounting of their stewardship.

THE AGNEW ANALYSIS:
FALSE PREMISES, WRONG CONCLUSIONS

(On November 3, President Nixon's) words and policies were subjected to instant analysis and querulous criticism.

MIKE WALLACE: The fact of the matter was that the speech was in the hands of the analysts . . . two hours ahead of time, and they all went over to be briefed on his speech by Henry Kissinger. Then they . . . listened to the speech and made their comments. So it was hardly any more instant analysis than the kind . . . that is done by overnight newspapers.

HERBERT KLEIN: I'd have to agree with that.

—Sixty Minutes, CBS-TV, November 25.

When President Kennedy rallied the nation in the Cuban missile crisis, his address to the people was not chewed over by a roundtable of critics. . . .

Would the Vice President believe Sander Vanocur, Ray Scherer, Frank McGee, David Schoenbrun, Roger Mudd, George Herman, Richard C. Hottelet, and Douglas Edwards? The date on that is October 22, 1962.

—Fred W. Friendly, speech, November 21.

We do know that to a man these commentators and producers live and work in the geographical and intellectual confines of Washington, D.C., or New York City. . . . We can deduce that these men read the same newspapers. They draw their political and social views from the same sources.

It is true that we live in New York . . . but not a single one of the network newsmen . . . comes from New York or even from that Eastern Establishment area: David Brinkley (is) from North Carolina; (Chet) Huntley from Montana; Howard K. Smith from New Orleans; Dan Rather from Houston, Texas; Eric Sevareid from North

---

The analysis of Vice-President Agnew's attacks on network news, the *New York Times* and *Washington Post*, is used here with the permission of *Columbia Journalism Review*, where it first appeared in the Winter, 1969-70 issue.

Dakota; Harry Reasoner from Iowa ... Frank McGee from Oklahoma. This is a cross section of America in its own way.

—Walter Cronkite, Sixty Minutes.

Is it not fair and relevant to question its (TV news') concentration in the hands of a tiny, enclosed fraternity of privileged men elected by no one ...?

No, I was not elected. But I submit that I could not have arrived at my present post without two score of news executives having made individual and independent judgments about me along the way. And I might add that none of these men ever asked me about my personal opinions. ... Had I ever violated their trust, I would not have been in their employ the following day.

—Elmer Lower, president, ABC News,
speech, December 10.

Do they allow their biases to influence the selection and presentation of the news?

Well, we all have our prejudices, we all have our biases, we have a structural problem in writing a news story or presenting it on television as to time and length, position in the paper, position on the news broadcasts, and these things are all going to be affected by our own beliefs, of course they are. But we are professional journalists. This is the difference. We are trying ... to be objective.

—Walter Cronkite, Sixty Minutes.

As with other American institutions, perhaps it is time that the networks were made more responsive to the views of the nation and more responsible to the people they serve.

What does that mean, "made"? He could have said, "Perhaps it is time the networks became more responsive." ... It seems to be an implicit threat to station owners.

—Mike Wallace, Sixty Minutes.

I'm asking whether a form of censorship already exists when the news that 40 million Americans receive each night is determined by a handful of men responsible only to their corporate employers. ...

Censorship must be official, or it isn't censorship. Newsmen editing news is not censorship, even if they do their jobs badly. As for official censorship, it is Mr. Agnew who raises that specter.

—Reuven Frank, president, NBC News,
memo to staff, November 26.

If we are to believe a recent report of the House of Representatives Commerce Committee, then television's presentation of the violence in the streets (of Chicago) worked an injustice on the reputation of the Chicago police.

Police violence was a fact of convention week. Were the policemen who committed it a minority? It appears certain that they were—but . . . there has been no public condemnation of these violators of sound police procedures and common decency by either their commanding officers or city officials. . . .

> —*"The Walker Report," National Commission
> on the Causes and Prevention of Violence, 1968.*

But a single company, in the nation's capital, holds control of the largest newspaper in Washington, D.C., and one of the four major television stations, and an all-news radio station, and one of the three major national news magazines—all grinding out the same editorial line. . . .

The Washington *Post, Newsweek*, WTOP-TV, and WTOP radio decidedly do not "grind out the same editorial line." . . . They disagree on many issues. . . . Washington is one of the most competitive communications cities in America by any objective standards. It is one of only three cities left with three major newspapers under separate ownership, all of them first rate.

> —*Mrs. Katharine Graham, president,
> Washington Post Company, November 20.*

. . . . and this is not a subject that you've seen debated on the editorial pages of the Washington "Post" or the New York "Times."

In fact, in an editorial on March 13, 1969, headed "Competition and Monopoly," the *Times* stated, "The constitutional guarantee of freedom of the press provides the press with no warrant for seeking exemption from the laws prohibiting monopoly. If anything, the sanctity attached to press freedom by the First Amendment makes it the special obligation of the press to fight for the broadest extension of that freedom." This is a sentiment that the New York *Times* has expressed repeatedly and still holds.

> —*Arthur Ochs Sulzberger, president
> and publisher, New York* Times, *November 20.*

When 300 Congressmen and fifty-nine Senators signed a letter endorsing the President's policy on Vietnam, it was news—and it was big news. . . . Yet the next morning the New York "Times" . . . did not carry a word. Why? Why?

The New York *Times* printed the story. Unfortunately, it failed to make the edition that reached Washington but was carried in a later edition of the *Times*. Moreover, the *Times* has given considerable attention to that story as it developed.

—*Arthur Ochs Sulzberger, November 20.*

The day when the network commentators and even the gentlemen of the New York "Times" enjoyed a form of diplomatic immunity from comment and criticism of what they said is over. . . . (The) time for blind acceptance of their opinions is past.

Such a day, of course, had never dawned (at least) in the state whose punitive legislation against the *Times* some years ago produced the U.S. Supreme Court's controlling libel precedent.

—*Harry S. Ashmore, Los Angeles* Times.

I'm raising these questions so that the American people will become aware of—and think of the implications of—the growing monopoly that involves the voices of public opinion. . . .

If it was suspected from his initial speech . . . it was confirmed by the second: the rap was not against journalists but against liberals, actual or assumed. . . . If Agnew . . . were really interested in responsible news judgment and unbiased reporting, as he professed to be, he would have had to include *Time* magazine, the Chicago *Tribune*, and a host of right-wing newspapers with broadcast properties . . . which apparently earn their exemption through sympathy with the Administration.

—Variety, *November 26.*

* * *

Attorney General John N. Mitchell says the Nixon Administration has no intention of using the anti-trust laws to break up news media concentration. Questioned on a National Educational Television network program after Vice President Agnew's "monopolization" charge, the Attorney General said such action is "the last thing in the world we have under consideration."

—Publisher's Auxiliary, *December 13.*

The following are the statements of the presidents of the three major television networks answering Vice President Agnew's speech, as carried in the New York *Times* of November 14, 1970.

ABC: Leonard H. Goldenson

In our judgment, the performance of ABC news has always been and will continue to be fair and objective. In the final analysis, it is always the public who decides on the reliability of any individual or organization. We will continue to report the news accurately and fully, confident in the ultimate judgment of the American public.

CBS: Dr. Frank Stanton

No American institution, including network news organizations, should be immune to public criticism or to public discussion of its performance. In a democracy this is entirely proper. We do not believe, however, that this unprecedented attempt by the Vice President of the United States to intimidate a news medium which depends for its existence upon government licenses represents legitimate criticism. The public, according to opinion polls, has indicated again and again that it has more confidence in the credibility of television news than in that of any other news medium.

Our newsmen have many times earned commendations for their enterprise and for their adherence to the highest professional standards. Since human beings are not infallible, there are bound to be occasions when their judgment is questioned.

Whatever their deficiencies, they are minor compared to those of a press which would be subservient to the executive power of government.

NBC: Julian Goodman

Vice President Agnew's attack on television news is an appeal to prejudice. More importantly, Mr. Agnew uses the influence of his high office to criticize the way a government-licensed news medium covers the activities of government itself. Any fair-minded viewer knows that the television networks are not devoted to putting across a single point of view but present all significant views on issues of importance.

It is regrettable that the Vice President of the United States would deny to television freedom of the press.

Evidently, he would prefer a different kind of television reporting—one that would be subservient to whatever political group was in authority at the time.

Those who might feel momentary agreement with his remarks should think carefully whether that kind of television news is what they want.

IS THERE A NETWORK NEWS BIAS?

Interview with Howard K. Smith and Eric Sevareid

On Nov. 12, 1969, when the liberal media were angrily aboil over Vice President Agnew's blasts at the liberal left and its frequently violent crusades, a quiet voice on ABC-TV declared: "Political cartoonists have that in common with the lemmings, that once a line is set, most of them follow it, though it lead to perdition. The current cliche shared by them and many columnists is that Spiro Agnew is putting his foot in his mouth (and) making irredeemable errors. . . . Well, . . . I doubt that party line. . . . There is a possibility it is not Mr. Agnew who is making mistakes. It is the cartoonists."

One week later, on Nov. 19, 1969, when the liberal media were even more violently aboil over the climactic Agnew speech blasting bias in network news, that same quiet voice on ABC-TV once again was heard: "I agree with some of what Mr. Agnew said. In fact, I said some of it before he did."

The speaker was Howard K. Smith, ABC's Washington-based anchor man, ex-CBS European correspondent, and winner of a constellation of awards for foreign and domestic reporting. Mr. Smith had, indeed, said some of what Mr. Agnew said before Mr. Agnew had said it. For several years, despite his respect for network news departments and their achievements, he has been criticizing his colleagues—on the air and off—for falsifying U.S. political realities by means of biased reporting.

Mr. Smith is by no means an unqualified supporter of Mr. Agnew, and he has reservations about The Speech. To name the two most important: "A tone of intimidation, I think, was in it, and that I can't accept. . . . Also a sense that we do things deliberately. I don't think we do them deliberately."

Mr. Smith, however, says: "I agree that we made the mistakes he says we made." And he himself levels charges at the network news departments.

In fact, according to Howard Smith, political bias in tv reporting is of such a magnitude that it fully justifies the explosion we have seen. Here is this insider's analysis of the problem.

Eric Sevareid, the dean of television news commentators, and Howard K. Smith, also for years one of the most popular of newsmen, disagreed about the objectivity of the Vice-President. These interviews by Edith Efron and Neil Hickey are reprinted with the permission of *TV Guide*, copyright 1970, Triangle Publications, Inc. They also were reprinted in the June, 1970 *Seminar Quarterly*.

His candor begins at the very base of the network news operation—namely, with the political composition of the staff. Networks, says Mr. Smith, are almost exclusively staffed by liberals. "It evolved from the time when liberalism was a good thing, and most intellectuals became highly liberal. Most reporters are in an intellectual occupation." Secondly, he declares that liberals, virtually by definition, have a "strong leftward bias": "Our tradition, since FDR, has been leftward."

This is not to say that Mr. Smith sees anything wrong with being a leftist—"I am left-of-center myself." But he sees everything wrong with the dissemination of an inflexible "party line"; and this, he charges, is what liberal newsmen are doing today: "Our liberal friends, today, have become dogmatic. They have a set of automatic reactions. They react the way political cartoonists do with oversimplification. Oversimplify. Be sure you please your fellows, because that's what's 'good.' They're conventional, they're conformists. They're pleasing Walter Lippmann, they're pleasing the *Washington Post*, they're pleasing the editors of *The New York Times*, and they're pleasing one another."

He says a series of cartoonlike positive and negative reflexes are determining much of the coverage.

He names a series of such negative reflexes—i.e., subjects which newsmen automatically cover by focusing on negatives. Herewith, excerpts from his comments: [As noted by Miss Efron.]

Race: "During the Johnson Administration, six million people were raised above the poverty level. . . . And there is a substantial and successful Negro middle class. But the newsmen are not interested in the Negro who succeeds—they're interested in the one who fails and makes a loud noise. They have ignored the developments in the South. The South has an increasing number of integrated schools. A large part of the South has accepted integration. We've had a President's Cabinet with a Negro in it, a Supreme Court with a Negro on it—but more important, we have 500 Negroes elected to local offices in the deep South! This is a tremendous achievement. But that achievement isn't what we see on the screen."

Conservatives: "If Agnew says something, it's bad, regardless of what he says. If Ronald Reagan says something, it's bad, regardless of what he says. Well, I'm unwilling to condemn an idea because a particular man said it. Most of my colleagues do just that."

The Middle Class: "Newsmen are *proud* of the fact that the middle class is antagonistic to them. They're proud of being out of contact with the middle class. Joseph Kraft did a column in which he said: Let's face it, we reporters have very little to do with middle America. They're not our kind of people. . . . Well, I resent that. *I'm* from middle America!''

The Vietnam War: "The networks have never given a complete picture of the war. For example: that terrible siege of Khe Sanh went on for five weeks before newsmen revealed that the South Vietnamese were fighting at our side, and that they had higher casualties. And the Viet Cong's casualties were 100 times ours. But we never told *that*. We just showed pictures day after day of Americans getting the hell kicked out of them. That was enough to break America apart. That's also what it did.''

The Presidency: "The negative attitude which destroyed Lyndon Johnson is now waiting to be applied to Richard Nixon. Johnson was actually politically assassinated. And some are trying to assassinate Nixon politically. They hate Richard Nixon irrationally.''

If this is a sampling of the liberal reporters' negative reflexes, as seen by Howard Smith—what then are the positive reflexes? He provides an even more extensive set of examples—subjects on which, he says, his colleagues tend to have an affirmative bias and/or from which they screen out negatives. Again here are excerpts from his comments:

Russia: "Some have gone overboard in a wish to believe that our opponent has exclusively peaceful aims, and that there is no need for armaments and national security. The danger of Russian aggression is unreal to many of them, although some have begun to rethink since the invasion of Czechoslovakia. But there is a kind of basic bias in the left-wing soul that gives the Russians the benefit of the doubt.''

Ho Chi Minh: "Many have described Ho Chi Minh as a nationalist leader comparable to George Washington. But his advent to power in Hanoi, in 1954, was marked by the murder of 50,000 of his people. His consistent method was terror. He was not his country's George Washington—he was more his country's Hitler or Stalin. . . . I heard an eminent tv commentator say: 'It's an awful thing when you can trust Ho Chi Minh more than you can trust your President.' At the time he said that, Ho Chi Minh was lying! He was presiding over atrocities! And yet an American tv commentator could say that!''

The Viet Cong: "The Viet Cong massacred 3,000 Vietnamese at Hue alone—a massacre that *dwarfs* all allegations about My Lai. This was never reported on.''

Doves: "Mr Fulbright maneuvered the Gulf of Tonkin Resolution through—with a clause stating that Congress may revoke it. Ever since, he's been saying: "This is a terribly immoral thing.' I asked him: 'If it's that bad, aren't *you* morally obligated to try to revoke it?' He runs away! And yet Mr. Fulbright—who incidentally has voted against *every* civil-rights act—is not criticized for his want of character. He is beloved by reporters, by everyone of my group, which is left-of-center. It's one of the mysteries of my time!"

Black Militants: "A few Negroes—scavengers on the edge of society—have discovered they're riding a good thing with violence and talk of violence. They can get on tv and become nationally famous."

The New Left: "The New Left challenges America. They're rewriting the history of the Cold War.. Some carry around the Viet Cong flag. Some shout for Mao—people who'd be assassinated in China! They've become *irrational!* But they're not portrayed as irrational. Reporters describe them as 'our children.' Well, they're not *my* children. *My* children don't throw bags of excrement at policemen. . . .If right-wing students had done what left-wing students have done, everyone, including the reporters, would have called in the police and beaten their heads in. But we have a left-wing bias now, that has 30 years of momentum behind it."

What do Mr. Smith's examples of negative and positive biases add up to, politically? He says: "The emphasis is anti-American." In fact, as he portrays the pattern, it is a dual emphasis: This coverage as described by Mr. Smith is *anti*-American in that it tends to omit the good about America and focus on the *bad.* And it is also biased in *favor* of attackers-of-America by tending to *omit* the bad about them and focusing on the *good.* Mr. Smith has actually reconstituted here a loose variant of the New Left line. And New Left attitudes are influencing newsmen, he says. "The New Left," says Smith, "has acquired a grave power over the liberal mind."

This is not a new charge—it is the essence of the public outcry against network news, and it's the essence of the long-standing conservative charges against the newsmen. Mr. Smith himself, although he's been described as a "conservative" because he supports the war, is, as he says, a Leftist—indeed, a semisocialist who shares many views with economist John Kenneth Galbraith. He has been one of tv's most ardent fighters for civil rights—too ardent, Smith says, for CBS's tastes, which is one reason why, he adds, he is at ABC today. He is generally in disagreement with political Conservatives on virtually everything. And, for that matter, he finds it psychologically easier to defend tv news departments than to criticize them. But on this issue of anti-American, pro-New-Left bias in the network news departments, his observations are identical to those coming from the right.

His explanation of the causes of this pattern, however, are quite different from those which emerge from the right. Where conservatives are often inclined to see this pattern as a deliberate, conscious and intellectually potent conspiracy, Mr. Smith sees it as the opposite—as a largely unconscious phenomenon, stemming from intellectual impotence, from such qualities as "conformism," "hypocrisy," "self-deception" and "stupidity."

One of the chief conformist patterns, he says, is the automatic obedience to a convention of negativism in journalism itself, often for self-serving reasons. "As reporters, we have always been falsifying issues by reporting on what goes wrong in a Nation where historically, most has gone right. That is how you get on page one, that is how you win a Pulitzer Prize. This gears the reporter's mind to the negative, even when it is not justified."

But how about the opposite form of bias—a chronic omission of negatives and the unremitting focus on the good in our country's enemies? Here Mr. Smith tackles the New Left influence head on. He attributes it to a mental vacuum in the liberal world:

"Many of my colleagues," he says, "have the depth of a saucer. They cling to the tag 'liberal' that grew popular in the time of Franklin Roosevelt, even though they've forgotten its content. They've really forgotten it. They don't know what 'liberal' and 'conservative' *mean* any more! They're forgotten it because the liberal cause has triumphed. Once it was hard to be a liberal. Today it's 'in.' The ex-underdogs, the ex-outcasts, the ex-rebels are satisfied bourgeois today, who pay $150 a plate at Americans for Democratic Action dinners. They don't know what they stand for any more, and they're hunting for a new voice to give them new bearings."

The search for a "new voice," he says, has catapulted such men into the arms of the New Left: "They want to cling to that thrill of the old days, of triumph, and hard fighting. So they cling to the label 'liberal,' and they cling to those who seem strong—namely, the New Left. The New Left shouts tirades, rather than offering reasoned arguments. People bow down to them, so they have come to *seem* strong, to *seem* sure of themselves. As a result, there's a gravitation to them by the liberals who are *not* sure of themselves. This has given the New Left grave power over the old Left."

It is this New Left "power" over many of the Nation's liberal reporters, he says, that underlies an anti-American and pro-radical bias in network coverage—and that underlies public anger.

What is the solution to this problem, as envisaged by Mr. Smith?

Let public protest rip, he says. He experiences a twinge of discomfort over the fact that his solution is identical to Mr. Agnew's: "There have been very unpleasant, even threatening, letters," he reports. "But, quite literally, what Mr. Agnew suggests is all right."

Public protest, he thinks, will knock these men back into contact with U.S. political realities.

"The networks have ignored this situation, despite years of protest, because they have power. And you know what Lord Acton says about power. It subtly corrupts. Power unaccountable has that effect on people. This situation should not continue. But I wouldn't do anything about it. I would let public opinion and the utterances of the alleged silent majority bring about a corrective. The corrective? Just a simple attempt to be fair—which many people have thrown aside over the last few years."

MR. SEVAREID AND MR. HICKEY

Q. Do you detect a wide polarization among many sincere and well-meaning Americans these days?

A. I don't think there's a deep polarization in the country as a whole, no, I don't. Everybody said that in 1968—that we were coming apart, that there would be a whole new politics. Then you had the election, which is the only kind of test we get on a national basis, and this didn't really show up. You see, I don't believe fundamentally that most Americans are alienated from their country or its system or their generation. There's an awful lot of irritation with a lot of things. But how deep it goes is very questionable.

Q. Some say the Nixon-Agnew policy toward the press is enhancing what polarization does exist here.

A. Well, it was a little surprising, coming after what the President advised everyone not to do, which was not to raise their voices. I thought his effort would be to heal these divisions between the protesters and the critics in general. Well, he didn't do that. With Vice President Agnew, he took the opposite line. This is what shook everybody. What he did in the Agnew speech is just what President Johnson always said he'd never do. I can remember Mr. Johnson saying this privately more than once. He used to say to critical people like me that, look my friend, if I want to I can make this a patriotic issue and start calling a lot of names. I can drive you people right into a corner. I can arouse a great mass of people with a very simple kind of appeal. I can wrap the flag around this policy, and use patriotism as a club to silence the critics. But he said, I'm not going to do it. And he never did it. And I think this is what Agnew's been doing. What this Administration has been doing. And I must say, it shook me a great deal.

Q. Why did it shake you a great deal?

A. Because it adds to the exacerbation of the situation. It brings even a little more polarization. It has benumbed the opposition for a while and this is what he wanted. He won some time. But won it at what later might prove to be a very high price.

Q. There's a conviction around the country that most tv newsmen tend to be liberal and therefore more friendly to dissenters.

A. Yes, Mr. Agnew feels that obviously. I'm not quite so persuaded. I think news values and judgments are something different from personal bias. If television puts a lot of protesters on, I don't think it's necessarily because a lot of editors and producers and reporters are all for the protesters, in their private, political hearts. Some may be. I think myself we have fallen into at least some shallow ruts on this matter of what looks like news as it pours into our offices, and there's this great struggle to sort it out every day. And I've raised my private views about this inside CBS more than once. But to assume that this process of what's happening in the country, or that it's done out of a radical bias by a few, I really don't believe that.

I don't know what the word liberal means, except a kind of open-mindedness, a basic humanitarian view of life and concern for people. I don't know how people generally think of me. The most pointed criticism I've had in the mail has come from the left. Youth groups, protester groups, radical groups, professors, saying that I'm much too conservative, that I'm really an old square, that I don't understand the youth. And now suddenly I'm clobbered by Mr. Agnew and the right wing. So I don't know.

Q. Why do you suppose so many people think they detect a large portion of bias in tv journalism?

A. A lot of people say a lot of things. A majority of the daily newspapers in this country supported Mr. Nixon. It seemed to me the networks were right down the middle, just as fair and impartial as they could be. I will defy anybody to go through my scripts during that campaign and come out with any feeling that I was trying to push for Humphrey or for Nixon or for Wallace. I don't think you can do it.

Q. In the last year or so the so-called Silent Majority has bubbled to the top like carrots in a stew. What do you make of it?

A. It exists all right. There is a frustration with a lot of things. What Agnew did, you see, he overstepped the line of a proper democratic dialogue. He resorted to demagoguery. He gave these people to believe that there is some sort of conspiracy, an unelected elite. Well, if he means the dozen or so people who have been mentioned, of whom I am one, we rarely ever see each other, to tell you the truth.

Q. You don't conspire together every night?

A. Oh, God, I haven't had a serious conversation with Howard K. Smith, I suppose, in 10 years. I haven't run into Huntley or Brinkley in two or three years. It's ridiculous. Howard and I deeply disagree about the Vietnam War, for one thing. But you see, what Mr. Agnew did is very easy to do. I say it's demagoguery when you do that. The conspiracy theory of history, the devil theory, always finds a ready response when a lot of people are frustrated, baffled by a complexity of things. I'm not impressed with claims that a great majority of the country thinks that the war protesters are wrong. Joe McCarthy had a majority of Americans convinced that this government was crawling with Communists. It simply was not so. But a tremendous number of people believed it was, because it was an easy answer. They were disappointed and upset by many of the results of the war. The public mood of the moment is not necessarily right, nor is it necessarily going to last. A great majority believed in this Vietnam intervention, when people like me were in a minority. Mr. Agnew says we should all more closely reflect the majority feeling in the country. But majorities change. That's not *our* business. Suppose we *were* elected. You'd have an absolute shambles in communications. I think there should be some changes in the way we do various things. I've always wanted to have on the air regular programming of rebuttal—either by letters from viewers or having the people on themselves. There must be a way to do this. Well, suppose you'd had that system for the last few years on a regular basis, where all kinds of objections to what was said on television were voiced by ordinary people. Maybe a lot of this feeling would have been dissipated. That's one of our difficulties here. People are confronted by great big organizations and they can't answer back—whether it's the press, big government, big business. I think we should have found ways to get our audience's views on the air. I think we should do it now. There must be a way to do it in an attractive, listenable form.

Q. What do you think of the idea of spectrum commentary, that is, having analysts from all across the political spectrum employed on television?

A. Oh, we went through that in radio days. CBS came to the conclusion it was not a good way to do it. The emphasis has to be, in a job like mine, one of exploration, of elucidation, more than advocacy. You can't keep opinions out of it entirely. But that has to be the approach. People confuse objectivity and neutrality. You may go at something very objectively but come to a conclusion about it. If you come to a conclusion, then you hold an opinion. If you hold an opinion, then you're biased, according to various people.

Q. The Violence Commission, as other commissions have suggested in the past, would like to see a national board of review to survey the performance of the news media. What do you think of that?

A. I don't believe in that. Television is already the most heavily monitored, scrutinized, criticized medium of communication there's ever been. Everybody is an expert on tv. Let me ask you why, when nearly every daily paper in this country gets the great bulk of its nondomestic news from two wire services—the UPI and AP—there's no running critique of their performance.

Q. And you feel, obviously, that television news is entitled to precisely the same First Amendment guarantees as are afforded the print medium.

A. Absolutely. Absolutely. I can't see why there should be any difference. The issue has never been resolved nor faced properly because broadcasting is in this anomalous legal position. We've always lived on this thin ice. The stations have to get approval to operate every three years. I just do not believe that the power of the press and television has been vastly increased in recent years. This statement of Mr. Agnew's quoting some FCC Commissioner that the media in this country have a power equal to the local, state and Federal governments—it's a silly statement. It's the power of *government* in my adult life that has grown far more than the power of media or business or any other big entity.

Q. I've discovered in talking to people on the left that there's a broad streak of approval among many of them for a lot of the things Mr. Agnew said. They're hostile to tv news because they feel it doesn't come to grips with the real issues, while the right wing tends to feel that tv news disseminates far too much of this, mostly bad news.

A. That's right. It's just the opposite criticism. Look, FCC Commissioner Nicholas Johnson and all kinds of people on what I'd guess you'd call the left in this country, and many intellectual groups, have been hammering and hammering at television, for what? Because they say we just reflect Establishment, middle-class values. You know the litany on that. That we're not dealing enough with the poor, the blacks, the underprivileged. The Agnew criticism is the exact reverse of this. Now how do you satisfy this?

Q. The Violence Commission used the expression "crisis of confidence" between the media and the public, and said that some means should be found to make the media more responsive to the public.

A. More responsive to the public! What are they talking about? That's what Mr. Agnew says, in effect. I'm not about to adjust the work I do according to the waves of popular feeling that may come over the country. No responsible person can do that. They ought to be out of this business if they do.

Q. On the 60 Minutes program you said: "Nothing that the Communist enemy in North Vietnam could ever do to us could equal the damage we are doing to ourselves because of this war, and in my own view this damage has been increased by the Agnew speeches." What did you mean by that?

A. Well, the war has torn up a lot of things here. It's knocked the whole economy out of gear for one thing, played hell with the youth, made the draft something to be avoided. It's been a ghastly business because it's essentially a failure, that's one reason. The Agnew speech was absolutely unnecessary. This Administration was not doing that badly with the press. But this attack has exacerbated things, made lots of people angry. It's scapegoat politics.

Q. Many people seem to feel that television doesn't look on the bright side, that bad news drives out good.

A. I don't think this is necessarily political bias. The bad news is what's news because you assume normalcy. If you assumed nothing but upheaval, then only good news would be real news. But, nevertheless, there is some point to that criticism. I think we tend to get caught in these ruts, yes, I do. We argue about this all the time inside this company. But I don't think it's necessarily bias. That's one reason I say I wish we had an hour. Then you're not just trapped and engulfed every day by all kinds of fantastic events, many of them violent, happening all over the world, which you can't ignore.

Q. Is there anything to USIA director Frank Shakespeare's idea that the networks might wish to consider "a man's ideology" before hiring him as a newsman?

A. No, I don't think you can do that. Frank has nice neat divisions in his mind about what's conservative, what's middle of the road, and what's left, you see. I think in that sense he's rather primitive. You might as well argue that the business community in this country or the White House is too full of conservatives.

Q. It seems to some critics that tv newsmen haven't liked a President since Kennedy, and have trouble covering up that fact in their reports.

A. Oh, these generalizations about news people—I've been hearing these things for decades. I don't see it. That's another thing people do not understand about professional journalists: that even those who have very passionate private political views—when they come down to doing their job of reporting the news—they are professional enough to get on with the real matter, and leave the rest out of it. I've voted for lots of Republicans and lots of Democrats, yet all kinds of people are firmly convinced I'm a left-liberal in their terms, and to all kinds of others I'm a conservative square. Roosevelt and Kennedy were very upset about many things written about them. They would express virulent opinions about working newspaper people.

Q. But anyway, the opinion is abroad now that the Nixon Administration would like gentler treatment at the hands of the press.

A. I think they're had very decent treatment. Very decent. Good Lord, every time the President wants air time even for a minor ceremony, they give it to him. They give him too much, I think. That's been going on for years. Mr. Johnson abused it, I think, terribly. And I think we *let* him abuse us by taking too much air time. I don't think all three networks should have put Mr. Agnew on live, pre-empting their news shows and everything else. I don't think a President of the United States, unless he's declaring war, or some other terribly critical thing, ought to have all three networks at the same time. We've given too *much* time, and as a result anyone in power thinks of tv as an open conduit for his use.

Q. There are about a dozen men in this country, of whom you are one, who are considered to have disproportionate influence on the country's affairs because of their privileged position in the broadcast world. How do you feel about being one of these "unelected elite"?

A. I don't think they handle this power irresponsibly, these people you talk about, this dangerous dozen or whatever we're supposed to be. I don't think anybody regularly employed by a major network does use or would be *allowed* to use the invective and the epithets that Mr. Agnew used. I think we're more responsible than he is. Considerably so. I think his speech was an irresponsible utterance. Some say we're feared. I don't get that from people, and I get an awful lot of mail.

Q. So you detect no overt bias on the air waves?

A. You find some in the H.L. Hunt radio stuff which goes out from hundreds of radio stations. But Mr. Agnew had no objection to that, apparently. He had no objection to newspaper-tv monopoly situations where they are conservatives, and there are more of those than there are *Washington Posts* or *New York Times.* You see, all he was concerned about when he talked about bias or monopoly were those elements he feels in the press have been critical of his President. Every letter I've ever received in my life that accused me of bias was simply someone who disagreed with me. I have never had a letter yet from anybody who says, "I agree with you but you were not fair to the other side." Never. Never.

Q. It's not easy, is it, after a major Presidential address, to jump right in with a comprehensive analysis?

A. Well, one of the problems is you don't have enough time when you come on, and you have to do it in a very few minutes. That's difficult. But opposing points of view *have* to be presented, otherwise we're just a conduit for any government in power. That's what they really want television to be.

Q. In the future, are you still in favor of coming on after Presidential addresses and engaging in what Mr. Agnew calls "instant analysis"?

A. Well—I've had my doubts about it, where we have not had advance copies of the speech. In the Nov. 3 speech we did, as you know; we had a couple of hours. I would much rather that maybe an hour went by, or a half hour, so that you could do a real job. I think this way, not so much because we're apt to be unfair to a President, although that can happen certainly, but we're unfair to ourselves and unfair to the listeners. It's a practical problem.

MAKING A TELEVISION NEWS SHOW

Daniel St. Albin Greene

At 9:40 one dreary November 1969 morning, the only visible action in Room 508 of the RCA Building was on the screens of the mute television sets all over the place. As Ed Newman delivered a silent monolog in front of a model of the moon surface on one screen, Donna Reed was having a spat with her video hubby on another. But nobody was paying any attention to them. The five well-groomed men in the bright, wall-to-wall- carpeted office were quietly reading the morning papers and reams of news-service copy to find out what was happening in the world. Soon they would begin the long process of deciding what, and how, to inform more than 20,000,000 people about those events on *The Huntley-Brinkley Report.*

Ostensibly, it was the start of a typical week at NBC News. But things were not the same, and every newsman at the three giant television networks knew it. For they were not only covering the news the previous week—they had been part of it. And many of them were deeply worried about the possible consequences of the controversy that had suddenly engulfed them following an indictment of tv news coverage by the Vice President of the United States.

As Karlton "Jerry" Rosholt, a veteran field producer for *The Huntley-Brinkley Report*, put it: "None of us is the same man he was two weeks ago. Some will be more cowed from now on, some will be more antagonistic. But we all have to wonder if what we're doing is going to hasten Government censorship."

Censorship? In Spiro T. Agnew's now-famous Des Moines speech, he made it clear he was not advocating Federal censorship. But what he did say sent shivers through the television industry just the same.

An "elite" and like-minded group, Mr. Agnew declared, "numbering perhaps no more than a dozen anchormen, commentators, and executive producers, settle upon the 20 minutes or so of film and commentary that's to reach the public. . . . They decide what 40,000,000 to 50,000,000 Americans will learn of the day's events in the nation and in the world. We cannot measure this power and

Daniel St. Albin Greene's *National Observer* article on how difficult it actually is to put together a television show was later reprinted in the March, 1970 *Seminar Quarterly*. It is published here with the permission of *National Observer*.

influence by the traditional democratic standards, for these men can create national issues overnight. They can make or break, by their coverage and commentary, a moratorium on the war. They can elevate men from obscurity to national prominence within a week. They can reward some politicians with national exposure and ignore others."

By the Vice President's description, the tv-news bigwigs are a few stars, backed up by several shadowy figures behind the scenes, who live and work within "the geographical and intellectual confines of Washington, D.C., and New York City," spend a lot of time together, read the same newspapers, and share the same social and political viewpoints.

Mr. Agnew did not say so, but members of the Nixon Administration privately admit that they like NBC News least of all. So with the Agnew depiction of tv-news personages graphically outlined in my mind, I showed up at the Manhattan headquarters of *The Huntley-Brinkley Report* during a Monday morning rerun of *The Donna Reed Show* on CBS and an Apollo special on NBC. My assignment: to observe how "a tiny, enclosed fraternity of privileged men"—to borrow Mr. Agnew's words—decides what to show and tell the tv audience about the day's news, and then filters it "through a handful of commentators who admit to their own set of biases."

If any members of the Huntley-Brinkley staff were plotting to make or break anybody or anything that day, it was not apparent. In fact, there was a lot of morning conversation about why the networks had decided to limit their coverage of the previous weekend's antiwar demonstration to their regular news programs.

The decisions not to provide live coverage of what turned out to be the biggest demonstration of its kind in U.S. history had been made sometime before Mr. Agnew's speech, which was delivered the evening that the demonstration began. For the October moratorium, notes Reuven Frank, president of NBC News, the network did a 90-minute special program, covering all sides of the issue, as well as devoting half of a *Huntley-Brinkley Report* to the protest. "This time it was no longer unique," says Mr. Frank. "There was no purpose to be served. We covered it as a news event, which it was."

But to many people, including some newspaper columnists, the conspicuous dearth of tv cameras during the November demonstration suggested retreat by an intimidated medium. "How many marches and demonstrations would we have," Mr. Agnew had asked, "if the marchers did not know that the ever-faithful tv cameras would be there to record their antics for the next news show?"

David Brinkley (top, talking to student editors) worked with Chet Huntley for 14 years on NBC. Following Huntley's retirement Brinkley moved into a "roaming commentator" position, while John Chancellor (middle left) became solo anchorman and Frank McGee (middle right) replaced Hugh Downs on the morning news-talk "Today" show. At ABC, Howard K. Smith and Harry Reasoner (bottom left) shared the evening news assignment and the popular Frank Reynolds provided on-the-spot coverage (used with permission of NBC and ABC).

Walter Cronkite, considered the "dean" of television newscasters, thinks of himself as a "managing editor" and disputes the contention that television had a "star system." But like it or not "Uncle Walter" is the star of CBS. Shown here with the nightly war coverage, and preparing copy at his busy desk, Cronkite teams with another "dean," commentator Eric Sevareid (bottom left) and reporters like White House correspondent Dan Rather (bottom right—photos used with permission of CBS).

Some of the Huntley-Brinkley staff, including executive producer Wallace Westfeldt, conceded that the networks' limited coverage looked suspicious. "Suppose 200,000 hawks demonstrated now," postulated Jerry Rosholt. "By the same logic, we couldn't cover that live either."

But producer Lester M. Crystal, Mr. Westfeldt's second in command, was concerned with more immediate matters. He was reading wires from correspondents describing film packages that were en route to New York from various parts of the world. By 10 o'clock he had a seven-page list of story possibilities for that day and assignments for stories to be used on later shows.

Film reports that had already arrived or were on the way included the student riots in Tokyo ignited by Premier Eisaku Sato's departure for Washington; the sabotage of an Israeli ship by Arabs; an interview with Ian Smart of the Institute for Strategic Studies in London; and a Vietnam report. Other stories that NBC correspondents would be covering this day: Premier Sato's arrival in Washington; Joseph Kennedy's imminent death; Klan leader Robert Shelton's release from prison; congressional debate over the appointment of Clement Haynsworth to the Supreme Court; the opening of strategic arms limitation talks (SALT) in Helsinki, which would be reported by satellite transmission; reaction to the Mobilization; the Chicago conspiracy trial; and the Apollo flight.

Some of these stories would be covered by news teams directed by people assigned full-time to *The Huntley-Brinkley Report*, which has a staff of 35 producers, writers, news editors, and film editors. But this small unit is supported by the largest broadcast-news organization in the world, numbering more than 1,000 people in and outside of the United States. More than half of NBC News personnel are based in New York City, and 104 are in Washington.

The hub of it all is on the fifth floor of the RCA Building, far below the lofty executive suites of the men who run the Radio Corporation of America, which owns the National Broadcasting Co. And since *The Huntley-Brinkley Report* is the network's prime daily-news showcase, the hub of the vast news-gathering system most days is, more precisely, right here in Room 508.

This is a news room furnished with 23 identical gray metal desks with simulated wood tops. Six of them are arranged in a "T" at the far end of the room. One of the four executive offices opening into the news room belongs to Les Crystal, but he spends most of the day at a desk in this cluster in order to be at the center of things. Wally Westfeldt works out of his private office, though he is seldom alone there. David Brinkley, who is based in Washington, occupies the middle office when he is in town. And the office closest to the main door belongs to Chet Huntley.

Outside of the executive offices, the walls are devoid of pictures except one of the two stars. But decorating one wall is a poster that reads, "The Vietnam War Continues," and lists the casualty figures as of September.

A little after 10, Les Crystal took a call from Henry Griggs, his associate producer in the Washington bureau, and handed me an extension phone. Mr. Griggs reported that no big news was expected out of the Haynsworth debate, but he was assigning an artist to cover it anyway. He and Les agreed to dispatch film crews to get an interview with the former GI who prompted an investigation of a mass killing reported in Vietnam; to try to locate people charged in that case; and to cover a press conference by moratorium leaders and a congressional hearing on black-market operations in Vietnam.

10:20. Chet Huntley, a tall man with a sagging, leathern face and graying brown hair, arrived and went in for a chat with Wally Westfeldt.

On high shelves attached to the walls at either end of the news room, twin tv sets played constantly, though usually without sound. At 10:30 the volume was turned up on one of the sets carrying NBC programing; each morning at this time, the last *Huntley-Brinkley Report* is reshown on closed-circuit television for those who missed it. Beside each of the screens showing Huntley-Brinkley, the *Beverly Hillbillies* made silent foolishness in a CBS rerun.

Shortly before 11, Mr. Crystal got a call from Garrick Utley in London. They discussed a story in the works about the financial plight of the royal family, which would include filmed interviews with people in a pub and some footage of Prince Philip playing polo.

11:15. Mr. Crystal, four other staff members, and I gathered in Mr. Westfeldt's small office for the daily editorial meeting. While *Sale of the Century* played on his floor-model color set, the executive producer briefly went over the list of stories that would probably make up the evening newscast; then they discussed a few ideas for future stories.

Before winding up the meeting, Mr. Westfeldt revealed that the Washington bureau was trying to run down a report that Presidential aides, not the Vice President's regular speechwriter, had authored Mr. Agnew's blast against the networks.

The Vice President's criticism of tv news coverage in general, and of the caustic way the network commentators reviewed Presi-

dent Nixon's Vietnam speech in particular, had prompted Chet Huntley to dig up a letter Mr. Nixon sent him last January. Wally Westfeldt had been cheering up some of his troops by reading it to them,
and after the meeting it was shown to me.

In the letter, Mr. Nixon expressed his gratitude for the way
NBC covered the election campaign, and suggested that "the balanced coverage I received from the electronics media" probably "tipped the scales in my favor." Then he took a realistic look into the
future:

"In the years ahead, I realize there will be occasions when you
may not agree with the policies of the new administration. I want
you to know that I will appreciate receiving the benefit of your
criticism as well as your praise. . . . Above all, I want ours to be an
open administration—open to new ideas—listening and respecting
those who disagree with us as well as those who agree with us."

Messrs. Westfeldt, Crystal, and Rosholt were on their way up-
stairs to look at a color film taken of bomb-scarred villages in rural
North Vietnam, and I tagged along. NBC had bought the film from
the Canadian Broadcasting Corp. for possible showing, in install-
ments, on *The Huntley-Brinkley Report.* Impressed by the quality of
the film, they decided to use it with minor editing of the sound
track.

On the way back to 508, Jerry predicted resignedly: "We'll get
a lot of calls on this one from people who want to know why NBC
insists on showing propaganda from Hanoi."

Noon. Associate producers in Washington, Chicago, Burbank,
and Cleveland were on the line for the daily bureau conference call.
Henry Griggs in Washington said he was trying to get a follow-up on
Attorney General John Mitchell's condemnation of the Mobilization
leaders for not preventing the militant Crazies' attack on the Justice
Department.

"Do we have any film of the violence left?" Mr. Crystal asked.
"Would there be any point in running it now?"

"Using it now would in effect support what Mitchell says," Mr.
Griggs replied.

Les Crystal agreed: "It would probably just exaggerate the situation."

A news team in California had filmed an interview with the
young man who had blown the whistle on the soldiers allegedly
involved in the killing of the Vietnamese civilians. Mr. Crystal suggested that somebody go after the accused men's lawyers.

Chicago reported that Robert Shelton's release had been filmed,
but there was no sound. The other bureaus had nothing to offer.

Henrik Krogius, who was concentrating on the Apollo mission, invited me to accompany him to the videotape room to see the pictures that had been transmitted from the command module. Mr. Krogius, a tall, handsome man with a dashing brown beard but little hair on the top of his head, was born in Finland 40 years ago. He studied architecture at Harvard, specialized in psychological warfare in the Air Force, took a master's degree in journalism at Columbia University, and joined NBC News eight years ago. Married and the father of two boys, he pleads "guilty to being an Eastern liberal" and a Democrat. But he assured me that his political sentiments would not influence his choice of which parts of the Apollo tape to show on the air that evening.

Vice President Agnew had asked: "What do Americans know of the men who wield this power? Of the men who produce and direct the network news, the nation knows practically nothing."

Perhaps so, but during lunch downstairs at Charley O's, the two most important members of the decision-making "elite" behind *The Huntley-Brinkley Report* were as willing to talk about themselves as any of their famous on-camera colleagues would be.

Wallace Westfeldt, who has been executive producer of NBC's evening newscast since last January, is a strapping, 6-foot-4 man with wavy brown hair and rugged good looks. A native of New Orleans, he served in the Marine Corps in World War II and the Korean War, finally getting out as a major; was graduated from the University of the South in Sewanee, Tenn.; and roamed the South for eight years as a civil-rights reporter for the Nashville Tennessean, before joining NBC News in 1961. At 46, he is a Democrat, a "backslid" Episcopalian, married and the father of an 11-year-old daughter, an omnivorous reader, and a journalist "obsessed" with his work.

Mr. Westfeldt scoffs at Spiro Agnew's intimation that network news brass are a tightly knit circle. "We're competitors, not friends," he says. "I wouldn't know Les Midgley (his counterpart on CBS' Walter Cronkite show) if I saw him."

Les Crystal, who co-ordinates things for Mr. Westfeldt, is a slender, 35-year-old transplanted Minnesotan who still considers himself a Midwesterner. After taking a master's degree at Northwestern University, he worked as a tv newsman in Chicago, Altoona, Pa., and Philadelphia before becoming a member of the New York Huntley-Brinkley staff in 1967. He describes himself as a "mildly observant Jew." Mr. Crystal and his wife Toby have three young children.

Both producers acknowledge being liberals, though not in a strict ideological sense. "People in this business tend to have a preoccupation with social problems," Mr. Crystal explains. "We get around and see the results of these problems firsthand. It would be hard for anybody to see these things and not get emotionally involved."

Yet the conscientious tv journalist tries harder than most people to control his emotions and prejudices, Mr. Westfeldt adds: "All of us have spent years trying to suppress our feelings. There is not a man on my staff who could not go out and do an honest reporting job on an issue that he was personally opposed to."

By the time we got back, soap operas were unfolding on every video screen, and several typewriters were clattering away. While Les and Wally talked on the phone to correspondents, I occupied myself reading the bulletin board. Two items related to Chet Huntley. One was a newspaper article about a speech he gave in Memphis: The United States entered the Vietnam War with the "purest of motives," he was quoted as saying. "Our mistake was to send more troops than necessary, and to leave them there too long." The other was an interdepartmental memo from Reuven Frank verifying that Mr. Huntley, who is 57, would probably leave NBC in 1971 to go into the resort business in his home state of Montana.

Mr. Huntley invited me to his office for a chat. The Old West look of his haven, with its vintage furniture and spittoons, was a refreshing contrast to the functional modernity of the other offices. He sat at a heavy, roll-front oak desk that his father had used for a half-century on the Northern Pacific Railroad. A moment before, he had been banging away on the oldest typewriter in the vicinity.

Mr. Huntley admitted that his first reaction to Mr. Agnew's speech was "semi-shock at the acute sensitivities of this administration." Now, however, his mood was reflective: "Maybe we have been remiss in not finding enough positive things to report. But news, by its very nature, is usually not a happy thing. It deals with social and political irregularities. It is the exciting, the violent, the flagrant, the unusual that is news."

There is no doubt that Chet Huntley was one of those he had in mind when the Vice President posed his rhetorical question: "When a single commentator or producer, night after night, determines for millions of people how much of each side of a great issue they are going to see and hear, should he not first disclose his personal views on the issue as well?"

Mr. Huntley drew thoughtfully on his pipe. "It would be a miracle if my views didn't creep into what I said on the air occasionally," he acknowledged. "But it would be so subtle that it couldn't change anybody's mind. I rarely see any of the film before it is shown on the air. And the only copy I usually read before the show is what I've written." He took another puff. "The average American," he concluded, "is a hell of a lot more intelligent than Agnew thinks he is."

3:20. Les Crystal and Wally Westfeldt were in the executive producer's office plotting out the lineup of stories for the newscast. Beside each story listed on a yellow pad, Wally jotted the number of minutes and seconds he had allotted it. Shortly before 4 o'clock, he dictated the schedule to Pat O'Keefe, a shapely production assistant, who then added up the allotted time: 22 minutes.

"Will this program upset folks?" I wondered out loud.

"Well, anything we say about the moratorium is going to make somebody mad," Mr. Westfeldt replied. "And I'm sure we'll get criticized for even reporting the Vietnam killings. But we've got to report the news; what are we here for?"

After this, the office tempo quickened. News editor Gil Millstein, a stocky 54-year-old native New Yorker who used to write for magazines, was busy turning out copy for Chet Huntley to read on the air. Mr. Huntley was in his office finishing up a couple of pages he had written himself. David Brinkley, regarded by many as the best news writer in television, writes his own material.

Up on the ninth floor, news editor Tom MacCabe, who has the mien of a high-school principal, was still in a screening room editing film to fit designated time slots. In the Broadcast Operations Control room, Jerry Rosholt and Bob Lissit were waiting for NBC's turn to transmit its Helsinki report via communications satellite. When John Chancellor's report finally came though, it was simultaneously taped for later showing.

6 o'clock. The "remotes"—filmed and live studio reports electronically transmitted by NBC bureaus—were being shown on closed-circuit tv in the news room. As an artist's sketches of the "Chicago Eight" trial filled the screen, the correspondent quoted a defense attorney as saying, "It is impossible to prepare our case not knowing who in our office to trust," and later observed that a witness "didn't seem quite so sure about whom was attending which meetings."

Gil Millstein, the resident grammarian, yelled, "He's got his 'who' and 'whom' mixed up!"

Mr. Crystal, on the telephone to Chicago, pointed out the mistakes. Eventually, on the third try, the reporter got through his narration without a grammatical slip.

6:27. Charles Coates, a 39-year-old New Jersey native who used to work with Mr. Westfeldt on the *Nashville Tennessean*, was still batting out "pad"—news shorts that can be read to use up whatever time remains at the end of scheduled reports—as we rushed for the elevator. We got to the eighth-floor control room, adjoining the studio where Mr. Huntley sat in front of a battery of cameras and lights, just in time to hear: "Chet Huntley, NBC News, New York." "And David Brinkley, NBC News, Washington."

For the next 28 minutes, Mr. Huntley and his wry partner in Washington read copy and introduced picture reports that represented countless independent decisions by scores of producers, writers, correspondents, cameramen, and editors in far-flung parts of the world. Somehow, it all came together, piece by piece, in a miracle of timing and precision that no one had seen in its entirety before everyone saw it.

Some of these decisions and efforts paid off handsomely. Viewers were shown interviews with a moratorium leader in Washington and the Vietnam vet in California; film on the Tokyo riots and the Sato trip; the Arab sabotage film; Apollo pictures; the illustrated progress report on the conspiracy trial; and John Chancellor's satellite report from Helsinki. But other hoped-for contributions, such as interviews with the accused soldiers' lawyers, never came through.

As a videotape of the newscast was being transmitted to the 56 NBC affiliates that don't carry the live telecast, we rushed back downstairs to catch the 7 p.m. broadcast of the Cronkite show. Most of the major stories were covered by both networks. But CBS had a few things that NBC lacked or had chosen not to use: an interview with Robert Shelton; Hubert Humphrey excoriating Spiro Agnew for excoriating the media—and an interview with the lawyer of the captain involved in the Vietnam killings.

No sooner had Les Crystal seen this than he was on the phone trying to find out why NBC hadn't been able to get to a lawyer that CBS had. It was 7:45 before he learned the sad news: The NBC affiliate in Salt Lake City had an interview with the lawyer, recorded the week before, but NBC didn't know it.

As I left Room 508 at the end of the long day, calls were still coming in from people who didn't like what they had seen on the week's first *Huntley-Brinkley Report*. Somebody in the office was saying, "Well, thanks for calling anyway, and I'm sure Mr. Agnew will be glad to hear from you."

Chapter X

POWER OF THE PRESS

THE MONTGOMERY SPEECH

Spiro T. Agnew

One week ago tonight I flew out to Des Moines, Iowa, and exercised my right to dissent.

This is a great country—in this country every man is allowed freedom of speech, even the Vice President.

Of course, there's been some criticism of what I said out there in Des Moines. Let me give you a sampling.

One Congressman charged me with, and I quote, "a creeping socialistic scheme against the free enterprise broadcast industry." Now this is the first time in my memory that anyone ever accused Ted Agnew of having socialist ideas.

On Monday, largely because of that address, Mr. Humphrey charged the Nixon Administration with a "calculated attack" on the right of dissent and on the media today. Yet it's widely known that Mr. Humphrey himself believes deeply that the unfair coverage of the Democratic convention in Chicago, by the same media, contributed to his defeat in November.

Now his wounds are apparently healed, and he's casting his lot with those who were questioning his own political courage a year ago. But let's leave Mr. Humphrey to his own conscience. America already has too many politicians who would rather switch than fight.

There were others that charged that my purpose in that Des Moines speech was to stifle dissent in this country. Nonsense. The

Vice President Agnew does not limit his criticism of the news media to television. He often has included newspapers and in Montgomery, Alabama on November 20, 1969, he made some scathing remarks about the *New York Times* and *Washington Post* before the Chamber of Commerce, similar to the remarks made in Des Moines and reprinted earlier in this section.

expression of my views has produced enough rugged dissent in the last week to wear out a whole covey of commentators and columnists.

One critic charged that the speech was disgraceful, ignorant and base; that leads us as a nation, he said, into an ugly era of the most fearsome suppression and intimidation.

One national commentator, whose name is known to everyone in this room, said: "I hesitate to get in the gutter with this guy."

Another commentator charges that "it was one of the most sinister speeches that I've ever heard made by a public official."

The president of one network said that it was an unprecedented attempt to intimidate a news medium which depends for its existence upon Government licenses. The president of another charged me with a appeal to prejudice, and said that it was evident that I would prefer the kind of television that would be subservient to whatever political group happened to be in authority at the time.

And they say I have a thin skin.

Here indeed are classic examples of overreaction. These attacks do not address themselves to the questions I raised. In fairness, others, the majority of the critics and commentators, did take up the main thrust of my address.

And if the debate that they have engaged in continues, our goal will surely be reached, our goal which of course is a thorough self-examination by the networks of their own policies and perhaps prejudices. That was my objective then, and that's my objective now.

Now let me repeat to you the thrust of my remarks the other night and perhaps make some new points and raise a few new issues.

I'm opposed to censorship of television, of the press in any form. I don't care whether censorship is imposed by government or whether it results from management in the choice and presentation of the news by a little fraternity having similar social and political views. I'm against, I repeat, I'm against media censorship in all forms.

But a broader spectrum of national opinion should be represented among the commentators in the network news. Men who can articulate other points of view should be brought forward and a high wall of separation should be raised between what is news and what is commentary.

And the American people should be made aware of the trend toward the monopolization of the great public information vehicles and the concentration of more and more power in fewer and fewer hands.

Should a conglomerate be formed that tied together a shoe

company with a shirt company, some voice will rise up righteously to say that this is a great danger to the economy and that the conglomerate ought to be broken up.

But a single company, in the nation's capital, holds control of the largest newspaper in Washington, D.C., and one of the four major television stations, and an all-news radio station, and one of the three major national news magazines—all grinding out the same editorial line—and this is not a subject that you've seen debated on the editorial pages of *The Washington Post* or *The New York Times.*

For the purpose of clarity, before my thoughts are obliterated in the smoking typewriters of my friends in Washington and New York, let me emphasize that I'm not recommending the dismemberment of the Washington Post Company, I'm merely pointing out that the public should be aware that these four powerful voices hearken to the same master.

I'm raising these questions so that the American people will become aware of—and think of the implications of—the growing monopoly that involves the voices of public opinion, on which we all depend for our knowledge and for the basis of our views.

When *The Washington Times-Herald* died in the nation's capital, that was a political tragedy; and when *The New York Journal-American, The New York World-Telegram* and *Sun, The New York Mirror* and *The New York Herald Tribune* all collapsed within this decade, that was a great, great political tragedy for the people of New York. *The New York Times* was a better newspaper when they were all alive than it is now that they are gone.

And what has happened in the City of New York has happened in other great cities of America.

Many, many strong, independent voices have been stilled in this country in recent years. And lacking the vigor of competition, some of those who have survived have—let's face it—grown fat and irresponsible.

I offer an example: When 300 Congressmen and 59 Senators signed a letter endorsing the President's policy in Vietnam, it was news—and it was big news. Even *The Washington Post* and *The Baltimore Sun*—scarcely house organs for the Nixon Administration—placed it prominently in their front pages.

Yet the next morning *The New York Times*, which considers itself America's paper of record, did not carry a word. Why? Why?

If a theology student in Iowa should get up at P.T.A. luncheon in Sioux City and attack the President's Vietnam policy, my guess is that you'd probably find it reported somewhere in the next morning's issue of *The New York Times*. But when 300 Congressmen endorse the President's Vietnam policy, the next morning it's apparently not considered news fit to print.

Just this Tuesday when the Pope, the spiritual leader of half a billion Roman Catholics, applauded the President's effort to end the war in Vietnam and endorsed the way he was proceeding, that news was on Page 11 of *The New York Times*. The same day a report about some burglars who broke into a souvenir shop at St. Peter's and stole $9,000 worth of stamps and currency—that story made Page 3. How's that for news judgment?

A few weeks ago here in the South I expressed my views about street and campus demonstrations. Here's how *The New York Times* responded:

"He (that's me) lambasted the nation's youth in sweeping and ignorant generalizations, when it's clear to all perceptive observers that American youth is far more imbued with idealism, a sense of service and a deep humanitarianism than any generation in recent history, including particularly Mr. Agnew's generation."

That's what *The New York Times* said.

Now that seems a peculiar slur on a generation that brought America out of the great depression without resorting to the extremes of Communism or Fascism. That seems a strange thing to say about an entire generation that helped to provide greater material blessings and more personal freedom—out of that depression—for more people than any other nation in history. We have not finished the task by any means—but we are still on the job.

Just as millions of young Americans in this generation have shown valor and courage and heroism fighting the longest, and least popular, war in our history, so it was the young men of my generation who went ashore at Normandy under Eisenhower, and with MacArthur into the Philippines.

Yes, my generation, like the current generation, made its own share of great mistakes and great blunders. Among other things, we put too much confidence in Stalin and not enough in Winston Churchill.

But, whatever freedom exists today in Western Europe and Japan exists because hundreds of thousands of young men of my generation are lying in graves in North Africa and France and Korea and a score of islands in the Western Pacific.

This might not be considered enough of a sense of service or a deep humanitarianism for the perceptive critics who write editorials for *The New York Times*, but it's good enough for me. And I'm content to let history be the judge.

Now, let me talk briefly about the younger generation. I have not and I do not condemn this generation of young Americans. Like Edmund Burke, I wouldn't know how to draw up an indictment against a whole people. After all, they're our sons and daughters. They contain in their numbers many gifted, idealistic and courageous young men and women.

But they also list in their numbers an arrogant few who march under the flags and portraits of dictators, who intimidate and harass university professors, who use gutter obscenities to shout down speakers with whom they disagree, who openly profess their belief in the efficacy of violence in a democratic society.

Oh yes, the preceding generation had its own breed of losers and our generation dealt with them through our courts, our laws and our system. The challenge is now for the new generation to put its house in order.

Today, Dr. Sydney Hook writes of "storm troopers" on the campus: that "fanaticism seems to be in the saddle." Arnold Beichman writes of "young Jacobins" in our schools who "have cut down university administrators, forced curriculum changes, halted classes, closed campuses and set a nationwide chill of fear all through the university establishment." Walter Laqueur writes in *Commentary* that "the cultural and political idiocies perpetuated with impunity in this permissive age have gone clearly beyond the borders of what is acceptable for any society, however liberally it may be constructed."

George Kennan has devoted a brief, cogent and alarming book to the inherent dangers of what's taking place in our society and in our universities. Irving Kristol writes that our "radical students find it possible to be genuinely heartsick at the injustice and brutalities of American society, at the same time they are blandly approving of injustice and brutality committed in the name of 'the revolution.'" Or, as they like to call it, "the movement."

Now those are not names drawn at random from the letter head of Agnew-for-Vice-President committee. Those are men more eloquent and erudite than I, and they raise questions that I've tried to raise.

For we must remember that among this generation of Americans there are hundreds who have burned their draft cards and scores who have deserted to Canada and Sweden to sit out the war. To some Americans, a small minority, these are the true young men of conscience in the coming generation.

Voices are and will continue to be raised in the Congress and beyond asking that amnesty—a favorite word—amnesty should be provided for these young and misguided American boys. And they will be coming home one day from Sweden and from Canada and from a small minority of our citizens they will get a hero's welcome.

They are not our heroes. Many of our heroes will not be coming home; some are coming back in hospital ships, without limbs or eyes, with scars they shall carry for the rest of their lives.

Having witnessed firsthand the quiet courage of wives and parents receiving posthumously for their heroes Congressional Medals of Honor, how am I to react when people say, "Stop speaking out, Mr. Agnew, stop raising your voice?"

Should I remain silent while what these heroes have done is vilified by some as "a dirty, immoral war" and criticized by others as no more than a war brought on by the chauvinistic anti-Communism of Presidents Kennedy, Johnson and Nixon?

These young men made heavy sacrifices so that a developing people on the rim of Asia might have a chance for freedom that they obviously will not have if the ruthless men who rule in Hanoi should ever rule over Saigon. What's dirty or immoral about that?

One magazine this week said that I'll go down as the "great polarizer" in American politics. Yet, when that large group of young Americans marched up Pennsylvania Avenue and Constitution Avenue last week, they sought to polarize the American people against the President's policy in Vietnam. And that was their right. And so it is my right, and my duty, to stand up and speak out for the values in which I believe.

How can you ask the man in the street in this country to stand up for what he believes if his own elected leaders weasel and cringe.

It's not an easy thing to wake up each morning to learn that some prominent man or some prominent institution has implied that you're a bigot or a racist or a fool.

I'm not asking immunity from criticism. This is the lot of a man in politics; we wouldn't have it any other way in a democratic society.

But my political and journalistic adversaries sometimes seem to be asking something more—that I circumscribe my rhetorical freedom while they place no restriction on theirs.

As President Kennedy observed in a far more serious situation: This is like offering an apple for an orchard.

We do not accept those terms for continuing the national dialogue. The day when the network commentators and even the gentlemen of *The New York Times* enjoyed a form of diplomatic immunity from comment and criticism of what they said is over.

Yes, gentlemen, the day is passed.

Just as a politician's words—wise and foolish—are dutifully recorded by press and television to be thrown up at him at the appropriate time, so their words should be likewise recorded and likewise recalled.

When they go beyond fair comment and criticism they will be called upon to defend their statements and their positions just as we must defend ours. And when their criticism becomes excessive or unjust, we shall invite them down from their ivory towers to enjoy the rough and tumble of public debate.

I don't seek to intimidate the press, or the networks or anyone else from speaking out. But the time for blind acceptance of their opinions is past. And the time for naive belief in their neutrality is gone.

As to the future, each of us could do worse than to take as our own the motto of William Lloyd Garrison, who said, and I'm quoting: "I am in earnest. I will not equivocate. I will not excuse. I will not retreat a single inch. And I will be heard."

THE SECRET PENTAGON PAPERS: 1ST AMENDMENT AND NATIONAL SECURITY.

THE NEED FOR A CANTANKEROUS PRESS

Judge Murray L. Gurfein

" . . . . This Court does not doubt the right of the Government to injunctive relief against a newspaper that is about to publish information or documents vital to current national security. But it does not find that to be the case here. . . .

"For I am constrained to find as a fact that the *in camera* proceedings at which representatives of the Department of State, Department of Defense and the Joint Chiefs of Staff testified did not convince this Court that the publication of these historical documents would seriously breach the national security. It is true, of course, that any breach of security will cause the jitters in the security agencies themselves and indeed in foreign governments who deal with us. But to sustain a preliminary injunction the Government would have to establish not only irreparable injury, but also the possibility of success in the litigation itself. It is true that the Court has not been able to read through the many volumes of documents in the history of Vietnam, but it did give the Government an opportunity to pinpoint what it believed to be vital breaches to our national

The Supreme Court split 6-3 in favor of allowing the *New York Times* and *Washington Post* to continue publishing the text and documents from a highly classified Pentagon study dealing with the origins of the Vietnam War. But the nation's highest court did not rule that "prior restraint" could never be initiated by government and the courts, although two justices wanted the historic June 30, 1971 decision to include that unequivocal statement. Defeated, the Nixon administration began to pursue the possibility of criminal convictions of those involved in this bizzare episode which for the first time in the history of the Republic saw courts stop newspapers from publishing (*New York Times, Washington Post, Boston Globe* and *St. Louis Post-Dispatch*). In that sense, the *New York Times'* James Reston mused, the 1971 case was a dangerous precedent. Because even though the Supreme Court had ruled the federal government had not proven its case that the papers had harmed national security, future officials could note that courts did stop papers from publishing while the case was being decided. District Judge Murray L. Gurfein's ruling denying a preliminary injunction against the *Times* in the early days of the case deserves consideration, because of the sense and spirit of his language. The lesson for all: the press can be charged with violations after publication but prior restraint runs counter to the grain of the Constitution.

security of sufficient impact to contravert the right of a free press. Without revealing the content of the testimony, suffice it to say that no cogent reasons were advanced as to why these documents, except in the general framework of embarrassment previously mentioned, would vitally affect the security of the Nation. . . .

"The First Amendment of a 'free press' must be read in the light of the struggle of free men against prior restraint of publication. From the time of Blackstone it was a tenet of the founding fathers that precensorship was the primary evil to be dealt with in the First Amendment. Fortunately upon the facts adduced in this case there is no sharp clash such as might have appeared between the vital security interest of the Nation and the compelling Constitutional doctrine against prior restraint. If there be some embarrassment to the Government in security aspects as remote as the general embarrassment that flows from any security breach, we must learn to live with it. The security of the Nation is not at the ramparts alone. Security also lies in the value of our free institutions. A cantankerous press, an obstinate press, a ubiquitous press must be suffered by those in authority in order to preserve the even greater values of freedom of expression and the right of the people to know. . . .

"These are troubled times. There is no greater safety valve for discontent and cynicism about the affairs of Government than freedom of expression in any form. This has been the genius of our institutions throughout our history. It has been the credo of all our Presidents. It is one of the marked traits of our national life that distinguish us from other nations under different forms of government. . . ."

IN ONE WORD: CENSORSHIP

The Los Angeles Times

The publication by the *New York Times* of secret government documents about the Vietnam war, and the government's attempt to prevent the *New York Times* from publishing them, raise three questions of great importance to the people of this country.

The *Los Angeles Times*, one of more than a dozen other newspapers to publish excerpts from the Pentagon Papers, defended the *New York Times* when it became apparent the Nixon administration would attempt to have further publication banned by the courts. This editorial summed up the initial reaction of the world's leading newspapers, prior to the Supreme Court's decision. Hailed along with the *Times* was reporter Neil Sheehan, who originally obtained the study.

Those questions are: the documents themselves and what they reveal about the war; the judgment of the *New York Times* in publishing them even though they were classified "Secret" and "Top Secret"; and judgment of the government in attempting to stop the publication of further articles.

To the first, what the documents show, the answer is that they show not much that is wholly astonishing. The arguments of the principals within the Johnson Administration about the war are seen pretty much as they have been understood.

But the documents published to date do indeed show details that were not known before. Incomplete as they are, the documents show that the men of that administration moved sooner than the public knew toward an involvement in the war deeper than the public knew. They show further that the Johnson Administration engaged in, at best, dissimulation, and, on a few occasions, deliberate deception of the people of the United States, in a course of action of great importance to those people. The documents document the "credibility gap."

It was, as we all know by now, a tragic series of acts by the government, tragic in the real sense because what the government did in those years was done from the highest motives of idealism, of patriotism. How it was done, and what can be learned from the way it was done, and how to avoid doing anything like it in the future as best we can avoid it—these are the questions illuminated by the publication of those documents. That they are accurate, and that they touch on the deepest issues confronting the people—war and peace—no one can deny.

The question then is the judgment of the *New York Times* in publishing them. The *New York Times* argued simply that "it is in the interest of the people of this country to be informed." The American government is the servant of the people; what the government does is the public's business. With that general statement no one can quarrel. To protect the freedom of the citizens to know what their government is doing, and to dispute it if they wish, and to keep the government in the hands of the citizens to whom it is responsible—it was for these purposes that the First Amendment to the U.S. Constitution was adopted. Not for the press as an industry, but for the citizens.

Is the press then at liberty to publish whatever it wants to no matter what the consequences? Of course not. It is restrained by the laws of libel; it is restrained by sensible governmental regulations— and it is restrained finally by its own good judgment and sense of fairness.

The record of the American press in refraining from publishing confidential information affecting the security of the country and the lives of its citizens is, we can say in all candor, excellent. With one lamentable exception, the press went through the Second World War, when censorship was a reasonable and necessary regulation, without breaching security; so, too, on the whole, in the Vietnam War, where there is no censorship.

No newspaper we know of would knowingly compromise the national security interest of the country or the lives of its citizens; and the government has its "Secret" and "Top Secret" and other classifications to keep confidential that kind of information. The Executive Orders establishing those classifications are specific and reasonable about what kind of information is not to be made public.

By no standard of either those classifications or of common sense can the documents published by the *New York Times* yet be said to endanger the security of the country or the lives of its citizens. The documents are past history. They reveal old arguments, not present intentions or future operations.

Yet the Justice Department contends in its suit that with the continued publication of the information, the "nation's security will suffer immediate and irreparable harm."

Some embarrassment, yes; some personal anguish, certainly. But there is no evidence yet offered to show that the security of the country is in any way endangered by the publication.

Unnamed government spokesmen have suggested that the verbatim publication of actual messages exchanged abroad may enable the Soviet Union to break American codes. If so, and if the government asserts and proves that in court, it would be a different matter; then the argument could well be made that the publication of the texts verbatim did indeed endanger national security.

The government claims also that the publication endangers the confidentiality of communications with other governments. That is a consideration. It would be much more a consideration if democratic governments around the world did not continually spill the diplomatic beans about their negotiations; and if officials of the American government, from Presidents down, did not tell state secrets as they saw fit and for their purposes.

Which is what the present controversy is all about, really; the history of the war in Vietnam, and how we got into it. It is a history already being told, in part, in books and memoirs. The current publication of documents merely adds more pieces to that history. It is all coming out, anyway; and it will continue to, as the participants to

Preventive Detention

The press chief of the *Washington Post* signaled victory, holding the "first edition" which told of the Supreme Court's decision in favor of the *Post* and the *New York Times.* William Frazee and pressroom workers on all of the papers publishing the Pentagon Papers had to go back many years to match the excitement and suspense. (Used with permission of Wide World Photos, Inc.)

those decisions tell their versions of one of the most difficult episodes in the American experience.

It was astonishing, therefore, that the government sought to stop publication. On the arguments so far brought by the government, there is no evidence that the national security is endangered. There is only the evidence that the government does not like what is being published.

That, in a word, is censorship. The government is relying on the Espionage Act to enforce against the newspaper a law that perhaps was never intended to be used against the press; that certainly never has been so used; and that, we firmly believe, cannot, under the Constitution, be so used in this case.

The government's action is almost without parallel in the history of the nation. It is a sweeping assertion of government power, and, on the evidence produced so far, an assertion of power that challenges the basic right of the people to be informed about the activities of their government.

REGULAR USE OF CLASSIFIED INFORMATION

Max Frankel

The government's unprecedented challenge to the *Times* in the case of the Pentagon papers, I am convinced, cannot be understood, or decided, without an appreciation of the manner in which a small and specialized corps of reporters and a few hundred American officials regularly make use of so-called classified, secret and top-secret information and documentation. It is a cooperative, competitive, antagonistic and arcane relationship.

Without the use of "secrets" that I shall attempt to explain in this affidavit, there could be no adequate diplomatic, military and political reporting of the kind our people take for granted, either abroad or in Washington, and there could be no mature system of communication between the government and the people. That is one reason why the sudden complaint by one party to these regular dealings strikes us as monstrous and hypocritical—unless it is essentially perfunctory, for the purpose of retaining some discipline over the federal bureaucracy.

Max Frankel, chief of the *New York Times'* Washington Bureau, submitted an affidavit in U.S. District Court, excerpts from which explain the unique relationship of government documents and the flow of information.

Presidents make "secret" decisions only to reveal them for the purposes of frightening an adversary nation, wooing a friendly electorate, protecting their reputations. The military services conduct "secret" research in weaponry only to reveal it for the purpose of enhancing their budgets, appearing superior or inferior to a foreign army, gaining the vote of a congressman or the favor of a contractor. High officials of the government reveal secrets in the search for support of their policies, or to help sabotage the plans and policies of rival departments. Middle-rank officials of government reveal secrets so as to attract the attention of their superiors or to lobby against the orders of those superiors. Though not the only vehicle for this traffic in secrets—the Congress is always eager to provide a forum—the press is probably the most important.

In the field of foreign affairs, only rarely does our government give full public information to the press for the direct purpose of simply informing the people. For the most part, the press obtains significant information bearing on foreign policy only because it has managed to make itself a party to confidential materials, and of value in transmitting these materials from government to other branches and offices of government as well as to the public at large. This is why the press has been wisely and correctly called the Fourth Branch of Government.

I turn now in an attempt to explain, from a reporter's point of view, the several ways in which "classified" information figures in our relations with government. The government's complaint against the *Times* in the present case comes with ill-grace because government itself has regularly and consistently, over the decades, violated the conditions it suddenly seeks to impose upon us—in three distinct ways:

First, it is our regular partner in the informal but customary traffic in secret information, without even the pretense of legal or formal "declassification." Presumably, many of the "secrets" I cited above, and all the "secret" documents and pieces of information that form the basis of the many newspaper stories that are attached hereto, remain "secret" in their official designation.

Second, the government and its officials regularly and customarily engage in a kind of *ad hoc, de facto* "declassification" that normally has no bearing whatever on considerations of the national interest. To promote a political, personal, bureaucratic or even commercial interest, incumbent officials and officials who return to civilian life are constantly revealing the secrets entrusted to them. They use them to barter with the Congress or the press, to curry favor with foreign governments and officials from whom they seek information in return. They use them freely, and with a startling record of impunity, in their memoirs and other writings.

Third, the government and its officials regularly and routinely misuse and abuse the "classification" of information, either by imposing secrecy where none is justified or by retaining it long after the justification has become invalid, for simple reasons of political or bureaucratic convenience. To hide mistakes of judgment, to protect reputations of individuals, to cover up the loss and waste of funds, almost everything in government is kept secret for a time and, in the foreign policy field, classified as "secret" and "sensitive" beyond any rule of law or reason. Every minor official can testify to this fact.

Obviously, there is need for some secrecy in foreign and military affairs. Considerations of security and tactical flexibility require it, though usually for only brief periods of time.

But for the vast majority of "secrets," there has developed between the government and the press (and Congress) a rather simple rule of thumb. The government hides what it can, pleading necessity as long as it can, and the press pries out what it can, pleading a need and right to know.

Some of the best examples of the regular traffic I describe may be found in the Pentagon papers that the government asks us not to publish. The uses of top secret information by our government in deliberate leaks to the press for the purposes of influencing public opinion are recorded, cited and commented upon in several places of the study. Also cited and analyzed are numerous examples of how the government tried to control the release of such secret information so as to have it appear at a desired time, or in a desired publication, or in a deliberately loud or soft manner for maximum or minimum impact, as desired.

PROTECTION AND INTEGRITY

LET'S PROTECT OUR DYING FIRST FREEDOM

Bryce W. Rucker

If I am successful during the minutes allotted to me, you probably will be angry . . . at me or someone. I expect that some of you will stalk out, probably slamming the door behind you. Others will want to read me out of the AEJ for heresy. At the risk of these and other repercussions, I want to talk with you about some things I learned while writing *The First Freedom*. Figures cited come from that source. Having forewarned you, I shall launch forth.

> *It seems to me it is time journalism teachers rejoined the human race as thinking, participating, responsible citizens. For years we have stood mute, occasionally whispering fears that all is not well. A few, all too few, have timidly ventured forth for fleeting seconds to lament practices all of us know are harmful to our nation and to mass communications. But almost invariably we have retreated, even recanted at the first opposition to our stances.*

At the 1967 AEJ convention you heard pleas that national, regional, and local press councils be established to serve as the watchdogs over the communications media. Some proposed an association-wide press council. Quite obviously the odds against forming an AEJ national council approach zero, and were it organized it is highly doubtful if it would function with even a modicum of effectiveness. Undoubtedly, this explains why the Mellett Fund has invested in local councils. Two of the first four of which, incidentally, were formed through Southern Illinois University's Journalism Department. And while I shall not discuss those two councils, I can assure you that they have succeeded beyond the wildest dreams of those who established them.

Bryce W. Rucker, senior journalism professor at Southern Illinois University, originally intended to deliver these words at a national journalism convention (AEJ) but due to a misunderstanding they appeared instead in *Grassroots Editor*, September-October, 1968. The plea is reprinted here with the permission of *Grassroots Editor;* some of the data has changed although not substantially and the thrust of the comments still deserves attention.

Instead of attempting to organize a national press council, I would urge that we as individuals become deeply involved in righting some of the serious problems which plague the mass media. Here I refer to the ever-expanding chains; they control half of the daily newspapers, three-fourths of the television stations, and a third of the radio stations, and virtually all of the magazines in the United States. To illustrate, the British-Canadian Roy Thomson has expanded his United States newspaper ownerships during the past six years from 3 to 36, Gannett from 15 to 30, Scripps-League from 16 to 27, Newhouse from 19 to 22, Donrey from 14 to 21. The 19 largest chains, those owning 10 or more newspapers, now own more than 330 dailies. Roy Thomson said this year he sees no reason why he should not own 100. [Editor's Note: by 1971 these figures and others in the article had not changed drastically, a fact which doesn't diminish the author's point.]

Quite frankly, I find such crass money-chasing at the expense of press freedom reprehensible.

I refer also to the serious problem of local monopolies; in all but 64 of the 1,547 daily newspaper cities one ownership controls all of the newspapers. In 85 cities the owners of the only daily newspaper also hold financial interests in the only AM radio station; in 27 cities the owners of the only daily newspaper also have interests in the only VHF (channels 2 to 13) television station. In three cities (Rock Island, Ill.; Temple, Texas; Zanesville, Ohio) the only daily newspaper owns majority interest in the only AM radio station and the only VHF television station.

I refer to the plague of cross-media ownerships. Newspaper interests own 10 per cent of the AM and almost 15 per cent of FM radio stations and a third of the VHF television stations. Among newspaper chains which own broadcasting facilities are Newhouse, Chicago Tribune, Gannett, Triangle, Glassman, Lindsay-Schaub, Harte-Hanks, Cox, Donrey, Scripps-Howard, Ridder, Cowles, John P. Harris, Corinthian, Lee Enterprises, Stauffer Publications, Booth, Panax, Ottaway, Steinmen, and many, many more. Cross-media ownerships entwine magazines, too, as you will recognize from several of the above listings, notably Newhouse, Hearst, and Cowles. Add to these Time-Life, Meredith, Crowell-Collier, and Hunt. You will, no doubt, recognize several large book publishers in the above lists. Indeed E.B. Weiss warned recently that with RCA, NBC, IBM, General Electric, Xerox, and others expanding into "giant electronic publishers" we may well need "new federal regulations to insure freedom of expression in the public interest."

So much for size. Equally important is who owns the mass media. Did you know that control of two of our large cross-media giants now is held by liquor interests? Time-Life has been taken over by Seagram distilleries. And that firm recently bought control of Metro-Goldwyn-Mayer. Norton Simon has recently linked his McCall's magazine empire and his Hunt Foods and Industry complex with Canada Dry, distillers of brandy, gin, scotch, vodka, and whisky. Theater interests of RKO and Stanley Warner and Schenley have been merged.

Did you know that the chief publicly stated reason International Telephone and Telegraph gave for wanting to absorb American Broadcasting Company was to "improve its image in the United States?" How many of you lifted a finger to oppose that travesty on communications?

Did you know that advertising agencies are buying into the mass media, even to the extent of obtaining newspaper-radio monopolies, so they may use them as "test markets?"

Did you know that religious groups use broadcasting for profit and propaganda? The largest two—the Roman Catholic and Mormon churches—earn huge profits on their radio-television holdings on which they, as religious bodies, are required to pay little or no tax. Of the remaining commercial broadcasting licenses held by religious groups, approximately 80 per cent are in the hands of fundamentalist sects. This isn't to mention their "educational" broadcasting chains. I'll give two examples—Northwestern College of Minneapolis (enrollment about 300 students) operates AM-FM combinations in Minneapolis, Fargo, N.D., Sioux Falls, S.D., and Waterloo, Iowa. Then there is Alma White College (50 students) and its Pillar of Fire chain with stations in Cincinnati, Denver, and Zarepath, N.J. Even Oral Roberts, the faith healer, through his "university" owns an AM-FM in Tulsa. And how about those who enrich themselves by selling healing rags and other trappings over the air, some earning a million dollars a year. One charlatan even sold "autographed pictures of Jesus Christ."

We are talking about valuable natural resources the Federal Communications Commission has licensed to broadcast "in the public interest."

Do you know the story behind the demise of the *Herald Tribune, World Telegram & Sun,* and *Journal American* and their offspring the *World Journal Tribune,* owner John Hay Whitney; his story is so fantastic I doubt if anyone could fabricate it.

Did you know that our supposedly competitive media owners are linked into cartels? They entwine such respected names as Hearst, Scripps-Howard, Newhouse, Block, Pultizer and others.

Did you know that John S. Knight of the Knight chain recently asked the Michigan Legislature to pass a law making it illegal to start a new newspaper in the territory of an established newspaper closed during a strike? All in the name, no doubt, of freedom of the press.

Many large newspaper publishers have operated beyond the pale of the law so long they assume they are immune. Then when they are called to task they rush to Congress pleading for relief.

You know, of course, that owners of the mass media own oil interests, mining, airlines, railroads, farm lands, patent medicine, munitions manufacturing, even ice shows. Some are prime government contractors. And you realize that broadcasters are increasingly buying into professional athletics so they may assure themselves of daytime, weekend programming. If you think this is limited to CBS's ownership of the New York Yankees, you are underinformed. Communicators own interests in professional football, professional basketball, professional soccer, professional ice hockey, and, of course, other major league baseball teams. Approximately half of the franchises for a proposed professional boxing league have been assigned to broadcasters.

> What is to come of the mass media as they increasingly fall into the hands of those who use them to promote their wares and bar competitors from their use, oppose legislation which might more equitably tax and regulate their holdings, push bond issues which will further their economic interests, ad infinitum. And the suckers, the general public, doesn't even know what's going on. They're not aware of the special interest holdings of their news-information sources.
>
> And here we sit. Assuming our proper role is to provide a trained, cheap labor supply to the industry, all to the noble purpose of informing the public.

No wonder our brighter students are protesting about the kind of education we provide them. No wonder so few journalism graduates remain in the newspaper industry after graduation. They resent being used by those who are the greatest threats to our basic freedom, the selfish, expanding, egoistic mass media owners whose driving force is the dollar. (I must emphasize that these and other charges do not refer to the large number of honest, responsible, concerned media owners.) The ends, extra-legal and illegal, to which some have gone to bankrupt their competitors to forge monopolies is one of the saddest chapters in journalism history, but our journalism history texts ignore it. Reading U.S. Department of Justice cease-and-desist orders involving newspapers is enough to sicken strong men.

Here, then, lies the major threat to press freedom.

Is it too late? Has press freedom been lost? Nicholas Johnson of the FCC says he fears it has. Yet instead of joining battle against these forces we let media owners distract us with such claptrap as the Reardon Report, governmental news management and closed city council meetings. And we, Pavlovianly bay in unison at the moon; indeed we justify their crimes by mouthing their propaganda that "monopoly makes for better newspapers." If you have swallowed that line, just check any list of the 10 or 15 outstanding U.S. news-papers and see how many are monopoly rags. Even worse, we have been willing tools in media owners' ignoble acts, most recently by supporting the ANPA's so-called "failing newspaper bill." If Congress adopts anything resembling that politically-bought bill, we will have even more "failing newspapers." The moneyed communicators will see to that.

So let's admit we have been duped. Then let's each one of us, join the fight to prove Nicholas Johnson wrong. Keep an eye on your local mass media. Learn who owns them and what their other owner-ships are. Analyze the media to learn if they are being used for the owner's economic gain. Become aware of pressures being applied by one medium to another. Often it is painful, as in the case of the recent profit-sharing exposure of the esteemed St. Louis *Post-Dispatch* and Newhouse's St. Louis *Globe-Democrat.* But I sincerely believe our basic freedoms become more secure and our mass media better through this cleansing process. So let's expose the crooks. It is our duty. We could aspire to no greater public, indeed socially re-sponsible, service.

> All of us should become involved. We have too long left this dirty task to one or two men, and we, in our stupidity, have ridiculed them. The undertaking is too great and too important for us to remain silent. But let me caution you. Smitten media owners fight back. Since we at Southern Illinois University have become increasingly involved in various of these skirmishes we have lost a few scholarships, lost an oil-sponsored national contest, lost support on a couple of other projects, received pressures and threats from some of the giant monopoly-chain-crossmedia owners, heard hints of legal action, received crank "You dirty Communist" letters. How-ever, we sleep better at night, new friendships and support have come from unexpected sources both inside and outside the profession, we have gained governmental and nongovernmental contacts throughout the country who have helped implement change. And through it all, our students have gained a deeper respect for egg-head professors, journalism education, and education in general.

During 1968 we have been involved in a diversity of activities, among them opposing the FCC-approved ITT-ABC merger. That battle was won. We helped rally support and otherwise fought the so-called "Failing Newspaper Bill." The shockwaves from that ill-conceived power play have alerted members of Congress, the Justice Department, the Federal Trade Commission, and possibly even the FCC to the grave monopoly dangers in the mass communications media. The Justice Department recently announced new merger guidelines which will limit horizontal mergers. The SIU Journalism Department chairman, Dr. Howard R. Long, has been deeply involved in the oil shale controversy from the outset. Without his help and that of others it is doubtful if J.R. Freeman would have achieved the limited success he has. Now you know why The American Oil Company withdrew its contest. But which is more important, the recognition and publicity gained through conducting a national contest or blocking a multi-trillion dollar government giveaway to the oil industry.

> *Despite my pleas, I fear you will not become involved. Indeed, I suspect that those of us at SIU enmeshed in these and other fights could not have done so at many of your schools. That is the most depressing prospect of all.*

Every one of us knows that educators in other disciplines contribute heavily to and frequently criticize their professions. University law professors and law journals regularly stimulate the development of the law. Medical progress would be stymied without the research and experimentation conducted at university medical schools. Much current economic and political theory have been developed on campus. These educators have recognized and so must we that we can rely on business and industry to undertake research, introduce reforms, develop new ideas only in areas where the expectation of profits accrues.

> *If my message were to be summarized in a simple thought it would be, Our basic freedoms are in grave danger because we have entrusted them too long to those whose primary concern is with profits. We share a high responsibility to protect these precious birthrights. The hour is late; much has been lost. We must shoulder our burden.*

CAN JOURNALISM SCHOOLS IMPROVE THE PRESS?

John Tebbel

While critics of the press have lately been running through litanies familiar since the colonial political authorities complained that the first newspaper in America embarrassed their foreign policy (and promptly shut it down), those professionally involved with the media have been speculating about how to improve performance in a time of challenge and widespread disbelief.

No one doubts that the performance of both broadcast and print journalism could and should be improved. The improvement, however, ought to come from professional concern and knowledge, and not through pressure by laymen who want to implant their own standards of news judgment. As one eminent editor has observed, few people outside the professions of law and medicine would have the presumption to tell lawyers how to argue a case or surgeons how to perform an operation, but every Tom, Dick, and Spiro appears to feel qualified to tell media people how to perform their jobs, even though many of these critics, from the White House on down, are unable to perceive any grammatical difference between "media" and "medium."

When one looks at the real and not the imaginary faults of the press, the true meaning of that abused omnibus word "communications" becomes more apparent. No matter what medium carries them, words are the essence of communication, and more and more it appears that the *quality* of what is being transmitted is being overshadowed by *quantity* and by sheer technology. If the media can be said to have two major faults, one would certainly be the prevalence of careless, even trivial writing. The other would be the inability or unwillingness of so many media people to dig below the surface of the news. Taken together, these constitute formidable obstacles to conveying the news of our troubled times and to giving it perspective.

These are major faults and no doubt account in part for the general dissatisfaction with press performance among readers and viewers, although these audiences attribute their discontent to other factors, most of them self-serving fantasies. There is also to be con-

John Tebbel, whose article on radio-television representatives appeared earlier in this book, is a journalism professor with strong views regarding the role of the "J-school." This article appeared January 17, 1970 and is used with permission of *Saturday Review* Inc., copyright 1970.

sidered the fact that most of the public is completely ignorant of how news is gathered and edited, as is clearly evident from the nature of recent attacks on the media. The communications industry has a large job of education confronting it in this respect.

But if the quality of the media is to be improved, we must look in two directions—toward the media managers, who need to be aware of their problem and determined to do something about it, and toward the chief source of supply of writers and editors, the nation's schools and departments of journalism.

When the Nieman Fellowships at Harvard were first announced, *The New Yorker* viewed with disdain their proclaimed purpose of elevating the standards of journalism. After all, said the magazine, Hearst had gone to Harvard, and he couldn't elevate the standards of journalism with a derrick. This stylish piece of acidity turned out to be as shallow as a Hearst editorial. The fellowships *did* raise standards, because they made good newspapermen better informed and more thoughtful about what they were doing. Other fellowship programs in various parts of the country, funded by the Ford Foundation, are performing a similar service today. But the numbers involved in these programs are small, and the hope for any widespread improvement rests on the increasing number of J-school graduates who are staffing the newsrooms and who today dominate the major newspapers and networks. What, one may reasonably ask, are the schools doing to improve the profession further?

There is one way in which they are not helping, and that is the continued and increasing production of Ph.D.'s in communications. Leaving aside the "chi squares vs. green eyeshades" controversy, it could hardly be argued that any but a few of these graduates are qualified to gather and edit the news, nor should they be expected to do so. They have been trained in a different discipline, and their vocation lies in another direction. A few may have a talent for media writing, but most communicate in the professional language of the sociologist and the psychologist, an intramural tongue hardly understood by others.

Yet, it is commonplace for journalism professors, deans, and heads of departments to find in their small advertisements of faculty openings from other institutions in which the specifications often read: "Must have media experience, and also have, or be near to having, the Ph.D. degree." To the advertisers, there apparently is no contradiction in these demands, but it is common observation that the number of people worth having with any kind of media experience who are also Ph.D.'s, or likely to be, is infinitesimal. Many of the best writers and editors never went beyond the simple B.A., and a few did not reach even that stage.

Professional instruction in journalism takes place largely on the undergraduate level, and its quality is directly related to the media experience of the instructor, as well as his ability to convey what he knows. Inevitably, some schools assemble highly qualified faculties; others simply make do with what they have. Here the dead hand of academicism can be felt in the unprofessional approach of some administrators, and in accrediting procedures that place more value on faculty members' degrees than upon their experience. A school or department with a brilliant assemblage of working practitioners of the craft on its part-time staff can nevertheless be threatened with non-accreditation, if these faculty members do not have the proper academic "union cards." Supposedly, journalism students are being trained for a profession in which the use of words is the vital essence. Writing is what journalism is all about. It seems only simple logic that it should be taught by experienced writers and editors, regardless of their academic backgrounds.

Surprisingly, the idea that journalism training should be on a high vocational level, like that for doctors and lawyers, is gaining new acceptance today, after being sneered at so long by the academicians. "Relevance," the word without which the young would be speechless, has put journalism in a new light; as the current arguments over the media testify, there are few things more relevant today than the communications business.

In the restructuring of curricula taking place everywhere, journalism is now mentioned without an accompanying sneer even in the sacred precincts of Harvard, where it is being discussed as a possible new course of study. Except for Columbia, the Ivy League schools have always disdained journalism in following their traditional classical patterns of education, but the student revolt has changed that, among other things.

Existing journalism curricula are also subject to change, sometimes without much notice, in these hectic days. The problems are not easy. Some student needs and demands are logical and not difficult to meet through revisions that should have been made long ago. Others are far too permissive to be useful to people who intend to work in the media. As any experienced writer or editor knows, it is essential to have as broad a background as possible, especially in political and cultural history, yet more and more students try to concentrate their work in a single narrow field of individual interest, and many are so ignorant of the past that they find themselves quite unable to deal with any kind of writing not concerned with contemporary social problems. Many, too, have little respect for the craft of writing itself, as the pedestrian rhetoric of the New Left and the semi-literate prose of the underground press amply testify.

Here again the J-schools are not equipped to deal with some new kinds of students who appear in their classes. The black student, for example, whose ambition is to establish and operate a ghetto newspaper, will probably find little that satisfies him, or even helps him much, in most curricula. The dedicated activist who thinks of the newspaper (or any other medium) only as an instrument of social protest whose purpose is to help bring about social changes will not find anything to interest him in classes that talk about getting the news and presenting it as fairly and accurately as possible. Among a good many students there is an utter disdain for that concept, which has dominated the best newspapers of this century.

Most journalism training elsewhere in the world is based more or less on this idea, even in countries whose press is not particularly dedicated to the proposition, as in France. Journalism education abroad is often in the hands of editorial trade unions, or in a partnership of those unions with government, as in Holland. In Britain it is controlled by a coalition of the government and the newspaper proprietors. In these and other countries, the objective is recruitment of trained personnel for the business. Only in a few places is such education within the province of faculties of philosophy or law, and in these the curriculum is taken up largely with communications methodology, and such training as exists is left to the media, who do little or nothing about it.

England remains the one country where every effort to date to make journalism education a part of university training has failed. This may be less surprising when one considers that only recently have the Oxbridge authorities agreed to recognize sociology as an academic discipline and have permitted it to be taught. Those who have fought hard to gain a similar recognition for journalism were not even listened to seriously by Oxbridge, and the Redbricks, though at least willing to talk, have not opened their arms. The opposition has come not only from the universities, but from the newspaper proprietors and the trade unions. Even the kind of on-the-job training for young journalists that the National Council for the Training of Journalists has done so well may soon disappear in the new educational bureaucracy controlling British universities.

Nothing of that sort can happen here. Journalism education is too long established and in too healthy a condition to be shot down by old-fashioned editors or a few anachronistic university administrators. But it is suffering from that fashionable contemporary affliction, an identity crisis. Those who want to isolate it from the real world of the media as an academic discipline unrelated to professional performance will have little but sympathy to offer to newspapers and broadcasters who are under attack from critics of every variety, and who hope to fight back by improving their product.

On the other hand, those who want to improve professional training and adapt it to present needs, in an effort to raise the quality of the media by strengthening their personnel, find their intention impeded both on and off the campus, and often by their own students.

Some journalism educators, at least, are coming to understand that it is irrelevant to argue about whether the news judgment of a politician, a political administration, a minority, or a great silent majority should be substituted for that of reporters and editors. Whatever mistakes of judgment the latter may make, it seems obvious that a free press in a democracy cannot operate except through unfettered control by people who are obligated to no one but themselves. Responsibility, yes, and provision for a broad spectrum of opinion in the press as a whole—but these things we already have in about as much measure as is possible in our society. What we do not have is a press that is adapting itself rapidly enough to changing times, and that often lacks writers and editors sufficiently skilled to use the word, with which knowledge begins, to inform readers and viewers as they must be informed.

It seems equally plain that there is nowhere else the media can turn to for help in improving their product and fulfilling their obligations, implied by the same First Amendment that protects their freedom, than the journalism schools. If the schools are to continue to justify their long existence, it is a problem to which they might well address themselves.

MEDIA AND MESSAGES

Joseph P. Lyford

It was in 1958 that Edward R. Murrow delivered a classic blast at the broadcasters. A rereading of the statement leaves the general impression that in television nothing much changes except the quality of the picture tube. The broadcasters are still talking about their special rights under the First Amendment and their sacred responsibility to make as much money as possible; most of the shows are the same old plots dressed up with new titles; and the Federal Communications Commission is still busily supervising the buildup of the mass-media monopolies, mergers, and concentrations of ownership it is supposed to be heading off. At least we can be grateful that there are two commissioners, Nicholas Johnson and Kenneth Cox, who are needling the industry, and we have some highly literate press critics around in *Harper's*, *The Atlantic Monthly*, and the *Columbia Journalism Review*. But the quality and frequency of the criticism drop off sharply from here. The fact is that with all the talk about the mass media these past years, we still have only the foggiest notion of what they are up to; this is partly because most of the criticism is neither systematic nor continuous and is either vague or centered on isolated cases. Confusion is also generated by the vast quantity of data graciously supplied by the people who run the media and hire researchers who tell us—to use the vernacular of the tobacco industry—that there is no demonstrable link between television and the health of the people who smoke it. Any doubts as to the extent to which the broadcasters influence the character of the mass-media discussion should be dispelled by the F.C.C. chairman's recent admission that the Commission does "lean" rather heavily on the broadcasting industry for pertinent data. And the American Newspaper Publishers Association, to prove it isn't asleep at the switch, assured its members at one convention that while it doesn't have an official lobby in Washington, its suggestions about pending legislation affecting the press usually result in desirable modifications.

One of the main difficulties in trying to understand even the most basic facts about the mass media is that communications technology and the people making money out of it are moving so fast

Joseph Lyford's article probing the mass media business is reprinted by permission from the September, 1969 issue of *The Center Magazine*, Vol. II, No. 5, a publication of the Center for the Study of Democratic Institutions in Santa Barbara, California, for which Mr. Lyford is a consultant.

that by the time we get a full-fledged debate going on some problem, the problem is obsolete or has dwindled to secondary importance. While the F.C.C. fiddled around with ways of getting UHF receivers on sets to open up competition a little, cable television was already threatening to push UHF aside and American Telephone & Telegraph was getting an unbreakable hold on the satellite program for good. Now Congress has been ruminating about how to save failing newspapers when in fact it ought to be worrying about healthy ones like the *San Francisco Chronicle*, which has grabbed off a rich TV channel, set up a shady housekeeping deal with the city's only other daily, and gained control of about three-fourths of cable television interests in the San Francisco area.

Another weakness of the discussion about the mass media is the collection of wobbly assumptions on which much of the talk is based. One such assumption is the idea that commercial broadcasters, newspaper publishers, bank presidents, corporation board chairmen, and all the others who control communications properties will respond to vague threats or appeals to their corporate consciences.

If there are going to be any revolutions in the communications business, they will come about because of changes in technology, not conscience.

Since we can't very well get hold of exactly what is happening to the media, it seems more interesting to speculate what is happening to the consumers of the media. We are right back in the thicket of wobbly assumption here, too. Contrary to the widely held belief that TV and newspapers can change or modify our opinions, many respectable people who make a good living counting and analyzing public opinion cite "studies" which show the mass media have no influence whatever on our attitudes—that we are receptive only to those messages which reënforce our convictions. The ad men who spend all those millions on TV spots obviously don't believe this, but it is quite unsettling to writers and teachers who adhere to the quaint idea that exposure to alleged facts and sales talks determines to some extent how a man feels about Volkswagens or about Richard Nixon after the Checkers extravaganza. Young people hearing an exchange between a journalist and a public-opinion expert are also confused. After two hundred and fifty Berkeley undergraduates listened in shocked silence to Harry Ashmore's description of how Mr. Nixon packaged himself to the Presidency with twenty million dollars' worth of mass-media plugs, they were advised by a Ph.D. in mass-communications research to forget it, that all those carefully contrived TV spots we saw during the Pat Brown-Ronald Reagan California gubernatorial campaign were a waste of money because we had already decided how to vote. There was a further acceleration of confusion some months later when, after pollster Donald Muchmore predicted most people had made up their minds to vote Tom Bradley in as Los Angeles mayor, election day turned out to be Sam Yorty Day. By this time the Ph.D. was safely off campus and unavailable for questions.

It might be good to get things right out on the table and say the mass-media researchers don't know what they are talking about. Certainly some of their "scientific studies" have a peculiar ring to them; it is not convincing, for instance, to be told that because several days' propaganda over Cincinnati's TV stations did not increase U.N. popularity in the viewer sample, therefore TV didn't change opinions. What other influences were at work during the test period that might have neutralized the U.N. messages, or simply redirected the viewer's attentions? And how does a researcher calibrate the date of birth, or mutation, or the texture and shape of something as delicate as an opinion? A little delving into the literature of attitude measurement arouses a feeling that some aspects of the business come perilously close to shamanism—any professional body, for instance, that can take a book like *Unobtrusive Measures* in all seriousness needs some looking into.

Suspicious as one might be of the mind-inspectors, it has to be admitted that at least they have some evidence to present, while nobody on the other side has any airtight data proving that a blizzard of antismoking commercials has any effect on our thought processes. And there is some support for the idea that we are worrying too much about being exposed to large amounts of information. Reflecting on his experience with mescaline, Aldous Huxley wrote, in *The Doors of Perception*, that he found himself agreeing with the eminent Cambridge philosopher C.D. Broad that "we should do well to consider more seriously than we have hitherto been inclined to do the type of theory which Bergson put forward in connection with memory and sense perception. The suggestion is that the function of the brain and nervous system and sense organs is in the main eliminative and not productive. Each person is at each moment capable of remembering all that has happened to him and of perceiving everything that is happening anywhere in the universe. The function of the brain is to protect us from being overwhelmed and confused by the mass of largely irrelevant and useless knowledge by shutting out most of what we should otherwise perceive and remember at any moment, and leaving only that very small and special selection which is likely to be practically useful."

Huxley implied that the brain and nervous system perform involuntarily the censoring activity which McLuhan advises us all to do very self-consciously to protect our sanity against a bombardment of data. In Huxley's view the whole universe of impressions is funneled through a mental reducing valve, and what comes out at the other end is a "measly trickle of the kind of consciousness which will help us stay alive on the surface of this particular planet." This should be of some comfort to those of us who try hard to keep up with everything that is supposed to be going on. But questions persist. How does Huxley's reducing valve decide what is "likely to be practically useful" at any given time? Does the rejection process change as civilizations are revolutionized by technology? And if, as Huxley says, there are chemical ways of bypassing the reducing valve, may not psychological means for circumventing it or breaking it down be devised?

Huxley's reducing valve will assuredly be tested by the techniques future communicators will develop to get their messages into our heads, come hell or high water. Past technical improvements in film, videotape, and sound will seem rudimentary by comparison. We may discover that the mass media can accomplish by mechanical and psychological means what Huxley felt was possible only by drug-induced changes in the supply of sugar to the brain. We have a very mild scent of what is to come in the vast realism of the film "2001," which has even changed audience seating patterns. Despite the huge screen, many people like to sit in the front rows where they are swaddled in the action, projected into space along with the capsule. The illusion of participation will be enormously expanded by the introduction of such inventions as the living-history film envisioned by Leopold Godowsky, the inventor of Kodachrome, who has predicted that under controlled viewing conditions an audience will be unable to avoid the conviction it is actually confronting the subject of the film. Godowsky's original purpose in developing the film was to use it in interviews with important world leaders, which would become the basis of visual-history archives, but its adaptation to television—and the technical changes TV can make to facilitate transmission of this visual reality—will be a radical step to erase what is left of the boundaries between fantasy and reality.

There can be little doubt that new visual information systems will have the power to subject individual or mass audiences to enormous, unpredictable shock—something film can do now but with much less intensity. We probably need not be as concerned about overt assaults as we are about subliminal or disguised attacks on our equilibrium. Added to the technical perfections of film, tape, and what displaces tape, will be radical new styles of treating subject matter to intensify reality. It seems likely that some of these new methods will be built on *cinema vérité*, which abolishes the artificiality of staging; other methods will use sophisticated abstractions, and still others will use abstraction to hammer home a specific, tangible point. Another change which will enforce the illusion of reality is the magnification of the viewing surface. The enlargement of TV screens to the point where images are bigger than life size will not only increase the persuasive power of the film but it can work the sort of transformations suggested in Robert Snyder's "Small World," a documentary on insects in which the magnification brings the viewer to the edge of extreme revulsion. There is no way of knowing how far the impact of TV can be expanded once it breaks out of its present confines, but it is not difficult to imagine the mind penetration which could be accomplished by a twenty-first-century parallel to Leni Reifenstahl's "Triumph of Will," or by an on-the-spot piece of living history, full size and color, as it unfolds a sequel to Watts or Detroit. One might ask, then, what protections other than Huxley's overworked filter are needed against overt or subtle distortions, or the subliminal effects that can transform opinion into truth. How is one to be defended against the overwhelming crash of reality?

Confronted with these and other riddles, what are the critics of the mass media to do if they want to keep their jobs? They follow the example of the man at the computer who assembles all the sense data and then transforms it into the logical base for all subsequent computations—the very act of faith that propelled early Christians into the Colosseum. The critic leaps over all the riddles in order to get on with the discussion. There is something very reassuring to such people about the current Senate investigation of violence on TV and how it affects children. In the course of such rambling inquiries it is impossible to detect whether any given remark has a bearing on the subject, what the subject precisely is, or whether the remark has any internal validity of its own. In such discussion, nobody should feel inhibited. The politician Senator Pastore, after taking a number of indistinct positions, concludes his investigation with a suggestion that "scientific studies" will provide the answers. At some distance from the hearing room, in California, the scientist Joshua Lederberg replies that this is nonsense, the entire scientific literature on the subject can be read in an afternoon and is shaky and inconclusive to boot. At this point some of those paying attention may remember psychiatrist Bruno Bettelheim's announcement that violence on TV may be good for youngsters because it gives them a look at reality—to which educator Robert Hutchins responds (in the person of his synthetic philosopher Dr. Zuckerkandl) that on television nothing is real because the function of television is to eliminate pain so that we can watch natural disasters and the massacre of subject peoples in our living room without the slightest feeling of discomfort. One escapes from the controversy over TV, violence, and children only by concluding that since all children are destined to be frightened out of their wits a good deal of the time, television might as well be doing the job as the local movie theater or parents who read them *The Pit and the Pendulum* and *Grimm's Fairy-Tales.*

It is, of course, no more possible to talk about the "effects" of television on children than on any other group. To the child deprived of an alternative the set can become the only source of daylight, and many deprived children, in both Westport and Harlem, adopt TV as a substitute parent at infancy. Children with a great many other resources seem to regard TV as just another piece of furniture. They are more selective than many adults who have had to "learn" television in middle age and they are sometimes better at getting the main, if not the most obvious, point of what they see. Otherwise how does one explain the insistence of a child, watching the funeral of President Eisenhower, on finding out who shot him? The fact that these children show a preference for imaginative commercials over "Gunsmoke" is a tribute to their taste and an indication that they may be growing up with the same contempt for regular television programming their parents have for the newspapers.

If increased familiarity with television does breed boredom and distrust, it might be worthwhile to think some more about the Paul Lazarsfeld-Robert Merton thesis that the mass media reenforce social norms and status symbols. A good many black children who have gone through their teens watching patriotic newscasts and the exploits of honest white policemen seem to have missed the point of all this folklore. One wonders whether television is promoting any norms. There is no question but that a great deal of air time is given to people who are criticizing the Establishment and not all of these critics are apoplectic black ministers. In June, 1969 NBC reporter Nancy Dickerson raked the American Medical Association over the coals in very explicit terms following the President's veto of Dr. John Knowles for a post in the Department of Health, Education, and Welfare, and she seemed to feel quite at ease in doing so. Certainly Senator Hugh Scott did not feel CBS was enforcing social norms when he attacked the network in 1967 (inaccurately) for featuring more Negro militants than moderates. And one could ask what norms were reënforced by CBS's coverage of the last Democratic Convention? The norms of politics-as-usual? Of Mayor Daley's Chicago?

When accepted norms have become an object of suspicion even to a white, blue-collar class, television has no choice but to tell us about it. Controversy, action, fury still are what makes a top news story on TV or in the papers, and the dissenters have learned how to exploit news media tied to these standards. Sometimes the result of the exploitation has been an oversupply of fake news-drama, but occasionally we have been given some splendid television reporting— on Martin Luther King in Birmingham, Selma, Washington, D.C., and Cicero, and in CBS's documentaries on migrant farm workers and on hunger in America. Television has as many possibilities as a theater of discontent as it does a forum for complacency. In the very process of illuminating, it affects the course of the history with which it is dealing. The stage, transferred to television, becomes a very different sort of theater, in which the effects of manipulating sound and light, of closeups, intercutting between cameras, selection of personalities, timing, a multiplicity of observation points can invent mythology or history for millions of people. It isn't necessary any longer for us to test and age our heroes, because television can manufacture and peddle them overnight. It has also cut to nothing the time lag between the conception of stereotype, its mass adoption, its elevation to the ultimate, and its quick replacement by something newer. Television's decisions about what is topical and significant have an immediate impact on public and private conversations. So there is always the question as to whether television enforces norms, or is contributing to an impression that whatever is in style today will be gone tomorrow.

It would be an injustice not to acknowledge that television has experimented with the arts many times during the past decade in a very creative way. One of the most exciting of these happenings was NBC's magnificent taping of the Boston Symphony's last 1967 Tanglewood concert, in which many cameras were so integrated with the music that they could have been part of the orchestra itself. Perhaps there will be an increase in these efforts in the future when audiovisual electronic technology approaches perfection in picture transmission. The possibilities of new experiments with the fine arts are especially exciting. The new technology will make it possible to present painting and graphics with such spectacular reality that viewing fine art will surpass the museum experience. If television takes advantage of the technical possibilities, for the first time painting and still photography can be brought within reach of mass audiences with the same fidelity as music, long ago liberated from the concert hall by recordings and television staging. Until now the fine arts have had to depend on book and magazine reproduction, which even at its best (in the Skira and Abrams books) loses the critical ten or twenty per cent of the texture and color of the originals, and which have not been able to approximate the originals in size. In addition to truer reproduction, music has had another advantage over the plastic arts, in that the production of musical sounds is a kinetic theatrical event of short duration—all of which has made the musical performance peculiarly suited to television. And music on TV has had such inspiring and lucid translators as Dmitri Mitropoulos and Leonard Bernstein—in contrast to the fine arts, desperately handicapped by the inarticulate verbal confusions of the Robert Motherwells and Elaine de Koonings. With magnification and perfect reproduction, television's projection of painting might significantly promote the integration of the fine arts with modern life, greatly expanding their effect as a means of education and communication. The fine arts will never become popular, regardless of the excellence of transmission, but historically—notably in the Italian Renaissance—they have played an important part in the education of the spirit and the transformation of cultures.

Television's preoccupation with ratings and entertainment shows is not the only reason we have not had more creative, significant reporting on television. Television news producers also have an unhealthy tendency to rate technical excellence ahead of significance of content. They are also convinced that unless something moves it isn't news. Taken together, the obsessions with technique and motion mean that television reporting often misses what Henri Cartier-Bresson calls the "decisive moment" of a story—the single revealing picture which can be studied in its frozen state. Yet the documentary, created from a sequence of still photographs, which does not appeal to movie-minded TV producers, is an inexpensive and more focused way to get at the heart of the subject. An example is the televised photo-essay on Manolete, the bullfighter. Television's "motion sickness" also accounts in part for a reluctance to deal with abstractions or invisible happenings like the technological invasion of the environment.

Television news coverage has also been hampered by internal disagreements over what constitutes "responsible" reporting. The Kerner Commission, as well as members of Congress, have criticized the networks for the way in which they covered the 1967 urban riots, suggesting that television actually contributed to the spread of the disturbance. CBS's Frank Stanton has said that any agreement or "consortium" between networks designed to suppress live coverage of potentially violent events would not serve the public interest, no matter how worthy the motive for such suppression might be. Yet not long after the 1967 disorder the three major television networks reached an informal understanding, according to *The New York Times*, that they would not give live coverage of the anti-war demonstrations at the Pentagon, the idea apparently being that such coverage might have inflammatory effects. In the wake of this decision, edited film reports on the Pentagon affair gave an extremely distorted picture of what happened and were accompanied (notably in Washington, D.C.) with vituperative commentaries attacking the demonstrators but ignoring the violence of sheriff's deputies and soldiers.

It is certain that the sharp criticism of CBS's coverage of the Chicago Convention has added to the networks' uncertain state of mind about live coverage of volatile demonstrations, and the networks are proceeding very cautiously. That this should not necessarily be a cause for rejoicing is shown by past cases where the mass media have exercised "restraint" in the national interest. The possibility that the hour-long TV embargo on reporting of the Detroit riot left the field open to dangerous rumor-mongering was conceded by the Kerner Commission.

Caution has been pretty much a life-style for the networks since the beginning. With television right behind automobiles and drugs as the biggest industrial moneymakers, there is little likelihood that the next decade will give the network new courage. But somewhere, usually out of sight, is the talent and imagination to be daring. The NBC White Papers produced under Irving Gitlin, many of them directed by Arthur Zegart, made few compromises in its programs on the exposé of Newburgh, New York's welfare practices (which resulted in a lawsuit against the network), studies of gambling, of state legislatures, and of police corruption in Boston (which also brought NBC into the courts). Also, to the credit of CBS, were the unvarnished and often unbearable reports on Vietnam which brought that war home in its full reality—reports finally softened as the result of protests by Americans who found it too hard to take. And while on the subject of television's better moments, one has to mention those one-hour UNICEF films of Danny Kaye's and Marian Anderson's visits with children around the world, David Brinkley's look at the

Mississippi River, the memorable film of Nikita Khrushchev in retirement, and the documentary on the contrasting boyhoods of James Baldwin and Hubert Humphrey.

Recently there have been the two excellent "magazine" shows: "First Tuesday," which has shown us the rituals of life and death in New Guinea, the Nigerian civil war, the massacre of sheep in Skull Valley by poison gas, and "Sixty Minutes" (Venice, the dying city, and an interview with Marshal Tito). In drama we had Lee J. Cobb in *Death of a Salesman*, the Shakespeare series of plays sponsored by Esso and produced by the BBC, and NBC's grand tour of the Louvre. Children's programs reached a high peak with the imaginative Sunday-night Disney films, the long-awaited cartoon appearances of Charlie Brown, the Christmas productions of "Amahl and the Night Visitors," and—every morning, except Sunday, for years—Captain Kangaroo with puppets, paintings, dancing, animals, and music, from *Carousel* to Beethoven. There were many more good things, but taken all together they weren't enough to make television a very satisfying experience for the young.

If speculation on the future technology of television, if not its quality, is a bit exciting, contemplation of the newspaper business, past, present, and future, is a depressing one. With the usual exceptions, the big daily newspapers are not getting any better, even in those cities where they no longer have to worry about a competitor (which means almost everywhere). The slippage is unmistakable from front to back. Local coverage is mainly the memorializing of pseudo-events, official announcements, and press releases; national and international stories are also slighted and when used are written in the uninformative and purposefully dull prose of the wire services. Many papers which do subscribe to *The New York Times* or the *Washington Post-Los Angeles Times* services ignore their most interesting offerings or gut the pieces unmercifully. Most depressing is the bad writing that we now associate automatically with the sight of newsprint: no section of the newspapers from the columnists and critics to the feature writers is free of the blight. In a talk to Harvard's Nieman Fellows twenty years ago, the late A.J. Liebling declared that newspapers are specially devised for the destruction of style. Liebling echoed Van Wyck Brooks, who claimed that no writing talent can survive more than a year in a city room. A few years later, Professor Theodore Morrison tried again to plead the cause of the reader, with his attack on the "hugger-mugger sentences," the fake emotionalism of journalese, and reporters who cannot come face-to-face with an idea. But such outbursts are valuable only as collectors' items in a country where the newspaper business resolutely refuses to engage in self-criticism and is run by publishers who consider the classified advertisement as the ultimate in paragraph structure.

One prediction that can be made with some assurance about the bulk of existing dailies is that they will continue to resist change even if it means their extinction. Like service on the subways, they become shoddier as the price goes up. At some point, the newspaper will undergo a physical mutation at the hands of the electronics industry, which will put newsboys out of business forever: facsimile editions will unroll from our TV sets, thus making official the fact that newspapers are a tail on the television dog for most people. There is an irony to the fact that while TV news broadcasts adopted the very worst traits of the newspapers, the newspapers tried to compete with the newscasters at their own game—with neither medium able to match the other's peculiar talent for trivialization.

There are all sorts of reasons why per capita newspaper readership in America is declining, and runs well behind readership in many European and Asian countries, but the most important reason is that American newspapers are boring, petulant, distrusted, and run in the main by people who are milking them. Of course television competition for advertising has hurt the papers, but publishers and bad writing and third-rate reporters were killing newspapers long before TV was invented. The trouble with newspapers is that they are managed by the same sort of people who run railroads. For years conservative publishers have put out papers which, by opposing adequate financing of public education, have thereby ensured the decline of the literacy on which newspapers depend. By misreporting or underreporting the extent and effects of urban and rural poverty and racial discrimination, they have accelerated the deterioration of their cities and the departure of their advertisers and readers to the suburbs. Faced with vast population and economic changes in the cities, the newspapers have failed to adjust. There are exceptions—the *Washington Post* and the *Baltimore Sun*, for instance, are trying to replace their vanishing middle-class circulation by offering systematic coverage of the minority group communities. *The New York Times*, always a fine newspaper, has improved immeasurably in an effort to serve the needs of the world's most tortured city. But most of the urban dailies—and they include some of the traditionally "great" ones—see the ghetto mainly as a source of crime and riot stories.

It may be true that our biggest cities have become just as impossible to report on as they are to govern, and that newspapers, like government, ought to decentralize and assign reporters on a very different basis. The "storefront" reporter, visible in his neighborhood, could be a collector of volunteered information as well as a perennial observer on a new sort of beat. Despite its old reputation for gray impersonality, *The New York Times* has been doing a great deal of prospecting in the city's neighborhoods, on an irregular basis. There is an intimate and very appealing quality to some of its reporting as a result.

Oddly enough the same closeness to subject is frequently achieved in two newspapers thought of as being national rather than local in character—the *Christian Science Monitor* and the *Wall Street Journal.* When they examine a local situation the resulting story is well rounded, colorful, and quite personal in tone. But these are rare examples. A main contention of critics now is that the big dailies and urban TV stations are not in touch with the special problems of their own constituencies, and that they are behaving just like another centralized bureaucracy.

One effect of the urban news factory, heavily weighted with official events, pressure-group propaganda, and "national" stories, has been the raising of the trajectory of people's attention toward remote events, far from their immediate environment. Such material may combat provincialism, but too heavy a diet of it leaves the reader in ignorance about what is taking place next door. And with newspapers and television increasingly directing his attention to "big" issues over which he feels he has no control, his sense of helplessness grows and his inclination to intervene actively in the affairs of his community declines.

The big press and TV news factories are in direct contrast to the underground press, which has built up its circulation primarily by appealing to small and neglected communities, sometimes political, sometimes social. A former *Berkeley Barb* reporter, Stewart Glauberman, compares that newspaper to a sympathetic parent at the breakfast table listening to his son's account of being busted by the cops: what is important is not the facts, it is that in his own home the son is believed and his story will be told to the neighbors as gospel. But one has to look past the established examples of the underground press to find a true community newspaper—the *Barb*, the *Express Times*, and the *East Village Other* are so propagandistic that even their own readers can't afford to trust them. A good example of an insurgent newspaper that tries to serve an unrepresented community is the monthly *Freedom News*, which with volunteer help is flourishing as an antidote to the conservative dailies published in affluent Contra Costa County near San Francisco. *Freedom News* muckrakes, in factual and conversational style, gives the defendant's side of an arrest story, and even has its own columnist on what the Establishment is doing to the natural environment.

Another newspaper that has kept its community flavor in spite of its success is the *Village Voice*, whose encouragement of debate, reporting, and criticism has given it a respectably large citywide and national audience. *El Malcriado*, the organ of Cesar Chavez' United Farm Workers Organizing Committee in Delano, California, is something of a disappointment as a community newspaper. Published in Spanish and English, as the union's voice to its own membership, and supposedly as a plea for the attention of the outer community, the paper is a far cry from that classic community journal, *Indian Opinion*, founded in South Africa by Gandhi, whose philosophy deeply influenced Chavez. Of *Indian Opinion*, Gandhi wrote that it was "an open book to whoever wanted to gauge the strength and the weakness of the community, be he a friend, an enemy, or a neutral." The workers had realized at the very outset that secrecy had no place in a movement where one could do no wrong, where there was no scope for duplicity or cunning, and where strength constituted the single guarantee of victory. . . .

"One thing we (the staff) have endeavored to observe most scrupulously: namely, never to depart from the strictest facts, and in dealing with the difficult questions that have arisen . . . we hope that we have used the utmost moderation possible under the circumstances. We should fail in our duty if we wrote anything with a view to hurt. Facts we would always place before our readers, whether they be palatable or not, and it is by placing them constantly before the public in their nakedness that the misunderstanding between the two communities in South Africa can be removed."

Indian Opinion had a far different historic and political role to play than the newspaper of a contemporary American city, but the words Gandhi used to describe the standards and community responsibilities of his journal might serve as a text for modern publishers who consider their newspapers primarily as business properties. The failure of their newspapers to speak directly to their readers and to report about local life in a systematic and credible manner has contributed to the general distrust of the press. If a newspaper does not cultivate familiarity with the problem of that great majority of individuals who are "unimportant," it will not have the capacity to understand them when their actions suddenly become "important"—that is, disruptive, eccentric, or tragic.

The coverage of campus disturbances is a good example of how the press has distorted the nature of those fragile communities and what problems the universities face as they resist suffocation by the larger society. The TV or newspaper reporter casually assigned to a confrontation is no more equipped to understand the bare essentials of violence than he was when dispatched to the rioting in Newark and Detroit. Like a fixed camera, he does not view things in the round, and he is intellectually immobile as well. The fragments he offers his papers as the comprehensive truth will contradict the experience of any reader who has had personal contact with the event; thus the level of distrust is raised again and again.

The trend is not likely to be reversed, because newspapers and TV are fascinated with the characteristic rather than the typical, the spectacular rather than the intangible, and the easily categorized rather than the complex. To operate with such criteria means, obviously, that the most important information about almost everything is lost. On very few newspapers are reporters or editors permitted to become students of the society they tell us about. We are being educated by a professional secretariat, and the notion that reporters are supposed to record only "the facts" is, of course, an old notion, but it is not an old-fashioned one.

Only a few months ago, the executive head of the United Press International observed that the purpose of reporting is to "hold a mirror to the world." With such a philosophy, it is not surprising that in all echelons of the mass media there is suspicion of any young journalist who displays a minimum of creative vitality in his writing or in his way of approaching a subject. Such young people can complicate the life of an editor who wants people who can get the gist of anything in an hour, and who can be deployed quickly to trouble spots, like policemen. It is no wonder, then, that the mass media have turned out in force to cover the various wars, declared and undeclared, that are ripping up the world, from Watts to Vietnam, while we are left in ignorance about what is happening across town. Or that hundreds of correspondents every day jam Washington press conferences while the side effects of "scientific progress" that are destroying our air, water, and land have gone largely unreported until recently. And there should be nothing mysterious about the fact that, despite all the newsprint devoted to college riots, Americans understand their educational system no better than they did in 1900.

All of the above observations are questionable, of course, because they are generalizations. Nobody can overlook the diversity of a newspaper press that includes a *New York Times* and a *Daily News* in the same city, or a TV medium which can invent a *Newspaper of the Air* (KQED-TV, the San Francisco educational station) along with the sleek newscasts of its neighboring KRON-TV (owned by the *San Francisco Chronicle*). Also, if pressed, a critic can pick out of the record of the past ten years some examples of change for the better. *Time* and *Newsweek* have both improved their vision as well as their English. *The New Yorker* magazine is giving us all sorts of penetrating insights into life all over the country in the best journalistic prose around. Washington, D.C.'s *Star* and *Post* are getting better all the time. Some individual TV stations are doing a good job of local coverage. Interesting people like Joan Baez pop up on the "Today" show as well as fusty congressmen. But the hopeful signs are scarce. While the range is great, the overwhelming weight of television is as riddled with blah as it was when Ed Murrow took it to task for its unadulterated commercialism.

And a cross-country reading tour of our city newspapers shows them to be at least as trivial, if less plentiful, as they were when the Commission on a Free and Responsible Press issued its criticisms in 1947. The saddest fact of all about our newspapers and our TV programs is that there is nothing new to say about them.

Chapter XI

TREATMENT OF MINORITIES IN THE MASS MEDIA

JOURNALISM: THE WAY IT IS, AS SEEN BY BLACK REPORTERS AND STUDENTS

Melvin Mencher

In mid-October, 1968, I set out on a trip that I hoped would tell me how more members of minority groups could become journalists and how they fared after they were employed. That six-week trip was followed by two others and by many weeks of correspondence. In all, I visited 16 campuses, six of them black, and spoke to journalism teachers, college deans, admissions officers and faculty members; student journalists, black and white, and members of black student unions, associations and alliances. I talked to editors, publishers and reporters on newspapers and broadcast stations in a dozen cities.

Five months later, a few certainties, several probabilities, and many possibilities emerged as I read through a suitcase of notes.

Some black and Spanish-speaking Americans have moved from pushing brooms and jockeying elevators to sitting in swivel chairs at formica-topped desks. Their posture may have changed, but has their position really changed? Young blacks ask this question rhetorically. They talk about window dressing and tokenism.

"Right after I went to work," said a black radio newsman in Connecticut, "I was introduced to every one of the people in the place, the only time that had ever happened. I was the only reporter taken to the state broadcasting association dinner."

Melvin Mencher, journalism professor at the Graduate School of Journalism, Columbia University, and former newspaperman and Nieman Fellow, undertook this research in connection with Columbia's Interracial Reporting Program. The article is used with permission of *Journalism Quarterly*, where it appeared in the Autumn, 1969 issue, Vol. 46, No. 3.

To him, and to many others I spoke to, this kind of treatment is more demeaning than menial labor.

Blacks talk about moving up in journalism. Again, they are scornful. The facts on decision makers in journalism are clear. There are few members of minority groups at key spots on newspapers and broadcast stations. Whites are in charge.

The situation is the natural result of years of almost all-white newsrooms. Since promotions are usually based on seniority, the white man is often selected because he is closest to the top of the ladder. But does discrimination hold back the able black?

A black reporter on the staff of a newspaper in Kentucky has been handling minor assignments for three years. Is she window dressing?

"If it takes us another three years, we will make her a reporter," said the newspaper's publisher.

Melvin Lewis is a general assignment reporter for the Kansas City *Star*. He is 49 years old and a retired army sergeant. As a youth in the South, he would hang around a stringer for a Negro newspaper, running errands. Occasionally, he wrote news notes. In the service, Lewis worked on several army newspapers, including *Stars and Stripes*.

In 1966, when he was about to retire, he sent out letters seeking employment as a newsman. The Kansas City *Star* hired him.

"At first they had me writing obituaries," he said. He did not resent the work, which is usually assigned to cub reporters. "It's a good way to get to know the paper's style."

Later they sent him out on an interview. "They liked it and I got a raise," he said. Then came a period in which he was kept in the office. Lewis was disturbed.

"I went over to the city editor and I asked him, 'Look, is there something wrong? Why don't you send me out on stories?'

"He told me, 'You're an all-around reporter. We want to keep you here for the big stories.' I suppose he means it.

"Look, I'm black. I know I have to be better than the average guy. I have to show I'm better here, just as I did on the army newspapers. I have to get out on stories to show them.

"But even when I do, I know they're saying, 'That's a pretty good nigger.' Or else they say, 'He's a good boy.'

"Boy, boy, boy. I'm a boy to them. They'd like me to spend my life going around kissing whitey's ass. I'm not built that way."

Lewis is tall, dark and reserved. He is a formidable figure, sometimes aloof—perhaps too formidable, too aloof to be sent out on assignments to white Kansas City. Lately, Lewis has been sent out on stories a white reporter for the *Star* describes as "our recently discovered subculture, the black community."

Paul Miner, the president of the *Star*, said the newspaper uses blacks "as we do whites, on any sort of assignment that comes up, and on Negro community news only when skin color may be of some assistance in coverage.

"Using Negro staff members exclusively to cover Negro news circumscribes their effectiveness. Sometimes, news sources seem to react more favorably to the Negro staffer than to the white," Miner said.

Miner is anxious to hire more black reporters, to do more about reporting the black community. But the past cannot be erased easily, and the *Star's* readership—conservative and often southern in outlook—is a check on change. The newsroom still has its quota of old timers who find it difficult to say Negro and compromise on Nigra. Their decisions are based on years of tutelage by men who, like editors everywhere, ignored the blacks and Spanish-speaking next door. In fact, one of the *Star's* black reporters, Helen Gott, describes herself as the conscience of the staff.

"I'm a watchdog over the paper. Sometimes they will do something without thinking about it, and I'll go marching up there. But the paper is trying to make up for the past. A Negro death sometimes used to end up in the wastebasket, and when I first came we didn't have Negro brides," she said.

Some blacks and Spanish-speaking newsmen expressed the feeling that they may come on too strong for their white editors, that if they were to be sent out on important stories or given decision-making positions they might inject a strong point of view in their work.

"Sometimes you have to compromise, to lay low," said a black television newsman from Seattle.

The Connecticut newsman put it this way:

"Look, the people in this town don't want to admit they have a ghetto. The news editor says he doesn't want me to be a 'race reporter,' which is nice. But if they did let me get out into the ghetto, I might upset everybody by talking about the reality here."

A television reporter in New York City described being admonished by an editor:

"He told me, 'You've got to forget you're a Puerto Rican'."

Then she added, "But how can I forget what I am?"

And the television newsman from Seattle said, "I've developed a philosophy of telling the man (whites) to go to hell without his knowing it. I'm a beginner, so I'm not as fast as the man, but I'm figuring out how to beat the system. I'm going to learn what the man knows.

"You can compromise too much, but as long as you always remember what you are—as if you really ever forget it—you're all right."

At this time, when for the first time black youths have an opportunity to make career choices, many able young men and women see the press as a "tool of the establishment to keep blacks down on the plantation," as one college student put it. It has little relevancy for them.

Wesley Brown, a senior and the editor of the *Lincolnian*, the student newspaper at Lincoln University in Pennsylvania, said his first job will be as a teacher in the Philadelphia ghetto.

"The public schools are deficient. There is great need there," he said.

Had he considered journalism? "Yes," he replied. "But I don't want to write, what do you call it . . .?"

"Objectively?"

"Yes. I want to be subjective, to give the facts but to tell it the way it really is. Like Joe McGinnis of the (Philadelphia) *Inquirer.* He used to tell the truth about race. He said he quit to write a book. But I think he had to go because he was writing things the paper didn't like.

"We had a demonstration here to support some girls who had a problem with the dean of women. One of the Philadelphia papers covered it by calling the public relations office."

Next to Brown at a small table in the dormitory parlor where we were talking sat another black student, Carl Word, Brown's assistant editor. Word's light skin and his volubility were counterpoints to Brown's blackness and deliberate speech.

"The black student talks about merit and money," Word said. "He wants to be considered for jobs and promotions on the basis of merit. But he wants money, too. Money first, then 'Swaar,' which means, 'Once I got mine, the hell with Whitey'." ("Swaar" seems to be a corruption of bon soir.)

Word applied to Princeton to study social psychology.

"That's a field that there is a lot of consulting in. They want black people for that. I'll teach maybe 10 hours a week, do some consulting and then have time for my writing."

He estimates he will earn $20,000 a year.

"Journalism doesn't pay, and besides they change what you write."

He was given a tour of *Time* along with some other black editors, and he said he was told that everything that is written is edited by the senior editors. That convinced him that a strong point of view never gets past the editor. He wants what he writes to get into the paper.

Later, he confided, "I can't write well. Someone has to teach me to write. Do you think they can do that at a school of journalism?"

He described his goal as being a "part time revolutionary."

He stopped for a breath and repeated, "Journalism just doesn't pay enough money, and they change what you write.

"Lots of companies send black public relations and personnel people here to recruit, but only the Philadelphia *News* sent a man down, and who wants to work for them?

"I'm a separationist until things change," he said.

Does that mean he wants to return to the ghetto to work?

"Look man, it's up from rats and roaches for me."

I heard Word's ambivalence toward journalism repeated and restated in many other conversations I had with black students.

Jefferee James is the news editor of the *Herald* at Texas Southern University. He is a pharmacy major but is thinking about journalism.

"How much money can I expect to earn as a newspaperman?" he asked. He grimaced at the answer.

Then he began to talk about the journalism course he is taking.

"It's pertinent now," he said. "Last year we wrote about flowers. This year our teacher has us interviewing poor people."

The local newspapers do not do much with the poor, he said.

"They just don't give a damn about the black community."

The editor of the *Herald*, Jane Manning, is the campus correspondent for the Houston *Post*.

"When we had the demonstrations here, the police and the education reporters covered the campus," she said. (A policeman was killed in the disruption.)

"I helped the education reporter, and I saw some of the copy being written. It went into the causes of the disturbances here.

"But the *Post* preferred the police reporter's copy. The newspaper did not want to look into the causes of the situation."

Neither she nor any of the other journalism students indicated any interest in working for the Houston newspapers.

John S. Evans Jr. is no longer a student at Ohio State University. He was suspended after he had been indicted for illegal detention and blackmail, among other charges, as a result of a demonstration on the campus April 26, 1968, and he faces some 300 years in prison if he is convicted of all the charges and is given the maximum sentences.

He turned in his chair and offered me a copy of the BSU's newsletter, *The Black News Notes.*

"We tell the truth in that," he said. "You can't get the truth out of the *Lantern* (the campus newspaper). It's a bad newspaper. They want it that way. The editor is picked by six faculty members, and she's a member of the Young Americans for Freedom.

"Black students wrote lots of letters, but not one has been run. They keep saying the letters are over the maximum of 250 words they set.

"Black students read the *Lantern*, which doesn't tell the truth, and they say, 'What's the sense of going into journalism?'

"The Columbus papers are right-wing also. Preston Wolfe controls the paper, a radio-television set up, and he runs the Ohio National Bank, which runs Ohio. He's a Bircher.

"We don't get an even break in the news, and when I told the journalism dean I wanted to discuss the *Lantern* with him they had pigs (police) all over the place when I walked over there. The campus pigs carry guns here, you know."

(William Hall, the director of the Ohio State University School of Journalism, said the committee that chooses the editor of the *Lantern* has six members, five from the journalism staff and the outgoing editor. He denies that the editor is a member of the Young Americans for Freedom. Professor Hall describes the meeting with Evans as follows:

> A member of the Black Student Union called me early in May and asked for a meeting at 3 p.m. on Wednesday, May 15. The group, which got there 40 minutes late, began by cussing and discussing the *Lantern* and then spent most of our meeting denouncing the white racist press. The police weren't called because a few Black Student Union leaders were in my office. The morning of the meeting we began getting calls from the local radio and television stations who said they have been tipped there would be a mass demonstration at the J-School at 3 p.m. Earlier, there had been threats by activists groups both inside and outside of the Journalism Building "that we'll take care of the *Lantern.* " With about 200 students in class in the building at that time and with another 50 working in the *Lantern*, I felt my responsibility was to keep the demonstrators out of the building. I notified campus police of the information we had received. Had there been no calls about a demonstration, there would have been no

police. Remember this occurred just 14 days after the Administration Building had been taken over. The situations appeared to be similar. A small group asks for an appointment, and then a larger group infiltrates. I carefully explained to the boys that while it might damage their egos, the police were not there because of their visit. In their shoes I'd find that hard to believe myself, especially since the demonstration failed to materialize.)

At the University of Kentucky members of the Black Student Union said the local newspaper had until recently carried a special column of news events of the black community entitled, "Colored News and Notes." The title was changed but not the content, they said.

But they said the Louisville *Courier-Journal* and the campus newspaper, the *Kernel,* are considered good newspapers by the black students.

"The *Kernel* has printed a lot of our material," a BSU official said. "We consider it has been fair to us. The editor is interested in what we are doing."

Then he wagged his finger.

"And what do you think has happened? The *Kernel* is in trouble. As soon as a newspaper treats us fairly it gets into trouble."

He was correct. The editor, Lee Becker, and his staff were meeting the night I was on the campus to consider the pressure that had been building up against the newspaper from student groups, the alumni association, the trustees, and, they were convinced, the governor.

"We don't print enough of their kind of news," said Guy Mendes, a member of the editorial staff. "Fraternity dances. Club notices. They want us to give less attention to race and the SDS and politics. The same old story."

The *Kernel* staff was not seeing devils behind the draperies. An administrator told me that the University president had been able to hold off the *Kernel's* critics, "but the kids don't know when to lie low for a while."

A letter to the *Kernel* from A.B. Chandler, a former governor and now a member of the board of trustees, further provoked the students. He wrote:

"Unless you can make arrangements to clean it (the *Kernel*) up at the earliest possible moment, it is my thinking that the stinking sheet ought to be abolished. . . .

" . . . unless you gain a semblance of decency in short order, you will soon disappear from the scene."

There is only one black student majoring in journalism at the University of Kentucky.

Some editors see the black journalist, or the Chicano in the west and southwest, as a potential subversive, and they are not ready for the confrontations this new kind of journalist might bring about. Barely able to meet the demands that they report social change, the news media are hardly anxious to examine their possible role as instigators of change. The black, who lives outside the affluent industrial society and is its victim, could perceive of journalism in a new way—new, that is, to many newspapers and broadcast stations.

The reluctance of employers to hire minority group journalists or, once hired, to permit them to cover the community in depth and to promote them to responsible positions is not limited by geography, circulation or wattage.

An assistant to the publisher of one of the largest daily newspapers in California told me why his newspaper is not anxious to print too much about the ghetto.

"Look, we want to reach people who spend their weekends skiing, the couple that flies to London for a vacation. Our advertisers expect that kind of reader," he said. "They're not paying to reach poor people."

Blacks sense this resistance to face the bedrock reality of their lives. Some of those who would make excellent journalists find it hard to adjust to jobs that on close scrutiny turn out to prop up the assumptions, values and myths that support the status quo.

Post Script

"Why would a bright Negro student want to go into journalism?"

—From an interview with Hideya Kumata, director of the Institute of International Communication at Michigan State University.

Why would *any* bright student want to go into journalism?

The question is almost rhetorical, for many bright students do not make journalism their careers, even those who are campus journalists. In a study I made of the career choices of college editors, I found some 60% of the editors at large state universities go into journalism; 40% of the editors on small campuses become journalists. How many of these are bright or dim is impossible to determine. However, I did select a group of students whose newspapers were outstanding, and I interviewed them.

An editor of the *Michigan Daily* said:

> I'll be very hesitant to go into journalism. I don't know whether I'll be able to strive for the kind of depth of writing for which we strove on the *Daily*. I find commercial journalism infuriatingly superficial in communicating the important issues of the day. Much of the press is obviously "kept," either by the priority of business concerns or by a willingness to become the tool of establishments, or both. But beyond that most newspapers are simply anti-intellectual; they feed off society's sickness and were, I believe, greatly responsible for such idiocies as the Goldwater candidacy and the Vietnam war. Most newspapers neither dig nor reflect. They mirror, and that's a process I couldn't be part of.

He went on to Yale to study history and is now at Harvard.

Janet Wells, a former managing editor of the Georgia State College *Signal*, was of two minds about staying in journalism. She had been watching the southern press cover desegregation, and she was not happy about what she saw. In a letter to the author, she wrote:

> I do not believe that the press is now doing a good job, and unfortunately the reason seems to be an attitude toward the current civil rights movement or a reaction to black power. I know that the Negro revolution and I have both changed in five years, but it seems to me that the Atlanta newspapers, particularly the *Constitution*, have also changed. I was raised a segregationist in Albany, Georgia, with all the prejudices that entails. Hero-worship of John Kennedy softened my ideas a little, but it was on beginning to read the Atlanta *Constitution* daily when I was 16 that I became almost overnight, an avowed integrationist who would later do volunteer work for a civil rights group. While I was still in high school my greatest goal was to one day work for the *Constitution* and help it carry on the great struggle for racial justice. Now, at 21, having lived two years in Atlanta and being fairly well assured of a job on the *Constitution*, I am seriously wondering if I like journalism well enough to give up the opportunity to pursue my ideals in some more liberal field.
>
> The Atlanta papers led a courageous battle for progress in this city, and now they seem shocked that Negroes aren't willing to stop at the limited goals that were set when desegregation was the movement's only object. They deride Carmichael without trying to explain him to the indifferent white public that is moved only when it is personally threatened. The paper's attitude toward black power is almost like the segregationist's view of the whole movement a few years ago: Ignore it hard enough and it will go away. They simply can't present the total picture until they acknowledge the little girls in pink dresses who are going to grow up with their chins tilted a little bit higher because Stokely Carmichael made them proud to be themselves. Understanding between the races today and in the immediate future requires that whites respect the basic goals of the black power advocates even if they don't accept them, and the papers are not providing a constructive medium of explanation.

Watching the newspaper, press service and radio-TV reporters on the tennis courts that day, I understood Carmichael's contempt for them and was glad that I was there as an interested spectator and not as a representative of the commercial press. The only serious reporter there, the only one who would capture such essentials as the look in the eyes of the Negro father who asked his little girl if she had seen Stokely Carmichael, was a young man from the *Southern Courier*. The others were chuckling over the fact that Carmichael was wearing a suit instead of denim and making light of everything he said—which was taken so seriously by the much-wronged people around him. The reporters were unable to see him as he is, or to significantly interpret what was happening, and that hurt their ability to cover the event. Their editors had the same opinion and buried the story on page 20 in the second section. (The *Journal* got the story off the wire. The anti-Vietnam address by Dr. King that same day was on page 15 of the *Constitution* the following morning, on page one of the *New York Times*.)

In short, the papers aren't doing the public service I once thought they were.

COLOR AND THE COMICS

Jack E. White, Jr.

Leaf through the daily newspaper looking for black people. You'll probably find some in the news columns, maybe even on page one. But chances are you won't find a black face in the comics. Of more than 175 comic strips with wide syndication, only four feature blacks with any regularity. They are *Dateline: Danger*, *Wee Pals*, *Mandrake the Magician*, and *The Phantom*. Perhaps five others show blacks occasionally and then only in incidental roles.

Various reasons are advanced for this "comic strip apartheid." from conversations with comic art directors, the explanations go something like this: "We'd like to have some black characters because the times have changed. But we can't make them major characters in our existing strips because our readers might think it manipulative. We can't feature them in story segments because they'd eventually disappear and that would be tokenism. So, we'll create a new strip that's integrated from the beginning. It can't be a humor strip, because jokes directed at the black character might be inter-

Jack E. White, Jr. is a staff writer for the Race Relations Information Center in Nashville, Tennessee, which publishes a bi-monthly newsletter, *Race Relations Reporter*. The Winter, 1969-70 issue of *Columbia Journalism Review* carried the article, which is reprinted with permission of Mr. White and the *CJR*.

preted as racist. So it will be an adventure strip. But we can't have the character do anything that might offend Southerners, because then we couldn't sell the strip in the South."

Fear of offending anyone is the driving emotion at the syndicates. Sylvan Byck, comics editor at King Features, puts it this way: "We have tried to keep away from race and ethnic humor because you don't know if you'll offend anybody. It's not just blacks, but other ethnic groups like Jews and Italians. If you make the villain in an adventure strip an Italian or a Mexican, you're in trouble. So we try to keep our villains out-and-out WASP." Byck could have said the same thing about the vast majority of comic heroes.

During the so-called "Golden Age" of comics, black characters appeared in a number of strips. There was Smokey, Joe Palooka's faithful retainer; Asbestos, the race track buff in *Joe and Asbestos;* and Hambone, the homespun philosopher in *Hambone's Meditations.* One thing these and other black characters had in common was stereotype. Usually they had big white lips on solid black faces with big white eyes. Frequently black characters were cannibals. They spoke like this:

> Sis Mandy's gal bin 'way to collidge, an' cain' nobody now understan' whut she talkin' 'bout!

> *(Hambone's Meditations,*
> by Cal and J.P. Alley, Jr.)

> Moon: Oh, well, I saved myself 25 bucks!
> NEGRO: Less $10 foh de doctah—pretty good business, ah'd say, boss.

> *(Moon Mullins,* by Frank Willard)

When blacks protested against the stereotyped portrayal, the usual response of a syndicate was to eliminate the Negro character altogether. On the other hand, fear of offending the South prevented the syndicates from using blacks in less distorted roles. And there the situation rested until recently.

There were exceptions. In 1963, after the Cleveland chapter of the Congress of Racial Equality protested Asbestos' "minstrel" type character, Ken Kling changed him overnight. He became "almost handsome" and spoke like a college professor. In 1961, Leonard Starr featured a black music director in his popular show business strip *On Stage.* The strip excited the curiosity of a number of readers, who wrote to ask if the character was really a Negro. He was.

A number of elements have contributed to new interest in integrated comic strips. One of the most important, although editors might be reluctant to admit it, was the long hot summers. Morrie Turner, creator of *Wee Pals*, said many newspapers contracted for his strip in the wake of the Martin Luther King assassination. Another factor is that integrated strips apparently are now salable. "There's a general feeling that perhaps now the public has come to a point where you can show a black character and a white character within the same frame of a comic strip without insulting anyone," says William Sexton, editor of Publishers-Hall Syndicate. "Years ago, I guess this wasn't true."

Despite this feeling, the syndicates have been cautious. There is a feeling that going too far too fast might create a glut on the market, somewhat analogous to the "white backlash." Said King Features' Byck: "We would like to have a new strip with black characters, but we would like to have one which is a good strip, marketable. We have been working with someone on such a strip, but we don't know yet if it is going to be something that will sell."

In a sense, a strip is like a Broadway play; many scripts are submitted, but few are produced. The average syndicate looks at nearly 1,000 new strips a year, and may decide to buy only one or two. It is not surprising, then, that so far only one strip has been created from scratch as a racially integrated adventure story. It is *Dateline: Danger* by John Saunders and Al McWilliams and syndicated by Publishers-Hall. Both Saunders and McWilliams are white. [Editor's Note: At least one more might qualify in 1971, *Friday Foster*, the strip featuring a black girl photographer who has one adventure after another with her white friend named Shawn.]

"The credit has to go to Bob Hall, the president of Publishers-Hall," said Saunders. "He came to Toledo in June, 1968, to talk with my father, Allen Saunders. He's sort of the dean of comic writers. Bob Hall told him he wanted to do a strip with a black character and my father said, 'Well, that's fine, but I haven't got time. I'm already writing three strips. But you could go talk to my son!' " Hall did, and John Saunders accepted, reluctantly. He was not sure he could sensitively develop a black character.

Saunders met with Art Egerton, a black TV reporter, and talked about the strip. What finally emerged in November, 1968, was the story of a biracial team of news reporters who go all over the world in search of stories. The strip appears to be an unabashed attempt to capitalize on the success of the TV show *I Spy*. Its black character, Danny Raven, bears a striking resemblance to Bill Cosby. After an initial segment overseas, "to get the readers used to seeing an integrated situation," the two heroes came back to an American city, complete with ghetto, black militants, unemployment, white gangsters, pro football heroes, pretty girls and a multi-millionaire black businessman who made his fortune selling spareribs.

Dateline: Danger is now carried in 130 newspapers, even appearing in Capetown, South Africa. Several newspapers in the South carry the strip. "The strip is an easy sell," said Sexton, but a hard cancel, unless editors want to open themselves to the charge of racism. Two other syndicates are reportedly trying to catch up with integrated strips of their own.

Meanwhile, *Mandrake the Magician* and *The Phantom*, both syndicated by King Features, are being "changed in keeping with the times," says Byck. In *Mandrake*, this means that the hypnotist's longtime sidekick, Lothar, no longer runs around half-naked speaking in monosyllables. "Now he looks a little like Harry Belafonte, if Belafonte had more muscle," according to Byck. Lothar has also been granted equal prominence in the strip and no longer serves only as a muscular foil to Mandrake's "hypnotic gesturing."

The major change in *The Phantom* is the integration of the Jungle Patrol. This police force used to be the all-white fount of justice in a black African nation. Now the chief is black, and the patrolmen seem equally distributed between the races. However, there are still anomalies like the black African native girl, whose hair is as long and straight as that of Diana Palmer, girlfriend of the "Ghost Who Walks."

Only one widely syndicated strip regularly breaches the "integration-in-adventure-only-rule": *Wee Pals*, drawn by Morrie Turner. Based loosely on the vastly popular *Peanuts*, it has a multi-racial cast, including a Negro, a Chicano, an Italian, and a Jew. The humor is gentle but frequently touches on race relations. "I try to play the cultures against one another, but without bitterness," said Turner. "If there's philosophy, it is that we can all get along together." The strip, introduced four years ago by the Register and Tribune Syndicate, appears in a number of Midwestern newspapers, but still does not run anywhere south of Louisville.

Turner is distressed because "one of the strange things that's happened since I started is that they (the syndicates and newspapers) have placed the integrated strips in competition with each other," rather than with other strips in their own broad class. Thus, *Wee Pals* doesn't compete with *Peanuts*. "I guess it's because each editor feels 'We've got our token strip and we don't need any others'," he said.

"It's the syndicates who really control this kind of thing," says

Marge D. Devine, who has been scribe of the National Cartoonists Society for twenty-six years. "The willingness of the cartoonist to do it was one thing, but the willingness of syndicates to accept it was another."

Black characters have appeared in a number of strips without severe reaction. Charles Schulz has introduced a black character "Franklin"; Milton Caniff's *Steve Canyon* has had one or two black faces; there was a black FBI agent in *Buz Sawyer* by Roy Crane; and the irrepressible Al Capp has included black entertainers in *Li'l Abner*. In one of the most celebrated comic stories in recent years, Mary Worth was peripherally involved in the romance of a Mexican-American stewardess and a Kennedy-like U.S. Senator with presidential ambitions, The story was controversial for two reasons: Senator Edward Kennedy's celebrated automobile accident coincided with a similar accident in the strip, and it was perhaps the first attempt to portray a member of the Chicano community in human terms. As such, it represented a daring step on the part of the strip's author, Allen Saunders.

Whether these small steps toward integration of the comics will lead to more action is questionable. Said Turner: "I thought after Schulz did it everybody would." But at a seminar on integration of the comics held last year by the Newspaper Comics Council in New York, Allen Saunders got only "blank stares and quiet clearing of throats" when he suggested that the industry was "kidding themselves if they will not print integrated comics, because you can't walk down the street of any city in this country today and see only white faces. They said 'By golly, you're right,' but I don't know if they're going to do anything about it."

Part of the answer may be provided by the fate of *Butter and Boop*, an all-black strip created by Black Light, Inc., in Kansas City, Mo. The firm is supported by the Faultless Starch Corp., of Kansas City, whose president, Gordon Behan III, thought that the lack of black figures in comics might have a detrimental effect on the psychological development of children. Behan donated money to a group of Midwestern and Southern black youths and gave them a mission: create a black comic strip. After some personnel difficulties, the strip has now become a moderately well drawn and reasonably amusing view of the lives of black ghetto children. Much of the action takes place in tenement alleys.

"We wanted to hit pretty close to the ghetto," explained artist Edward Carr. "We felt that by getting into the alleys and other places where ghetto kids live and play that we could get some real feeling into the cartoons."

Butter and Boop could be a watershed. It is the first trip that deals with the lives of ghetto children, the first that attempts to get at the black humor revolving around scraggly dogs, hustlers, unemployment, poor schooling, and unequal opportunity. The strip now is carried in only five newspapers, including the black Chicago *Defender*, but if it can be syndicated and circulated, it might spell the beginning of the end of a story that seems to be grinding along as interminably as some of the episodes in *Winnie Winkle*.

Chapter XII

CHANGING CONTENT OF STORIES
AND PHOTOS

MEDIA MYTHS ON VIOLENCE

Terry Ann Knopf

Several years ago a resident of a small Northern town kept insisting to a local newspaper reporter that a policeman had been shot and killed during a racial disturbance there. The reporter checked and rechecked but was unable to substantiate the story. In fact a policeman had been killed, but in another city. The man simply had heard a garbled version of the story—not an unusual occurrence in the confusion that prevails during crises.

Crisis situations increase the need for news. During most serious disturbances, news media are bombarded with calls from anxious citizens wanting information, clarification, verification of what they have heard. So important is the flow of news through established channels that its continued absence can help precipitate a crisis. In 1968 in Detroit the absence of newspapers during a protracted strike helped create a panic: there were rumors in the white community that blacks were planning to blow up freeways, kill suburban white children, and destroy public buildings; in the black community, that white vigilantes were coming into the area to attack the residents. Gun clubs sprang up in the suburbs; black leaders urged preparation of survival kits. On March 7—nearly four months after the strike began—Mayor Cavanagh had to go on TV to plead for calm.

As racial disorders have become a familiar part of the national scene the media have demonstrated a growing awareness of their responsibilities and a healthy willingness to experiment with new

Terry Ann Knopf, a research associate at the Lemburg Center for the Study of Violence, Brandeis University, demonstrates some improvements in press performance but also some shortcomings. This article appeared in the Spring, 1970 *Columbia Journalism Review* and is used with permission of that publication.

policies and procedures. Technical improvements also have been made. The City of Detroit, for example, has built a press room large enough for 150 people, with independent telephone lines. Operational techniques have been modernized—the Pittsburgh police, among others, have on occasion provided a helicopter for the press. And central headquarters or "press centrals" have been established to help eliminate conflicting reports. Moreover, a number of cities have adopted or revised guidelines for reporting. These guidelines—sometimes formal, sometimes informal—urge that unnecessary interpretation be minimized, rumors be eliminated, unverified statements be avoided, and superlatives and adjectives in "scare" headlines be excluded. One set of guidelines put the matter simply: "Honest and dispassionate reporting is the best reporting."

In accordance with these guidelines, newspapers have tended to move away from the "shotgun" approach—the front-page buildup, complete with splashy pictures and boxscores of the latest "riot" news. Dramatic but meaningless predictions have also largely disappeared. In May, 1967, *U.S. News & World Report* declared that Newark was "not expecting trouble," while Cleveland was voted the city "most likely to explode—again." Cleveland failed to erupt in 1967, but Newark experienced one of the most massive outbursts in our country's history. This kind of journalism is much less common today.

There is also evidence of greater sympathy and sensitivity toward blacks. How far have we come? Consider the following comment from the New York *Times* on July 23, 1919, concerning the violent disorder in Washington, D.C.:

> The majority of the negroes (sic) in Washington before the great war were well behaved. . . . More of them admitted the superiority of the white race, and troubles between the two races were undreamed of. Now and then a negro intent on enforcing a civil rights law would force his way into a saloon or a theatre and demand to be treated the same as whites were, but if the manager objected he usually gave in without more than a protest.

These changes represent considerable improvement. But serious problems remain. Glaring instances of inaccuracy, exaggeration, distortion, misinterpretation, and bias have continued at every level—in newspapers and newsmagazines large and small, Northern and Southern, liberal and conservative.

The wire services are probably the most underexamined segment of the media, although as much as 90 per cent of the news in some newspapers on a given day may come from the wires. One error in a wire service report from one city may be repeated in hundreds of newspapers and newscasts. In York, Pa., in mid-July, 1968, for instance, incidents of rock- and bottle-throwing were reported. Toward the end of the disturbance UPI in Harrisburg asked a stringer to get something on the situation. A photographer took a picture of a motorcyclist with an ammunition belt around his waist and a rifle strapped across his back. A small object dangled from the rifle. On July 18, the picture reached the nation's press. The Washington *Post* said:

> Armed Rider—Unidentified motorcyclist drives through heart of York, Pa., Negro district, which was quiet for the first time in six days of sporadic disorders.

The Baltimore *Sun* used the same picture and a similar caption:

> Quiet, But . . . An unidentified motorcycle rider, armed with a rifle and carrying a belt of ammunition, was among those in the heart of York, Pa., Negro district last night. The area was quiet for the first time in six days.

The implication of this photograph was clear: The "armed rider" was a sniper. But since when do snipers travel openly in daylight completely armed? Also, isn't there something incongruous about photographing a sniper, presumably "on his way to work," when according to the caption the city "was quiet"? Actually the "armed rider" was a sixteen-year-old boy who happened to be fond of hunting groundhogs—a skill he had learned as a small boy from his father. On July 16, as was his custom, the young man had put on his ammo belt and strapped a rifle across his back, letting a hunting license dangle so that all would know he was hunting animals, not people. Off he went on his motorcycle headed for the woods, the fields, the groundhogs—and the place reserved for him in the nation's press.

More recently, an AP man in Dallas filed a story on a student takeover at Southern Methodist University. The Fort Worth *Star-Telegram* in its evening edition last May 2, put the story on the front page and gave it a banner headline:

BLACKS SEIZE OFFICE OF S.M.U.'S PRESIDENT

Police Are Called to Stand By

> Dallas (AP)—Black students with some support from whites took over the office of the president of Southern Methodist University today and swore to remain until their demands are met. . . .

> Reports from the scene said from thirty to thirty-five students were in control of (President) Tate's office.
>
> The takeover occurred during a meeting of Tate and a campus organization, the Black League of Afro-American and African College Students.

The story had one major flaw—it wasn't true. While about thirty-five students had met with the university president, they were not "in control" of his office; nor had they "swore to remain" until their demands were met. No such "takeover" had occurred. Glen Dromgoole, a staff writer for the *Star-Telegram*, later reported what really happened. The black students had met with the president for more than five hours discussing recent demands. The talks were more friendly than hostile. (At one point hamburgers were brought in.) By the end of the meeting, agreement had been reached on most of the issues. Apparently the wire service reporter had accepted the many rumors of a student takeover.

Martin Hayden of the Detroit *News* has suggested "an almost mathematical relationship between the level of exaggeration and the distance of news transmission." Edwin Guthman of the Los Angeles *Times* maintains that the early wire service report "is at the crux of the news media's problem." However, it is more likely that instances of misreporting remain a problem at *every* media level. The Lemberg Center for the Study of Violence, in investigating twenty-five incidents in which the news media had alleged sniping, found that, along with the wire services, local and nationally known newspapers bore a heavy responsibility for imprecise, distorted, and inaccurate reporting.

While treatment of racial disorders is generally more restrained today, the news media continue to overplay the more violent or sensational aspects of a story. The central media concern during the disorder at Cornell University last April, for example, was the emergence of the blacks from the student union. A picture of the students carrying rifles and shotguns, splashed across the nation, had a distorting effect on public opinion. The New York *Times* put the picture on page 1, and *Newsweek* used it on its cover the following week. Certain facts were largely ignored: prior to the disorder a cross had been burned in front of a black women's dormitory; the students had heard radio reports that carloads of armed whites were moving toward the campus; when the students emerged from the building their guns weren't loaded. What was basically a defensive response by a group of frightened students came across in the media as a terrorist act by student guerrillas. [Editor's Note: Richard M. Warshauer, senior editor of the *Cornell Daily Sun*, in a letter to the editor of the *Columbia Journalism Review* (Fall, 1970), claimed:

I agree with the author that the now-famous picture of the armed blacks emerging from the student union may have given many people the erroneous impression that the building was seized at gunpoint. Nevertheless, the fact that they thought it necessary to arm themselves at any time is without a doubt the crux of the story.

Approximately one hour after the crucial judiciary meeting ended a burning cross was discovered and extinguished by an Ithaca police detective. To say that that event was "largely ignored" reveals a lamentable narrowness of reading habits. It was well reported in *Life*, the New York *Times*, and AP stories to name a few. John Kifner of the *Times* was one of the first reporters on the takeover story because he was dispatched to Ithaca right after the cross incident.

The alleged "radio reports" that carloads of armed whites were moving toward the campus never existed. It is true that friends of the black students on campus had relayed such *rumors* to them, but there was never any truth to them; I am happy to say that local radio stations had the news judgment not to broadcast such inflammatory stories without checking their accuracy.

In stating that the guns were not loaded, the author fell for the transparent fiction given out by the Cornell administration. Although Cornell Vice President for Public Affairs Steven Muller positively stated that the guns were not loaded, a large group of reporters, including me, saw that the guns were indeed loaded as Muller signed an agreement with the black students.]

Aspects of the disorders are dramatic and do merit extensive coverage. But the media still tend to equate bad news with big news and to confuse the obvious with the relevant. Thus when sixty-five students at Brandeis University took over a building in 1969, it rated a story on the front page of the New York *Times*—despite the fact that there was no violence, that classes continued, and that the university suffered only minor inconvenience. I was on campus then. My only recollection of anything unusual was that on the first day or two an attendant asked to see my identification, and for the next week and a half I noticed large numbers of reporters, press cars, cameras, and other equipment. I sometimes wondered if there weren't more reporters outside than students inside the building.

The *Times*, along with most newspapers, missed the unusual climax at Brandeis. In a war of nerves with the students, President Morris Abram showed consummate skill in handling the situation, remaining flexible on the issues, mobilizing the support of the student body and faculty, and, above all, refusing to call in police. Eleven days after the crisis had begun the students quietly left the building—a dramatic victory for the Brandeis community, a dramatic example of how to handle a university crisis in contrast to fiascoes at Columbia and San Francisco State. Yet the students' departure merely merited a *Times* story about three inches long, well off the front page.

Disparities between the headlines and news stories are another problem. Often much less occurs in the story than the headline would indicate. Also in 1969, for example, some concerned parents in Jacksonville, Fla., removed their children from Kirby Smith Junior High School after a local radio station had broadcast an exaggerated report of a fight between black and white students. The school principal later indicated that "classes continued and there was no panic." Nevertheless the Miami *Herald* headlined its story April 25: MOMS MOB SCHOOL AFTER RIOT 'NEWS.' Sometimes no violence occurs in the story, dramatic headlines to the contrary. A story appearing in the Boston *Globe* last May 10, told of a peaceful rally by a small group of students at a local theological seminary. According to the *Globe*, the rally was "brief and orderly." But the headline above the story read NEWTON CAMPUS ERUPTS.

The use of the word "riot" presents another problem because it has no precise meaning in terms of current disorders. *Webster's* defines a "riot" as a "tumultuous disturbance of the public peace by three or more persons assembled together and acting with a common intent." The difficulty is that "riots" have become so frequent and come in so many sizes and shapes as to render the word meaningless. There is something ludicrous about lumping together as "riots" Detroit, with forty-three deaths, 7,000 arrests, and $45 million in property damage, and an incident in which three people break a few store windows. Yet this is precisely what the news media still do. The continued media use of the term contributes to an emotionally charged climate in which the public tends to view every event as an "incident," every incident as a "disturbance," and every disturbance as a "riot." Journalists would do well to drop the word from their vocabulary altogether.

No law says the media have to interpret and not simply report the news, but having assumed this responsibility they have an obligation to make reasonable judgments based on careful analysis. Unfortunately, journalistic attempts in the direction of social science research have been rather amateurish, particularly where new trends and patterns are concerned. The case of the Cleveland "shoot-out" is a good example. On July 23, 1968, an intense gun battle broke out between the police and a group of black nationalists led by Ahmed Evans. Before the disorder was over 16,400 National Guardsmen had been mobilized, nine persons had been killed, and there was property damage estimated at $2.6 million. The Cleveland *Press* on July 24, 1968 compared the violence to guerrilla activity in Vietnam:

... it didn't seem to be a Watts, or a Detroit, or a Newark. Or even a Hough of two years ago. No, this tragic night seemed to be a part of a plan.

A reporter writing in the New York *Times* of July 28, 1968, stated:

It marks perhaps the first documented case in recent history of black, armed, and organized violence against the police.

More recent reports have revealed that the "shoot-out" was something less than a planned uprising and that the situation was considerably more complicated than indicated initially. Unfortunately, following the events in Cleveland, disorders in which shots may have been fired were immediately suspected by the press of being part of a "wave." A series of errors involving a handful of cities became the basis of a myth—that the pattern of violence in 1968 had changed from spontaneous to premeditated outbreaks. Few of the nationally known newspapers and newsmagazines attempted to verify sniping reports coming out of the cities and over the wire services; few were willing to undertake independent investigations; and far too many were overly zealous in their assertions of a new "trend" based on limited and unconfirmed evidence. Unwittingly or not, the national media had constructed a scenario on armed uprisings.

Although having more time to check and verify reports than daily newspapers, the newsmagazines were even more vocal in their assertions of a "new pattern." On September 13, 1968, *Time* took note of an "ominous trend" and declared that the violence "appears to be changing from spontaneous combustion of a mob to the premediated shoot-outs of a far-out few." The story went on to indicate that "many battles" had begun with "well-planned sniping at police." Nearly a year later, on June 27, 1969—long after investigation by a task force of the National Commission on the Causes and Prevention of Violence, by the Lemberg Center, and by the New York *Times* (which reversed itself on the Cleveland question) had cast serious doubt about premeditated outbreaks in Cleveland and elsewhere—*Time* still was talking about the possibilities of a "guerrilla summer" and reminding its readers of the time in Cleveland when "police were lured into an ambush." Once started, myths are difficult to extinguish.

The most recent myth created by the media involves an alleged "shift" in racial disturbances from large to small cities. Last July 25 a syndicated reporter for the News Enterprise Association (NEA) noted:

The socially sizzling summer has begun—but unlike recent history, it seems to be the minor, not the major, cities which are sweltering.

In a article entitled "Riots, 1969 Style," *Newsweek* declared on August:

... the traditional riot scenario is still being played out this summer—with one major difference. This season the stage has shifted from the major population centers to such small and disparate communities as Kokomo, Ind., Santa Ana, Calif., Cairo, Ill., Middletown, Conn., and Farrell, Pa.

Last September 9 the New York *Times* captioned a picture:

New Riot Pattern: Rioting in Hartford, Conn., last week . . . underscored the fact that smaller cities this summer have had more racial trouble than the big ones.

Similar stories appeared about the same time in scores of other newspapers, including the *Wall Street Journal*, the Baltimore *News American*, the Woburn, Mass., *Times*, and the Pittsburgh *Press.*

In fact, racial disorders occurring over the past few years—not just during the summer of 1969—have been concentrated in smaller cities. About 75 percent of all outbreaks recorded in 1968 by the Lemberg Center's Civil Disorder Clearinghouse occurred outside the 100 largest cities. For the first six months of 1969 and also for the summer no appreciable change in the percentage was noted. Furthermore, many of the cities cited as prototypes of this latest "new pattern"—Hartford and Middletown, Conn., Cairo, Ill.—have had disorders in previous years. The difference is that such outbreaks were completely overshadowed by a few enormous outbreaks in large cities such as Newark and Detroit.

Discovering the origin of these and other myths would be useful—a faulty wire service report, an inept reporter, an unreliable source. But aside from the fact that such a task would be almost impossible, it would miss a central point—that the system of reporting ensures that errors of fact and interpretation may be repeated, compounded, and reformulated as myths. In recent years the various components of the media have become extremely intertwined and dependent upon one another. The wire services, the nationally known newspapers, and the newsmagazines feed one another news and information. While the system undoubtedly speeds the flow of news to the public, it has encouraged a parrot-like character in which the various media segments tend to reproduce rather than examine one another's views.

In this respect the New York *Times'* caption proclaiming a NEW

PATTERN assumes greater significance. Prior to its appearance in the *Times*, I talked with Jack Rosenthal, who had been working on a story on the relatively cool summer. When the subject of a new "shift" in violence came up I indicated that such allegations were false and misleading. Rosenthal wrote a thoughtful story, dwelling on police-community relations, civic programs, and the new community spirit among blacks. His story made no mention of a "new riot pattern." Apparently the caption writer had paid more attention to what *Newsweek* and the *Wall Street Journal* were saying than to his colleague at the *Times*.

The failure of the media to tell the complete story in the case of Cornell or the right story in the case of Cleveland goes beyond a lack of initiative or an inclination to sensationalize. It also indicates a bias—one which, notwithstanding Vice President Agnew's declarations, cuts *across* political and geographical lines. The media are no more aware of this bias than is the general public aware of its own. In part, we could call it a class bias in that those who comprise media staffs—reporters, editors, headline writers, etc.—are part of the vast American middle class and, as such, express its views, values, and standards.

Both the general public and the media share the same dislike of protestors; both are unable to understand violence as an expression of protest against oppressive conditions; both prefer the myth of orderly, peaceful change, extolling the virtues of private property and public decorum. People are expected to behave in a certain way; they just don't go around yelling and cursing or throwing rocks. Both will grant that it took a revolution to secure our independence and a civil war to end slavery (at least officially), but that was all long ago and somehow different. The bias also has elements of racism in that color is never far from the surface. It is difficult to say where the class bias begins and racist bias ends. These elements are inseparable and reenforce each other, and both manifest themselves in the thinking of the public and media alike.

A growing body of research shows that racial disorders are a part of the social process. The process includes an accumulation of grievances, a series of tension-heightening incidents such as police harassment, and a precipitating event such as an arrest which crystallizes the tensions and grievances that have mounted—the "last straw" that triggers the violence. The "typical rioter" is young, better educated than the average inner-city black, and more dissatisfied. He wants a better job but feels that prospective employers will discriminate against him. He is likely to be a long-term resident of the city.

(In a survey in Detroit, 90 per cent of those arrested were from Detroit, 78 per cent lived in the state, and only 1 per cent lived outside the state.) He is extremely proud of his race and is politically conscious. He is more interested in and informed about politics than blacks who are not involved in a disorder. He is also more inclined toward political activism. (In one survey, nearly 40 per cent of the participants in the disorder—as compared to only about 25 per cent of the nonparticipants—reported having been involved in civil rights activity.) Finally, he receives substantial support from the rest of his community, which does not participate but regards the violence as necessary and beneficial.

As important as the findings in these studies are, they have made virtually no impact on the vast majority of the public. Most Americans continue to believe that violence is caused by a tiny and insignificant minority, that "outside agitators" and "criminal elements" are mainly responsible for isolated outbursts that have little or no social significance. Intellectuals must share a portion of the blame for this situation. Having completed their studies, they have been notoriously reluctant to roll up their academic shirtsleeves and assume leadership in presenting their ideas to the public. There is a trace of condescension in their assumption that good ideas from above will somehow trickle down to the "masses of asses," as one academic I know calls them.

Greater responsibility for the failure to confront the public's resistance rests with the news media. They have failed to commit their power and prestige on behalf of such studies. They have failed to place the ideas before the public and push for reform in an aggressive, effective manner—settling for a splash of headlines and stories initially, and little followup. Instead the media have opted for the status quo, reflecting, sustaining, and perpetuating outworn beliefs of their predominantly white audience.

Historically the notion of plots and conspiracies has always had great currency in this country—and in other countries, too. Prior to the Civil War, Southerners frequently viewed abolitionists as "outside agitators" trying to stir up the happy slaves. Violent interracial clashes during World War I were said to have been instigated by the Bolsheviks, and the outbreak in Detroit in 1943 was attributed to an "Axis plot." The current wave of disorders has been blamed on individuals such as Stokely Carmichael and H. Rap Brown or, for those who like a more international flavor, "Communist infiltrators." In a survey of six Northern cities by the Lemberg Center, 77 per cent of all whites interviewed believed that "outside agitators" were a major contributing cause of disorders. When Los Angeles Mayor Sam Yorty blamed a rash of school disorders on a conspiracy of the Black Student Union, the Students for a Democratic Society, Communist sympathizers, and the National Council of Churches, he was following a long—though not very honorable—tradition.

Such allegations are usually made without a shred of evidence, except for an occasional "someone told me so." Nevertheless the media have frequently taken their cues from the public in formulating and circulating such reports. Misinterpretations of the events in Cleveland, along with assertions of a "new pattern" of premeditated violence, are blatant examples of this form of bias. But more often the bias is expressed in more subtle ways. For example, when rumors circulated that "outside agitators" were involved in a disturbance in Omaha, Neb., a news story appearing in the Arkansas *Gazette* June 27, 1969 made reference to the rumors but also mentioned that the mayor had no evidence to support such reports. Yet, the headline above the story read: 'OUTSIDERS' LINKED TO OMAHA RIOTING.

A look at the way in which the disorders are written up reveals, tragically, that the majority of the media and the public share essentially the same view of the violence—as meaningless, purposeless, senseless, irrational. Media treatment of the disorders following the assassination of Rev. Martin Luther King, Jr., illustrates the point. The sense of loss and injury among blacks at the time of the assassination was extremely great—far greater than among whites. The unprecedented wave of disorders—approximately 200—was expressive of the anger, bitterness, resentment, frustration that black people everywhere felt.

How did the media handle the disorders? Stories in just two newspapers analyzed—the Buffalo *News* of April 9, 1968 (the day of Dr. King's funeral), and the Trenton *Times-Advertiser* one day later—are fairly typical. No attempt is made to place the violence in a social context. The reference to the assassination of Dr. King is perfunctory, with only a passing mention of his funeral and a few shouts about his death. Value-laden words receive unusual emphasis. The participants are "marauders," not men; they "rove" instead of run; they move in "gangs," not groups; they engage in "vandalism," not simply violence.

We have all grown so used to viewing blacks as stereotyped criminals that it is difficult to picture them in any other role; hence such frequent press concoctions as "roving gangs," "roving vandals," roving gangs of rampaging teenagers," or, for variety, "a window-smashing rampage of roving gangs of Negro youths." The New York

Times assertion last July 1 that "roving bands of ruffians" were involved in a disturbance in Middletown, Conn., seems somewhat feeble by comparison. The effect of such treatment by the media is to pander to the public's prejudice, reenforcing stereotypes, myths, and other outmoded beliefs. The media not only frighten the public but confuse it as well.

And let us not forget the effects on the news media. The proliferation of underground newspapers, radical publications, black journals, as well as underground radio stations of FM bands held by churches and universities, indicates that the media are failing to reach certain groups, and that they still lack sensitivity, sophistication, and skepticism commensurate with their important and strategic position. [Editor's Note: The following report accompanied the original article.]

Reporting conflict in an age of change. . . .

Conflict is part of the crucible of change. It may yield progress or repression. But conflict is not a state of social equilibrium. Whether conflict is resolved by violence or cooperation will depend in part upon the actors' perceptions of the world about them. Providing an accurate perception of that world is the media's most important responsibility. . . .

Collectively, and within their own organizations, the news media can accomplish much before . . . disorder starts. Indeed, how much they do may determine whether it starts at all or how much it grows. . . .

The most controversial and difficult issue for radio and television centers on the delay of news. Where the news event is of a kind likely to symbolize past injustices to any significant group in the community, there is a danger that such an event may trigger a large-scale disorder. Moreover, once a crowd has begun to gather at the scene of such an event, immediate broadcast of the event and its precise location is likely to draw additional persons to the area and add to crowd-control problems of the police, thereby contributing to the likelihood of a violent outbreak and its severity if it does occur. . . .

Once it is decided that the incident is potentially inflammatory or may attract a crowd to the scene, most of the newsmen with whom we have discussed the problem suggest a delay of at least thirty minutes to confirm the story, make sure the facts are clear, and to avoid exaggeration. Under particular circumstances it may require a delay of an hour or longer. Media transmittal of unconfirmed reports, emotional or unbalanced accounts, and visual portrayals of violence without perspective can do at least as much damage as news delay.

Where communitywide guidelines are in effect, it is best to designate one journalist representative to determine the length of the embargo. Such centralization eliminates the competitive pressures that tend to undermine this policy. A complete embargo beyond one hour, and preferably beyond thirty minutes, probably cannot be justified. . . .

In reporting both incidents that may grow to disorders and the disorders themselves, the media can make additional preparations within their own organizations. Some TV stations, for example, have already made the decision not to cover riots with live mobile television units. Rather than send conspicuous shoulder-braced sound cameras to a riot, they can plan to send the much smaller, hand-held silent camera, plus a man with a tape recorder to pick up random sound. Similarly, they can use black and white instead of color film, which requires more light; in this way, they can reduce the need for crowd-attracting lights and apparatus. They should plan in advance the deployment of manpower within the news organization, what the process for assimilation shall be, and who shall exercise responsibility at each stage.

A neighborhood fight should not be called a riot. A disturbance should not be designated racial without confirmation. Accuracy should have priority over speed. The story, particularly its violent aspects, should be kept in perspective. . . .

If, for example, the police radio carries a report of a National Guardsman being shot, it is tempting to put this on the air, because it has the surface authenticity of a police report. Many of these reports are based on rumors and are simply requests for confirmation by a police officer. The story is skimpy; no details substantiate it. During the tension of a riot, the police can act hastily and carelessly. Moreover, the day is past when everything the police say should be broadcast as "truth." The report must be confirmed. . . .

News is the unusual, the extraordinary; it is something that doesn't happen every day. The media have no need to report each airliner that arrives safely; it is not a matter of general public interest. The objection, however, is not that the media focus upon the unusual; rather it is that they focus on the unusual aspects of the unusual. Recall, for example, the coverage of the meeting at Watts, devoted to discussing grievances and what could be done to calm a tense racial situation. The media focused on the extremist statements of one sixteen-year-old-boy. This was not a representative portrayal of a legitimate news event. . . .

The media have properly rejected the suggestion that they report "good" news simply because it is good. It apparently has not occurred to very many newsmen, however, that events should not go unreported simply because they involve a nonviolent resolution of conflict. One function of the media is to aid in coordinating society's response to change. They can fulfill this function in part by telling the public how conflicts are resolved nonviolently and by giving such resolutions the same prominence they give the violent manifestations of conflict. . . .

The press does provide a marketplace for ideas, but it is not of the sort commonly supposed. The increased level of violence in this country today is partially owing to the sluggish response of our institutions to social change; but the press shares in this sluggishness, and an important part of its inadequacy is the inability of new and different voices to gain routine and peaceful access to the centralized news media. . . . It should become habitual editorial policy to display fairly and clearly the opinions, analyses, and solutions offered by a wide variety of people, expert and non-expert, covering the spectrum, regardless of the proprietor's personal position.

Too many news organizations fear social ideas and social action. As a result, they stimulate, dissatisfy, and arouse anxiety only to fall silent or limit themselves to irrelevant cliches when thoughtful solutions are required. Alternative solutions to our most urgent social problems, based on the work of our most imaginative social thinkers, and written with the clarity that only a good journalist can produce, ought to be standard. . . .

America can look forward to change—the only certainty. This will require not only information about events, violent and nonviolent, but ideas about what to do about these events. . . .

Specifically we recommend:

A. The Corporation for Public Broadcasting be provided with a budget for news and public affairs programming comparable to that of the television networks. . . .

B. The Justice Department and the Federal Communications Commission should scrutinize carefully all mergers, license applications, and license transfers which would result in greater concentration of media ownership. . . .

C. Perhaps most important is that the government must stay abreast of new technological developments in the communications industry and be prepared to assure that further concentration of control does not occur. This is particularly important with respect to CATV. . . .

D. There is a good deal of confusion, particularly among practicing broadcast journalists, about what the fairness doctrine requires. . . . We recommend that the FCC clarify this ambiguity and resolve it along the lines indicated.

E. Each year the Federal Communications Commission must pass on approximately 2,500 broadcast license renewal applications. . . . If the Commission is to effectively discharge its mandate, it must develop at least broad guidelines for such determinations in order that its staff can bring to the Commission's attention those cases that raise serious questions. . . .

F. Journalists should reexamine the degree to which existing news judgments incorporate obsolete standards, including a tendency to report violence because it is sensational, rather than because it is significant. Moreover, in reporting conflict, the press should develop a special sensitivity to the danger of overstating the degree of conflict.

G. Beyond reexaming existing standards for reporting violence, newsmen should reconsider the contemporary utility of well established newsgathering practices. Perhaps most important is the interpretive news stories—which can be written with time for calm reflection and balanced judgment—be allocated more resources and be given greater prominence. For newspapers, this means running such stories regularly on page 1. . . .

H. We strongly recommend: (1) that the media hire and train increased numbers of newsmen from minority groups; (2) that the the media provide the kind of regular surveillance of minority group activities which it applies to other segments of the community; (3) that the media provide information to local groups about preparing press releases and, more generally securing access to the media through traditional channels short of demonstration, confrontation, and violence; (4) the use of ghetto "stringers"; (5) inclusion of members of miniority groups in day-to-day news, such as births, deaths, weddings, business promotions, opening of new businesses, and social functions; (6) more background and in-depth stories on social issues and particularly those stories dealing with facets of the American scene with which the majority of the audience have little actual experience.

I. There is a need for greater interaction between the news media and the community and for responsible criticism of media performance. There are a number of ways in which this can be brought about:

(1) News organizations should establish and publicize the existence of grievance machinery or internal appeal boards to hear the complaints of persons who feel that their viewpoint has been unfairly excluded from the press or that the press coverage of an event in which they were involved is inaccurate. Such a program has worked well at the Louisville *Courier-Journal.*

(2) News organizations should encourage local press councils to provide a continuing exchange of views between the news media personnel and representative members of the community.

(3) Journalism schools should ingrain in their students a tradition of continuous reexamination and self-criticism through, *inter alia,* the establishment of journalism reviews and programs designed to prepare the student to apply new findings in communications theory to the practical problems of communicating the news.

(4) The establishment in other major metropolitan areas of publications like the *Chicago Journalism Review* which provide a forum for public debate on news media performance.

(5) News organizations should freely criticize other news organizations and report on their performance the same as they would any other institution in our society. . . .

J. We endorse the mid-career training programs offered at some universities and urge that more media owners and operators, particularly television, make time and funds available to their newsmen to take advantage of these programs.

K. We recommend that every news medium establish a code or other form of guideline to be followed in the coverage of riots or other events involving group violence. . . .

L. We recommend that news organizations resist those critics who would have them deny coverage to protest. The news media can reduce substantially whatever incentive they provide for violence by providing balanced treatment of at least four aspects of demonstrations:

(1) The purpose of the demonstration. What is the nature of the grievance? Why are the demonstrators there?

(2) The events leading up to the demonstration. Have other remedies been sought; if so, what has been the response of those addressed?

(3) The demonstration. How many people were present? How did they conduct themselves? Do not focus only on the most extreme conduct or dress.

(4) The provocations, if any, and the official response. Why were the demonstrators trying to provoke the police? Did the police use more force than necessary to maintain order? Were there any extenuating circumstances, such as physical exhaustion or personal security of political candidates?

The standard for determing whether an event will be covered should place more emphasis on the nature of the grievance, the number of people affected, the severity of the grievance and less emphasis on the willingness of the aggrieved to engage in violence or the likelihood that they will. . . .

—*Mass Media and Violence*,
Report to the National Commission
on the Causes and Prevention of Violence.

IS ANYTHING UNPRINTABLE?

Lee H. Smith

When Michael McClure's play, *The Beard*, opened in New York in late 1967, the daily reviews were unanimous on two points. They didn't like the play very much and they didn't want to talk about it very much. The reason for the latter seems clear. The play, a fanciful sex duel between Jean Harlow and Billy the Kid not only contained a good deal of verbal obscenity, it also ended in one of the most startling scenes ever staged. *The New York Times* described that finale as "a highly publicized sexual act" (referring, somewhat cryptically, to the notoriety the play had received in San Francisco). The *Daily News* called it "an unorthodox sex act." The *New York Post* glided over it as "a sexual act that can't be described in a family newspaper." What the reviews couldn't say—or wouldn't say—was what the fuss was all about: an act of cunnilingus.

For better or for worse, American society has become increasingly concerned with its sex life and more and more eager to talk about it in public. The taboos against strong language and references to sex are vanishing with such staggering speed that it is often hard to remember what last year's taboos were. Two years ago, the movie *Who's Afraid of Virginia Woolf?* created a stir when Richard Burton said "hump the hostess." Today, the film *In Cold Blood* uses much earthier language and no one bothers to mention it. Norman Mailer was an iconoclast when he wrote the verb "fug" in *The Naked and The Dead*. In his latest novel, *Why Are We In Vietnam?*, he uses much more explicit obscenities much more often and hardly anyone is surprised.

Lee H. Smith studied the standard of editing for "family" consumption while an associate editor at *Newsweek*, **specializing in the coverage of the news media. His Spring, 1968 article is used here with permission of** *Columbia Journalism Review*.

Candor is not restricted to the arts. Women hem their skirts well above their knees and trot off to cocktail parties where "The Pill" has replaced breastfeeding versus bottlefeeding as the favorite topic of conversation. Homosexuals have emerged from the shadows to parade in front of the White House and the Pentagon to demand equality, including the right to serve in the armed forces. August state legislatures openly debate the pros and cons of relaxing the laws for abortion—a word that used to be anathema almost everywhere. Schools across the country are beginning to feel the pressure to provide sex education, even for grammar school pupils.

The sexual revolution is real enough. For responsible newspapers, magazines, and radio and television stations that presents a problem: How can they report the revolution without compromising their standards? Some publications, of course, have a vested interest in cheering the revolution on. Magazines such as *Playboy* and its female counterpart, *Cosmopolitan*, often seem to be leading the way. But many more editors seem to be thoroughly confused. They want to keep up with what's happening but they aren't quite certain how to do it. More and more editors are faced with the problem of separating what is pertinent from what is simply prurient and trying to define the line between good reporting and bad taste. Some publications have been extremely bold, others far too reticent. And surprisingly, television—usually thought of as the meekest of the media—may be on its way to establishing a standard that accepts progress and yet maintains good taste; it may help the so-called "family" publications decide what can be said and what cannot.

Government censorship doesn't offer much guidance. The Supreme Court in recent years has decided it will allow just about anything short of what it considers hard-core pornography or (in the case of Ralph Ginzburg's conviction) hard-sell titillation—boundaries most editors have no intention of approaching. A few publications are exploring and exploiting that frontier, most recently the growing band of underground newspapers scattered in hippie enclaves from New York's East Village to San Francisco's Haight Ashbury district. The *East Village Other*, one of the most successful undergrounders, recently displayed, for example, a somewhat fuzzy photograph of what appeared to be an act of homosexual fellatio. And in the classified pages anyone can put his sexual appetites on the block. One ad in the same issue ran: "Attention!!! Dominant male wishes to meet docile female, gay or straight. We will have a whipping good time." As a result of such frankness, the Brooklyn District Attorney's office seized 1000 copies of the paper and the editors of *EVO* are going to have to defend their candor in court.

The older *Village Voice*, which straddles the underground and the Establishment, draws the line at peddling perversion in its classifieds. "If you allow those," says editor Daniel Wolf, "suddenly you discover you're running an adjunct to Bellevue." But by most standards the *Voice* is unabashedly frank. "We have always been more open than most papers," observes Wolf. The *Voice* has used the common four-letter words freely for years. Lately the *Voice* has started running front-on photographs of nudes, collected by *Voice* photographers making the rounds of Greenwich Village dances and art shows. "We didn't sit around and discuss it," says Wolf. "We had the pictures and we just said 'what the hell' and shoved them in."

At other publications such decisions are momentous, even when an editor knows he is reaching a limited, sophisticated, and well-educated audience. Robert Manning, editor of *The Atlantic*, recalls pondering over a reportorial piece on Harlem in which the writer quoted a young boy sticking his head out the window and shouting "Fuck you, white cop." Says Manning: "I looked at it, stared at it, and finally decided the only way to convey the full gut of it was to use it. The idea that a Negro boy of four, five, or six was already conditioned to that extent seemed to me to be something worth conveying. Dots would have undercut the impact."

Manning declines to allow four-letter words in fiction, but Willie Morris, editor of *Harper's*, says he will permit four-letter words in fiction or nonfiction when they are used by established authors. "This is something we would never do lightly," says Morris, "but times have changed. American readers are now infinitely more sophisticated than at any other time and they even demand more of the language than at any other time." Morris turned over the entire March issue of the magazine to Norman Mailer—an act that would make most editors shudder—for his journalistic report, "The Steps of the Pentagon." The report is witty, moving, and, in part, scatological. [Editor's Note: Morris was fired from *Harper's* in early 1971 and seven editors quit in support. But contrary to popular opinion, the disagreement did not arise solely from his turning over the entire March issue, 48,000 words, to Mailer for a rebuttal to Women's Liberation spiced with four-letter words. It was, said *Saturday Review*, caused more by a philosophical argument over "how to edit an intellectual magazine in today's market."]

Intellectual monthlies such as *Harper's* and *The Atlantic* can proceed rather boldly without worrying about offending large groups of readers. Candor becomes a real problem for general circulation newspapers and magazines that reach mass audiences. Advertising departments are particularly nervous. They diligently "ink in" clothes on unclad starlets in movie ads and edit out the explicit language underneath. When the Yugoslav film *Love Affair—Or The Case of the Missing Switchboard Operator* opened in New York in February the *Times* and the *Post* were sent an ad displaying a nude woman lying face down on a bed. Both newspapers "draped" a towel over her and the *Post* added a brassiere as well. This cover-up seemed reasonable enough. The ad was nothing but a cheap come-on.

Often, however, advertising departments are over-zealous. When the Yale University School of Drama opened its season last fall, the school routinely sent out an ad that listed the plays, including John Ford's seventeenth-century tragedy *'Tis Pity She's A Whore.* The *New Haven Register* reformed the lady somewhat and changed the title to *'Tis Pity She's Bad.* The *Hartford Courant* turned her into a mystery woman by truncating the title to read *'Tis Pity She's.* Donald Spargo, advertising director for the *Register,* explained that the wording of the ad was read to him over the phone and that if he had realized it was a title, he probably wouldn't have touched it. But Sidney Kaplan, advertising manager for the *Courant,* stood fast. "We just didn't run it period," he snapped. "We try to run a clean newspaper."

The New York Times Book Review recently became alarmed that a deluge of ads for marriage manuals and other non-fiction works dealing with sex was giving the book review a bad image. As a result, the *Times* decided to close the *Review,* probably the country's major display case for publishers, to all non-fiction sex books—the important as well as the trivial and the titillating.

Editors are similarly fearful that the wrong word or picture is going to bring them reprisals from their readership. Over the past twenty years or so they have been slowly and cautiously scratching out such euphemisms as "social disease," "illegal operation," and "assault" and penciling in the more specific "syphilis," "abortion," and "rape." In some cases they have moved boldly. *Newsweek* magazine put a partly nude Jane Fonda on its cover to illustrate its special report on "The Permissive Society." *Life* magazine ran an excerpt from *The Naked Ape* in which British zoologist Desmond Morris examines man as a primate. The first paragraph of the excerpt included the sentence: "He [man] is proud that he has the biggest brain of all the primates but attempts to conceal the fact that he also has the biggest penis, preferring to accord this honor falsely to the mighty gorilla." (That same observation was to cause a considerable amount of trouble for other publications later.)

Some newspapers have been equally outspoken. Unfortunately, one of the best of them is now dead: the *New York Herald Tribune.* When Dr. William H. Masters and Mrs. Virginia Johnson published *Human Sexual Response,* a physiological study of the sexual act, in 1966, the *Herald Tribune* science editor, Earl Ubell, was unabashed in his summary and consequently helped dispel some disturbing myths about sexual performance. In paraphasing the book's conclusions Ubell included such paragraphs as: "Neither the size of the male sex organ, the penis, nor that of its corresponding anatomical part in the female, the clitoris, has any relation to the adequacy of the man or woman as a sex partner."

The New York Times was more reticent, for which the *Times* is now apologetic. "I think we were wrong," says *Times* managing editor E. Clifton Daniel. "This was a serious work and it would have been perfectly acceptable to quote words such as penis and clitoris."

The *Times* has become more candid recently and such sensitive topics as homosexuality are reported liberally. And in its recent series on the drug-obsessed society the *Times* quoted a girl who said she took amphetamines to prolong her sexual activities. "I once stayed in bed for three days with a man," the girl was quoted as saying, "taking pills to keep going and smoking pot to enjoy myself." Still, the *Times* proceeds cautiously. When theater critic Clive Barnes reviewed *The Beard* he first wrote the word "cunnilingus." Metropolitan news editor Arthur Gelb asked him to take the word out: "It wasn't a big argument but at this time I just don't think we should use it. That might not be the case a month from now."

Other newspapers, perhaps a majority, are much more conservative. A former reporter on one of the largest papers in upstate New York says her movie reviews were consistently bowdlerized. In discussing *A Guide for the Married Man* she tried to convey the tone of the film by referring to "bouncing bosoms and fannies." The phrase was softened to read "flouncing females." In outlining the plot of *The Family Way* she said of the young bride: "After six weeks of marriage she was still a virgin." The desk changed it to read: "The marriage was not consummated"—a throwback to 1953 when the word "virgin" made *The Moon Is Blue* a "dirty" movie.

Usually, such editing is carried out quietly. But in January 1968 two of the nation's most influential publications—*The Chicago Tribune* and *The Washington Post*—were caught editing in public. The two papers decided to recall some 1.7 million copies of *Book World,* the Sunday book review supplement they have published jointly since last September, when they spotted a page-one review they found offensive.

Peter Farb, a New Yorker who writes science books for laymen, reviewed Morris's *The Naked Ape* and paraphrased some of the book's conclusions, including: "The human male and not the gorilla possesses the largest penis of all primates; the human's preferred face-to-face mating is due to the frontal position of sexual signaling devices."

In New York, *Book World's* editor, Byron Dobell, a former managing editor of *Esquire* magazine, approved the review and dispatched it to be printed for the *Post* in Philadelphia and to Chicago to be printed for the *Tribune*. *Tribune* editor W.D. Maxwell and publisher J. Howard Wood picked up copies from an early press run and apparently carried them off to the *Tribune* board of directors' meeting in Fort Lauderdale, Florida. Five days before the book review was scheduled to appear, Maxwell put in an urgent call to Thomas Furlong, managing editor in charge of features. Maxwell's order was to kill the review. Some 3,000 copies had already been sent to bookstores, libraries, and publishers, but the *Tribune* managed to collect more than a million copies that had been sent to distributors or were still in the plant. The page-one review was killed and a review that was scheduled to have run the following week was substituted. (Estimates of the cost of the kill ranged from $30,000 to $100,000.) The *Post* did not kill the review but did strike out the lines referring to penis from its 500,000 copies. (The *Post* had been much bolder in 1966 when it ran Ubell's review of *Human Sexual Response.*)

The *Tribune's* kill seemed to be consistent with Maxwell's policy. The story goes that in 1961 he was given a copy of *The Carpetbaggers* by a well-meaning friend who thought it was a Reconstruction Novel. Maxwell was so shocked that he ordered the book eliminated from the *Tribune's* best-seller list and, to exclude similar works, he changed the name of the section to "Among the Best-Sellers." *Tribune* readers were thus "protected" from a significant—if depressing—scrap of sociology: The American public buys a lot of trash.

Because it does so much of its editing in public—"bleeping out" of offensive words—television often seems to be the most cautious of the media. But lately the bleeps have been fading and television has been growing much bolder. Five years ago, David Susskind invited a group of panelists that included *Playboy* editor and publisher Hugh Hefner and psychologist Dr. Albert Ellis to discuss "The Sexual Revolution in America." The show was taped but Bennett Korn, then a vice president of WNEW, refused to let it go on the air. Last year Susskind taped an even more delicate discussion, "Homosexuality: Perversion or Sickness?", with two psychiatrists and Dick Leitsch, president of the homosexual Mattachine Society. The show was broadcast to thirty cities across the country without objection from station managements.

Earl Ubell, who is now science editor for WCBS-TV, believes that he has been just as frank on television as he was on the *Herald Tribune* and that his only restraint is to make certain he delivers his information on sex soberly with no hint of a snicker or a raised eyebrow. And recently, Johnny Carson demonstrated that even a mass audience of network viewers will accept a serious discussion of sex. Carson interviewed Desmond Morris on *The Tonight Show* and needled *The Chicago Tribune*. "You talked about his [man's] penis," Carson said to Morris. "And they took that out of the paper in Chicago, because it would offend people. . . . And I don't understand it, in this day and age, that you could not use that in a family newspaper." No bleep. No outraged phone calls to local television stations. Ernest Lee Jahncke Jr., NBC's vice president for standards and practices, explains why the network didn't bleep the reference. "This wasn't a lot of quipping and kidding around," he says. "It was a serious discussion, an adult discussion."

Television seems to be developing an "adult" standard for coping with the problem of sexual candor. Newspapers and many magazines persist in feeling inhibited by "family" standards. Even *The Wall Street Journal*—hardly a publication one passes on to the children—falls back on this excuse. When Edmund Fuller reviewed Mailer's *Why Are We in Vietnam?* for the *Journal* last fall he said: "Whether or not this newspaper is a family one depends, we suppose, on the family. But it is enough of one that we are restricted from offering you a slice of this pungent literary haggis for your own revulsion." [Editor's Note: The *Washington Post* once ran a news story, editorial and cartoon about a controversy over a four-letter word but never revealed directly or indirectly what word was at issue. A quote from the editorial:

> People who propose to take sides on the titanic scandal at McKinley High School over the classroom use of an essay entitled *The Case for Retiring Our Most Overworked Four-Letter Word* might be well advised to read the essay. Most of them, we surmise, will find it instructive (though perhaps not edifying), provocative, amusing, rather sensible and slightly shocking—but not dirty, obscene or pornographic within any reasonable meaning of those painfully overworked terms.]

The premise that mass publications must be edited for "families" always seems to ignore the fact that families are growing up. Also, it begs the question of why publications should be edited for the most innocent reader. Most readers (if Marshall McLuhan is right, all readers) are adults and want to be written to as adults. Furthermore, the "family" standard is an unprofessional one that isn't applied to other areas of coverage. Any correspondent who filed from Saigon that he is witnessing a war that can't be talked about in a family newspaper would be hastily recalled.

This does not mean that editors should discard good taste and indulge themselves in titillation and gratuitous obscenity. On the contrary, it means that they should use good taste as a standard— their own good taste—and not waste their time trying to anticipate the most hysterical reaction of the most sensitive reader. The story of the candid society is too big to be ignored and from all indications it will run for a long time.

PORNOGRAPHY AND PROPAGANDA

John Thompson

For all I know, the "Frank Newman" who wrote *Barbara* may actually be named Frank Newman, and the "Odette Newman" credited with *So You Think Sex Is Dirty?* may be a real name too. Who is Norman Singer, author of *The Babysitter, The Hungry Husband, The Lay of the Land*, and other titles in the various series of dirty books now published in America by Maurice Girodias? Vladimir Nabokov, author of the *Lolita* which Girodias published in the old Traveller's Companion editions in Paris, is a real name; and so (I believe) is J.P. Donleavy, credited with *The Ginger Man* when it was first published there. For *Candy*, though, Mason Hoffenberg and Terry Southern chose to use a pseudonym. So one doesn't know, anymore than one knows the bibliographical data on Grove Press books like *A Man With A Maid*, advertised first as underground Victoriana and then as being "in the tradition of" those kind of dirty books—and now honored with a sequel which seems to be pirated. No, pirated is not quite

John Thompson, member of the English faculty at State University of New York, Stony Brook, Long Island, regularly reviews fiction for *Commentary*. His August, 1969 article is reprinted with permission from *Commentary*, copyright 1969, by the American Jewish Committee.

the word: what is it when an additional volume borrowing the title and form of the original is published with the claim that it is an extension of the original? In this case, probably just a hoax upon a hoax.

Thus the old aura of the surreptitous manages to cling to dirty books even though in the name of truth and liberation they now offer publicly for sale material that goes far beyond anything that I, at least, ever saw of the old-fashioned secret printings. If Girodias and Barney Rosset confess to their publishing enterprise, many of their authors do not; and if the dirty book shops flourish openly, not only in Times Square but in other parts of town, they are not usually engaged in the general book trade. My small acquaintance with the old Traveller's Companion Series in Paris was gained by finding them here and there among other books in regular book stores or in stalls on the quais; the dirty book shop I have been patronizing on the Upper West Side has nothing but this one specialty. Signs proclaim No Browsing. Fee of $2.00 For Looking at Magazines if No Purchase. The clerk sits high in a sort of observation perch. When I was in there the other day, some innocent appeared asking for the Monarch Review series. His instinct was somehow correct, for these trots also used to be thought indecorous and students didn't bring them to class. The clerk said, "This is a erotic book store. We got nothing here but erotic sex books." What you buy he seals in a plain brown paper sack.

The recent outcropping of dirty weekly papers was peddled openly, in New York at least, on regular newsstands, and purported to be leading a crusade against the older and acceptable type of dirty papers on these stands, those that have headlines like "She Boiled Her Baby and Ate It." With their raucous barracks language, graffiti-like art works, and homosexual pin-ups, these strange publications also seemed to be assaulting the kind of old-fashioned fraternity-house view of sex presented in *Esquire* and *Playboy*. Unlike the snub-nosed monsters who coyly display their balloon-like mammary glands in those magazines, the women in the dirty papers had pubic hair and genitals, and as often as not pimples, soiled feet, and breasts as detumescent as the male organs also photographed there with all the art of a *Daily News* car-crash report. The crusaders acted so boldly, meanwhile plastering bright labels on their covers reading: "Warning—Adult Sex Material. If you are liable to be offended by such material kindly lay off and place back on pile neatly. Thank you. This literature is not intended for minors and under no circumstances are they to view it, possess it, or place orders for the merchandise offered herein." This plea, apparently intended as justification under recent court rulings, is perhaps less a copping out than itself an advertisement; still, it is something less than a real declaration of sexual independence.

The aura clings also to your fearless reviewer, bringing to the pages of a respectable magazine notices of a kind of literature the magazine would never publish nor most of its readers purchase anywhere. The only reviews of these books I have seen were in the dirty weekly papers which seem now finally to be suppressed after several previous attempts failed. And as an indication of the ambiguity to say the least of this reviewer's attitude, let me tell how I was speaking to a friend of mine who also collected these curiosities with as much interest and amusement as I did. I told him of the most recent "bust"; there was a moment of telepathic communication; and we both said, "Good." What we wordlessly confessed was, of course, that if everyone could get this stuff it was not going to be fun anymore.

* * *

No doubt most other educated persons know more of biology than I do, and certainly I could relieve at least a part of my ignorance with a few more hours in the library. But that is not what I mean. I mean such knowledge as I have available at any moment in my mind for the notions and decisions about sex that come to bemuse or frighten me. But doesn't it seem that the human race might well be content with what nature has arranged for us in this matter? Certainly our system of reproduction is fantastically, even, as we are so often told now, threateningly successful. We are indeed attracted to one another, male and female, we manage the physical mechanics of fertilization with appalling success, and as if this were not enough, we have almost universally among our species a mating system which insures for most of us the constant availability of a willing sexual partner, an availability furthered not only by our family system but (which came first?) by the fact that unlike other mammals we are not dependent on cycles of female estrous for sexual stimulation. Folklore, gossip, and Kinsey assure us that we can if we wish go through the motions of the act of reproduction every day of our lives practically from the onset of puberty. Yet who would not laugh to hear me say now, What more do we want?

The first and obviously correct assumption of the dirty books is that we want a great deal more. We want sex in the head, if I may be permitted D.H. Lawrence's old phrase, invented by him when it could mean something it would not mean today, at least in dirty books. We want to know how other people do it, we want to hear them talk about it, we want to talk about it, we want to see it, or see pictures of it; many if not all of us want not just the genital contacts of the reproductive process but strange mockeries of the process which (in my innocent biology) I believe the other mammals not in "domestic" or other captivity find little time for. This kind of curiosity is one thing the dirty books satisfy.

And this seems to me useful. The ignorance of even sophisticated people cannot be overestimated. Recently, among some of my literary friends, I have found I am likely to be asked not about some play or film or some new novel but rather this, "Have you read *Barbara* yet?" I wanted to recite this simple question first only in the connection of how topical these dirty books are; but in this other connection, in that of our ignorance, the query has a sequel. The lady asking the question, a novelist of some note, went on to inquire if I knew whether one of the complex couplings described in that work was really physically possible. It was that of simultaneous vaginal and anal penetration of a woman by two men. I am not prepared to say why she should know that or why she should not, but she did not, anymore than I myself only a few years ago knew what Norman Mailer meant when he said that behind the discreetly closed bedroom door, in that once fearsomely dirty book, *The Deer Park*, three of his characters made a "sandwich." Well, what if they did, why do we care? I am sure many people have led long and happy lives never dreaming of such triples.

I have purposely chosen for these few remarks a kind of relation that probably has a minimal overt attraction for most people. Few men I know like to share their women, few women would care to serve what might seem to them two men's interest in one another rather than in her. Still I think we all have a nearly unbounded curiosity about the permutations and combinations of human sex, and who is to say we should be in ignorance of them—if for no other reason than for the protection of those who may decide to remain personally if not intellectually innocent of these practices.

My example, however, if by no means extreme among the well-rehearsed team-plays that abound in these new dirty books, still admittedly is not of the same sort as those benign instructions and vicarious pleasures offered to us by a book like *Fanny Hill*. Almost all of us now, I would guess, might think this a kind of period tableau of marzipan dolls which we wouldn't even hide from the children. Another remark, this time by a distinguished British writer known also for his homosexuality. Quite shyly he said, "Yes, *Fanny Hill* is charming, and I think now that had I been able to read it when I was a boy, had I known women might be like that, it might have made all the difference to me." There is also in these books much instruction for middleaged Middlewesterners, like myself, in how to conquer the terrible squeamishness we were brought up in. Not in *Fanny Hill*, of course. There is nothing there to offend even our so spotlessly scrubbed souls.

Most of the dirty books I have read are, like most other books, produced by idiots for idiots, and who am I to say that those with low thresholds should not be given these to enjoy, as others blessed by easily available imaginations are satisfied by *Airport* or similar respectable fantasies. It is difficult to imagine them doing any harm, unless you believe that masturbation is harmful. Somewhat more literate than most (although not much better printed—our modern requirements in book arts for pornography are certainly nothing like those of the fabled 19th-century collectors) are the books signed Norman Singer. They have some humor of a crude kind, and some social observation of about the caliber of a routine mystery story, that is, easily indicated varieties of cliche, the bored middle-class housewife, the blustering father-in-law, the plain girl who becomes a siren when she removes her—her eyeglasses. The plot is that of an innocent person seduced first into illicit and physically complex heterosexual acts, each partner possessing bodily attributes of Homeric proportions. For most of these encounters a libretto for the reader's mental processes is provided with "oohs" and "ahs" and, "Aw man, he was starting to tremble all over!" Then the innocent is further seduced into homosexual acts, by surprise, drugs, force, or other means, and he finds he likes that too. From there on there is nowhere to go but into further repetitions. Sexual freedom is praised by all concerned, but drugs, in these books, are dangerous and one heavy user of them, although possessing the same prodiguous sexual capacities as the other characters, commits suicide.

Barbara has the same sort of progression, a scenario that provides for the presence of at least one innocent or new partner (the reader) at each of the progressively-complicated and presumably outrageous orgies. *Barbara*, however, has pretensions both to genuine social observation and to social purpose. The scene is Provincetown, the society is that of painters, writers, various visitors and tourists, college and high-school kids, and a few dogs. The right clothing and wrong clothing is described with all the narrow-eyed fervor of *Harper's Bazaar;* the right places, the right food, the right interior decoration, all these important matters are definitively dealt with. When they observe this obsessive preening of a certain trendy kind among other males, men call this the taste of faggots. *Barbara* is a handbook of one variety of faggot chic.

The hero of the book is one Max, and his primary function is to serve as orgy-master for the accumulation of these rituals as the book proceeds. In this role he would seem to be, by the standards of the other books I have read, sufficiently inventive, gathering to himself and to those about him large numbers of male and female homosexuals and persons of various races and ages, all of them of course magnificently endowed in physique and temperament for their demanding tasks. In *Barbara* there is more than the usual provision, for a dirty book, of motive, individual reaction, and of setting for these occasions. On an imaginary critical scale, I should suggest these provisions of extracurricular interest match those provided by an average television serial to stitch together its essential elements of beatings, knifings, and shootings. This puts it, of course, far above the average dirty book should we wish to invoke this scale.

But further distinguishing *Barbara* from its neighbors on the sex-shop shelves is its declared social purpose. It is not for me to say what the intention of this dual presence might be, to say whether the familiar Laocoon-like writhings of the orgy are supposed to seduce us to the doctrines about society, or whether these doctrines are to seduce us to assent (in our "heads"?) to the oral and anal outrages. I know why I doubt, though, the avowed intent claimed for the book by its publisher, Girodias, in his preface—his claim that *Barbara* is the manifesto of a new breed whose boasted political and sexual freedom will at last set things right in our rotten bourgeois culture: sexual freedom is now ready to undo the old Puritan bonds, and the connection of sex and social criticism is thus essential. I doubt him because he sounds like a man cashing in. And I doubt the author of *Barbara* because he messes up pornographic pleasures with propagandistic messages. But finally I doubt him because I believe both the sexual propaganda and the social propaganda are in truth only homosexual propaganda.

I realize that to say this today among people who read without moving their lips is about as barbarian as pasting a decal of the American flag on one's automobile, and I realize that it would be popular among those who move their lips without reading. Furthermore, I realize that there is something a bit silly about this whole project, this solemnity about dirty books. To intellectualize on the subject is little better than prowling into them in order to censor, to collect one's own pornography so that one may better command the burning of that of others.

And I can see, doubtless far less clearly than my readers will have seen already, that when I voice my final objection to these books it will be based on some all-but-unconscious concatenation of the various anecdotes I have chosen to present here. My simultaneous pleasure in dirty books and my objection both to their easy availability and to their present tendency is clearly derived from boyhood, from attitudes of that boyhood culture that it would be stupid to call anything but homosexual. Boys enjoy talking to one another about sex, they enjoy using dirty words. Some of them, of course, enjoy mutual overt acts too; but it seems to me that this is something different. This talk is a form of bluster, really, of bluster and giggling, and we can enjoy it always with other men, products of the same culture that formed us, wherever we go. Its real utility I do not mean to consider here: I am speaking of pleasures. Every man I know enjoys this kind of talk. But very few men I know enjoy acting-out giggles or acting-out bluster, and even fewer enjoy seeing other men do it. If this be morality, make the most of it.

Therefore I do not enjoy seeing our boyish bluster and giggles transformed into propaganda, which tries, I believe, to strike us at that level which we cannot in faith to ourselves and to our friends deny. To make objections to dirty jokes or dirty words in the company of other men would be unmanly—that is to say, unboyish—but to object to their widespread public display, to their open publication, or to the public performance of the fantasies embedded in this boyish talk—to object to that is not unmanly, above all it is not unboyish. It is no treason. Those who perform these things, who seek to present them in imaginative productions as something possible to perform—for clearly in our boyhood talks they were totally impossible—those who do this are the dumbbells who never understood. They are the kind who would probably become sexually aroused during the recital of a dirty joke and would laugh during a good voyeuristic spectacle like a blue film. They simply did not understand and they never will.

Nor am I impressed by the argument, quite as explicit in this dirty book *Barbara* as in the works of Norman O. Brown, that the vile hinges of civilization will rot and fall if only "queer power" could prevail, and that the ensuing period will be one of the lion lying down with the lamb, the lady with the Doberman-Pinscher, all the boys with all the girls, and everybody will perform superhuman deeds of sexual athletics.

A few months ago in these pages I made the rash statement that few of us, however enthusiastic about Eros, ever argued in favor of abolishing the incest taboo, which we should have to do if we seriously proposed healing this wound to man's erotic life that Freud said was perhaps the most maiming ever inflicted on us. "Few of us" was an evasion: I didn't really know of any. Still, it leaves me not completely caught out by my then ignorance of *Barbara*. But I must now, briefly, before explaining that remark, tell a bit about the indoctrinations given us by Frank Newman, or to be somewhat more fair, by his hero Max. Max lives in an open beach shack, eats brown rice with bits of fish, lives by occasional jobs as "an expert bartender, a good auto mechanic, a first-rate typist. About twice a week something would come in the mail for him—a book or jazz record to review, a manuscript to edit or proofread." He is also an expert petty thief, crawls under the door in pay toilets, and charges phone calls to his enemies' numbers. (Oh ambivalence, thy presence is everywhere. I began this list thinking what a revolting figure of old-fashioned Village daydreaming this Max was, and now I see how charming he must be. A first-rate typist crawling under the toilet stall door!)

But to return to my serious and, I still insist, derisive purpose: Max instructs his neophytes, after having trained them in karate, tantra, Bhagavad-Ghita, Che, and other arcane matters: "Right, when you leave here. All of you, Barbara and Franz, all love commandoes, freaking people out once and for all. What more can you do?"

Well, they can make their final assault on Western, if not World, civilization. At the final orgy of the Provincetown season, just as they are to depart with their love-commando commissions, Barbara and Franz (already lovers as brother and sister) are presented with their mother and their father with whom they proceed to commit in mother-daughter and father-son combinations oral-genital perversions. Can you not hear the giggles of "Frank Newman" as he thought of mailing that last page off to Girodias?

THE STORY EVERYONE IGNORED

Seymour M. Hersh

I was asked to write this article—to tell editors how they missed one of the biggest stories of the year—by an associate editor of one of the biggest newspapers in America, one of the newspapers that was very slow to fully realize the significance of the alleged massacre at Songmy. That irony, in itself, is important to me—for it convinces me that editorship, like democracy, is not dead . . . yet.

The fact that some thirty newspapers in this country, Canada, and abroad did publish my first and subsequent Dispatch News Service stories on Songmy is further proof that the nation's press is not as gutless as all that. I honestly believe that a major problem in newspapers today is not censorship on the part of editors and publishers, but something more odious: self-censorship by the reporters.

There is no doubt that many reporters had heard of the Pinkville incident (at least many have told me so). In talking to some Pentagon officials before I wrote my first story (they talked then), I was told by one general officer: "Pinkville had been a word among GIs for a year. I'll never cease to be amazed that it hasn't been written about before." Another general officer who was attached to headquarters in Saigon in 1968 said he had first heard talk of Pinkville soon after it happened. Of course, an outsider can also be amazed that generals would hear of such incidents and not demand an investigation, but the notion that *those* men thought that the press had somehow fallen on the job is, well, significant.

As everyone knows, the first mention of the incident was provided by the public information officer at Fort Benning, Ga., who released a brief item September 6 announcing that Lt. William L. Calley, Jr., had been charged with murder in the deaths "of an unspecified number of civilians in Vietnam."

The AP man in the area promptly put in a query; when the Pentagon did not gush forth with all of the details, that was that. No other questions were officially asked of the Pentagon about the Cal-

Seymour M. Hersh won the Pulitzer Prize for the story he describes in this article. A former Associated Press Pentagon reporter, he now is a reporter for *Dispatch News Service*, the agency which broke the news of My Lai. This personal account is adapted from a report in the *Bulletin of the ASNE* and is reprinted here with permission of Mr. Hersh and *Columbia Journalism Review*, where it appeared in the Winter, 1969-70 issue.

Poll reports more Americans disturbed over My
Lai publicity than My Lai massacre itself.

ley story until I offered some carefully hedged queries around October 23. The Washington *Post* queried the Pentagon about Calley on November 6; by that time I had arranged a number of interviews—with Calley, among others—and was well on the way. The New York *Times* also began asking some questions shortly before the first story broke early November 12 for the next morning's papers.

The initial Pentagon dispatch was put on the wire by the AP and appeared Saturday morning in many major newspapers in the country, including the Washington *Post*, the New York *Times*, and Los Angeles *Times*. It would be wonderful to say I noticed it immediately, saw its significance, and dashed out with pencil and pad in hand. Of course not. I was tipped around October 20 by a source with Pentagon connections. My source simply told me that the military was planning to court-martial an officer at Fort Benning, Ga., for the murder of about seventy-five Vietnamese civilians.

What made me drop everything (I was then finishing *The Ultimate Corporation*, a book on the Pentagon for Random House) and begin pursuing the story? For one thing, my source was good—but certainly no better than others who must have told newsmen about the incident in the twenty months since it took place. Another, more important reason, I think, was my experiences with chemical and biological warfare (CBW). I had written a book on CBW (*Chemical and Biological Warfare: America's Hidden Arsenal*, Bobbs-Merrill) that was published in mid-1968 but somehow failed to make much of a mark at first. The public and the press seemingly did not want to believe that the United States was stockpiling nerve gas at Army commands overseas, nor did they want to believe that American military men would be capable of shipping trainloads of nerve gas through the American countryside without telling anyone. My book prompted very little investigative reporting.

So, I believed the story about Pinkville. And I also knew—or thought I knew—that newspapers would probably be the last to believe it. Thus I began my searches with an eye on *Look* and *Life* magazines. I won't tell who gave me leads, but suffice to say that I managed to find out who Calley was, and where his lawyer was located. I decided that the telephone was a bad interviewing instrument on the Pinkville story, and therefore interviewed every important witness or near-witness in person. I applied for and received a limited travel grant (about $2,000 en toto) from the Philip Stern Fund for Investigative Journalism in Washington, and began flying around to locate witnesses. (In all, I traveled more than 30,000 miles via air.)

By early November I had a pretty good picture of what had happened, at least solid enough so I could write. I knew Calley had been charged with 109 deaths and I had the precise wording from the charge sheets. I contacted *Life;* they said they weren't interested (little did I know that they had turned down Ronald Ridenhour, the twenty-three-year-old California college student whose letters first prompted the Army to study the incident). Then I went to *Look*. A senior editor there was very interested; I wrote a sketchy, but explosive, memo on what I had. They, too, decided to pass—I think, charitably, because of their four- to six-week lead time.

I really didn't know where to turn, so I simply kept doing research. David Obst, general manager of Dispatch and a Washington neighbor and fellow touch football player, had learned from me about Pinkville and was insistent on handling it. I had written a few Sunday pieces for his news service and been moderately successful; as many as six or eight responsible newspapers (including the Baltimore *Sun*) had published one or more of my earlier works. So in the end, I turned to Dispatch and committed myself to its syndication.

Why? I was convinced that if I walked into a major newspaper and laid out my story, the editors, to verify my information, would have to repeat the painstaking interview-and-more-interview process I had gone through, and then write their own story. I could respect this, but I simply wanted my story for myself. And I wanted it to be credible, which ruled out smaller magazines. This wasn't an article for a journal of opinion, like the *New Republic*, or *National Review*, for that matter—it was hard news that should be written as such.

That left Obst and Dispatch. Amazingly, as is well known, it worked. Of about fifty newspapers contacted, thirty-two or so eventually ran my first story citing the charges against Calley. This was not done on a whim; the papers carefully checked me and as many of the facts as possible. That was to the newspaper world's credit.

What happened after the first story is not. Only the New York *Times*, which had its own story, chose to follow up independently on the story, by sending Henry Kamm from its Saigon bureau to the Pinkville area to interview survivors (ABC-TV and *Newsweek* also went along). The *Times* decided to treat Pinkville as a major story and do its own reporting from the outset. Other papers avoided any hint of investigatory research and it was left to me to seek out Ridenhour (who, after my first story, had told newspapers about his role) and to interview him in California. Although he had first revealed his part in the story Friday, November 14, and I did not see him until the following Monday afternoon, amazingly I was the first reporter to personally interview him. The New York *Times* and AP had talked briefly to him by telephone, but the Los Angeles *Times*—barely thirty miles away in downtown Los Angeles—did not send a reporter. And none of the papers realized how important Ridenhour was—he had a list of eyewitnesses, many of whom were out of the service and willing to talk.

Ridenhour gave me the names and addresses of some of the eyewitnesses he had spoken to about Pinkville (he did not actually participate in the incident), and off I went. After personal interviews in Utah, Washington, and New Jersey—conducted within twenty-four hours—my subsequent story, for newspapers of November 20, was well received by the nation's press. [Editor's Note: The first publication of My Lai photos came in the November 20 Cleveland *Plain Dealer*, which later reported many readers who phoned within twenty-four hours disapproved of publication of the photos.] After that second story, newspapers generally were still reluctant to comment editorially on Pinkville (with the New York *Times* and Chicago *Sun-Times* being notable exceptions), although they were playing the story big. It all had suddenly become much more credible when the Army announced in late November that Calley had indeed been charged with the murder of 109 Vietnamese civilians.

The last newspapers vestiges of resistance disappeared when Paul Meadlo of Terre Haute, Ind., submitted to a Dispatch interview and told how he had calmly executed, under orders, dozens of Vietnamese civilians. Dispatch provided information on Meadlo to CBS-TV, which ran a long interview on the Walter Cronkite show. It was a crash deal for Dispatch, with Meadlo, who had been fully informed of the possible dangers to him and his rights in the matter, not being paid one cent; but even more important was the fact that television was needed—that somehow just relying on newspapers to sear the conscience of America hadn't been working, or had been working too slowly. It took three newspaper stories and one television interview to make Pinkville a national issue; it shouldn't have.

After Meadlo came a flurry of newspaper stories quoting former members of Calley's platoon and his company. The newspaper industry, in one of those collective changes of mind that can only be found in the business, decided each man's testimony was important enough to play all over the front pages. The indiscriminate use of eyewitness statements was amazing to me; I had carefully attempted to get some kind of "feel" from each of my interviewees before quoting them. GIs are notorious liars (that point is based on a personal recollection), particularly when talking about their combat days. I think some of those who came forward did not tell all the truth.

This, of course, leads right into the issue of pre-trial publicity; a major dilemma facing newspapers today. I was impressed by how important this issue was for some newspapers when they were deciding whether or not to run my first few Dispatch stories; and then surprised at how quickly the same newspapers forgot about such rights and began splashing stories across their newspaper once Pinkville became a big issue. Dispatch handled the pre-trial publicity question by retaining a prominent Washington law firm and relying on it for advice. The advice generally was that the public's right to know far outweighed any disadvantages to some involved individuals. Even if a court-martial became an impossibility and some men had to be turned free, this seemed preferable to not having as full and as responsible a debate as possible—and "responsible" to me simply meant when I quoted a source I firmly believed him to be telling the truth; it was not always a question of just quoting someone accurately.

What made some responsible and careful newspapers publish my stories and others, equally as responsible and careful, not publish them? I think part of the answer is instinct, the instinct many reporters and editors feel for a story or a source. There are many blind sources one can trust, even over a telephone, while others need careful checking.

One newspaper with which I became involved was the Washington *Post.* I met with top editors of the paper early on the morning of November 12, when Dispatch broke the story. The meeting was chaired by Ben Bradlee, the *Post's* executive editor. My story was passed around, read by all, and I answered some direct questions on the legal aspects of the charges against Calley. No one asked what seemed to me to be the obvious question: "Is this true?" After I left, I learned later, Bradlee handled that aspect by telling his staff, "This smells right." His instinct was working, at least that morning.

Nevertheless, I knew things had changed for most of the nation's press after the Meadlo interview; at least six friends in the Washington newspaper corps called me at home over the next few evenings seeking tips on where to go next or leads on involved GIs or officers who might be living in their local areas.

When the nation's newspapers begin wanting their hometown mass murderer, things are well in hand.

TONKIN: WHAT SHOULD HAVE BEEN ASKED

Don Stillman

On the stormy night of Aug. 4, 1964, the U.S. Navy destroyers *Maddox* and *C. Turner Joy* were cruising the Gulf of Tonkin off North Vietnam when the *C. Turner Joy* reported radar detection of ships closing in fast for a possible attack. Sonarmen reported tracking torpedoes from the ships. Seaman Patrick Park, the main gun director of the *Maddox*, scanned his sensitive radar for signs of the enemy. But as the destroyers maneuvered wildly for three hours in heavy swells he detected nothing. Then suddenly he reported picking up a "damned big" target, and was ordered to fire. Park recalled later:

> Just before I pushed the trigger, I suddenly realized: that's the *Turner Joy.* This came right with the order to fire. I shouted back, "Where's the *Turner Joy?*" There was a lot of yelling, "Goddamn" back and forth, with the bridge telling me to "fire before we lost contact. . . . " I finally told them, "I'm not opening fire until I know where the *Turner Joy* is." The bridge got on the phone and said, "Turn on your lights, *Turner Joy.*" Sure enough, there she was, right in the crosshairs. I had six five-inch guns right at the *Turner Joy*, 1,500 yards away. If I had fired, it would have blown it clean out of the water. In fact, I could have been shot for not squeezing the trigger. . . . People started asking, "What are we shooting at? What is going on?" We all began calming down. The whole thing seemed to end then.

But it didn't end there for Park, whose statements were reported by Joseph Goulden in his excellent book *Truth Is the First Casualty*, or for the rest of the world. Hours later, President Johnson ordered the first U.S. bombing raids against North Vietnam. Within the week, he had demanded and received a Congressional resolution that authorized him to "take all necessary steps" to "prevent further aggression" in Vietnam.

The massive American buildup in Vietnam dates from that crucial week in the Gulf of Tonkin, and in retrospect the events there proved to be a turning point in the war. At the time of the incidents, only 163 Americans had died in action in Vietnam, and the 16,000

Don Stillman ends this book on a significant note with an article related directly to the one by Seymour Hersh. He is a member of the West Virginia journalism faculty and editor of the Appalachian monthly *The Miner's Voice*, a publication calling for reform within the United Mine Workers. The piece is reprinted here with his permission and that of *Columbia Journalism Review*, where it appeared in a special Vietnam issue, Winter, 1970-71.

American troops there ostensibly were serving as "advisers" rather than full combat soldiers. But within a year President Johnson began to use a Congressionally approved "Tonkin resolution" as a functional equivalent of a declaration of war in an escalation that ultimately brought more than half a million U.S. troops to Vietnam. More than 40,000 were killed.

What really happened that dark night is unclear; but persistent digging by Senator J.W. Fulbright and his Foreign Relations Committee staff, by then-Senator Wayne Morse, and by a handful of persistent reporters like Joseph Goulden has given us a view of at least part of the iceberg of deception that remained hidden for years.

Reporting of the first attack on the *Maddox* on Aug. 2 and the second alleged attack on both the *Maddox* and the *Turner Joy* on Aug. 4 was extremely difficult because the only real sources of information were Pentagon and Navy officials and the President himself. Slowly and painfully over four years, as the private doubts of Senators and reporters became public, the American people learned that in fact the *Maddox* was not on a "routine patrol in international waters," but was on an electronic espionage mission to gather intelligence information on North Vietnamese radar frequencies. As part of that mission, the *Maddox* would repeatedly simulate attacks by moving toward the shores of North Vietnam with its gun-control radar mechanisms turned on to stimulate enemy radar activity. In addition, years after the incidents stories revealed that the territorial waters recognized by North Vietnam (twelve miles) were repeatedly violated by the *Maddox*.

Two days before the first attack on the *Maddox*, the South Vietnamese for the first time conducted naval shelling of North Vietnam. Using U.S. "swift boats," they attacked the islands of Hon Me and Hon Ngu. The night following the raids, the *Maddox*, approaching from the same direction as the South Vietnamese, came within four nautical miles of Hon Me. The captain of the *Maddox* intercepted North Vietnamese messages reporting the possibility of "hostile action" because the enemy believed the *Maddox* to be connected with the South Vietnamese shelling of the islands. The *Maddox* cabled: CONTINUANCE OF PATROL PRESENTS AN UNACCEPTABLE RISK. That day it was attacked.

The *Maddox* was joined by the *Turner Joy* and, after again requesting termination of the mission because of the likelihood of attack, it reported two days later that the two ships had been ambushed by North Vietnamese PT boats. The black clouds and electrical storms during that night prevented any visual sightings of hostile craft, and contradictory sightings on radar and sonar added to the confusion. The commander in charge cabled:

> Entire action leaves many doubts except for apparent attempted ambush. Suggest thorough reconnaissance in daylight by aircraft.

After lengthy questioning of crew members on both ships, the doubts grew larger. The commander cabled:

> Review of action makes many reported contacts and torpedoes fired appear doubtful. . . . Freak weather effects and overeager sonarmen may have accounted for many reports. No actual visual sightings by *Maddox*. Suggest complete evaluation before any further action.

That evaluation did not occur, and hours later American bombers took off for North Vietnam.

Thus the espionage mission of the *Maddox*, its violation of territorial waters, its proximity and relationship to South Vietnamese shelling, and major questions about whether the second attack occurred, all combine to give a much different picture of the incidents than the Administration fed the country through the news media. How well did the media handle reporting and interpretation of the Tonkin incidents?

Perhaps the worst excesses in reporting were committed by *Time* and *Life*. Both viewed the event as if the *Maine* itself had been sunk. The week after the encounter, *Life* carried an article headlined FROM THE FILES OF NAVY INTELLIGENCE that it said was "pieced together by *Life* correspondent Bill Wise with the help of U.S. Navy Intelligence and the Department of Defense." Wise was clearly fed only a small smattering of cables that contained none of the doubts about the second attack. He stated (Aug. 14, 1964):

> Despite their losses, the [North Vietnamese] PTs continued to harass the two destroyers. A few of them amazed those aboard the *Maddox* by brazenly using searchlights to light up the destroyers—thus making ideal targets of themselves. They also peppered the ships with more 37 mm fire, keeping heads on U.S. craft low but causing no real damage.

Senator Wayne Morse, in a speech on the floor of the Senate Feb. 28, 1968, denounced the Pentagon's "selective leaking of confidential information" and *Life's* gullibility in accepting it. "I don't know who leaked, but I can guess why," he said. "The 'why' is that someone in the Pentagon decided that the American people should see some of the messages confirming that an unprovoked attack had occurred on innocent American vessels. . . . The *Life* magazine reporter was taken in. He was 'used.' The press should be warned."

The next issue of *Life* went even further in embellishing events.

It carried a picture spread headlined HEROES OF THE GULF OF TONKIN that praised the pilots who had bombed North Vietnam. "Most of the young Navy pilots had never seen combat before, but they performed like veterans," *Life* said. The planes, with two exceptions, "got back safely and their pilots, the nation's newest battle veterans, would be remembered as the heroes of Tonkin Gulf."

This kind of irresponsible puffery was evident in *Time*, too. Despite thorough and restrained files from its Washington bureau, *Time* (Aug. 14, 1964) constructed its typical dramatic scenario of events which, though lively, was grossly inaccurate:

> The night glowed eerily with the nightmarish glare of air-dropped flares and boats' searchlights. For three and a half hours the small boats attacked in pass after pass. Ten enemy torpedoes sizzled through the water. Each time the skippers, tracking the fish by radar, maneuvered to evade them. Gunfire and gun smells and shouts stung the air. Two of the enemy boats went down. Then, at 1:30 a.m., the remaining PTs ended the fight, roared off through the black night to the north.

Joseph Goulden, one of the few writers to interview crew members, reports that when the *Maddox* and *Turner Joy* arrived at Subic Bay several weeks after the incidents, one crew member had occasion to read both the *Life* and *Time* accounts. He quotes the seaman as stating:

> I couldn't believe it, the way they blew that story out of proportion. It was like something out of *Male* magazine, the way they described that battle. All we needed were naked women running up and down the deck. We were disgusted, because it just wasn't true. It didn't happen that way. . . .

Newsweek, which generally waved the flag far less than *Time* in its coverage of the Vietnam War, was just as overzealous in its dramatization of the second Tonkin incident (Aug. 17, 1964):

> The U.S. ships blazed out salvo after salvo of shells. Torpedoes whipped by, some only 100 feet from the destroyers' beams. A PT boat burst into flames and sank. More U.S. jets swooped in. . . . Another PT boat exploded and sank, and then the others scurried off into the darkness nursing their wounds. The battle was won. Now it was time for American might to strike back.

Even the usually staid New York *Times* magazine was caught up in the adventure of the moment. Its Aug. 16 picture spread on the Seventh Fleet, which had launched the planes that bombed the North, had the look of a war comic book. Headlined POLICEMEN OF THE PACIFIC, it showed planes streaking through the sky, missiles being fired, and Marines landing on beaches. It carried captions such as, "A component of the Marines is always on sea duty, ready when the call comes."

The New York *Times* news sections handled the story with restraint and, after the Aug. 2 attack, even mentioned claims that U.S. destroyers like the *Maddox* "have sometimes collaborated with South Vietnamese hit-and-run raids on North Vietnamese cities." The Washington *Post*, like the *Times*, was thorough and incisive in its reporting. Murrey Marder's superb accounts even mentioned the South Vietnamese shelling on Hon Me and Hon Ngu as a possible cause for the then seemingly irrational attack on the *Maddox*.

Because transcripts of TV news shows from this period are not available it is difficult to evaluate broadcast media performance. But the accounts of TV coverage printed in government bulletins and elsewhere indicate that some perceptive reporting did occur. NBC carried an interview with Dean Rusk Aug. 5 in which Rusk was pressed on the question of whether the U.S. ships might have been operating in support of the South Vietnamese shelling units. But for the most part the broadcast media, while perhaps more responsible than some print outlets, fed viewers the same deceptive Administration leaks.

Editorial comment almost universally supported the President's response. The New York *Daily News* speculated that "it may be our heaven-sent good fortune to liquidate not only Ho Chi Minh but Mao Tse-tung's Red Mob at Peking as well, presumably with an important assist from Generalissimo Chiang Kai-shek and his Nationalist Chinese forces on Taiwan."

The Los Angeles *Times* praised U.S. actions as "fitting in selectivity, proper in application, and—given the clear, long-standing statement of U.S. intentions—inevitable in delivery." William Randolph Hearst, Jr., praised the bombing as a "fitting reply to one of the more outrageous—and implausible—aggressions committed by communism in many years." He went on to suggest that rather than limit the bombing it might be better to continue until the North Vietnamese surrendered.

The New York *Times* said: "The attack on one of our warships that at first seemed, and was hoped to be, an isolated incident is now seen in ominous perspective to have been the beginning of a mad adventure by the North Vietnamese Communists." But the *Times* did warn that "the sword, once drawn in anger, will tend to be unsheathed more easily in the future." When the Tonkin resolution went before Congress, the *Times* perceptively cautioned that "it is virtually a blank check."

The Washington *Post's* editorial page saw the Tonkin resolution much differently. Earlier editorials mentioned "the atmosphere of ambiguity" that surrounded the first attack on the *Maddox*, but when the resolution was considered the *Post* said: "That unity (against Communist aggression) has been demonstrated despite the reckless and querulous dissent of Senator Morse. There is no substance in Senator Morse's charge that the resolution amounts to a 'predated declaration of war'. . . . This means of reasserting the national will, far short of a declaration of war, follows sound precedent. . . . "

One of the few newspapers to attack the President's account was the Charleston, W. Va., *Gazette*, which stated that the Tonkin attacks were probably caused by the South Vietnamese naval strikes and complained of the "air of unreality" about the incidents. But the overall failure of the press to raise questions about the incidents in the editorial columns, although in keeping with the mood of the country at the time, was part of the general breakdown of the media's responsibility to act as a check on the actions of the Government.

Foreign coverage of the incidents raised some of the significant points being ignored in this country. *Demokreten*, of Denmark, stated:

> To create a pretext for an attack on Poland, Hitler ordered the Germans to put on Polish uniforms and attack a German guard. What the Americans did in North Vietnam was not the same. But the story sounds doubtful. . . . Why was the vessel off North Vietnamese coasts? In any case its presence there could indeed be interpreted as provocative.

New Statesman of Britain also raised doubts:

> There is so little trust in official [U.S.] accounts about Vietnam that suspicion is surely understandable. . . . Is it not possible that the destroyers could not be distinguished from South Vietnamese craft that were engaged in another raiding mission?

One American journalist who raised continuing doubts about the veracity of the Administration's accounts was I.F. Stone. In his small, outspoken sheet, Stone reported the South Vietnamese attacks on Hon Me and Hon Ngu. He was the only one to cover in detail the charges raised by Senator Morse about the incidents and the Tonkin resolution, and he even raised questions about whether the second attack even occurred. While *Time* and *Life* were adding readable embellishments to the nineteenth-century theme of "they've sunk one of our gunboats," I.F. Stone was asking the crucial questions.

One of the major shortcomings of columnists and opinion writers was their failure to ask the broad question: does the punishment fit the crime? The total damage in both attacks was one bullet hole in the *Maddox*. No U.S. ships were sunk, no American boys were killed or even wounded. In turn, we not only claimed to have sunk four North Vietnamese vessels but went on to the bombing of the North, sinking the major part of the North Vietnamese navy, and wiping out more than 10 per cent of its oil storage tanks.

The overwhelming response of the editorialists was that President Johnson should be commended for his restraint in limiting the bombing. Among Washington journalists only Stone opined that indeed the American response was "hardly punishment to fit the crime." His small-circulation sheet received little attention.

The record of the media improved measurably as public doubts about the Tonkin incidents began to grow. Senator Fulbright, who managed the Tonkin resolution through Congress for President Johnson, began to question the facts and, in May, 1966, wrote in *Look* that he had serious doubts about the Administration's account. But the media didn't follow this up very extensively. Despite the importance of the Tonkin incidents, they were content to pass over opportunities to interview crew members of the two ships—the only firsthand witnesses—some of whom had left the service or were otherwise accessible for interviews. The first real breakthrough came in July, 1967, when Associated Press sent a special assignment team headed by Harry Rosenthal and Tom Stewart to interview some three dozen crew members. Their superb 5,000-word account was the first real enterprise reporting on the Tonkin affair.

AP revealed for the first time that the *Maddox* was carrying intelligence equipment, and also cited for the first time that the *Maddox* had not fired any warning shots, as claimed by Secretary McNamara, but had shot to kill instead. The crew interviews indicated that there was a great confusion on board the two ships during the incident. At this point, however, there was little client interest in the story. Urban riots broke out the day it was to run. As a result, the AP report was not used by major metropolitan newspapers such as the Washington *Post*, Washington *Star*, New York *Times*, or others which might have given it the exposure it deserved. The story did appear in the *Arkansas Gazette*, however, where it was read by Fulbright, who by this time was devoting much of his attention to uncovering the true story of Tonkin.

The AP account was followed in April, 1968, by an article in *Esquire* by David Wise, who also interviewed the crews and cast further doubt on the Administration's account. These two reports and another AP account by Donald May were the only real enterprise stories that turned up new information. But John Finney, the able New York *Times* reporter, raised further questions in *New Republic* early in 1968, as did John Galloway in *Commonweal*. (Galloway has just done a splendid source book, *The Gulf of Tonkin Resolution*.)

By this time Fulbright and Morse were generating much breaking news as they prepared for the Foreign Relations Committee hearings held in February, 1968. But even during those hearings the press failed to distinguish itself. When Morse, through the *Congressional Record*, released important segments of a top-secret study done by the Foreign Relations staff, based on cable traffic and new data from the Defense Department, it took the Washington *Post* two days to recognize the significance of his statements.

The final credit for tying together the whole thread of deception surrounding the incidents must go to Joseph Goulden, whose book appeared in early fall of 1969. While covering the 1968 Tonkin hearings for the Philadelphia *Inquirer*, Goulden had filed a story on the controversial testimony of Secretary McNamara, who appeared to contradict some aspects of his 1964 testimony. The *Inquirer* rewrote the lead to make it read:

> The United States did not provoke the 1964 Gulf of Tonkin incident, previously secret naval communications indicated Saturday.

Goulden left the *Inquirer*, sought out crewmen and others involved in the incident, and wrote his detailed and insightful account.

This, then, is the record on the Tonkin affair. Given its lessons, one may hope that the media will not fail so grandly if similar incidents occur. The reporting on the *Pueblo* and the *Liberty* give reason for hope. But the Fourth Estate must establish a far more independent and critical stance on government actions if hope is to become reality.

The Media and Vietnam: comment and appraisal

In preparing [the issue on Vietnam, *CJR* asked 12] news media observers and practitioners—"hawks" and "doves," conservatives and liberals, Americans and foreigners—to appraise U.S. news media performance on Vietnam.

On thirteen specific subjects, rated as "good" or "poor," newspapers, magazines, and radio-TV all were ranked "good" by most in presentation of the war's historical context, the nature and extent of U.S. antiwar sentiment, and analysis of "the many hopeful prognoses" by public officials. Radio-TV won slightly greater approval than rival media for coverage of Congressional debates over troop buildups. All the media were rated predominantly "poor" in covering the Gulf of Tonkin incidents, the economic/social impact of the war on the South Vietnamese, U.S. involvement in Thailand and Cambodia, various peace "feelers" and the Paris negotiations, and the present Vietnamese economic/political situation. There was little consensus in other categories except for rating radio-TV "poor" in coverage of the Diem government, Americans' early involvement as "advisers," and the impact of heavy bombing of the North.

Overall, magazines and newspapers were rated highest in performance, with no one marking magazines as "poor." Most rated radio-TV "average" to "poor," and several marked it "excellent." Among comments:

George E. Reedy, Fellow, Woodrow Wilson International Center for Scholars; former press secretary to President Johnson: "My overall impression is that all of the media have done as well as they could in covering the Indochina War and, in view of economic realities, have devoted considerable resources to the project. . . . The problem is that the news media are primarily channels of information, and play—and can only play—a severely restricted role in the field of basic education. Those engaged in the production of newspapers, magazines, and radio-TV shows assume—and generally the assumption is correct—that the interested audience has a fund of background information which enables it to make some form of sense out of the facts presented. In the case of Indochina the assumption had no validity whatsoever. To most Americans the area did not even exist until a few years ago. Aside from a minute group of specialists, our citizens had no conceptions of the land or its people—not even the romantic misconceptions that we have of other areas of the world.

"Many newspapers and magazines recognized this problem and made a valiant effort to plug the gap with backgrounders. Some of them were superb. But even the best could not make up for the many decades of total indifference to Indochina on the part of our society. It was not a question of presentation, explanation, or background but of education, without which the foregoing are useless.

"Added to this was the unusual nature of the war—no front lines; no clear-cut objectives; and no easily recognizable distinction between friend and foe. And finally, the official explanations were less than candid, perhaps because officialdom was having almost as much trouble as the press in finding familiar patterns. . . ."

Barry Zorthian, president, Time-Life Broadcast, Inc.; former U.S. military information officer, Saigon: "Some combat coverage and coverage of problems of the U.S. and Vietnamese military were outstanding. Particularly poor to my mind was political and economic coverage of the period of political chaos in 1965-66, the general internal situations in 1967, and problems and perspectives of the Vietnamese. . . . I think the media's continued skepticism about the official 'line' was healthy; was essential. The media should be skeptical about government. One of the beefs I have about press and government is that they spend too much time criticizing each other and too little in self-examination.

"If I had to make one criticism of the press, with all the drawbacks of generalization—and my reservations are very real—it has to do with reporters' qualifications. There were some superbly qualified people in Vietnam, but an awful lot of people with major outlets just were not prepared to cover the war, and by the time they were qualified—had picked up experience—they were transferred. . . ."

Senator J.W. Fulbright, chairman, Senate Foreign Relations Committee: "The press has, I believe, performed very well throughout the war and has rendered a great public service in the process. Reporters have questioned government pronouncements and policy more thoroughly than has been the case on any other major issue since I have been in public office. The press has been an invaluable source of information to the Committee throughout the course of the war and has been, in my view, our prime source of information on what was really taking place in Southeast Asia. . . ."

Louis Heren, deputy editor, the Times of London: "Generally speaking, I think the U.S. media, with one or two outstanding exceptions, were slow to question official policy and, indeed, some of the old ideas of patriotism. The majority appear to have been inhibited by the old anti-Communist ideology. The slowness to appreciate the situation was the most serious weakness. . . . Finally, and this is a constant complaint of mine, too little attention was—and is—given to Congress. The New York *Times* has three or four men covering the Hill. The London *Times* has about twenty men in Parliament.

"Outstanding examples of coverage and/or interpretation? The New York *Times*, especially in the early days with David Halberstam, and the report from North Vietnam on the bombing, by Harrison Salisbury. Also the Los Angeles *Times* series on the peace initiative 'Marigold.' Some TV and press photography also was excellent.

"Particularly poor or objectionable examples? Mainly the lack of interest in the consequences of the war for the South Vietnamese—especially the effect of the bombing and defoliants."

James J. Kilpatrick, syndicated columnist: "I think, on the whole, the press has given us almost more information about what was going on in Vietnam than could reasonably be absorbed. This war has gone on so long it's like the war in *1984*—nobody can remember exactly when it started, or who is fighting whom. We see the movements of men and casualties, and one day tends to blur into another in coverage. . . . I think coverage has been competent and workmanlike and on the whole quite fair. . . ."

William Porter, chairman, Department of Journalism, University of Michigan: "This generally has been a good chapter in U.S. journalism. . . . Our worst reporting was in the earlier stages of deep involvement, and the real digging out of that story should have been done in Washington. That David Halberstam-Charles Mohr-Malcolm Browne had to turn on the light from 9,000 miles away, thanks primarily to finding some discontented officers, is more than anything else an indication of the lack of initiative in a lot of Washington bureaus. . . ."

Noam Chomsky, professor of linguistics, MIT: "In my opinion many war correspondents have done a very honest job of reporting what they themselves have seen. However, to learn something of the social and political context of events in Southeast Asia one must turn to the French press, particularly (though not exclusively) *Le Monde*. . . .

"As to analysis of government propaganda, it is virtually nonexistent. Consider, for example, Laos. The scale and character of the air war in Laos have been known to American newsmen for some time, and they have sufficient information available to them to refute conclusively the official government pronouncements on this subject. They have not done so.

"To mention just one example of gross neglect, President Nixon announced in March that a North Vietnamese invasion had raised the North Vietnamese troop level to 67,000 men, obliging the U.S. to respond with heavy air strikes and so on. A few weeks later Evans and Novak raised it to 70,000, and Robert Shaplen to 75,000. In fact, every newsman in Vientiane, unaware of the 'invasion,' was giving out the figure of 50,000 troops, as for the preceding year. To my knowledge, this fact appeared only in a side remark by D.S. Greenway in *Life*. Furthermore, most correspondents were aware that these alleged 50,000 troops were largely support and supply units that consist, to a large measure, of women and old men. All knew that only about eighty North Vietnamese prisoners had been captured since 1964 (eight in the alleged 'invasion').

"Similarly, when the Symington Committee hearings on Laos were released, with the Government claim that only military targets were being attacked in Northern Laos (April, 1970), the claim could have been refuted by any correspondent who has interviewed refugees, or any editor who has read such reports (say, those introduced by Kennedy into the *Congressional Record* in late April, 1970). The matter is of immense importance. On this turns the whole question of the nature of the air war in Laos since 1964 (virtually unreported in the media).

"A Kennedy subcommittee staff report of September, 1970, merely reports what is common knowledge in Vientane when it reveals that a primary purpose of this war has been to destroy the social and economic structures of the Pathet Lao. Apart from a column by T.D. Allman about a year ago, I have seen nothing in the American press—apart from small magazines—that clearly explains this, the dominant feature of the American war in Laos for the past several years. Similarly, Jacques Decornoy's eyewitness account (June, 1968) received no notice, to my knowledge, in the American media. And so on and so on."

Wayne Danielson, Dean, School of Communications, University of Texas; president, Association for Education in Journalism: "In large terms I want to emphasize what the media learned. . . . They learned something from Vietnam just as they learned something from the McCarthy era. Both lessons were hard. . . ."

Prof. Karl Deutsch, Harvard University; president, American Political Science Association: "I think what was missing was better reporting on the decision process. If you read the book by Townsend Hoopes, *The Limits of Intervention*, there was a lot of information there that the press had not caught. . . .

"In television, even the best do not use the full force of the medium. TV should give you much more detail of the kind the Pentagon does with visual aids. Visual aids are hardly ever used to the maximum on TV. . . ."

Clayton Kirkpatrick, editor, Chicago Tribune: "There were occasional lapses into superficial, naive reporting, but the level of reporting by all media was the best in our history of war reporting. . . ."

Ron Dorfman, editor, Chicago Journalism Review: "While researching a magazine article on the strategic hamlet program in 1962 I discovered that the only general-circulation publications in the U.S. that were paying consistent attention to the war were the New York *Times* and *New Republic.* The wire services apparently had men in Saigon fulltime, but hardly any papers were using their files—at least not with any regularity. It was only with the Buddhist uprising of 1963—the burning monks, the street demonstrations, and finally the assassination of Diem—that the media started paying attention. . . .

"Meanwhile, the Washington coverage was absurd: Why should it have taken I.F. Stone to put the lie to so much of the propaganda from State. the Pentagon, and the White House? This was particularly evident in connection with the alleged 'truce violations' and the Gulf of Tonkin. . . .

"Until very recently the press was also bamboozling us on the question of our brave boys in the boondocks. . . . . The scope and nature of GI dissent, the dope-smoking on patrol, the racial divisions among GIs and between GIs and the 'gooks' went as unreported as the profiteering . . . and the history and causes of the conflict itself."

Peter C. Newman, editor, Toronto Star: "It seems strange to me that the most memorable insights on Vietnam came out of a novel—David Halberstam's *One Very Hot Day.* But perhaps it's that kind of a war."

DISCUSSION QUESTIONS

1. Do you think a sensitive television industry over-reacted to Vice President Agnew's statements about television news?

2. What chance would there be for the characters in Daniel St. Albin Greene's article to plot in preparing the news?

   What impressed you the most about the daily operation of a television news show?

3. Did you agree with the Supreme Court's decision regarding publication of the secret Pentagon Papers in June, 1971? Do you think a line can be drawn in all instances between prior restraint and post-publication prosecution?

4. Discuss ways in which your particular "J-School" can better prepare for the complex world of the 1970's. Take into account some of Professor Tebbel's observations while discussing needed course changes, campus media operations and job opportunities.

5. Because there is much bitterness on the part of minority persons, how could the mass media better treat minority persons in the presentation of commercials, news items and entertainment? What is the biggest complaint regarding media careers?

6. Terry Ann Knopf's strong criticisms of news treatment of violence causes some natural questions. Do you think her expectations are too high regarding the possibility of reporting errors?

7. The Vietnam War shaped the nation's foreign and domestic affairs for years to come. What part can the news media play in the future regarding "sensitive" stories like those described by Seymour Hersh and Don Stillman? What obstacles will remain to the gaining of such vital information? Should such news be published or was this harmful to the nation's future in the long run?

PROJECT

Using these articles and books like *To Kill A Messenger* (William Small's personal account of television news), *Free Press, Free People* (John Hohenberg's story of the press), *The Kingdom and the Power* (Gay Talese's picture of the *New York Times*), and other historical works, pinpoint the exact role of the news media in our society. Use examples from recent or past journalism history to describe the successes and failures of the media (see Appendix for other examples).

FURTHER READINGS

Perhaps the most interesting because they contain the most controversy are the readings in Part III. Some additions to this section follow:

"Words to the Wise Newspapermen." *Broadcasting* 79 (November, 1970):167.

"Pressure on the Media." *Nation* 212 (April, 1971):420-21.

Arnold, Edmund. "The Editor and the Educator." *Quill* 58 (December, 1970):18-20.

Bagdikian, Ben. "The Future Content of News." *Bulletin of the American Society of Newspaper Editors, No. 550* (April 1971).

Brucker, Herbert. "Can Printed News Save a Free Society." *Saturday Review* 53 (October, 1970):52-55, 64.

Chittick, William O. "American Foreign Policy Elites: Attitudes Toward Secrecy and Publicity." *Journalism Quarterly* (Winter, 1970):689-96.

Clay, Grady. "The Death of Centrality." *Nieman Reports* 24 (December, 1970):3-5.

Diamond, Edwin. "How the White House Keeps Its Eye on the Network News Shows." *New York* (May, 1971):45,47-49.

Fallaci, Oriana. "What Does Walter Cronkite Really Think?" *Look* 34 (November, 1970):57-62.

Frank, Reuven. "Freedom of the Broadcast Press: An Artificial Innocence." *Vital Speeches, given at Yale University* (February 17, 1970).

Hersh, Seymour. "How I Broke the My Lai Story." *Saturday Review* 53 (July, 1970):46-49.

Kauffmann, Stanley, "On Obscenity." *New Republic* 163 (October, 1970):20.

Kristol, Irving. "Pornography, Obscenity and the Case for Censorship." *New York Times Magazines* (March, 1970):2-5.

MacNeil, Robert. "The News on TV and How It Is Unmade." *Harper's* 237 (October, 1968):72-80.

Singer, Benjamin D. "Violence, Protest and War in Television News: U.S. and Canada Compared." *Public Opinion Quarterly* 34 (Winter, 1970):611-16.

Witcover, Jules. "Salvaging the Presidential Press Conference." *Columbia Journalism Review* 9 (November-December, 1970):27-34.

Part Four

APPENDIX

"NATIONAL CENTER FOR STUDY OF THE MEDIA" (see page 62 for reference)

In summary, several financing possibilities are available and should be explored. The criteria for ideal funding are: widespread and direct individual participation, freedom from government or industry control, sufficiency, and stability.

The center should be authorized by its charter to perform a broad spectrum of related tasks. Its basic functions would include collecting, studying, storing, and disseminating information about the performances, practices, and values of the mass media of the United States.

Among other tasks, the center would undertake the following investigations:

A. The analysis and evaluation of media standards—The processes and substance of voluntary media standards, both internal and industrywide, would be subjected to continuing consideration.

B. Collection of data concerning the media—The center would conduct or fund continuing collection of data on national media fare. Moreover, the center could conduct spot surveys of local media fare. The availability of such data would encourage further experiments, surveys, and study by interested researchers.

C. The monitoring and evaluation of media performance—In the broadcast media, the center could evaluate the degree of adherence to standards as well as measure the extent to which broadcasters meet their commitment (in licensing applications to the Federal Communications Commission) to provide specified amounts of public-interest programming. The center should also examine from time to time the accuracy, integrity, and relevance of the broadcast rating services.

In the print media, the center could monitor standards for inclusion of news in newspapers and magazines and standards for the national wire services and syndicates. In all media, standards for granting access should be evaluated.

D. The evaluation of media grievance machinery—The center might well contribute to the development of workable procedures to ensure access to the media for significant dissident groups.

The responsiveness of the media to complaints and requests for the opportunity to present alternative views on public issues could be monitored and evaluated by the center. To the extent that the media undertake to develop professional grievance machinery such as press or broadcasting councils, the center could contribute to their development and effectiveness by evaluating their responsiveness. Consideration could well be given to a "right of reply" for redressing grievances.

E. Analysis of the institutional and economic structure, trends within, and practices of the media—A thorough examination should be made of the relationship between the mass media and the advertising business, politicians, and policymakers in local, state, and national governments. The impact of economic concentration should be an intensive, continuing concern of the center.

F. Analysis of media employment practices—The center should monitor practices and trends in media employment. As the Kerner commission and others have observed, the quality of reporting on minority-group problems is directly related to the extent to which minority-group members are employed in substantive journalistic capacities.

G. The evaluation of the effectiveness of government agencies charged with media-related responsibilities—Certain government agencies are charged with the responsibility of overseeing specific aspects of the media's activities. These agencies in turn would benefit from a continuing examination of the performance of these functions.

H. Development of standards and programs for ameliorating community-press relations—As the Kerner commission suggested, "the institute could undertake the task of stimulating community action" and "could serve as a clearinghouse for an exchange of information on police-press relations."

I. The conduct of funding of journalism training in areas of critical social significance—The center should be authorized to conduct or fund programs for the training of minority-group journalists, as well as for the training of nonminority-group members in techniques for reporting on minorities and on social economic, and environmental problems generally.

J. The stimulation of public-interest coverage through grants and awards—The center's impact should not be limited to the negative sanctions of critical evaluation and condemnation. To the extent that its resources permit the center should engage in affirmative programs to stimulate media coverage in the public interest through grants. Such grants may be particularly appropriate for local media projects which may lie beyond the resources of local newspapers or commercial broadcasters to perform without financial assistance.

In addition, the center must appropriately develop a program of awards for outstanding public-interest coverage or other performance.

K. Long-term study of the social effects of media entertainment and news practices—The center should study and evaluate the social effects of media entertainment content to the benefit of both the media and society: a reasoned and dispassionate analysis could overcome much of the hyperbole that has attended accusations and denials that the effects of the media injure society.

In addition, the center should conduct studies in three major areas of the news media to determine, much as in the case of the entertainment media, (a) news-media content, (b) the effects of news content, and (c) the ways in which the news media function. Content analysis would include the decisionmaking process in news operations. Effects analysis would emphasize group effects but would also include individual effects. Functional research should include research on the mechanical and business aspects of news and would also deal with both the internal and external regulatory mechanisms applicable to the media.

L. The conduct and funding of research—The center should conduct a modest research program with its own research staff. Most research under the aegis of the center, however, should be done by others, encouraged and supported by center grants and contracts. The research board of the center would provide advice and counsel to the center director in research matters.

POWERS OUTLINED

In Section 6 (see full staff report) we include detailed suggestions for the organizational structure of the center. In addition to these suggestions, the center should be granted certain minimal powers:

A. Authority to publicize findings and conclusions—The center would be expected to seek the widest possible dissemination of its statements and reports. While the center should be authorized, if necessary, to purchase media time or space to publish its findings, the media would normally be expected to provide adequate coverage for institute releases.

B. Authority to request data and reports through government agencies—The center should have access to relevant data from such agencies as the Securities and Exchange Commission, the Federal

Proposed Center for Media Study

A nonprofit corporation to be chartered under the laws of the District of Columbia.

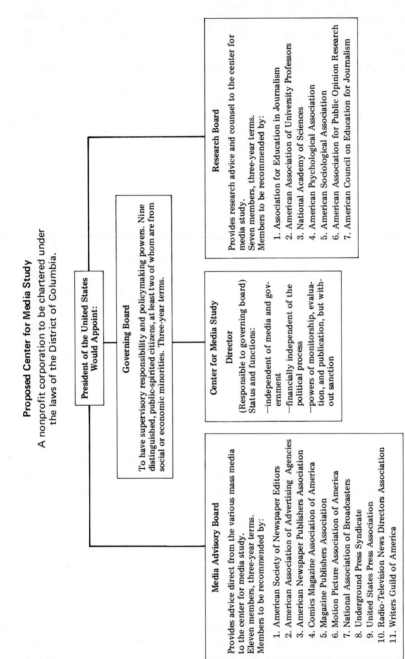

President of the United States Would Appoint:

Governing Board

To have supervisory responsibility and policymaking powers. Nine distinguished, public-spirited citizens, at least two of whom are from social or economic minorities. Three-year terms.

Center for Media Study

Director

(Responsible to governing board) Status and functions:

—independent of media and government

—financially independent of the political process

—powers of monitorship, evaluation, and publication, but without sanction

Media Advisory Board

Provides advice direct from the various mass media to the center for media study.
Eleven members, three-year terms.
Members to be recommended by:

1. American Society of Newspaper Editors
2. American Association of Advertising Agencies
3. American Newspaper Publishers Association
4. Comics Magazine Association of America
5. Magazine Publishers Association
6. Motion Picture Association of America
7. National Association of Broadcasters
8. Underground Press Syndicate
9. United States Press Association
10. Radio-Television News Directors Association
11. Writers Guild of America

Research Board

Provides research advice and counsel to the center for media study.
Seven members, three-year terms.
Members to be recommended by:

1. Association for Education in Journalism
2. American Association of University Professors
3. National Academy of Sciences
4. American Psychological Association
5. American Sociological Association
6. American Association for Public Opinion Research
7. American Council on Education for Journalism

Courtesy of Russell Lenz, chief cartographer.

Communications Commission, the Department of Health, Education, and Welfare, and the Federal Trade Commission.

Finally, to provide a check on its own activities, as well as a formal occasion for evaluation of overall performance of trends within the media, the center should be required to prepare and make available to the public an annual comprehensive report detailing its activities and rendering its judgments.

THE NEWS MEDIA AND RACIAL DISORDERS

THE KERNER REPORT*

The President's charge to the Commission asked specifically: "What effect do the mass media have on the [1967] riots?"

The question is far reaching and a sure answer is beyond the range of presently available scientific techniques. Our conclusions and recommendations are based upon subjective as well as objective factors; interviews as well as statistics; isolated examples as well as general trends.

Freedom of the press is not the issue. A free press is indispensable to the preservation of the other freedoms this nation cherishes. The recommendations in this chapter have thus been developed under the strong conviction that only a press unhindered by government can contribute to freedom.

To answer the President's question, the Commission:

- Directed its field survey teams to question government officials, law enforcement agents, media personnel, and ordinary citizens about their attitudes and reactions to reporting of the riots;
- Arranged for interviews of media representatives about their coverage of the riots;
- Conducted special interviews with ghetto residents about their response to coverage;
- Arranged for a quantitative analysis of the content of television programs and newspaper reporting in 15 riot cities during the period of the disorder and the days immediately before and after;
- From November 10-12, 1967, sponsored and participated in a conference of representatives from all levels of the newspaper, news magazine, and broadcasting industries at Poughkeepsie, New York.

Finally, of course, the Commissioners read newspapers, listened

---

*From the *Report of the National Advisory Commission on Civil Disorders,* 1968.

to the radio, watched television, and thus formed their own impressions of media coverage. All of these data, impressions, and attitudes provide the foundation for our conclusions.

The Commission also determined, very early, that the answer to the President's question did not lie solely in the performance of the press and broadcasters in reporting the riots proper. Our analysis had to consider also the overall treatment by the media of the Negro ghettos, community relations, racial attitudes, urban and rural poverty—day by day and month by month, year in and year out.

On this basis, we have reached three conclusions:

First, that despite incidents of sensationalism, inaccuracies, and distortions, newspapers, radio and television, on the whole, made a real effort to give a balanced, factual account of the 1967 disorders.

Second, despite this effort, the portrayal of the violence that occurred last summer failed to reflect accurately its scale and character. The overall effect was, we believe, an exaggeration of both mood and event.

Third, and ultimately most important, we believe that the media have thus far failed to report adequately on the causes and consequences of civil disorders and the underlying problems of race relations.

With these comments as a perspective, we discuss first the coverage of last summer's disturbances. We will then summarize our concerns with overall coverage of race relations.

We have found a significant imbalance between what actually happened in our cities and what the newspaper, radio, and television coverage of the riots told us happened. The Commission, in studying last summer's disturbances, visited many of the cities and interviewed participants and observers. We found that the disorders, as serious as they were, were less destructive, less widespread, and less a black-white confrontation than most people believed.

Lacking other sources of information, we formed our original impressions and beliefs from what we saw on television, heard on the radio, and read in newspapers and magazines. . . .

As we started to probe the reasons for this imbalance between reality and impression, we first believed that the media had sensationalized the disturbances, consistently overplaying violence and giving disproportionate amounts of time to emotional events and "militant" leaders. To test this theory, we commissioned a systematic, quantitative analysis, covering the content of newspaper and television reporting in 15 cities where disorders occurred. The results of this analysis do not support our early belief. Of 955 television sequences of riot and racial news examined, 837 could be classified for predominant atmosphere as either "emotional," "calm," or "normal." Of these, 494 were classified as calm, 262 as emotional, and 81 as normal. Only a small proportion of all scenes analyzed showed actual mob action, people looting, sniping, setting fires, or being injured, or killed. Moderate Negro leaders were shown more frequently than militant leaders on television news broadcasts.

Of 3,779 newspaper articles analyzed, more focused on legislation which should be sought and planning which should be done to control ongoing riots and prevent future riots than on any other topic. The findings of this content analysis are explained in greater detail in Section I. They make it clear that the imbalance between actual events and the portrayal of those events in the press and on the air cannot be attributed solely to sensationalism in reporting and presentation.

We have, however, identified several factors which, it seems to us, did work to create incorrect and exaggerated impressions about the scope and intensity of the disorders.

First, despite the overall statistical picture, there were instances of gross flaws in presenting news of the 1967 riots. Some newspapers printed "scare" headlines unsupported by the mild stories that followed. All media reported rumors that had no basis in fact. Some newsmen staged "riot" events for the cameras. Examples are included in the next section.

Second, the press obtained much factual information about the scale of the disorders—property damage, personal injury, and deaths—from local officials, who often were inexperienced in dealing with civil disorders and not always able to sort out fact from rumor in the confusion. At the height of the Detroit riot, some news reports of property damage put the figure in excess of $500 million. Subsequent investigation shows it to be $40 to $45 million.

The initial estimates were not the independent judgment of reporters or editors. They came from beleaguered government officials. But the news media gave currency to these errors. Reporters uncritically accepted, and editors uncritically published, the inflated figures, leaving an indelible impression of damage up to more than ten times greater than actually occurred.

Third, the coverage of the disorders—particularly on television—tended to define the events as black-white confrontations. In fact almost all of the deaths, injuries and property damage occurred in all-Negro neighborhoods, and thus the disorders were not "race riots" as that term is generally understood.

Closely linked to these problems is the phenomenon of cumulative effect. As the summer of 1967 progressed, we think Americans often began to associate more or less neutral sights and sounds (like a squad car with flashing red lights, a burning building, a suspect in police custody) with racial disorders, so that the appearance of any particular item, itself hardly inflammatory, set off a whole sequence of association with riot events. Moreover, the summer's news was not seen and heard in isolation. Events of these past few years—the Watts riot, other disorders, and the growing momentum of the civil rights movement—conditioned the responses of readers and viewers and heightened their reactions. What the public saw and read last summer thus produced emotional reactions and left vivid impressions not wholly attributable to the material itself.

Fear and apprehension of racial unrest and violence are deeply rooted in American society. They color and intensify reactions to news of racial trouble and threats of racial conflict. Those who report and disseminate news must be conscious of the background of anxieties and apprehension against which their stories are projected. This does not mean that the media should manage the news or tell less than the truth. Indeed, we believe that it would be imprudent and even dangerous to down-play coverage in the hope that censored reporting of inflammatory incidents somehow will diminish violence. Once a disturbance occurs, the word will spread independently of newspapers and television. To attempt to ignore these events or portray them as something other than what they are, can only diminish confidence in the media and increase the effectiveness of those who monger rumors and the fears of those who listen.

But to be complete, the coverage must be representative. We suggest that the main failure of the media last summer was that the totality of its coverage was not as representative as it should have been to be accurate. We believe that to live up to their own professed standards, the media simply must exercise a higher degree of care and a greater level of sophistication than they have yet shown in this area—higher, perhaps, than the level ordinarily acceptable with other stories.

This is not "just another story." It should not be treated like one. Admittedly, some of what disturbs us about riot coverage last summer stems from circumstances beyond media control. But many of the inaccuracies of fact, tone and mood were due to the failure of reporters and editors to ask tough enough questions about official reports, and to apply the most rigorous standards possible in evaluating and presenting the news. Reporters and editors must be sure that descriptions and pictures of violence, and emotional or inflammatory sequences or articles, even though "true" in isolation, are really representative and do not convey an impression at odds with the overall reality of events. The media too often did not achieve this level of sophisticated, skeptical, careful news judgment during last summer's riots.

Our second and fundamental criticism is that the news media have failed to analyze and report adequately on racial problems in the United States and, as a related matter, to meet the Negro's legitimate expectations in journalism. By and large, news organizations have failed to communicate to both their black and white audiences a sense of the problems America faces and the sources of potential solutions. The media report and write from the standpoint of a white man's world. The ills of the ghetto, the difficulties of life there, the Negro's burning sense of grievance, are seldom conveyed. Slights and indignities are part of the Negro's daily life, and many of them come from what he now calls "the white press"—a press that repeatedly, if unconsciously, reflects the biases, the paternalism, the indifference of white America. This may be understandable, but it is not excusable in an institution that has the mission to inform and educate the whole of our society.

Our criticisms, important as they are, do not lead us to conclude that the media are a cause of riots, any more than they are the cause of other phenomena which they report. It is true that newspaper and television reporting helped shape people's attitudes toward riots. In some cities people who watched television reports and read newspaper accounts of riots in other cities later rioted themselves. But the causal chain weakens when we recall that in other cities, people in very much the same circumstances watched the same programs and read the same newspaper stories but did not riot themselves.

The news media are not the sole source of information and certainly not the only influence on public attitudes. People obtained their information and formed their opinions about the 1967 disorders from the multiplicity of sources that condition the public's thinking on all events. Personal experience, conversations with others, the local and long-distance telephone are all important as sources of information and ideas and contribute to the totality of attitudes about riots.

No doubt, in some cases, the knowledge or the sight on a television screen of what had gone on elsewhere lowered inhibitions or kindled outrage or awakened desires for excitement or loot—or simply passed the word. Many ghetto residents we interviewed thought so themselves. By the same token, the news reports of riots must have conditioned the response of officials and police to disturbances in their own cities. The reaction of the authorities in Detroit was almost certainly affected in some part by what they saw or read of Newark a week earlier. The Commission believes that none of these private or official reactions was decisive in determining the course of the disorders. Even if they had been more significant than we think, however, we cannot envision a system of governmental restraints that could successfully eliminate these effects. And an effort to formulate and impose such restraints would be inconsistent with fundamental traditions in our society.

The failings of the media must be corrected and the improvement must come from within the media. A society that values and relies on a free press as intensely as ours, is entitled to demand in return responsibility from the press and conscientious attention by the press to its own deficiencies. The Commission has seen evidence that many of those who supervise, edit, and report for the news media are becoming increasingly aware of and concerned about their performance in this field. With that concern, and with more experience, will come more sophisticated and responsible coverage. But much more must be done, and it must be done soon.

The Commission has a number of recommendations designed to stimulate and accelerate efforts toward self-improvement. And we propose a privately organized, privately funded Institute of Urban Communications as a means for drawing these recommendations together and promoting their implementation. . .

The Commission's major concern with the news media is not in riot reporting as such, but in the failure to report adequately on race relations and ghetto problems and to bring more Negroes into journalism. Concern about this was expressed by a number of participants in our Poughkeepsie conference. Disorders are only one aspect of the dilemmas and difficulties of race relations in America. In defining, explaining, and reporting this broader, more complex and ultimately far more fundamental subject, the communications media, ironically, have failed to communicate.

They have not communicated to the majority of their audience—which is white—a sense of the degradation, misery, and hopelessness of living in the ghetto. They have not communicated to whites a feeling for the difficulties and frustrations of being a Negro in the United States. They have not shown understanding or appreciation of—and thus have not communicated—a sense of Negro culture, thought, or history.

Equally important, most newspaper articles and most television programming ignore the fact that an appreciable part of their audience is black. The world that television and newspapers offer to their black audience is almost totally white, in both appearance and attitude. As we have said, our evidence shows that the so-called "white press" is at best mistrusted and at worst held in contempt by many black Americans. Far too often, the press acts and talks about Negroes as if Negroes do not read the newspapers or watch television, give birth, marry, die, and go to PTA meetings. Some newspapers and stations are beginning to make efforts to fill this void, but they have still along way to go.

The absence of Negro faces and activities from the media has an effect on white audiences as well as black. If what the white American reads in the newspapers or sees on television conditions his expectation of what is ordinary and normal in the larger society, he will neither understand nor accept the black American. By failing to portray the Negro as a matter of routine and in the context of the total society, the news media have, we believe, contributed to the black-white schism in this country.

When the white press does refer to Negroes and Negro problems it frequently does so as if Negroes were not a part of the audience. This is perhaps understandable in a system where whites edit and, to a large extent, write news. But such attitudes, in an area as sensitive and inflammatory as this, feed Negro alienation and intensify white prejudices.

We suggest that a top editor or news director monitor his news production for a period of several weeks, taking note of how certain stories and language will affect black readers or viewers. A Negro staff member could do this easily. Then the staff should be informed about the problems involved.

The problems of race relations coverage go beyond incidents of white bias. Many editors and news directors, plagued by shortages of staff and lack of reliable contacts and sources of information in the city, have failed to recognize the significance of the urban story and to develop resources to cover it adequately.

We believe that most news organizations do not have direct access to diversified news sources in the ghetto. Seldom do they have a total sense of what is going on there. Some of the blame rests on Negro leaders who do not trust the media and will not deal candidly with representatives of the white press. But the real failure rests with the news organization themselves. They—like other elements of the white community—have ignored the ghettos for decades. Now they seek instant acceptance and cooperation.

The development of good contacts, reliable information, and understanding requires more effort and time than an occasional visit by a team of reporters to do a feature on a newly-discovered ghetto problem. It requires reporters permanently assigned to this beat. They must be adequately trained and supported to dig out and tell the story of a major social upheaval—among the most complicated, portentous and explosive our society has known. We believe, also, that the Negro Press—manned largely by people who live and work in the ghetto—could be a particularly useful source of information and guidance about activities in the black community. Reporters and editors from Negro newspapers and radio stations should be included in any conference between media and police-city representatives, and we suggest that large news organizations would do well to establish better lines of communication to their counterparts in the Negro press.

In short, the news media must find ways of exploring the problems of the Negro and the ghetto more deeply and more meaningfully. To editors who say "we have run thousands of inches on the ghetto which nobody reads" and to television executives who bemoan scores of underwatched documentaries, we say: find more ways of telling this story, for it is a story you, as journalists, must tell—honestly, realistically, and imaginatively. It is the responsibility of the news media to tell the story of race relations in America, and with notable exceptions, the media have not yet turned to the task with the wisdom, sensitivity, and expertise it demands.

The journalistic profession has been shockingly backward in seeking out, hiring, training, and promoting Negroes. Fewer than 5 percent of the people employed by the news business in editorial jobs in the United States today are Negroes. Fewer than 1 percent of editors and supervisors are Negroes, and most of them work for Negro-owned organizations. The lines of various news organizations to the militant blacks are, by admission of the newsmen themselves, almost nonexistent. The plaint is, "We can't find qualified Negroes." But this rings hollow from an industry where, only yesterday, jobs were scarce and promotion unthinkable for a man whose skin was black. Even today, there are virtually no Negroes in positions of editorial or executive responsibility and there is only one Negro newsman with a nationally syndicated column.

News organizations must employ enough Negroes in positions of significant responsibility to establish an effective link to Negro actions and ideas and to meet legitimate employment expectations. Tokenism—the hiring of one Negro reporter, or even two or three—is no longer enough. Negro reporters are essential, but so are Negro editors, writers and commentators. Newspaper and television policies are, generally speaking, not set by reporters. Editorial decisions about which stories to cover and which to use are made by editors. Yet, very few Negroes in this country are involved in making these decisions, because very few, if any, supervisory editorial jobs are held by Negroes. We urge the news media to do everything possible to train and promote their Negro reporters to positions where those who are qualified can contribute to and have an effect on policy decisions.

It is not enough, though, as many editors have pointed out to the Commission, to search for Negro journalists. Journalism is not very popular as a career for aspiring young Negroes. The starting pay is comparatively low and it is a business which has, until recently, discouraged and rejected them. The recruitment of Negro reporters must extend beyond established journalists, or those who have already formed ambitions along these lines. It must become a commitment to seek out young Negro men and women, inspire them to become—and then train them as—journalists. Training programs should be started at high schools and intensified at colleges. Summer vacation and part-time editorial jobs, coupled with offers of permanent employment, can awaken career plans.

We believe that the news media themselves, their audiences and the country will profit from these undertakings. For if the media are to comprehend and then to project the Negro community, they must have the help of Negroes. If the media are to report with understanding, wisdom and sympathy on the problems of the cities and the problems of the black man—for the two are increasingly intertwined—they must employ, promote and listen to Negro journalists.

PRESS BEHAVIOR IN DALLAS

THE WARREN REPORT*

. . . If Oswald had been tried for his murders of November 22, the effects of the news policy pursued by the Dallas authorities would have proven harmful both to the prosecution and the defense. The misinformation reported after the shootings might have been used by the defense to cast doubt on the reliability of the State's

*From the *Report of the President's Commission on the Assassination of President John F. Kennedy*, 1964.

entire case. Though each inaccuracy can be explained without great difficulty, the number and variety of misstatements issued by the police shortly after the assassination would have greatly assisted a skillful defense attorney attempting to influence the attitudes of jurors.

A fundamental objection to the news policy pursued by the Dallas police, however, is the extent to which it endangered Oswald's constitutional right to a trial by an impartial jury. Because of the nature of the crime, the widespread attention which it necessarily received, and the intense public feelings which it aroused, it would have been a most difficult task to select an unprejudiced jury, either in Dallas or elsewhere. But the difficulty was markedly increased by the divulgence of the specific items of evidence with which the police linked Oswald to the two killings. The disclosure of evidence encouraged the public, from which a jury would ultimately be impaneled, to prejudge the very questions that would be raised at trial.

Moreover, rules of law might have prevented the prosecution from presenting portions of this evidence to the jury. For example, though expressly recognizing that Oswald's wife could not be compelled to testify against him, District Attorney Wade revealed to the Nation that Marina Oswald had affirmed her husband's ownership of a rifle like that found on the sixth floor of the Texas School Book Depository. Curry stated that Oswald had refused to take a lie detector test, although such a statement would have been inadmissible in a trial. The exclusion of such evidence, however, would have been meaningless if jurors were already familiar with the same facts from previous television or newspaper reports. Wade might have influenced prospective jurors by his mistaken statement that the paraffin test showed that Oswald had fired a gun. The tests merely showed that he had nitrate traces on his hands, which did not necessarily mean that he had fired either a rifle or a pistol.

The disclosure of evidence was seriously aggravated by the statements of numerous responsible officials that they were certain of Oswald's guilt. Captain Fritz said that the case against Oswald was "cinched." Curry reported on Saturday that "we are sure of our case." Curry announced that he considered Oswald sane, and Wade told the public that he would ask for the death penalty.

The American Bar Association declared in December 1963 that "widespread publicizing of Oswald's alleged guilt, involving statements by officials and public disclosures of the details of 'evidence,' would have made it extremely difficult to impanel an unprejudiced jury and afford the accused a fair trial." Local bar associations expressed similar feelings. The Commission agrees that Lee Harvey Oswald's opportunity for a trial by 12 jurors free of preconception as to his guilt or innocence would have been seriously jeopardized by the premature disclosure and weighing of the evidence against him.

The problem of disclosure of information and its effect on trials is, of course, further complicated by the independent activities of the press in developing information on its own from sources other than law enforcement agencies. Had the police not released the specific items of evidence against Oswald, it is still possible that the other information presented on television and in the newspapers, chiefly of a biographical nature, would itself have had a prejudicial effect on the public.

In explanation of the news policy adopted by the Dallas authorities, Chief Curry observed that "it seemed like there was a great demand by the general public to know what was going on." In a prepared statement, Captain King wrote:

> At that time we felt a necessity for permitting the newsmen as much latitude as possible. We realized the magnitude of the incident the newsmen were there to cover. We realized that not only the nation but the world would be greatly interested in what occurred in Dallas. We believed that we had an obligation to make as widely known as possible everything we could regarding the investigation of the assassination and the manner in which we undertook that investigation.

The Commission recognizes that the people of the United States, and indeed the world, had a deep-felt interest in learning of the events surrounding the death of President Kennedy, including the development of the investigation in Dallas. An informed public provided the ultimate guarantee that adequate steps would be taken to apprehend those responsible for the assassination and that all necessary precautions would be taken to protect the national security. It was therefore proper and desirable that the public know which agencies were participating in the investigation and the rate at which their work was progressing. The public was also entitled to know that Lee Harvey Oswald had been apprehended and that the State had gathered sufficient evidence to arraign him for the murders of the President and Patrolman Tippit, that he was being held pending action of the grand jury, that the investigation was continuing, and that the law enforcement agencies had discovered no evidence which tended to show that any other person was involved in either slaying.

However, neither the press nor the public had a right to be contemporaneously informed by the police or prosecuting authorities of the details of the evidence being accumulated against Oswald.

Undoubtedly the public was interested in these disclosures, but its curiosity should not have been satisfied at the expense of the accused's right to a trial by an impartial jury. The courtroom, not the newspaper or television screen, is the appropriate forum in our system for the trial of a man accused of a crime.

If the evidence in the possession of the authorities had not been disclosed, it is true that the public would not have been in a position to assess the adequacy of the investigation or to apply pressures for further official undertakings. But a major consequence of the hasty and at times inaccurate divulgence of evidence after the assassination was simply to give rise to groundless rumors and public confusion. Moreover, without learning the details of the case, the public could have been informed by the responsible authority of the general scope of the investigation and the extent to which State and Federal agencies were assisting in the police work.

While appreciating the heavy and unique pressures with which the Dallas Police Department was confronted by reason of the assassination of President Kennedy, primary responsibility for having failed to control the press and to check the flow of undigested evidence to the public must be borne by the police department. It was the only agency that could have established orderly and sound operating procedures to control the multitude of newsmen gathered in the police building after the assassination.

The Commission believes, however, that a part of the responsibility for the unfortunate circumstances following the President's death must be borne by the news media. The crowd of newsmen generally failed to respond properly to the demands of the police. Frequently without permission, news representatives used police offices on the third floor, tying up facilities and interfering with normal police operations. Police efforts to preserve order and to clear passageways in the corridor were usually unsuccessful. On Friday night the reporters completely ignored Curry's injunction against asking Oswald questions in the assembly room and crowding in on him. On Sunday morning, the newsmen were instructed to direct no questions at Oswald; nevertheless, several reporters shouted questions at him when he appeared in the basement.

Moreover, by constantly pursuing public officials, the news representatives placed an insistent pressure upon them to disclose information. And this pressure was not without effect, since the police attitude toward the press was affected by the desire to maintain satisfactory relations with the news representatives and to create a favorable image of themselves. Chief Curry frankly told the Commission that

I didn't order them out of the building, which if I had it to do over I would. In the past like I say, we had always maintained very good relations with our press, and they had always respected us.

Curry refused Fritz' request to put Oswald behind the screen in the assembly room at the Friday night press conference because this might have hindered the taking of pictures. Curry's subordinates had the impression that an unannounced transfer of Oswald to the county jail was unacceptable because Curry did not want to disappoint the newsmen; he had promised that they could witness the transfer. It seemed clear enough that any attempt to exclude the press from the building or to place limits on the information disclosed to them would have been resented and disputed by the newsmen, who were constantly and aggressively demanding all possible information about anything related to the assassination.

Although the Commission has found no corroboration in the video and audio tapes, police officials recall that one or two representatives of the press reinforced their demands to see Oswald by suggesting that the police had been guilty of brutalizing him. They intimated that unless they were given the opportunity to see him, these suggestions would be passed on to the public. Captain King testified that he had been told that

A short time after Oswald's arrest one newsman held up a photograph and said, "This is what the man charged with the assassination of the President looks like. Or at least this is what he did look like. We don't know what he looks like after an hour in the custody of the Dallas Police Department."

City Manager Elgin Crull stated that when he visited Chief Curry in his office on the morning of November 23, Curry told him that he "felt it was necessary to cooperate with the news media representatives, in order to avoid being accused of using Gestapo tactics in connection with the handling of Oswald." Crull agreed with Curry. The Commission deems any such veiled threats to be absolutely without justification.

The general disorder in the Police and Courts Building during November 22–24 reveals a regrettable lack of self-discipline by the newsmen. The Commission believes that the news media, as well as the police authorities, who failed to impose conditions more in keeping with the orderly process of justice, must share responsibility for the failure of law enforcement which occurred in connection with the death of Oswald. On previous occasions, public bodies have voiced the need for the exercise of self-restraint by the news media in periods when the demand for information must be tempered by other fundamental requirements of our society.

At its annual meeting in Washington in April 1964, the American Society of Newspaper Editors discussed the role of the press in Dallas immediately after President Kennedy's assassination. The discussion revealed the strong misgivings among the editors themselves about the role that the press had played and their desire that the press display more self-discipline and adhere to higher standards of conduct in the future. To prevent a recurrence of the unfortunate events which followed the assassination, however, more than general concern will be needed. The promulgation of a code of professional conduct governing representatives of all news media would be welcome evidence that the press had profited by the lesson of Dallas.

The burden of insuring that appropriate action is taken to establish ethical standards of conduct for the news media must also be borne, however, by State and local governments, by the bar, and ultimately by the public. The experience in Dallas during November 22—24 is a dramatic affirmation of the need for steps to bring about a proper balance between the right of the public to be kept informed and the right of the individual to a fair and impartial trial.

THE CHICAGO POLICE AND THE PRESS

THE WALKER REPORT*

Not only in Chicago, but also throughout the nation there has been a storm of controversy over the fairness of mass media coverage—and particularly television coverage—of the Democratic National Convention. We have not been charged with investigating that aspect of convention week. Our concern here is with instances of violence involving media representatives and police.

We address the following questions, and shall consider media coverage only insofar as it bears on them.

1. Was any news staged and manufactured by demonstrators and newsmen?

2. Were newsmen calculated targets of violence by police?

3. Were any police attacks on newsmen unwarranted and unprovoked?

---

*From the *Report to the National Commission on the Causes and Prevention of Violence*, 1968.

There is good reason to seek answers to these questions—of about 300 newsmen assigned to cover the parks and streets of Chicago during convention week, more than 65 were involved in incidents resulting in injury to themselves, damage to their equipment, or their arrest. . . .

Basic difficulties in providing coverage began weeks before the convention when a strike by the International Brotherhood of Electrical Workers (IBEW) against Illinois Bell Telephone Company held up most of the advance preparation of the convention hall facilities. The International Amphitheatre was the vital control and origination center for all media. Normally a minimum of ten weeks is required to install the complex cable systems, including microwave relay links for live remote coverage at key hotels and elsewhere. The impasse almost forced the convention elsewhere.

Microwave antennas, which dotted hotel roofs in Miami Beach for the Republican convention and allowed live television coverage inside and outside of hotels, could not be installed in Chicago. Seemingly endless union jurisdictional disputes on top of the three-month-old telephone strike left network news officials apparently convinced that there was virtually no chance of live pickups outside the convention hall and fearful that there might be none inside either.

The alternative in either case was reliance on video tape and film for television and on tape for radio. The procedure, according to network sources, could delay radio-TV transmissions for 20 to 30 minutes to an hour or more. Extent of the delay would depend not only on time needed to develop the film that was used—probably under 30 minutes—but also on transportation to the stations. Finally, a month before the convention was to start, a moratorium on the telephone strike was reached. The moratorium requested by city officials allowed IBEW volunteers to wire the Amphitheatre only. This blocked virtually all live coverage elsewhere. . . .

On Thursday prior to the convention Superintendent Conlisk directed the following order which was read at all roll calls for the next three days:

> During and prior to the Democratic National Convention there will be many out-of-town newsmen in the city who will not have Chicago police press cards but will carry other types of press credentials. These credentials whether issued by the Democratic National Committee News organizations or other police departments will serve to properly identify the bearers as newsmen. . . .

It is in the interest of the department and the City of Chicago that there be a harmonious relationship between department personnel and the news media representatives who will report the Democratic National Convention to the world.

But the press and Chicago officials, particularly the police, had disagreements just prior to the convention. The Chicago Fire Department inspected television equipment vans and ordered them re-wired, saying they did not conform to the Chicago code. Police imposed a parking ban on TV camera vans. They ordered TV cameras off sidewalk locations near the convention hotels and threatened, according to one TV technician on the scene, to take the cameras apart "piece by piece" if they weren't moved.

Frank Sullivan, a former Chicago newspaper reporter, and now director of Public Information for the police, denied the parking ban and aimed a stifling television coverage. "It is no device to block TV coverage," he said. "It is simply a matter of priority. The delegates need space to board buses and the delegates take priority over television." He said the police were working to locate nearby lots for television trucks. Some video tape trucks were already parked in a lot behind the Conrad Hilton Hotel. Cables were strung into the hotel to cameras, but no cameras were permitted on the sidewalk in front of the hotel or in open windows overlooking the front entrance. The police said that, because of security problems, cameras would not be allowed to shoot film out of hotel windows. In addition, no cameras would be allowed on the roof of the Amphitheatre.

At a meeting with top representatives of the TV industry in Mayor Daley's office on Saturday noon a compromise was reached. The Mayor instructed a city street official to give them what they wanted "as long as security measures aren't violated." As it turned out, the TV representatives wanted live cameras in Grant Park across from the Hilton. The Mayor approved, but the Secret Service vetoed the plan.

They also wanted to construct a wooden TV platform at the southwest corner of Balbo Drive and Michigan Avenue in front of the Haymarket Lounge. This was rejected on the grounds that cameras at that location would tie up traffic. Finally it was decided to allow cameras in certain fixed positions.

The mounting list of television network problems led Richard S. Salant, CBS News president, to say that they formed "a pattern well beyond simple labor disputes, logistics and security problems."

Minor friction between police and press continued over the weekend before the convention opened. Overhead camera shots from "cherry picker" units were discouraged. Mobile news vans were told to move along from chosen locations. Between the restrictions created by the IBEW strike and the denial of parking to news vans on the street, live coverage other than at the Amphitheatre and at O'Hare Field (where President Johnson might arrive) had been pretty effectively barred, and newsmen felt more and more "squeezed" by the overwhelming security measures. They speculated among themselves, "Was the Democratic Party trying to minimize coverage of violence in the streets, should it occur?"

The stage was set. Press facilities were operational, and newsmen were ready to cover the many-sided convention story, determined to do so despite whatever problems arose.

By the time the convention began, there were over 6,000 newsmen in Chicago, 4,000 of them from out of town. The TV networks sent, by far, the largest contingents; NBC had over 750 in its Chicago Task Force, CBS about 740 and ABC about 500. . . .

As has been documented, there were ample causes before and during the convention week for media-police hostility. The media representatives felt hampered and frustrated by the convention arrangement difficulties and the ever-present security precautions. The police are never enthusiatic about the presence of newsmen in large-crowd situations and their irritation during the week grew for the reasons described above. Police emotions were heightened by their impression, as they listened to radio, watched TV and read newspapers, that the media coverage was anti-Chicago, anti-Mayor Daley and anti-Police. . . .

The first instance of violence involving a member of the press in connection with the demonstrators took place Saturday night at about 11:45 p.m., at Clark Street opposite Menomonee Street on Chicago's Near North Side. *Chicago Daily News* reporter Lawrence Green came across some youthful demonstrators on the sidewalk who were shouting at police patrolling the street.

According to Green, he and other newsmen at the scene were ordered "in front" of the police lines and the police then charged the crowd on the sidewalk. Green said he was pushed, then stumbled, and another reporter fell on top of him. Green had his press credentials visible around his neck. As he scrambled to his feet, he said he held out his press card and yelled, "Press! Press! Press!" Nonetheless, a policeman came up to him and clubbed him on the back. Another police officer, seeing his credentials said, "Fuck your press cards."

Late Sunday night, the Chicago police cleared Lincoln Park of demonstrators. The demonstrators left the park and flowed into the

Old Town area of Chicago's North Side and later marched downtown to the Michigan Avenue bridge. In the process, several clashes with the press occurred. . . .

On Monday, before the convention started, the first reports of beatings of newsmen began circulating, and articles and pictures appeared in the newspapers late Monday.

Police Superintendent James B. Conlisk ordered an investigation of the reports of clubbing of newsmen and photographers, and a general order was issued emphasizing the order of the previous week and calling for complete cooperation with newsmen. . . .

Despite these precautions, Monday, August 26, was to be one of the most hazardous days for newsmen. On Monday afternoon, a TV reporter was warned by two police detectives, separately, that "the word is being passed to get newsmen" and "be careful—the word is out to get newsmen."

In the early afternoon, an ABC-TV crew assigned to cover the hippies and demonstrators went to Lincoln Park. The crew consisted of correspondent James Burns, cameraman Charles Pharris, electrician Jud Marvin and audio-man Walter James. All were neatly dressed, wearing suits, and had clearly visible press badges. They went to the park because Burns had heard a report that there would be self-defense exercises by the National Mobilization Committee To End War in Vietnam. They were the only crew there. Only a few police officers and demonstrators were present. About 2 p.m., the four were sitting on the grass when a squadrol moved into the park. A number of demonstrators gathered around the squadrol. The police jumped out and pulled Tom Hayden out of the crowd. Pharris, who was kneeling on the ground about 35 yards away, started to film the arrest. As he rose, a policeman rushed up behind him and clubbed the zoom lens of his camera, breaking it and knocking it to the ground. Then he struck Marvin on the back with his club, and ran away before any of the four could get a clear look at him. . . .

At 5 a.m. Tuesday *Newsweek* News Editor Hal Bruno dispatched the following telegram to Mayor Daley and Superintendent James Conlisk. The telegram was typical of others to follow.

> Newsweek Magazine hereby informs you that for the second night in a row our reporters and photographers were subject to unprovoked attacks by Chicago policemen. Three of our men were injured and we have evidence that individual policemen are deliberately assaulting newsmen. We can identify men and units and are anxious to cooperate with you so that immediate measures can be taken to safeguard newsmen in the performance of their duty. . . .

Wednesday morning, Chet Huntley on NBC radio broadcast nationally: "We in the calling of journalism have hesitated to talk about our problems in Chicago . . . but the hostility toward any kind of criticism, and the fear of telling how it is has become too much and it becomes our duty to speak out. . . . The significant part of all this is the undeniable manner in which Chicago police are going out of their way to injure newsmen, and prevent them from filming or gathering information on what is going on. The news profession in this city is now under assault by the Chicago Police."

On Wednesday night the violence broke out again. . . .

Chicago Daily News photographer Paul Sequeira was covering the demonstrations near the Hilton Hotel. After taking a picture of a police lieutenant spraying mace at people, he was himself maced by the same lieutenant. His camera blocked the spray, so he was not affected. (A picture relating to this incident appears in the photographic section.) A short while later Sequeira was following a police line moving north from the Hilton on Michigan Avenue. He wore a helmet marked "PRESS" and carried cameras around his neck. The police line turned west on Jackson Boulevard. As it did, Sequeira came upon the following scene:

A man in an army sergeant's uniform was beating a man dressed in white (identified as Dr. Richard Scott, intern at Presbyterian-St. Luke's Hospital). Approximately 12 policemen were standing around watching. Sequeira began photographing the incident. At least two policemen approached him saying, "Get out of here." Sequeira showed his press card and shouted "Press." He was hit on the helmet, arm and back by police and forced to his knees. Suddenly his helmet was on the ground. Sequeira tried to use a camera to fend off the blows to his head. Then, he curled up in the street and the police stopped clubbing him. His right hand was broken and he had head injuries. Despite his injuries, Sequeira continued covering the demonstrations. He took another picture of the "sergeant" (later identified as an AWOL soldier, but not a sergeant) about 20 minutes later. When the man demanded the film and tried to kick him, Sequeira stopped a police car. The police took the sergeant into custody. Sequeira was treated for his injuries at Passavant Hospital later that night. . . .

On the *Today* show Thursday morning, Hugh Downs asked his NBC-TV viewers if there was any word to describe Chicago policemen other than "pigs!" One viewer who objected was Frank Sullivan, the beleaguered press officer for the Chicago police. "I was so incensed that I asked Superintendent Conlisk if it would be o.k. for me to hold a press conference," he said.

At 10:30 a.m., speaking extemporaneously before a large and stormy gathering of newsmen, Sullivan described demonstration leaders as communist revolutionaries "bent on the destruction of the United States. They are a pitiful handful. They have almost no support. But, by golly, they get the cooperation of the news media. They are built into something really big. . . . Let's get this thing into perspective." He charged news media with bias and poor judgment in criticizing the Chicago police. . . .

Chicago's Mayor Richard J. Daley held a press conference of his own late Thursday morning. He publicly criticized both the media and the protesters. Reading from a prepared statement, and giving no opportunity for questions, Mayor Daley placed much of the blame for the street disorders on the news media. He said the media set the stage for the disruptions by detailing the advance plans of the demonstrators. He also claimed that the efforts of law enforcement agencies were "distorted and twisted" in news accounts. The Mayor further charged that television was a "tool" used in plans for "calculated disruption and rioting." . . .

Also, on Thursday, a federal appellate judge, responding to the appeal of photographers O'Sullivan, Berliant, Morrill and Schnell, issued an injunction. The order restrained police from interfering "by force, violence or intimidation" with the constitutional rights of newsmen to cover public events.

That night, in an appearance with Walter Cronkite on CBS, Mayor Daley challenged the television networks to cover the more positive side of the police-demonstrator story, rather than merely the violent aftermath of each incident. He contended that the cameras never showed the police reasoning with the marchers or showing them where they could move freely or safely. Nor did TV ever tell about the policemen who were hurt, he said. . . . [Editor's Note: only a few incidents were included here.]

A total of 49 newsmen are described as having been hit, maced, or arrested, apparently without reason, by the police. Forty-three were hit, three were maced and three were arrested. Of the newsmen involved, 22 were reporters, 23 were photographers and 4 were members of the TV crews.

In ten of these incidents, photographic or recording equipment was deliberately broken; in one, the police intentionally knocked a reporter's notebook out of his hand.

In over 40 instances, the newsman involved was clearly identifiable as such; that is, even aside from photographers carrying the identifying apparatus of their trade, newsmen wore helmets, carried visible press badges or press passes hanging around their necks. In only four situations do the facts indicate that the newsmen were so mixed in with the crowd that the police could have hit them under the mistaken apprehension that they were demonstrators.

Forty-five of the incidents occurred at night, four during the daytime. Fourteen of the newsmen were from Chicago and the balance were from out of town. The average age was about 31 years; 28 were in the 20 to 30 year age bracket; ten were from 31 to 35; seven were over 35. We do not know the ages of the other four.

Ten of the incidents took place on Saturday and Sunday. The greatest number—25—occurred on Monday. None occurred on Tuesday (except for the Dan Rather incident at the Amphitheatre, which is not represented in the above statistics). On Wednesday, however, the violence resumed: there were 14 incidents.

There is evidence of a number of other instances of police-press violence. In 12 of these incidents, newsmen were struck by police baton; in three their photographic equipment was damaged by police. These are not reported in this chapter either because they took place when the police were moving large crowds (making it possible that any injury to newsmen was accidental) or because we do not have enough information to warrant their inclusion in this report.

Index